THE SPORTING EXCEPTION
IN EUROPEAN UNION LAW

ASSER INTERNATIONAL SPORTS LAW SERIES

Editors
Robert C.R. Siekmann and Janwillem Soek

ISSN 1874–6926

T.M.C. ASSER INSTITUUT
ASSER International Sports Law Centre

THE SPORTING EXCEPTION IN EUROPEAN UNION LAW

by

Richard Parrish and Samuli Miettinen

T·M·C·ASSER PRESS

Published by T·M·C·ASSER PRESS
P.O. Box 16163, 2500 BD The Hague, The Netherlands
<www.asserpress.nl>

T·M·C·ASSER PRESS' English language books are distributed exclusively by:

Cambridge University Press, The Edinburgh Building, Shaftesbury Road,
Cambridge CB2 2RU, UK,
or
for customers in the USA, Canada and Mexico:
Cambridge University Press, 100 Brook Hill Drive, West Nyack, NY 10994-2133, USA
<www.cambridge.org>

ISBN 978-90-6704-262-8
ISSN 1874-6926

Cover photograph: Carlo Carrà, *Partita di calcio*, 1934, olio su tela, AM 1016, Roma Galleria
Comunale d'Arte Moderna e Contemporanea.
© 2008, Archivio Fotografico Galleria Comunale d'Arte Moderna e Contemporanea, Roma.

**T.M.C. Asser Instituut – Institute for Private and Public International Law,
International Commercial Arbitration and European Law**

Institute Address: R.J. Schimmelpennincklaan 20-22, The Hague, The Netherlands; Mailing Address:
P.O. Box 30461, 2500 GL The Hague, The Netherlands; Tel.: +3170 342 0300; Fax: +3170 3420 359;
Internet: www.asser.nl.
Over forty years, the T.M.C. Asser Institute has developed into a leading scientific research institute in
the field of international law. It covers private international law, public international law, including
international humanitarian law, the law of the European Union, the law of international commercial
arbitration and increasingly, also, international economic law, the law of international commerce and
international sports law.
Conducting scientific research, either fundamental or applied, in the aforementioned domains, is the
main activity of the Institute. In addition, the Institute organizes congresses and postgraduate courses,
undertakes contract-research and operates its own publishing house.
Because of its inter-university background, the Institute often cooperates with Dutch law faculties as
well as with various national and foreign institutions.

SUMMARY OF CONTENTS

FOREWORD

Sport is not mentioned in the EC Treaty. And yet sporting practices may have profound economic implications, and they may cut across basic assumptions of the EC
Treaty such as non-discrimination on the grounds of nationality, free movement
across borders and undistorted competition. So if the EC Treaty is to be interpreted
in a manner apt to achieve its objectives it cannot afford sport unconditional immunity from its scope of application. On the other hand, sport has characteristics which
are not shared by other sectors of the economy and, moreover, the Treaty is defi-
cient in setting out any helpful framework for understanding just what is 'special'
about sport. So the EU's institutions, most of all the Court and the Commission, are
wisely circumspect when invited to intervene in sport. Add in a host of actors with
incentives to argue for maximum autonomy for sport – sports federations and governing bodies, most obviously – and others, particularly those adversely affected by
the choices made by governing bodies, with incentives instead to promote the aggressive application of EC law, and the scene is set for the shaping of a fiendishly
complicated and hotly contested area of law and policy.

The European Court has a rather spotty record in keeping the law on track. Plenty
of sporting practices have been challenged but found to suffer no rebuke when
examined in the light of EC law. But *why* do some sporting rules escape condemnation under EC law? Usually, in my view, it is not because they exert no economic
effects. In fact there are few such 'pure' rules. Usually it is because their economic
effects are a necessary consequence of their contribution to the structure of legitimate sports governance. This is true of nationality rules governing the composition
of national representative teams, of rules governing selection for international competition, of 'transfer windows', of rules forbidding multiple club ownership, of
anti-doping rules and procedures, and so on. But in its first great case on sport,
Walrave and Koch, the Court referred to 'a question of purely sporting interest'
which 'as such has nothing to do with economic activity'. And it thereby introduced
the idea of rules which lie beyond the reach of the Treaty. For governing authorities
in sport this is a delightful notion, for it helps their interest in maximising the scope
of their autonomy from legal supervision. This is the widest possible version of the
'sporting exception'. But I think it is misleading. Most sporting practices *do* fall
within the scope of the Treaty – because they have economic effects – but this is not
to say they are incompatible with it. In my view the correct way to understand the
so-called 'sporting exception' in EC law is simply to regard it as the space allowed
to sports governing bodies to show that their rules, which in principle fall within the
EC Treaty where they have economic effects, represent an essential means to protect and promote the special character of sport. There is no blanket immunity. There
is case-by-case scrutiny. EC law applies, but does not (necessarily) condemn. And

I think that recently, in *Meca-Medina and Majcen* v. *Commission* the Court adopted this approach.

This is the territory explored by this very fine book. It examines the development of the law and it then applies the analysis to particular areas of controversy, including broadcasting and the labour market. It richly repays close reading and it is the product of deep thinking and conscientious research. Richard Parrish has already shown us the way in his pioneering book *Sports Law and Policy in the European Union* (2003), in which he built his narrative around the appealing notion of 'separate territories', according to which there is 'a territory for sporting autonomy and a territory for legal intervention' (p.3). In this book, with the reinforcement of his co-author Samuli Miettinen, Richard Parrish shows us a great deal of overlap between those territories, and the writers pore over the frictions that exist at the boundaries.

In general sports governing bodies remain wearyingly reluctant to engage seriously with the need to demonstrate intellectually durable reasons why their structures and practices should be treated as necessary and therefore compatible with EC law. Even today they frequently complain about having to do what every other commercially active party has to do – comply with the law. 'Sport is special!' They declare. So it is – but not *that* special. If governing bodies want to take seriously the space which EC law allows them to show why and to what extent sport is truly special, while also generating large amounts of money, then this book provides them, their members and their legal advisers with a platform from which to develop balanced and well-informed arguments. I congratulate Richard Parrish and Samuli Miettinen on their scholarship. This book is a terrific addition to the literature on sport and the law and, I am sure, will be welcomed by all those with a professional, regulatory and academic interest and stake in this developing and important subject.

Oxford, November 2007   Stephen WEATHERILL
                                               Jacques Delors Professor
                                               of European Community Law
                                               Somerville College
                                               University of Oxford
                                               United Kingdom

PREFACE

The Sporting Exception in European Union Law is the most recent addition to the nascent monograph literature exploring the interface between sport and European Union law. One of the first monographs, Parrish's, *Sports Law and Policy in the European Union*, was published in 2003 by Manchester University Press. In 2004 Halgreen's *European Sports Law* was published by Forlaget Thomson in which the author presented a comparative analysis of the European and American sports models. In 2005 Kluwer published Van den Bogaert's *Regulation of the Mobility of Sportsmen in the EU Post Bosman*, a book which investigated the application of free movement law to sporting contexts. These books were the first generation of EU sports law monographs, all being inspired by the 1995 European Court of Justice judgment, *Bosman*,[1] and all being the product of PhD research. In addition to these monographs, professor Weatherill's influential work on the subject was collected in *European Sports Law: Collected Papers*, published in 2007 in the Asser International Sports Law Series. Three developments justify the need to begin a second generation of monograph literature. First, the Court's 2006 judgment in *Meca-Medina*[2] is arguably as significant as *Bosman* as it establishes a new methodology for the application of competition law to sport. Second, the 2007 European Commission White Paper on Sport signals a major political impetus for the EU to intervene more directly in sport and makes a plea for further research to inform future debates. Third, this involvement will become constitutionalised in the form of an express competence if the Reform Treaty, unlike the 2005 Treaty establishing a Constitution for Europe, navigates the ratification process.

The 1974 judgment of the European Court of Justice in *Walrave*[3] established the 'sporting exception', a principle by which rules of 'purely sporting interest' were removed from the scope of the EC Treaty. This encouraged sports governing bodies to argue that sporting practices that could otherwise constitute infringements of Community law were 'purely sporting rules' and beyond the scope of Community law. The Court's 1995 *Bosman* judgment clarified that economic activities were governed by Community law even when they were located in the regulatory ambit of sports governing bodies, and established firmly that economic sporting practices did fall within the scope of Community rules on labour mobility. In its 2006 *Meca-Medina* judgment, the Court made explicit that the presence of some 'purely sporting' phenomena in the context of economic sporting activity did not altogether exclude sports governing bodies from the scope of competition law.

---

[1] Case C-415/93 *Union Royale Belge Sociétés de Football Association and others* v. *Bosman*, [1995] *ECR* I-4921.

[2] Case C-519/04 P *David Meca-Medina and Igor Majcen* v. *Commission* [2006] *ECR* I-6991.

[3] Case 36/74 *Walrave and Koch* v. *Association Union Cycliste Internationale* [1974] *ECR* 1405.

Engagement with the justificatory processes of Community law is therefore of critical importance for the governing bodies. Whilst modern Community law prohibits undertakings adopting restrictive practices, it places great emphasis on the strength of justificatory arguments. In free movement law restrictions can be objectively justified with reference to the attainment of proportionately pursued legitimate objectives. In competition law, the decision on whether a restriction is to be condemned must take account of the context in which the restriction was imposed. This analysis can render certain practices incapable of being defined as a restriction. Even if a practice that constitutes 'a restriction', the party imposing the restriction has recourse to the exemption criteria which provide opportunities to justify the existence of a restriction.

This book seeks to establish the definitive analytical toolkit explaining how 'specificity of sport' arguments can find expression within Community free movement and competition law. Chapter one explores the intellectual foundations of the specificity of sport argument by interrogating claims that sport is special from the perspective of its activities, rules and structures. Chapter two explores the articulation of these specificities within the emergent EU sports policy. Chapters three, four and five present an analytical framework on how specificity arguments may find expression within the Community legal framework. Chapter six explores the elaboration of specificity arguments within the context of sports broadcasting and chapters seven and eight do likewise in relation to the rules of the governing bodies affecting the rights of players and those rules pertaining to the organisation of sport in Europe. Chapter nine draws upon this analysis and presents an overview of the present state of the legal framework. It also draws some conclusions as to the questions which the Union's fledgling sports policy will need to consider in the future.

Some technical questions remain to be addressed. After some agonizing, the authors have settled for 'Community' rather than Union law, whilst retaining the terminology of 'Union' where the context so requires. The distinction will become anachronistic following the entry into force of the Reform Treaty. Some Commission documents already reflect a preference for 'EU law'. This book also admittedly has an emphasis on football. With few exceptions, only football is sufficiently commercialized to regularly raise issues in the context of Commission enforcement powers. UEFA is also active as a lobby group, and has raised the profile of many of the sporting-related issues considered here.

In writing this book, the authors received financial support from Edge Hill University's Faculty of Arts and Sciences Research and Knowledge Transfer Committee. In addition, the authors wish to acknowledge the support of Professor Alistair McCulloch, Dean of Research and Knowledge Transfer at the University. This book represents the first major publication of the Centre of Sports Law Research at Edge Hill University. We would like to extend our thanks to Francesco Rizzuto, Head of the Department of Law and Criminology. Without his support neither the Centre nor this book would have been possible. We also extend out thanks the editorial staff at T.M.C. Asser Press, in particular Robert Siekmann and Janwillem Soek, editors of the Asser International Sports Law Series, and Philip van Tongeren, publisher at T.M.C. Asser Press. Sincere apologies are owed to our families, whose support endured despite the many consecutive postponements of summer vacations.

Ormskirk, October 2007   Samuli MIETTINEN
                                                          Richard PARRISH

TABLE OF CONTENTS

Chapter 4

The Sporting Exception: Form and Substance

ABBREVIATIONS AND ACRONYMS

AGM	Corporation Annual General Meeting
AMSD	Audiovisual Media Services Directive
BSB	British Satellite Broadcasting
BSkyB	British Sky Broadcasting
CAS	Court of Arbitration for Sport
CFI	Court of First Instance
DG	Directorates General
DHB	German Handball Federation
DRC	Dispute Resolution Chamber
EBU	European Broadcasting Union
ECJ	European Court of Justice
ECVET	Vocational Education and Training
EEA	European Economic Area
EFAA	European Football Agents Association
EMAS	Eco Management Audit Scheme
ENGSO	European Non Governmental Sports Organisations
ENIC	English National Investment Company
ENPA	European Publishers News Association
EOC	European Olympic Committees
EPC	European Paralympic Committee
EPFL	Association of European Professional Football Leagues
EQF	European Qualifications Framework
FAPL	Football Association Premier League
FARE	Football against Racism in Europe network
FIA	Fédération Internationale de l'Automobile
FIBA	International Basketball Federation
FIFA	Fédération Internationale de Football Association
FIFPro	Fédération Internationale des Associations de Footballeurs Professionels
FIGC	Italian Football Federation
HEPA	EU Health-Enhancing Physical Activity
IGC	Intergovernmental Conference
IOC	International Olympic Committee
ITC	Independent Television Commission
NFL	National Football League
NOC	National Olympic Committees
OJ	Official Journal
SGEIs	Services of General Economic Interest
TAF	Arbitration Tribunal for Football
UCI	Union Cycliste Internationale
UEFA	Union des Associations Européennes de Football
UMTS	Universal Mobile Telecommunications System
URBSFA	Union Royale Belge des Sociétes de Football Association
WAADI	Netherlands Labour Market Intermediaries Act/Wet Allocatie Arbeidskrachten door Intermediairs
WADA	World Anti-Doping Agency
WHO	World Health Organisation

Chapter 1
Is Sport Special?

European Community law prohibits undertakings adopting restrictive practices, but in doing so it places great emphasis on the strength of justificatory arguments. In free movement law restrictions can be objectively justified with reference to the attainment of proportionately pursued legitimate objectives. In competition law, the decision on whether a restriction is to be condemned must take account of the context in which the restriction was imposed. This analysis can render certain practices incapable of being defined as a restriction. Even if it were, the party imposing the restriction has recourse to the exemption criteria which provides another opportunity to justify the existence of a restriction.

In *Walrave*, the European Court of Justice (ECJ) held that 'having regard to the objectives of the Community, the practice of sport is subject to Community law only in so far as it constitutes an economic activity within the meaning of Article 2 of the Treaty'.[1] In doing so the European Court of Justice established the 'sporting exception' in which rules of purely sporting interest were removed from the scope of the Treaty. Consequently, in the subsequent years the governing bodies of sport rarely engaged with the justificatory processes in Community law, instead relying on a standard 'of purely sporting interest' defence. The perception of the non-economic nature of sport was strengthened further by the amateur foundations of sport within the European model of sport which left 'a lasting imprint on the normative expectations of political stakeholders'.[2] The Court's judgment in *Bosman* dealt a severe blow to the non-economic argument.

In *Bosman*, the Belgian Football Association argued that only the major European clubs could be regarded as undertakings.[3] The European governing of football, the Union des Associations Européennes de Football (UEFA) argued that it is extremely difficult to distinguish between the economic and the sporting aspects of football and that a decision of the Court concerning professional sport may call into question the organisation of football as a whole.[4] Similarly, the German government stressed that in most cases a sport such as football is not an economic activity.[5] The Court rejected these arguments citing the narrowly construed non-economic exemption for national eligibility criteria in national team sports. The non-economic defence was ultimately

[1] Case 36/74 *Walrave and Koch* v. *Association Union Cycliste Internationale* [1974] *ECR* 1405, hereafter referred to as *Walrave*, Para. 4.

[2] H.E. Meier, *The Rise of the Regulatory State in Sport*, paper presented at the 3rd ECPR Conference, Budapest (8-10 September 2005) p. 5.

[3] Case C-415/93 *Union Royale Belge Sociétés de Football Association and others* v. *Bosman* [1995] *ECR* I-4921, Hereafter referred to as *Bosman*, Para. 70.

[4] Ibid. Para. 71.

[5] Ibid. Para. 72.

expunged in *Meca-Medina* in which the Court held that 'it is apparent that the mere fact that a rule is purely sporting in nature does not have the effect of removing from the scope of the Treaty the person engaging in the activity governed by that rule or the body which has laid it down'.[6] The legacy of the sporting exception is a reluctance on the part of the governing bodies to engage with more meaningful justifications on why sport should be afforded special status within the EU's legal framework. It contributed to their failure 'to provide an intellectually convincing account of why it should be allowed a partial or total immunity from the application of legal rules to which normal industries are subject'.[7] Following *Bosman* and *Meca-Medina*, the new agenda for the governing bodies is to fill this intellectual void.

This agenda forms the starting point of this book. In particular, this first chapter interrogates the intellectual foundations of the specificity of sport argument presented in the Commission's White Paper on Sport. In it, the Commission approached the issue of the specificity of sport from two angles. First, it argued that there exists specificity of sporting activities and rules such as separate competitions for men and women, limitations on the number of participations in competitions, or the need to ensure competitive balance in sport. In addition, the Commission cited examples of specificity of sports structure which includes the autonomy and diversity of sport organisations, the pyramid structure of the European model of sport, solidarity in sport, the organisation of sport on a national basis and the principle of a single federation per sport.[8]

1.1.   SPECIFICITY OF SPORTING ACTIVITIES AND RULES

1.1.1.   Mutual interdependence and the need for co-ordinated action

Sporting competition is argued to be distinct from economic competition. There are features of mutual interdependence in the success of sport, and because sporting action needs to be centrally co-ordinated. Much sport is organised on the basis of teams competing in leagues. This results in mutual interdependence between competitors being a common feature. For instance, sporting competition cannot take place unilaterally. It requires the participants or the league to co-ordinate activity over such issues as setting fixtures and establishing the rules of the game. Whilst these forms of co-ordinated activity are not commonly permitted in other industries, it is eminently reasonable to allow for limited cartelisation in sport. The question concerns how far cartelisation should extend. Whilst co-ordinated action over the setting of fixtures is not objectionable as having an opponent to play is a pre-requisite for engaging in the

---

[6] Case C-519/04 P *David Meca-Medina and Igor Majcen* v. *Commission* [2006] *ECR* I-6991 Para. 27. Hereafter referred to as *Meca-Medina*, Para. 27.

[7] S. Weatherill, 'Resisting the Pressures of "Americanisation": The Influence of European Community Law on the "European Model of Sport"', in S. Greenfield and G. Osborn, eds., *Law and Sport in Contemporary Society* (London, Frank Cass 2000) p. 158.

[8] Commission of the European Communities, *White Paper on Sport*, COM(2007) 391 final, p. 13.

activity, other forms of co-ordinated action have more pronounced economic impacts. For example, the inability of some clubs to individually exploit their broadcasting rights undermines competition between undertakings and has consequential impacts on other markets such as the broadcasting sector. Yet even in this realm of overtly economic activity, market objectives can be qualified by other considerations such as the need to collectively exploit broadcasting rights for the purposes of ensuring horizontal and vertical solidarity in sport. The economic impact of co-ordinated action in sport is examined more closely elsewhere in this book as is the legal analysis of such activity. Nevertheless, co-ordination is a necessary feature of the sports market and one that marks it out as being different from other sectors. As Flynn and Gilbert argue, 'there is no harm to competition from the co-ordination among the member teams when those teams are not economic competitors in a relevant market'.[9]

1.1.2. Competitive balance

Mutual interdependence between participants precludes the application of a cut-throat model of competition within leagues. The objective of team A is not to take market share from team B in order to effect team B's ultimate withdrawal from the market. It is argued that a position of perpetual sporting dominance does not serve spectators, leagues, or even the club itself. Sport, it is suggested, requires uncertainty of result to maintain public interest, the so-called outcome uncertainty hypothesis. Without public interest, revenue streams in sport would dwindle as fans stay away from matches, refuse to consume merchandising and as broadcasters switch their interest to other fields of entertainment. An inequality of resources can also lead to unequal competition and a concentration of success in a small number of teams. Redistributive mechanisms therefore promote greater outcome uncertainty. Consequently, 'the promotion of competitive balance is a legitimate policy concern for all sports governing bodies'.[10] Promoting competitive balance between participants requires co-ordinated activity not generally seen elsewhere. This can include the use of limits on the number of teams participating in a league, reserve clauses, draft rules, roster limits, salary caps, transfer windows, collective bargaining arrangements, revenue sharing, joint merchandising and the collective sale and reinvestment of broadcasting rights. The need for market intervention to protect competitive balance is regarded by many as a self evident truth and these arguments have filtered into the considerations of US and EU courts and competition authorities who have explored the legality of co-ordinated action in sport. In *Bosman* the ECJ stated that 'in view of the considerable social importance of sporting activities and in particular football in the Community, the aims of maintaining a balance between clubs by preserving a certain degree of equality and uncertainty as to results ... must be accepted as legitimate'.[11] Nevertheless, since the

---

[9] M. Flynn and R. Gilbert, 'The Analysis of Professional Sports Leagues as Joint Ventures', 111 *Economic Journal* (February 2001) F45.

[10] J. Arnaut, *Independent European Sport Review* (2006), see at <www.independentfootballreview. com> p. 47.

[11] *Bosman* Para. 106.

ECJ's judgment in *Meca-Medina*, the governing bodies need to re-articulate the case for cartelised action based on evidence supporting the indispensability of the co-ordinated for maintaining competitive balance.

Szymanski distinguishes between match uncertainty, seasonal uncertainty and championship uncertainty.[12] The first refers to the level of competition in a single match, the second refers to a single championship season and the third refers to there being a variety of champions over a period of years rather than a concentration of success. Reviewing the literature, Szymanski suggests that in the context of match uncertainty, demand for tickets peaks where a home team's probability of winning is about twice that of the visiting team. For seasonal uncertainty, Szymanski argues for caution depending on the methodology employed. Whilst some studies have identified a connection between attendance and uncertainty others reveal decreasing attendances in uncertainty. Szymanski argues that it may be impossible to isolate a single influence such as uncertainty of outcome when identifying causal relationships.[13] Little evidence exists on the question of championship uncertainty. The Arnaut Report suggested that '[w]orryingly ... in recent years there has been a significant decline in competitive balance in a number of top flight leagues across Europe, which is supported by statistical analysis'.[14] An examination of thirty years of English top division football reveals a tendency for one team to dominate certain time periods. Since the formation of the English Premier League in 1992 only four teams have won the title. Manchester United won nine times, Arsenal three, Chelsea two and Blackburn once. In the 15 seasons prior to the formation of the Premier League Liverpool won the championship eight times, Arsenal twice, Everton twice and Leeds United, Aston Villa and Nottingham Forest once. This indicates some diminution in competitive balance but reveals a tendency for a single club to dominate throughout certain time periods. An important distinction between these time periods is the impact of the UEFA Champions League which since 1992/3 has admitted teams not winning the national championship. Arguably this has heightened competitive imbalance in that it has widened revenue imbalances between those qualifying for the competition and those not.[15] The negative effect of the Champions League on competitive balance has led some to recommend its abolition.[16] Nevertheless, evidence of imbalance requires discussion on the consequences of imbalance. In the USA for example, concern at chronic competitive imbalance in Major League Baseball has not diminished its

---

[12] S. Szymanski, 'The Economic Design of Sporting Contests', 41 *Journal of Economic Literature* (2003) p. 1155.

[13] Ibid. p. 1156.

[14] J. Arnaut, *Independent European Sport Review* (2006), see at <www.independentfootballreview. com> p. 48.

[15] P. Massey, 'Are Sports Cartels Different? An Analysis of EU Commission Decisions Concerning the Collective Selling Arrangements for Football Broadcasting Rights', 30(1) *World Competition* (2007) pp. 101-104.

[16] S. Késenne, 'The Peculiar International Economics of Professional Football in Europe', 54(3) *Scottish Journal of Political Economy* (2007) pp. 398-399.

popularity.[17] A similar trend can be observed in European football with attendances continuing to experience growth.[18] Competitive imbalance therefore has not been conclusively proven to cause economic destabilisation of the sport as a whole.

Empirical evidence appears equivocal. Taking into consideration 22 studies where match, seasonal and championship uncertainty were at issue, Szymanski reports that ten offered clear support for the uncertainty of outcome hypothesis, seven offer weak support and five contradict it. Nevertheless, 'even supportive studies on the issue of match uncertainty seem to imply that attendance is maximised when the home team is about twice as likely to win as the visiting team'.[19] Szymanski then reviews the evidence on the effectiveness of certain types of restriction which purport to enhance competitive balance such as the reserve clause, the draft system, roster limits, revenue sharing, salary caps, luxury taxes, unionisation and restrictions on the number of teams in a league. Whilst some support the hypothesis that intervention is necessary to correct competitive imbalance, others suggest that intervention has either no effect or indeed has a negative effect. For example, critics of revenue sharing argue that this reduces the incentive for profit maximising team owners to compete thus producing a more uneven distribution of talent in a league which reduces competitive balance.[20] Others argue that restraints which are justified on the grounds of competitive balance are actually profit enhancing schemes by leagues.[21] The impact of the type of co-ordinated interventions in sport described above are dealt with throughout this book and reviewed elsewhere by Szymanski.[22] Nevertheless, the evidence on competitive balance is far from clear-cut and judicial bodies and competition authorities can be expected to exercise caution in permitting restrictions justified in terms of maintaining competitive balance.

The Arnaut Report stated that the need to address competitive imbalance in sport justifies non-financial measures such as squad size limits and/or local trained player requirements, and financially based measures such as greater revenue re-distribution based on collective selling and cost controls such as salary caps.[23] Such assumptions require greater research-based support. Furthermore, correcting competitive imbalance may not be in the best interest of those capable of affecting change. Noll indicates that governing bodies or leagues face financial incentives to maintain the

---

[17] S. Szymanski, 'Baseball Economics', in W. Andreff and S. Szymanski, *Handbook on the Economics of Sport* (Cheltenham, Edward Elgar 2006) p. 449.

[18] Deloitte, *Annual Review of Football Finance* (2007).

[19] S. Szymanski, 'The Economic Design of Sporting Contests', 41 *Journal of Economic Literature* (2003) p. 1156.

[20] S. Szymanski and S. Késenne, 'Competitive Balance and Gate Revenue Sharing in Team Sports', 52 *The Journal of Industrial Economics* (2004) pp. 165-166.

[21] S. Ross, 'Competition Law as a Constraint on Monopolistic Exploitation by Sports Leagues and Clubs', 19(4) *Oxford Review of Economic Policy* (2003).

[22] S. Szymanski, 'The Economic Design of Sporting Contests', 41 *Journal of Economic Literature* (2003) pp. 1137-1187.

[23] J. Arnaut, *Independent European Sport Review* (2006), see at <www.independentfootballreview.com> p. 41.

status quo.[24] Competitive imbalance generates significant revenues for governing bodies and the major clubs. In this connection, the governing bodies face resistance to change from the larger clubs who also benefit from the maintenance of competitive imbalance and who are increasingly becoming more influential through the G14 grouping of clubs. Consequently, whilst competitive balance serves as a useful mantra for those justifying restrictions in the labour market and the product market, the EU can be expected to take a more evidence based view as indicated in the Commission's White Paper package. A key question is whether the competitive imbalances flow not from the deregulation of the players' markets, but from the regulatory choices made by the governing bodies in the product market. In this connection, the Champions League itself appears to be a significant cause of imbalance rather than the abolition of the retain-and-transfer system. Finally, it must be questioned whether restrictions imposed in the player market and the product market are in fact intended as a means of controlling players' wages and mobility in order to secure maximal profits for clubs and governing bodies. Clearly, restrictions imposed on clubs and players cannot be justified simply on the grounds that they are profitable.

1.1.3. Ensuring the regularity and proper functioning of competitions

The primary responsibility of a sports governing body is to ensure they discharge their regulatory competence in relation to ensuring the regularity and proper functioning of competitions. At one level this entails ensuring the rules of the game are devised and observed. For example, in order to ensure consistency within and between leagues, it is important that the height of goal posts are standardised and the shape of the ball is uniform. It is also crucial that a governing body ensures that a fixture list is devised, officials are dispatched to the correct matches and infractions of the rules by players are recorded so that ineligible players are appropriately suspended. A governing body also has a duty to ensure the game is conducted safely with players, officials and spectators not subject to undue risk. As is discussed below, the governing bodies argue that the discharge of these responsibilities requires them to hold a position of regulatory dominance so that standardised conditions of play and enforcement can be achieved. Yet the manner in which regulatory choices have been made has attracted some criticism from those who identify the exercise of regulatory discretion as a mask for commercial protectionism.[25] For example, the choice to permit or exclude sports equipment will entail consequences on those companies who manufacture such equipment.[26]

---

[24] R. Noll, 'Broadcasting and Team Sports', 54(3) *Scottish Journal of Political Economy* (2007) p. 417.

[25] Commission Press Release IP/99/434, 30/6/99, 'Commission Opens Formal Proceedings into Formula One and Other International Motor Racing Series'.

[26] Commission Press Release IP/98/355, 15/04/1998, 'The Commission Conditionally Approves Sponsorship Between the Danish Tennis Federation and Its Tennis Ball Suppliers'.

1.1.4. Encouraging the training and education of young players

In addition to recognising the need to maintain competitive balance in sport, the court in *Bosman* also acknowledged the legitimate objective of the governing bodies of encouraging the recruitment and training of young players.[27] Again, the need to educate and train young employees is a common feature of all business activity but it seems only in the context of sport that specific interventions are pursued. The sports sector is argued to be unique in so far as participants are often at their prime in their early careers and the development of their talent begins at a very early age. Spending considerable time and money on players only to see them lost to a rival without compensation creates disincentives for clubs to nurture talent and would negatively affect the sector as talent is not brought through. Furthermore, the role of a well rounded education for young players takes on added significance in light of the very high proportion of young trainees failing to be offered professional terms, a situation the governing bodies argue is compounded by cross border labour migration. A European Commission report on the training and education of young players revealed that less than 10% of young English academy footballers were offered a professional contract.[28] The report also revealed a range of education and training models employed throughout the European Union. This was also a theme of the European Parliament's Belet Report on The Future of Professional Football in Europe. The Report pointed out that young players require general education and vocational training in parallel with their club and training activity, so that they do not depend entirely on the clubs. There is an inherent danger of social exclusion for young people who become dependent on their club only to fail to be selected.[29]

In the *Bosman* case, UEFA argued that the disputed transfer system was one such way of ensuring sufficient incentives were maintained encouraging clubs to educate and train young players. Whilst the court recognised that the prospect of receiving a transfer fee would encourage clubs to train young talent, the revenue streams from transfer fees could not be relied on by clubs given that it is impossible to predict the sporting future of young players. Furthermore, the fees were unrelated to the actual cost borne by clubs of training young players and less restrictive means of achieving the objective were available.[30] Consequently, the court ruled that the disputed transfer system was unlawful. Since *Bosman*, the transfer system has been revised and International Federation of Football Associations (FIFA) and UEFA are still concerned with the impact of the revised transfer regime on contract stability, supporters identification with teams composed of transient labour, and the question of the financial health of a sector whose clubs rely on the market, and not their academies, to fill squads.

---

[27] *Bosman* Para. 106.

[28] Commission of the European Communities, *Education of Young Sportspersons, Final Report*, A report by PMP in partnership with the Institute of Sport and Leisure Policy (Leicestershire, Loughborough University: August 2004), p. 49.

[29] European Parliament, rapporteur: Ivo Belet, *The Future of Professional Football in Europe*, European Parliament Committee on Culture and Education, 2006/2130(INI), Paras. 16-19.

[30] *Bosman* Paras. 108 and 109.

Whilst the details of the new transfer system raise some legal issues with respect to the application of Article 39 EC, the main point is that the EU considers the principle of encouraging the education and training of young players as a legitimate objective. Not all commentators agree with this assessment. Weatherill states, 'I cannot see any compelling reason for supposing that a football club is any less likely to train young employees because they might subsequently quit the company than a supermarket or a university would be'.[31] This line of reasoning sees sports clubs as no different to other businesses which nurture and retain talent through good employment practice rather than restraining their trade. Consequently, whilst Weatherill may be persuaded that the specificities of sport include mutual interdependence and ensuring competitive balance, he is not convinced that training and educating young employees marks sport out as at all different.

1.1.5. Promoting stadium attendance and participation at all levels

For spectators and players, sport is truly special when there is a vibrant atmosphere in the stadium. This is not in question. For Arnaut, it therefore follows 'that sports bodies have a legitimate interest in taking steps to protect and promote attendance at live matches'.[32] Traditionally this has manifested itself through the enactment by governing bodies of blocking rules which prevents a game from being broadcast on television at the same time as the event is being staged. This is further justified by reference to the need to ensure a healthy level of participation at all levels of the game, in other words encouraging children and amateurs to play sport at traditional times rather than simply watching sport live on television. Blocking rules have been a common feature of US and European sport but they do raise competition law concerns as they restrict the ability of broadcasters to transmit matches at times favourable to their schedules and they prevent national football federations, and potentially clubs, from freely marketing their transmission rights. Those who argue that live television has a negative effect on stadium attendance subscribe to the substitution theory which suggests that fans substitute stadium attendance for live television coverage. Alternatively, the complimentary theory asserts that live television compliments stadium attendance and has no adverse effect on it. The academic research on this question is inconclusive, the details of which are reviewed more fully elsewhere in this book. In April 2001 the European Commission found that allowing national associations to block the broadcasting of games during a two and a half hour slot on either Saturday or Sunday fell outside the scope of Article 81 as no appreciable restriction of competition could be identified.[33] Consequently, it cannot be gleaned from this decision that governing bodies have a legitimate objective in forming restrictive rules designed to protect stadium attendance, although neither can it be argued that they do not.

---

[31] S. Weatherill, 'Resisting the Pressures of "Americanisation": The Influence of European Community Law on the "European Model of Sport"', in S. Greenfield and G. Osborn, eds., Law and Sport in Contemporary Society (London, Frank Cass 2000) p. 166.

[32] J. Arnaut, *Independent European Sport Review* (2006), see at <www.independentfootballreview. com> p. 40.

[33] Commission Decision 2001/478/EC *OJ* L171/12.

1.1.6. Protection of national teams

There is no doubt that national team sports hold a special place in the affections of supporters. The strength of national competition is also a major source of revenue for the governing bodies, particularly in some sports such as cricket in which the financial viability of County teams is inextricably linked to the health of the national team. Elsewhere, Allen argued that 'the England national team's performances are important in affecting attendance at Premier League games'.[34] The importance of protecting national team sports is acknowledged by the European Court as a legitimate objective. In *Walrave* the ECJ held that the prohibition on nationality discrimination 'does not affect the composition of sport teams, in particular national teams, the formation of which is a question of purely sporting interest and as such has nothing to do with economic activity'.[35] Nevertheless, the ECJ did find that 'this restriction on the scope of the provisions in question must however remain limited to its proper objective'.[36] In Deliège, the Advocate General remarked, 'the pursuit of a national team's interests constitutes an overriding need in the public interest which, by its very nature, is capable of justifying restrictions on the freedom to provide services'.[37] Consequently proportionate rules designed by the sports governing bodies to protect national team sports are unlikely to be considered a breach of the EC Treaty. Nevertheless, some rules purporting to protect national teams have been criticised such as nationality restrictions in club football which purport to create a pool of talent eligible to play for the national team, the mandatory release of players from clubs to national associations, the fixing of the international match calendar and rules on the local training of players. Other rules, such as selection criteria for national teams, are more robust.

1.1.7. Ensuring the integrity of competition

Sport is only able to maintain public interest if spectators have confidence in the integrity of competition. Spectators, broadcasters and sponsors would question the value of watching, broadcasting and sponsoring a competition which is fixed, distorted by drug users or in which the unpredictability of outcome is seriously questionable. Consequently, governing bodies have devised rules which, whilst *prima facie* restrictive of commercial competition, are necessary to maintain public confidence and fair play. Such rules include anti-doping measures, club licensing schemes designed to ensure good governance, rules on the ownership, control and influence of clubs, rules regulating players' agents and rules restricting the times in which transfers can take place (transfer windows). Whilst each of these categories of rule impact upon the personal and commercial freedoms of individual stakeholders, they are defended on the

---

[34] S. Allen, 'Satellite Television and Football Attendance: The Not So Super Effect', 11(2) *Applied Economics Letters* (2004) p. 123

[35] *Walrave* Para. 8.

[36] Ibid. Para. 9.

[37] Joined Cases C-51/96 and C-191/97 *Deliège* v. *Ligue francophone de Judo et disciplines Associés Asb* [2000] *ECR* I-2549, Opinion of Advocate General Cosmas, point 84. Hereafter referred to as *Deliège*.

grounds that they serve the greater collective good and without them there could be no meaningful competition. The plea from the governing bodies is that the law should recognise the indispensability of these rules and remove them from judicial scrutiny.

1.1.8. Connecting with local communities

Sports clubs play a significant role within local communities. Clubs often assist with community initiatives and play a role in the education and training of local children and young adults. Furthermore, clubs offer an important source of entertainment for local communities with few leisure pursuits being able to lay claim to a loyal following of anything from a few hundred to many thousands of spectators. In this connection, sport performs important social and economic functions within local communities. Governing bodies claim that the law should respect sporting autonomy because of the local importance of sport. In this connection, debate has taken place over the extent to which clubs should be representative of the locality in which they are based. Rules requiring clubs to play their matches within their locality and rules requiring clubs to include within their squads a number of locally trained players have been debated within this context. The question is whether it is considered a legitimate objective for governing bodies to pursue rules designed to connect clubs with their locality and whether rules on local tying and locally trained players represent an apt and proportionate pursuit of these objectives. In this connection, the closest analogy came by way of *Bosman*. The Court found that

> 'a football club's link with the Member State in which it is established cannot be regarded as any more inherent in its sporting activity than its links with its locality, town, region (...) Even though national championships are played between clubs from different regions, towns or localities, there is no rule restricting the right of clubs to field players from other regions, towns or localities in such matches'.[38]

It matters not to supporters that teams are composed of players from other towns, cities and indeed countries. The performance of the team is key.

1.2.   SPECIFICITY OF THE SPORT STRUCTURE

1.2.1. Is sport a private matter?

The phrase 'sporting autonomy' assumes that sport and the law are separate realms, each populated by principles of limited exportability. Whilst sport is a social and cultural activity, practiced privately for amusement and entertainment, 'legal norms are fixed rules which prescribe rights and duties; relationships within the social world of sport are not seen in this way'.[39] Nationally and internationally sport is organised

---

[38] *Bosman* Para. 131.

[39] K. Foster, 'Developments in Sporting Law', in L. Allison, ed., *The Changing Politics of Sport* (Manchester, Manchester University Press 1993) p. 106.

by governing bodies many of which are unincorporated associations of members or private limited companies. Whilst this does not preclude the possibility of recourse to the courts for those involved in a dispute, the particular nature of the activities in question does limit litigants to a judicial field restricted to those located within private law fields. For example, within the UK, the actions of sports governing bodies are not subject to challenge by way of judicial review.[40] Traditionally in Britain at least, the executive and legislative have confined their involvement in sport to a narrow range of sporting issues which touch upon matters of public concern such as public health, public order and public safety. What is left is a matter of private concern in which the state does not wish to trespass. This has reinforced the perception that sport no only possesses values which are different from those which the law normally regulates but also that it possesses only limited public functions.

The pattern across Europe is similar with only a small number of states adopting interventionist sports policies although even here decentralist tendencies are evident.[41] For example, the French government has gradually scaled back its central co-ordination of sports policy towards a mixed model.[42] In Greece, another interventionist state, the government passed a 2006 sports act in order to reverse the suspension imposed on the Hellenic Football Federation by FIFA after complaints by football's world governing body that Greek sports legislation conflicted with FIFA statutes regarding the independence of member associations. In many other European countries, states have adopted non-interventionist sports policies and courts have generally been reluctant to intervene in disputes. Nevertheless, the labels of 'non-interventionism' and 'judicial reluctance' are under strain. Whilst there is not a trend towards wholesale statutory regulation of sport, governments and legislatures are increasingly recognising the public character of sport. For example, in France the state law on sport refers to sport being 'of general interest'.[43] In the UK, sports governing bodies are considered public bodies pursuant to the 1998 Human Rights Act. Recognising the public nature of sport has implications for regulatory environment sport finds itself within. Governments are now keen to use sport to implement broader social and economic policies. This has led to a greater focus on how public expenditure is targeted and there is now a general expectation that the sports governing bodies must respond to governmental objectives and translate state goals on good governance, anti-doping, non-discrimination and child protection into their constitutions. For example, in the UK, receipt of public funds is dependent on the governing bodies responding to these agendas. Promises of delivering state objectives can also affect the regulatory environment. For instance, the 2006 Independent European Sports Review explicitly linked the is-

---

[40] *Law* v. *National Greyhound Racing Club Ltd.* [1983] 1 *WLR* 1302; *R* v. *Jockey Club, ex p Mass-ingberd-Mundy* [1993] 2 *All ER* 207; *R* v. *Jockey Club, ex p Aga Khan* [1993] 1 *WLR* 909; *R (on the application of Mullins)* v. *Appeal Board of the Jockey Club*, [2005] EWHC 2197' *Flaherty* v. *National Greyhound Racing Club* [2005] EWCA Civ 117.

[41] A.N. Chaker, *Study of National Sports Legislation in Europe* (Strasbourg: Council of Europe Publishing 1999).

[42] J-F. Nys, 'Central Government and Sport', in W. Andreff and S. Szymanski, *Handbook on the Economics of Sport* (Cheltenham, Edward Elgar 2006) pp. 263-267.

[43] Sports Act, 16 July 1984.

sues of judicial oversight with those of good governance in sport.[44] Yet in the context of EU sports regulation, the lack of a public character to sport is immaterial. Referring to nationality discrimination, the ECJ in *Walrave* stated that the 'prohibition of such discrimination does not only apply to the action of public authorities but extends likewise to rules of any other nature aimed at regulating in a collective manner gainful employment and the provision of services'.[45]

A lack of good governance in sport points to the reason why 'judicial reluctance' is also strained. In the UK, when a sports governing body is subject to a private law challenge, the standards expected of that governing body are in effect the same as those demanded under judicial review. Whilst the courts would not want to substitute the knowledge and expertise of a governing body for that of the court, they do demand that governing bodies act rationally, proportionately and with procedural fairness and that they follow both the law of the land and their own rules. Clearly, membership of the European Union offers litigants in Member States a new venue through which the decisions of the sports governing bodies can be challenged either privately or via the public enforcement routes available by way of a complaint to the European Commission. The incursion of Community law into sport is a particularly unwelcome development for the governing bodies. As Duthie explains, the Court's decision in *Bosman* was 'considered by many in sport to be a significant invasion by European law into an area which it did not belong'.[46] Community law, lacking as it did and still does a reference point in the Treaty defining the specificity of sport, is considered a blunt instrument when dealing with the sector. This is, according to the governing bodies, compounded by the apparent inability of the Court and Commission to balance the question of the specificity of sport with the primacy of the fundamental freedoms which has 'plunged the labour market in professional sport deeply into economic liberalism'.[47] These criticisms are difficult to reconcile with the sizeable economic effects that flow from the decisions of sports governing bodies, the constitutional requirement for the Court and the Commission to uphold the *acquis* and the apparent willingness of these Community bodies to actually recognise the special characteristics of sport. This is elaborated most clearly in the *Bosman* judgment in which the Court referred to the 'considerable social importance of sporting activities and in particular football in the Community' and the need to recognise as legitimate the aims of 'maintaining a balance between clubs by preserving a certain degree of equality and uncertainty as to results and of encouraging the recruitment and training of young players'[48] as justifications for special treatment within internal market rules.

---

[44] J. Arnaut, *Independent European Sport Review* (2006), see at <www.independentfootballreview. com> pp. 129-140.

[45] *Walrave* Para. 17.

[46] M. Duthie, 'European Community Sports Policy', in A. Lewis and J. Taylor, eds., *Sport: Law and Practice* (London, Butterworths Lexis Nexis 2002) p. 313.

[47] J-C. Breillat and F. Lagarde, 'The Specificity of Sport and European Community Law: The Example of Nationality', in W. Andreff and S. Szymanski, *Handbook on the Economics of Sport* (Cheltenham, Edward Elgar 2006) p. 742.

[48] *Bosman* Para. 106.

1.2.2. 'Self regulation is effective, efficient and economical'

A corollary to the argument that sport is a private activity is that sports governing bodies claim that they are best placed to regulate their respective sports. In *Bosman*, Advocate General Lenz stated that 'sports associations have the right and the duty to draw up rules for the practice and organisation of the sport, and that that activity falls within the association's autonomy which is protected as a fundamental right'.[49] This right partly derives from the fact that the governing bodies have acquired an understanding of the sport far superior to that of external parties such as regulators and judges. English jurisprudence has historically recognised this. In *Flaherty* v. *National Greyhound Racing Club Ltd*, Scott Baker LJ referred to the sports governing bodies having an 'unrivalled and practical knowledge of the particular sport that they are required to regulate'.[50] Earlier in *Enderby Town Football Club Ltd.* v. *Football Association Ltd.*, Lord Denning MR considered that '[j]ustice can often be done in them better by a good layman than by a bad lawyer. This is especially so in activities like football and other sports, where no points of law are likely to arise, and it is all part of the proper regulation of the game'.[51] Furthermore, as Foster argues, with many sports regulators being former players, compliance with these rules is higher as rules are seen as legitimate.[52] In *Deliège* the European Court of Justice acknowledged that

> 'it naturally falls to the bodies concerned, such as organisers of tournaments, sports federations or professional athletes' associations, to lay down appropriate rules and to make their selections in accordance with them. [68] In that connection, it must be conceded that the delegation of such a task to the national federations, which normally have the necessary knowledge and experience, is the arrangement adopted in most sporting disciplines, which is based in principle on the existence of a federation in each country'.[53]

It has also been suggested by governing bodies that as entities not established within the EU, they should not be subject to Community law. Furthermore, some have claimed that even though established in the EU, they have responsibilities which reach beyond the confines of the EU. UEFA for example have 51 national associations as members. On the question of governing bodies being established outside the EU (UEFA is established in Switzerland for example), it has long been established that Community law applies to all legal relationships in so far as these relationships, by reason either of the place where they are entered into or the place where they take effect, can be located within the territory of the Community.[54] On the question of global regulatory responsibilities, Weatherill explains, 'one might respond, a global cartel

---

[49] *Bosman*, Opinion of Advocate General Lenz, point 216.

[50] *Flaherty* v. *National Greyhound Racing Club Ltd*, [2005] EWCA Civ 1117 Para. 21.

[51] *Enderby Town Football Club Ltd* v. *Football Association Ltd*, [1970] E. No. 2145; [1970] 3 *WLR* 1021 at 605.

[52] K. Foster, 'How Can Sport Be Regulated?', in S. Greenfield and G. Osborn, eds., *Law and Sport in Contemporary Society* (London, Frank Cass 2000) p. 278.

[53] *Deliège* Paras. 67-68.

[54] *Walrave* Para. 28.

may be more, not less, pernicious than a domestic or regional cartel and may require supervision in the public interest by any and every available regulator'.[55]

The juridification of sport creates incentives for parties to litigate and aggrieved parties will venue shop until they find redress. This creates legal uncertainty in the sports world and, for the governing bodies, this cannot be tolerated as the nature of sporting competition requires swift dispute resolution. Participants, supporters and broadcasters need to be satisfied that the outcome of a particular event is final. They cannot wait for lengthy legal proceedings to be exhausted as the time limited structure of championships does not allow for this. Furthermore, the career of many sportsmen and women is short and it is impractical for individuals and clubs to involve them- selves in lengthy judicial proceedings. For example, Jean Marc Bosman began his legal proceedings in 1990 with the European Court of Justice finding in his favour at the end of 1995. The case was then returned to the national courts for application with Bosman finally receiving a financial settlement in December 1998. This is one reason why bodies such as the Court of Arbitration for Sport have emerged. Court of Arbitration for Sport (CAS) offers relatively low cost and speedy access to justice although as Nafziger suggests,

> 'what would arguably be lost by formalizing the CAS process ... are several other ad- vantages of arbitration: confidentiality; relatively low cost; simplified procedures; speed; meditative quality; capacity to help restore; preserve and maintain relationships between disputing parties; flexibility and customization to particular circumstances and the wishes of the parties; and international enforceability'.[56]

The ability of sports bodies to self-regulate has important financial implications. Liti- gation is expensive and the costs of defending claims and settling disputes divert scare resources from the mainstream activities of sports governing bodies such as redistributing revenues throughout all levels of sport. There is also an argument that the costs of litigation should be borne by the sport in question and not transferred to the public.

1.2.3. The internalisation of sports law

Lord Denning's reference to justice being better served by a good layman than by a bad lawyer is the philosophy underpinning the creation of the CAS. In order to estab- lish more affordable and expedited dispute resolution, and as a means of fending off judicial encroachment from Courts uneducated in the ways of sport, the sports gov- erning bodies have created their own internal legal systems composed of disciplin- ary panels with appeals procedures. Courts have generally been unwilling to unpick the decisions of these quasi-judicial bodies so long as certain procedural standards

---

[55] S. Weatherill, 'Resisting the Pressures of "Americanisation": The Influence of European Com- munity Law on the "European Model of Sport"', in S. Greenfield and G. Osborn, eds., *Law and Sport in Contemporary Society* (London, Frank Cass 2000) p. 158.

[56] J. Nafziger, *International Sports Law* (Ardsley, New York State: Transnational 2004) p. 52.

are upheld. These include the requirement to act rationally, proportionately and with procedural fairness and that governing bodies follow both the law of the land and their own rules. As sport is a global phenomenon, new forms of international sports dispute resolution have emerged. Pre-eminent among them being the CAS. Established by the International Olympic Committee (IOC) in 1983, its statute coming into force in June 1984, the role of the CAS is, according to Beloff et al. a major source of 'the incipient international lex sportiva which ... is in the process of taking shape'.[57] This is 'a process that comprises a more or less distinctive body of rules, principles, institutions and procedures to govern important consequences of transnational sports activity'.[58] The involvement of the Olympic movement has imbued this emerging international sports law with normative, non-governmental features and legal principles distinct from other forms of international law negotiated between states or deriving from national legal systems. Indeed, as Kerr adds, 'sport is particularly special in its interaction with the law because of the unique position it occupies in international jurisprudence'.[59] Consequently, only international bodies such as the CAS can offer the legal certainty required for the proper functioning of sport, for over time the emerging *lex sportiva* serves to act as the basis for the harmonisation of rules thus guiding adjudicative awards in national courts, and guiding the nature of disciplinary hearings and arbitral awards within the sports world itself. It also offers the prospect of affecting the content of national sports legislation and even the prospect of influencing state behaviour in the international sporting environment.

The CAS has the ability to hear cases involving a wide range of issues including those of a purely sporting nature (such as disciplinary hearings) and issues of a more commercial nature. As the CAS itself claims, it is a body which offers specialist knowledge, low cost and rapid action and a means of resolving sports disputes adapted to the specific needs of the international sporting community.[60] The CAS also has the potential to overcome some concerns associated with dubious decisions of the disciplinary panels of individual sports.

Most of the international sports federations who are affiliated to the Olympic movement, including FIFA, refer cases to the CAS although some have their own Arbitral Tribunals. However, disputes involving sport are still frequently settled outside the 'sporting family' with the role of national judicial bodies and the EU being particularly problematic for the governing bodies. Nafziger argues that 'among the most difficult issues of international sports law today – perhaps the most difficult – is the role of national courts', particularly in relation to questions of jurisdiction, choice of law and enforcement of judgments.[61] If national courts, and indeed the EU's judiciary, are too active in controlling the actions of international sports bodies a fragmented

---

[57] M. Beloff, T. Kerr and M. Demetriou, *Sports Law* (Oxford, Hart 1999) p. 256.

[58] J. Nafziger, *International Sports Law* (Ardsley, New York State: Transnational 2004) p. 1.

[59] T. Kerr, 'Is Sport Special?', 9(1) *Sport and the Law Journal* (2001) p. 78.

[60] M. Reeb, 'The Role and Functions of the Court of Arbitration for Sport (CAS)', 2 *International Sports Law Journal* (2002) p. 21.

[61] J. Nafziger, 'International Sports Law as a Process for Resolving Disputes', 45 *International and Comparative Law Quarterly* (1996) p. 131.

international regulatory environment may arise and the construction of international sports law will be impeded. As Beloff et al. argue, national courts 'should intervene as little as possible, since otherwise the development of the international machinery will be hampered'.[62] However, if national courts shy away from intervention the rights of affected stakeholders may not be sufficiently protected.

For the governing bodies, the benefits of having such an international 'in-house' dispute resolution tribunal are clear. However, the organisation and financing of the CAS has raised some concerns relating to its independence and impartiality. In the 1994 *Gundel* case the Swiss Federal Tribunal drew attention to some potential conflicts of interest within CAS including its relationship with the IOC who financed the CAS, had the ability to modify the CAS statute and who retained considerable influence over the appointment of CAS members.[63] The case led to major reform within the CAS. However, the IOC still continues to fund the CAS although this burden is now shared with the other sports bodies.

There is suspicion that the sports governing bodies crave autonomy and self regulation and wish the CAS to develop and interpret the *lex sportiva* in this light. The role of the CAS in the emergence of a body of international sports law is receiving increasing academic attention, yet the very use of the term international sports law has come under scrutiny from Ken Foster.[64] Foster wonders whether the linkage between the term and the concept *lex sportiva* has been stretched too far. Foster reminds us that international law regulates relations between nation states and consequently international sports law can be defined as the principles of international law applicable to sport. But Foster argues that international sports law is wider than the general principles of public international law for it includes those 'constitutional safeguards' common to western democracies including clear unambiguous rules, fair hearings in disciplinary proceedings, no arbitrary or irrational decisions, and impartial decision making.[65] These do not amount to a *lex sportiva* as they are external legal sources not generated by the sports federations. They are the basic principles of law which must be respected by the federations and applied by the CAS on pain of litigation before national courts. Consequently, the autonomy of the federations is 'limited'.[66] Foster then examines rules that are generated by the international federations themselves. First, he identifies the rules of the game and rules designed to protect the spirit and integrity of the game. These he calls *lex ludica* and suggests they too should be distinguished and separated from the concept of *lex sportiva*. They are 'sporting laws'. For the most part, as evidenced by the jurisprudence of national courts, the EU and the

---

[62] M. Beloff, T. Kerr and M. Demetriou, *Sports Law* (Oxford, Hart 1999) p. 257.

[63] *G.* v. *FEI* CAS 92/63.

[64] K. Foster, 'What is International Sports Law?', 5(6) *Sports Law Bulletin* (2002) pp. 14-16; K. Foster, 'Is There a Global Sports Law?', 2(1) *Entertainment Law* (2003) pp. 1-18; K. Foster, 'Lex Sportiva and Lex Ludica: The Court of Arbitration for Sport's Jurisprudence', 3(2) *Entertainment and Sports Law Journal* (2006) and in I.S. Blackshaw, R.C.R. Siekmann and J.W. Soek, eds., *The Court of Arbitration for Sport 1984-2004* (The Hague, T.M.C. Asser Press 2006) pp. 420-440.

[65] K. Foster, 'Is There a Global Sports Law?', 2(1) *Entertainment Law* (2003) p. 2.

[66] Ibid. p. 7.

CAS, these are considered legally unchallengeable although questions continue as to where the rules of the game end and commercial rules begin. Consequently, one may identify a zone of autonomy here for the international federations to work within.

The second set of self-generated rules examined by Foster form the basis of 'global sports law', a transnational autonomous legal order created by the private global institutions that govern sport. These are norms created 'in the practice, rules and regulations of international sporting federations' and are distinct from those norms drawn from agreements by nation states or from national legal jurisdictions, a feature of international sports law.[67] These norms are developed by the CAS as the global forum for the resolution of disputes. The CAS becomes a 'standards council', not only interpreting the codes of the sports federations but selecting the best examples thus creating a set of harmonised codes of best practice which are applied to the federations either persuasively or through arbitral awards.[68] Furthermore, as these norms are self created by the transnational non-governmental sports movement, they create an 'immune system' that is respected by national courts. Whilst international sports law can be applied by the domestic courts, global sports law implies immunity from their reach.

1.2.4. The European model of sport

The argument that sport is an essentially private matter is contradicted by the simultaneous claim made by governing bodies that sport carries with it important social and cultural functions, the fulfilment of which is in the public interest. For example, in *Bosman*, the German government submitted that sport has points of similarity with culture. Article 128 of the Treaty provides that the Community shall contribute to the flowering of the cultures of the Member States, while respecting their national and regional diversity and that EU action should be aimed at, *inter alia*, the safeguarding of cultural heritage of European significance. Furthermore, Article 128 requires the EU to take cultural aspects into account in its action under other provisions of the Treaty. The implication is that if the sport as culture analogy can be sustained, the Treaty offers sport a means of protection from the application of single market laws. Without entering this debate, the Court rejected the cultural analogy by finding that the question submitted by the referring court did not relate to Article 128 but to the rights contained in Article 39.[69] Although the brevity of the Court's rejection is less than satisfactory, an assessment of the substance of the cultural analogy would lead to the same result. Van den Bogaert points out that cultural activities that are carried out, performed or delivered in return for remuneration are still considered to be economic activity and subject to the Treaty's prohibitions.[70] Article 128 is therefore no longer

---

[67] Id.

[68] K. Foster, 'Lex Sportiva and Lex Ludica: The Court of Arbitration for Sport's jurisprudence', 3(2) *Entertainment and Sports Law Journal* (2006) Para. 6.

[69] *Bosman* Para. 128.

[70] S. Van den Bogaert, *Practical Regulation of the Mobility of Sportsmen in the EU Post Bosman* (The Hague, Kluwer 2005) p. 19.

considered a potential location for sport within the Treaty that would sustain continued pleas for independence and pure self-regulation.

Even though the cultural analogy is strained, the social function of sport is stronger. In this connection, it is often stressed that an important feature ensuring the social function of sport persists of the organisational structure on which sport is based in Europe. The European Commission's paper 'The European Model of Sport' explored this structure.[71] The paper described the model of sport in Europe as a pyramid structure which refers to both the organisational and competitive dimensions to European sport. In organisational terms, the structure comprises European federations, national federations, regional federations and the clubs. In competitive terms, promotion, relegation and merit based as opposed to financially based access to European competitions are considered the central features of the European model.

At the pinnacle of the European pyramid are the European sports federations which are themselves usually affiliated to a world governing body. Affiliated to the European federation are the national associations which organise and regulate the sport in question within their national territory. Affiliated to the national federations are the regional federations and leagues. The European pyramid is supported at its base by the sports clubs, players and administrators, many of whom are not remunerated. Consequently, in theory at least, there is a strong connection within the pyramid between the professional game and grassroots sport and the governing bodies owe a duty to all levels in their capacity as guardian of the sport. In football, this structure translates into the UEFA being the European governing body for football which is a confederation of 53 national associations recognised by the FIFA, the games global governing body. UEFA is a society entered in the register of companies under the terms of Swiss Civil Code. FIFA is an association located in Zurich and also registered in accordance with the Swiss Civil Code. FIFA establishes the constitutional framework governing the organisation of the game globally whilst UEFA assumes responsibility for the governance of the game within Europe and settles disputes between national associations. In exercising their duties FIFA and UEFA draw up statutes and regulations and ensures their enforcement. Every person and organisation involved in the game of football, including UEFA, must observe the primacy of FIFA rules.

Clearly, the structure of the European model of sport places the governing bodies in monopolistic positions with regards the regulation of the sport in question. Channels of authority within the European model are vertical, with authority flowing in a top down manner from the global and European federations. The international governing bodies defend the structure on the grounds that they must be allowed to take decisions in their capacity as guardian of the sport, which includes a commitment to represent and protect the interests of all members from grassroots through to the professional game, including national team sports. The organisational efficiency and essential values of sport would be seriously undermined if commercially powerful stakeholders were able to exert too much influence over decision making processes.

---

[71] Commission of the European Communities, *The European Model of Sport*, Consultation Document of DG X (1998).

Furthermore, sports with multiple governing bodies loose public interest as the public prefer to associate with one national and international competition rather than with competing competitions. Another feature of the European sports model is the existence of promotion, relegation and qualification for European competitions. In order to protect this structure, the governing bodies require clubs to commit to the entire structure and impose sanctions on participants deterring the formation of, and participation in, rival structures.

Whilst not necessarily questioning the utility of maintaining monopoly structures in sport, some stakeholders have questioned the rigidity with which these structures are maintained. It is questionable whether it is strictly necessary for governing bodies to deny influence to major stakeholders on the grounds cited above. Some stakeholders within sport, such as clubs and players, argue that this structure is undemocratic in that it precludes horizontal patterns of stakeholder representation. They also complain that the structure leaves governing bodies unaccountable, particularly where decisions of a regulatory nature impact on the commercial freedoms of the stakeholders. These questions are illustrated by the dispute between FIFA and some sports stakeholders over the issue of mandatory player release rules for international football.[72] For the larger clubs, at issue is the imposition of a rule which is used to strengthen the commercial viability of international football whilst denying the clubs a voice in the framing of the rules or a direct share in the profits generated. In terms of the football product market, international football competes with club football, particularly in terms of attracting buyers for the broadcasting rights. Consequently, it can be argued that regulatory dominance is abusively employed as a mask for commercial protectionism.

These allegations are denied by FIFA and UEFA who argue that without mandatory player release rules, international football could not survive. FIFA and UEFA claim that clubs can channel their concerns through national associations and that they do adequately represent the stakeholders within football. Furthermore, they claim to confirm to the democratic principles of the separation of powers which sees a separation between their legislative, executive and judicial functions. For example, within UEFA, the Congress acts as the legislative body, the Executive Committee, Chief Executive and President act as the executive. The disciplinary bodies and the CAS act as the judicial bodies. Furthermore, in 2007 UEFA established the Professional Football Strategy Council which includes representatives of the Association of European Professional Football Leagues (EPFL), representatives of the European Club Forum whose members represent the interests of the clubs participating in the UEFA competitions, and representatives of International Federation of Professional Football Players (FIFPro) (Division Europe) who represent professional players in Europe.

---

[72] Case C-243/06 *SA Sporting du Pays de Charleroi, G-14 Groupment des Clubs de Football Européens* v. *Fédération Internationale de Football Association (FIFA)*, Reference for a preliminary ruling from the Tribunal de Commerce de Charleroi lodged on 30 May 2006. Hereafter referred to as *Charleroi/Oulmers*.

1.2.5. The Americanisation of the European model

The European model of sport is frequently contrasted with the American model.[73] US sport is dominated by the four main sports – basketball, football, ice-hockey and baseball although other sports such as golf, tennis and motor racing are major economic activities. The highest level of sport in the USA is organised on an overtly commercial basis with profit maximisation as the central objective. Sports teams are business franchises who are in the business of selling the product (sport) to fans, broadcasters and sponsors. The economic nature of this activity is not disputed. US sports is therefore analogous to the entertainment industry unlike its European counterpart which has traditionally stressed, with or without good cause, the more socio-cultural and non-commercialised aspects of its activity. Within the European model owners 'are not there to make money'.[74] Success on the field is considered as more important that profit maximisation. This distinction is under strain. Football clubs are commonly publicly listed companies and in the UK the increasing incidence of foreign ownership of clubs may be slowly altering the utility maximising, rather than profit maximising, objectives of clubs. The influence of television revenues is also important in changing owners' motivations as is the wealth generated by new forms of supranational competition such as that introduced by the UEFA Champions League.

Due to the mass popularity of sport in Europe and the emergence of new media platforms, governing bodies have also become significant economic actors. This may conflict with their role as regulatory bodies and their role in promoting grassroots sport. Clubs, which are regulated by the federations and bound by the governing body's rules on broadcasting contracts are beginning to demand a greater share of television rights. As discussed in Chapter 8, this has heightened interest in the possibility of the major clubs forming a European league independent of UEFA's regulatory control. One may therefore identify the possibility of a closed league system emerging in some European sports, particularly football. Financial, rather than merit-based criteria would regulate access to the competition as the larger clubs seek to play one another more frequently in order to maximise revenues. The 1992 Media Partner proposal for a European super-league attests to this. Furthermore, as sport commercialises some investment companies have expressed an interest in purchasing football clubs even though at present the governing bodies have adopted restrictive rules on multiple club ownership. The prospect of sports franchises is therefore raised also in Europe.

US sports franchises are organised into closed leagues with no provision for promotion and relegation. This also means that teams within these leagues do not compete outside that structure and players are not released for international representative duties. If a league expands, it is financial and not merit based criteria that is used to judge entrance suitability. In other words the new franchise buys a place in the league

---

[73] L. Halgreen, *European Sports Law, a Comparative Analysis of the European and American Models of Sport* (Copenhagen, Forlaget Thomson 2004).

[74] P. Sloane, 'The European model of sport', in W. Andreff and S. Szymanski, *Handbook on the Economics of Sport* (Cheltenham, Edward Elgar 2006) p. 300.

and the fee is distributed among the existing members. These league rules derive from the constitutional settlement agreed between the participating team franchises. A Commissioner heads each league and has considerable powers of constitutional enforcement. It is not uncommon for the league to own one or more of the clubs in a syndicate structure in which ownership is pooled and players can be allocated centrally to different teams thus maintaining a competitive balance within the league.[75] A more common feature is for a wealthy benefactor or a corporation to own franchises. Multiple club ownership is also a common feature in the USA in contrast to Europe where federation rules prohibit such arrangements as being potentially damaging to the integrity of the sporting competition. The European model of merit-based promotion and relegation is highly competitive and provides incentives for owners to achieve on-the-field success. This explains why European owners pursue a win maximising strategy as opposed to a profit maximising strategy, particularly given the intensity with which supporters follow their team. Promotion and relegation also removes the need for a franchise system to operate whereby clubs relocate to larger markets and it underpins the European model's single structure as it provides for fluidity between levels. Consequently, there is no need for competing leagues. Nevertheless, as is discussed above and elsewhere in this book the prospect of a European breakaway football super-league based on a closed model has been mooted.

The profit maximising philosophy in the USA, which does not entail a cut-throat model of sporting competition between teams, is favoured. Competition between leagues can be fierce as witnessed by the establishment of rival leagues and the same can be said of team (franchise) competition within a league. However, off-the-field competition between teams operating within the same league is moderated by a high degree of co-ordination in their activities. Owners of franchises recognise that fans will not want to watch sport if on-the-field competition is weak. Consequently, throughout the US leagues a range of solidarity and restraint mechanisms are in place to ensure balanced on-the-field competition. These include reserve clauses, draft rules, roster limits, salary caps, collective bargaining arrangements, revenue sharing, joint merchandising and the collective sale and reinvestment of broadcasting rights. These features are generally not widely employed in Europe although there is a growing debate on the utility of introducing some of these interventions in European sport. This is a major challenge for European sport given that EU labour law has been invoked to protect the rights of sportspersons in Europe. In this connection, the *Bosman* ruling has been widely identified as the principal cause of financial difficulties in European sports. Players, free from migratory restrictions, able to command higher wages thus placing pressure on wage-to-income ratios. Governing bodies and the clubs are exploring ways to place added restrictions on players in order to control such developments. These measures will be subject to scrutinised under both EU labour and competition law systems following *Meca-Medina* with a view to determining whether the restrictions are inherent to sport, thus requiring those imposing the restriction to justify the restraint.

---

[75] L. Halgreen, *European Sports Law, a Comparative Analysis of the European and American Models of Sport* (Copenhagen, Forlaget Thomson 2004) p. 78.

An alternative model to central governing body control, and one employed in the USA, is for representatives of labour and management to negotiate collective employment terms. This model is discussed in detail in Chapter 2. Articles 138 and 139 of the EC Treaty provide a mechanism through which such collective agreements in European sport can be achieved. Currently in Europe the FIFPro represents the players and the EPFL is the most representative employers grouping. In *Brentjens* the Court of Justice established that the social policy objectives of collective agreements would be undermined if agreements seeking to improve conditions of work and employment were subject to competition law.[76] This exemption is similar to the US non-statutory labour exemption. The White Paper on Sport endorses the use of social dialogue within the European professional sports sector and provides official support for such initiatives.[77]

1.2.6. Antitrust and sport: lessons from the US experience

In the USA, the legality of co-ordinated interventions in sport has been challenged by those claiming that they are incompatible with US anti-trust (competition) and labour law.[78] The US equivalent of the EC Treaty's provisions on competition law is the Sherman Act (1890). The Act was used as the model for EU intervention in this field when rules on competition were devised in the 1950's. Section 1 of the Act prohibits every contract, combination and conspiracy in restraint of trade or commerce among the several States, or with foreign nations. In applying the Sherman Act to sporting contexts US courts will consider two issues. First is the so-called rule of reason principle in which the court must examine the nature, purpose and effect of the restraint to determine whether it is on balance pro- rather than anti-competitive. The second is the *per se* approach in which courts will not enter into a rule of reason type analysis because the disputed measure is so inherently restrictive. If the courts determine that the Sherman Act has been breached, the Clayton Act allows the complainant to recover damages.

In *Federal Baseball Club of Baltimore*[79] the US Supreme Court established the famous baseball anti-trust exemption by declaring that baseball leagues and teams were not engaged in interstate commerce. In *Toolson* v. *New York Yankees*[80] the Supreme Court reviewed the anti-trust exemption in light of a challenge to the operation of reserve clauses in baseball contracts which place restrictions on the mobility of players. The Supreme Court argued that if baseball is to fall within the scope of the Sherman Act, Congress should legislate to this effect. A subsequent challenge to the reserve

---

[76] Joined cases C-115 to 117/97 *Brentjens* [1999] *ECR* I-6025.

[77] Commission of the European Communities, *White Paper on Sport*, COM(2007) 391 Final, p. 19.

[78] For a review of the case law, see A. Wise and B. Meyer, *International Sports Law and Business* (The Hague, Kluwer Law International 1997) and L. Halgreen, *European Sports Law, a Comparative Analysis of the European and American Models of Sport* (Copenhagen, Forlaget Thomson 2004).

[79] *Federal Baseball Club of Baltimore, Inc.* v. *National League of Professional Baseball Club* 259 US 200 (1922).

[80] *Toolson* v. *New York Yankees* 346 U.S. 356 (1953).

clause again failed in *Flood* v. *Kuhn*.[81] The extent to which the anti-trust exemption is a general exemption or only relates to the operation of the player reserve clause is a moot point following *Piazza* v. *Major League Baseball*.[82] Thus far, the anti-trust exemption has not been extended to others sports, a position confirmed in *Radovich* v. *National Football League*[83] and *Robertson* v. *National Basketball Association*.[84] However, other sports such as the NFL have a limited statutory antitrust exemption in the field of broadcasting.[85]

Despite the reach of the Sherman Act into sports other than Baseball, the Act does not prohibit single economic entities from adopting restrictive practices. This so-called single entity theory was invoked in *Fraser* v. *Major League Soccer* (2000).[86] In essence, as the league owns the clubs it cannot be said to conspire against itself. Similar principles exist in the context of Article 81 and the single entity theory, whereby a single undertaking is incapable of colluding with itself. Baseball's anti-trust exemption is therefore a curious construction. It has been recognised by the courts as being flawed but it has thus far not been repealed nor has it been extended to other sports. The Curt Flood Act[87] does however place some limits on baseball's antitrust exemption by subjecting league rules that restrict player movement or compensation to antitrust law, although in the 1996 *Brown* v. *Pro Football Inc.*[88] case the Supreme Court ruled in that unionized employees cannot file antitrust suits.

Whilst anti-trust law seeks to promote competitive forces in the business sector, labour law defends the rights of the employees. In particular, the Clayton Act specifies a statutory labour exemption in which labour unions are not considered combinations or conspiracies in restraint of trade and as such their activities may escape the reach of the Sherman Act. In order to reconcile the tension between anti-trust and labour law the Supreme Court established the non-statutory labour exemption which specifies that collective bargaining agreements escape the reach of antitrust laws if the agreement primarily affects only the parties to the collective bargaining relationship, deals with a matter that is the mandatory subject of collective bargaining and is the product of genuine bargaining.[89] Attempts to challenge the salary cap and college draft in basketball failed on these grounds in *Wood* v. *National Basketball Association*.[90] Consequently, labour law predominates over anti-trust law when a collective bargaining agreement exists.

---

[81] *Flood* v. *Kuhn* 407 U.S. 258 (1972).

[82] *Piazza* v. *Major League Baseball* 831 F. Supp. 420 (1993). See also J. Gray, 'Regulation of Sports Leagues, Team, Athletes and Agents in the United States', in A. Caiger and S. Gardiner, eds., *Professional Sport in the EU, Regulation and Re-regulation* (The Hague, T.M.C. Asser Press 2000) p. 278.

[83] *Radovich* v. *National Football League* 352 U.S. 445 (1957).

[84] *Robertson* v. *National Basketball Association* 389 F. Supp. 867 (S.D.N.Y. 1975).

[85] Sports Broadcasting Act 1961 U.S.C. 1291.

[86] *Fraser and others* v. *Major League Soccer* 97 F.Supp. 130 (2000).

[87] 15 U.S.C.A. Section 27a.

[88] *Brown* v. *Pro Football Inc* 116 S. Ct. 2116 (1996).

[89] *Mackey* v. *National Football League* 543 F.2d 606 (8th Cir. 1976).

[90] *Wood* v. *National Basketball Association* 809 F.2d 954 (2nd Cir. 1987).

1.3. CONCLUSIONS

Specificity of sport arguments touch upon two key questions. First, sport requires decision making autonomy so that certain welfare maximising policies can be pursued. These include the need to maintain competitive balance, to ensure the regularity of sporting competitions, to educate and train young talent, to promote stadium attendance and participation at all levels, to protect national teams, to safeguard the integrity of sport and to connect with local communities. Second, the nature of the European model of sport requires the formation of rules which are justified by reference to the pre-existing structure of European sports markets, the essentially private nature of sports organisations, the effective, efficient and economical benefits deriving from self regulation and the rule of law safeguards established by the creation of an internal legal system in sport based on adherence to the judgments of the Court of Arbitration for Sport. These are the twin arguments on which the plea for self-regulation is based. Chapter 2 explores how these arguments have found expression within the emerging sports policy of the EU. Chapters 3, 4 and 5 discuss the extent to which the EU's legal framework recognises these arguments, and the legal bases on which the treatment of commercial sport is founded. Chapter 6 explores the elaboration of these arguments within the context of sports broadcasting and Chapters 7 and 8 do likewise in relation to the rules of the governing bodies affecting the rights of players and rules pertaining to the organisation of sport in Europe.

Chapter 2
EU Sports Policy

In July 2007 the European Commission published a White Paper on Sport in which it sought to raise the status of sport within the EU and sensitise the institutions to the specific characteristics of sport. The White Paper does not represent the birth of an EU sports policy but consolidates a number of themes from a range of EU policy interventions in sport dating from the mid 1980's. The theme of greatest prominence concerns the question of how the special characteristics of sport should be given expression in Community law. In this connection, the EU has needed to reflect on whether contributing to this debate requires limited intervention by way of political guidelines on the application of law to sport or whether a more holistic and broad-based approach to sport needs to be pursued, possibly supported by a revision to the Treaty granting sport a legal base within the EU's constitutional framework of the European Union. This chapter reveals that the EU has been seduced by the more broad-based approach to sport in which the connection between sport and the wider socio-cultural context of European integration is considered. Thus far, this approach has not been supported by a revision to the Treaty granting authority for the institutions to elaborate a sports policy, although the 2007 Reform Treaty proposes such a move. The lack of a legal base in sport has constrained EU action in sport and placed limits on its ability to allocate budgetary appropriations to sport. In theory, EU sports policy should be limited to narrow questions concerning the provision of guidelines on the application of the EU's legal framework to sporting contexts. Despite this constitutional limit, the EU has pursued a gradual policy of linking its sports related activities to areas of the Treaty in which it does have a competence to act. Nevertheless, sport remains ancillary to wider questions of single market regulation and also to questions of socio-cultural integration.

This ancillary approach to sport makes policy coherence problematic. The EU is not a monolith pursuing an agreed agenda in sport. Each of the 27 Member States pursue divergent national sports policies which cannot easily find common expression at European level. Furthermore, as sport interacts with a wide range of policy areas, a large number of Commission Directorates General are brought into the policy debate. Attaining policy coherence within a framework involving multiple institutions with differing institutional missions is problematic. This diversity leads to decision making problems within the EU and contributes to vague, policy statements on sport based only on the pre-existing common ground as unanimous agreement is difficult to achieve. This ambiguity in the EU's approach to sport is compounded by the EU's reliance on a definition of sport deriving from the 1992 Council of Europe European Sports Charter. Article 2(1) of the Charter defines sport as 'all forms of physical activity which, through casual or organised participation, aim at expressing or improving physical fitness and mental well being, forming social relationships or obtaining results in competition at all levels'. This catch-all definition diversifies the number of interested sporting stakeholders drawn into the policy debate and precludes the adoption of a coherent policy on sport as the whole gamut of commercial and social sport is conflated.

This chapter interrogates these issues. It explores how the EU institutions have attempted to construct a policy on sport which reconciles the specificities of sport and the primacy of Community law. It does so by describing the impact of the EU institutions on sport and then interrogating the two dominant stands of EU sports policy, namely the use of the socio-economic impact of sport to underpin European integration and second, the elaboration of a position on how to reconcile the organisational rules of sport with EC law. In this connection, the chapter examines the impact of the *Bosman* judgment on EU sports policy, the influence of the Amsterdam and Nice Declarations, the findings of the 2006 Independent European Sport Review, the utility of establishing a legal base for sport in the Treaty. Finally it provides an overview of the Commission's 2007 White Paper on Sport and considers its particular emphasis on the prospects for social dialogue within sport.

2.1. THE EU INSTITUTIONS AND SPORT

Even though the EU has no Treaty competence to intervene directly in sports policy, the activities of the EU institutions do impact on sport. At the pinnacle of the EU's institutional structure is the European Council. Composed of the Heads of State and Government of the Member States and the President of the European Commission, the European Council's primary role is to provide the general context shaping the future development of the Union. The European Council infrequently intervenes in EU sports policy but its interventions are often influential, as for example the annexation of the Amsterdam Declaration on Sport to the Treaty of Amsterdam in 1997 and during the Nice Treaty deliberations in 2000 in which the Member States released a Declaration on the specific characteristics of sport in the form of a Presidency Conclusion.[91] Neither of these interventions were legally binding, although the decision to insert an article on sport in the Reform Treaty will provide a legally binding solution.

Whilst the European Council defines the broad direction of European integration, the sectoral Council of the European Union acts as the Community legislator, a role it shares with the directly elected Parliament. As there is no constitutional provision for the establishment of a formal Sports Council, the Council's impact on sport is limited. However, Ministers or their representatives have met informally to discuss a wide range of sporting issues. In 2004 the Member States established a rolling agenda for sport in order to define priority themes for discussions on sport and throughout 2005 and 2006. Expert meetings were held with Member State representatives and a

---

[91] Presidency Conclusions, *Declaration on the specific characteristics of sport and its social function in Europe, of which account should be taken in implementing common policies*, Nice European Council Meeting, December 2000.

number of EU sports working groups were established. As part of the rolling agenda, in 2006 a Ministerial Conference was organised jointly by the Commission and the Finnish Presidency.[92] The conclusions of this conference endorsed the publication of the White Paper on Sport and a White Paper Working Group was subsequently established which met for the first time in March 2007. Although the Council cannot pass sports legislation, its general legislative activity impacts on sport is indirectly. For example, legislation pertaining to labour mobility has an indirect impact on sport. There are also areas of Community regulation where sectoral special treatment can be authorised by way of a Council decision, for example in the field of state aid regulation. The establishment of the rolling agenda and the legal base in the Reform Treaty will sensitise Ministers to the special characteristics of sport even though these measures do not amount to a legal requirement for the Ministers to take sport into account in the framing of legislation. In other contexts, the Council's legislative activity in related fields impacts on sport. For example, the Council and Parliament adopted a decision to establish 2004 as the European Year of Education Through Sport, the title reflecting the EU's competence in education policy but lack thereof in relation to sport.

The rolling agenda and the Reform Treaty will add to the work of the European Sports Directors who are often from national ministries. This body prepares Council meetings and ensures a degree of co-ordination between the Member States on sporting matters. In particular, their role is important in terms of supporting the work of the Council Presidency, an EU body which assists with the smooth administration of business within the EU. Whilst the Presidency cannot unilaterally set the policy agenda during its six month term of office, it can prioritise business. For example, the British, Austrian and Finnish Presidencies were instrumental in establishing the EU working groups on Sport and Health, Sport and Economics and Non-Profit Sports Organisations which met throughout 2005, 2006 and 2007. Furthermore, the 2005 UK Presidency prioritised the ongoing issue of sports governance and initiated the Independent European Sports Review under the Chairmanship of José Luís Arnaut. The Review reported in 2006.

The work of the Commission also has a major impact on sporting activity despite the lack of a direct regulatory competence. A 1995 survey on sport and the EU found that three quarters of the Commission's Directorates General (DG's) had an impact on the sports sector.[93] Today, the inter-service work of the Education and Culture DG extends to 17 DG's.[94] The impact is indirect, in the sense that sport is not generally the intended target of their actions. For example, whilst not directed at sport, the activities of the Competition Policy DG have a significant impact on economic sporting activity. Elsewhere, sport has also become associated with a large number of other policy areas falling within the competence of the Commission including doping, public health policy, education, training and youth policy, equal opportunities and dis-

---

[92] The EU and Sport: Matching Expectations, Brussels 27-28 November 2006.

[93] Coopers and Lybrand, *The Impact of European Union Activities on Sport*, Study for DG X of the European Commission (1995), pp. 17-18.

[94] Commission of the European Communities, *Commission staff working document. Impact Assessment Accompanying the White Paper on Sport*, SEC 932, 11/07/2007, p. 6.

abilities policy, employment and free movement policy, environmental policy, media policy and cultural policy. The extent to which sport has become the unintended target of policy activity in these fields has drawn attention from the Employment and Social Affairs DG. It commissioned studies under budget heading B3-4000 into the prospect of a structured social dialogue taking place in European sport to minimise the some of the largely employment related effects of such activity. The formal responsibility for sport within the Commission lies with the Directorate General for Education and Culture. A specialist Sports Unit has been created within this DG to organise the sporting activities of the Commission. In particular, the Sports Unit is responsible for three tasks. First, it facilitates inter-service cooperation within the Commission and with other institutions on sport-related issues. Second, it cooperates with national and international sports institutions, organisations and federations. Finally, it holds bilateral meetings with sports institutions and organisations and international sports federations.

The European Parliament influences sport through the exercise of its legislative, budgetary and scrutiny powers. The Parliament has influenced legislation in fields related to sport as it did, for example imposing an amendment to the Television Without Frontiers Directive which included provision for Member States to develop lists of sporting events that must be broadcast on free-to-air television.[95] In budgetary terms the Parliament was influential in obtaining funding for sports related activities by way of its decision to establish the European Year of Education Through Sport project (2004). Its scrutiny of Commission business has contributed to a number of reports and resolutions which have been influential in informing the political debate on the application of EC law to sport. These include the Van Raay report, the Larive Report, Pack Report, the Mennea Report, the Manders Report and the Belet Report.[96] These reports have focussed on the extent to which specificity of sport arguments should be reflected in the decisions of the Court and Commission. Within the Parliament's committee structure, sporting issues are primarily discussed in the Committee on Culture and Education although the Committee on Legal Affairs, the Committee on Employment and Social Affairs and the Committee on Internal Market and Consumer Protection also debate issues relating sport. In a further effort to influence sports policy, in 1992 the Parliament also established a Sports Intergroup, a cross-committee, cross-party discussion forum for sports related matters.

---

[95] Art. 3a Directive 97/36/EC.

[96] European Parliament, rapporteur: J. Van Raay, *Report for the Committee on Legal Affairs and Citizen's Rights, on the Freedom of Movement of Professional Footballers in the Community* (1989); European Parliament, rapporteur: J. Larive, *Report on the European Community and Sport* (1994); European Parliament, rapporteur: D. Pack, *Report on the Role of the European Union in the Field of Sport* (1997); European Parliament, *Report on the Commission Report to the European Council With a View to Safeguarding Current Sports Structures and Maintaining the Social Function of Sport Within the Community Framework - The Helsinki Report on Sport* (2000); European Parliament, *Professional Sport in the Internal Market*, Commissioned by the Committee on the Internal Market and Consumer Protection of the European Parliament on the initiative of Toine Manders, project No: IP/A/IMCO/ST/2005-004; European Parliament, rapporteur: Ivo Belet, *The Future of Professional Football in Europe*, European Parliament Committee on Culture and Education, 2006/2130(INI).

2.2. Sport as a Vehicle for European Integration

The origins of EU sports policy lie, not in attempts to reconcile sport's special nature with EC law, but as a vehicle through which the European regional integration movement could find socio-cultural underpinnings. The idea of European unity has been historically driven by the ideology of federalism which promotes the construction of a European federation based on the creation of a democratic institutional arrangement in Europe through which nations would be incorporated into a central system of government on a constitutionally entrenched basis. Whilst historically, governments remained cautious of this project, fearing a diminution of state power, they have gradually acquiesced to further integration as the problems of managing modern interdependent economies have grown.

The location of sport within this Community structure raises intellectual and legal questions concerning the role of the EU in sports policy. Arguably sport is one of the few areas of social activity that genuinely both unites and divides Europeans. It is a passion shared by most Europeans yet an activity at the root of many national rivalries, a classic unity versus diversity dilemma often resolved by federal systems. Whilst sport therefore has the potential to feature within the European integration movement, there are also profound reasons why historically, politically, culturally and legally it should not. The EU has become increasingly aware that the creation of a federal Europe in the absence of popular support is unsustainable, hence the desire to use sport and other socio-cultural policies to promote the idea of European unity. Conversely, federalism implies a division of powers between the constituent units and in national contexts, sports policy has tended to be defined as an area of local concern. For example, in federal Germany, sports policy is largely the preserve of the Lander (States). Within the context of the EU, the tradition of decentralising sports policy implies that the nation states or their regions remain the competent authority when sports policy choices are made. To supranationalise sports policy would be to contradict the traditional role of the nation state and its sub units in sporting matters and ignore the legally enshrined doctrine in the EU of subsidiarity.

Article 5 EC places a constitutional constraint on the actions of the Community institutions. The principle of conferral specifies that the Community must act within the bounds of the competences that are conferred upon it by the Member States. Another constraint is Article 3 EC which defines those areas in which the EU has a competence to act. As the absence of sport in this list has not, until the Reform Treaty, been corrected by the Member States, one can only assume it has been the will of the Member States not to intervene in sport on a European level. Whilst Article 3 appears to preclude the development of a sport policy, it also establishes a commitment to (c) 'an internal market characterised by the abolition, as between Member States, of obstacles to the free movement of goods, persons, services and captial and ... (g) a system ensuring that competition in the internal market is not distorted'. These provisions are applicable to sport whenever it is practiced as an economic activity. This raises a problem for those seeking to promote the political uses of sport in the EU and raises a major problem for sports governing bodies. The Treaty promotes legal

intervention in economic sectors but it fails to constitutionally recognise the specificity of sport. In the absence of a Treaty based statement on the specificity of sport, the
EU institutions have pieced together a series of non-legal initiatives on sport which
they have attempted to elaborate a position on the role of EC law in sport. Ultimately,
these initiatives contributed to the Member States affording sport a legal base in the
Reform Treaty.

Although constitutionally hamstrung, the Community first pursued an interest in
sport in 1984 at the Fontainebleau Summit. The Adonnino Committee reported on
measures designed to 'strengthen and promote [European] identity and [The Community's] image for its citizens and for the rest of the world'.[97] It identified eight
categories of proposals, one of which concerned youth, education, exchanges and
sport. The report acknowledged that the administration of sport is predominantly the
responsibility of sports associations independent of government. In this respect, the
Report extended an invitation to them, rather than the EU, to consider a number of
initiatives including, the creation of European Community sports teams and events,
the wearing by sporting teams of the Community emblem in addition to their national
colours at major sporting events, encouraging exchanges of sportsmen, athletes and
trainers between the different Community countries, and encouraging support for
sporting activities, especially for the disabled.

Throughout the remainder of the 1980's the EU sponsored or promoted a number
of sporting events such as the European Sailing Regatta, the cycling Tour de l'Avenir,
the Tour Feminin, the Tour de France, the tennis tournament of Antwerp and a failed
attempt was also made at establishing the first European Swimming Championships
in 1987.[98] In recent years the EU has funded activities connected to the 2005 Alm-
ería Mediterranean Games and the 2007 Jaca European Youth Olympic Festival. For
some, the logical development of such initiatives would be the creation of European
teams or athletes competing under the EU flag, a goal expressed in the Adonnino
Report. This idea encountered derision from those questioning the effectiveness and
constitutional basis of such interventions although proponents point to the European
Ryder Cup golf team as an example of the success of supranational sports affiliation
and the effective use of the Community emblem.

The largely unsuccessful venture into sports policy in the 1980's was reviewed in
1991 as part of a policy statement on sport made by the Commission to the Council
and the European Parliament.[99] The review focussed on improving communication
with the sports world and providing funding opportunities for sport although it persisted with the idea that sport is 'an appropriate instrument of public relations'. In
terms of improving communication with the sports world the European Sports Forum
was established as an annual meeting held between members of the EU and the sports

---

[97] Commission of the European Communities, *A People's Europe, Reports From the Ad Hoc Committee*, (1984) COM(84) 446 Final.

[98] W. Tokarski et al., eds., *Two Players One Goal? Sport in the European Union* (Oxford, Meyer
and Meyer 2004) pp. 62-63.

[99] Commission of the European Communities, *The European Community and Sport*, SEC (91) 1438
of 31 July 1991.

world. In addition, the Coopers and Lybrand study on 'The Impact of European Union Activities on Sport' was commissioned.[100]

Whilst the EU had previously sponsored and promoted sporting events, the 1990's saw the development of a wider role for the Commission as it began to manage specific sports funding programmes, most notably Eurathlon and Sports for People with Disabilities. This took EU involvement in sport beyond mere self-promotion to one in which sport was being employed to implement other socio-economic and cultural policy goals. In this connection, sport could be employed as one element in attempts to narrow the EU's so-called democratic deficit and increase public support for European integration, two factors contributing to the problematic ratification of the Maastricht Treaty in 1992. However, this expansion of competence was legally questionable given the lack of a specific sports competence in the Treaty and following *UK* v. *Commission* the Commission was compelled to suspend its sports-related funding programmes.[101]

The Commission subsequently published a study examining ways in which sport could be integrated into other EU programmes. For example, the British Council Presidency in the first half of 1998 examined the use of sport in employment policy and policies designed to combat social exclusion and regenerate communities. Other Presidencies have focussed on the relationship between sport and EU policies on disabilities, health, education, vocational training, youth and media.[102] Furthermore, 2004 was designated the European Year of Education Through Sport, the linkage with education policy reflecting the existence of an EU competence in the field of education but not for sport. In the 2007 White Paper on Sport, the Commission reviewed the interaction between the Union and the socio-economic dimensions of sport. This paper establishes the likely future direction of EU sports policy and clearly envisages employing existing legal bases to support these actions. The key issues identified included public health, doping, education and training, volunteering, social inclusion, combating violence and racism, external relations, sustainable development, macro economic policy, public and private support for sport and regional development. Two policy themes can be distilled from this list. First, the EU has identified sport as a means through which it can respond to macro economic concerns about the state of the European economy. In economic terms, sport accounts for 3.7% of GDP and 5.4% of the labour force.[103] In this context it can contribute to the EU's Lisbon Agenda on European competitiveness. As an undoubted growth sector, sport has the potential to become an even more significant source of employment and wealth creation. In this connection, the Commission must take care in how it elaborates its approach. In traditional sectors the Commission would embark on a classic de-regulatory model in

---

[100] Coopers and Lybrand, *The Impact of European Union Activities on Sport*, Study for DG X of the European Commission (1995).

[101] Case C-106/96 *UK* v. *Commission ECR* [1998] I-02729.

[102] M. Duthie, 'European Community Sports Policy', in A. Lewis and J. Taylor, eds., *Sport: Law and Practice* (London, Butterworths Lexis Nexis 2002); Coopers and Lybrand, *The Impact of European Union Activities on Sport*, Study for DG X of the European Commission (1995).

[103] Commission of the European Communities, *White Paper on Sport*, COM(2007) 391 Final, p. 11.

which markets are liberalised. The sports markets tend to be structured along national lines with strong political and cultural resistance to such a model.

Second, although not explicitly referred to in these terms, the White Paper envisages sport being employed as a vehicle for achieving a post-national European identity and as a means of underpinning European integration. Employing sport as a means of promoting a European identity and integration entails a number of dimensions including employing sport within the context of the EU's external relations policy, using sport to tackle social issues such as in the field of public health, using sport as a vehicle for achieving greater social cohesion and employing sport as part of the EU Citizens agenda. In this context the Commission argued that sport could be as a tool to bring 'the EU closer to its citizens'.[104] Previously at the 1997 Amsterdam summit, the Member States referred to the ability of sport in 'forging identity and bringing people closer together'.[105] More recently, the 2004 European Year of Education through Sport project explicitly referred to sport as 'a vehicle for Europeanisation' and stressed the role of the national printed media in covering European football competitions and the ability of footballers to circulate within the territory of the EU without restriction. Furthermore, in a clear signal that the Commission retained its desire to employ sport for integrationist purposes, the Commission stated in the 2007 White Paper on Sport that it wished to 'reach out to citizens through a broad-based approach and to send a signal in support of the citizen dimension of sport'.[106]

The EU appears to suffer from a legitimacy problem as witnessed by low voter turnout at European elections, the rise of anti-EU political parties and movements and the rejections in France and the Netherlands of the Constitutional Treaty in public referendums. It is less accepted that socio-cultural policy interventions can correct such perceptions. In the early years of the Community, Transactionalist theorists focused on how a sense of identity within a political community could be forged by greater interaction between Europeans. This literature remains largely dominant today. Levermore and Millward suggest that initiatives taking place outside the EU framework may serve to promote a European identity. They argue that for supporters of Europe's larger clubs, 'there is evidence that suggests participation in the Champions League is opening up new horizons – competing in the "European space" is arguably more important than competing in the national leagues'.[107]

In this connection, Roche raises the question of whether the EU should focus not on the construction of a European identity through the use of symbols such as those espoused in the Adonnino Committee Report, but through its regulatory capacity.

---

[104] Commission of the European Communities, *Commission staff working document. Impact Assessment Accompanying the White Paper on Sport*, SEC 932, 11/07/2007, p. 16.

[105] Declaration 29 to the Treaty of Amsterdam.

[106] Commission of the European Communities, *Commission staff working document. Impact Assessment Accompanying the White Paper on Sport*, SEC 932, 11/07/2007, p. 25.

[107] R. Levermore and P. Millward, *Using Sport as a Vehicle to Help Build a Pan-European Identity*, paper presented to Europe in the World Centre International Workshop (University of Liverpool, July 2004) p. 11.

Roche refers to this as 'cultural Europeanisation through regulation'.[108] This might for example include providing an Article 81(3) exemption for the collective sale of sports broadcasting rights in exchange for governing body commitments on the redistribution of the revenues to grassroots football. Adopting a more interventionist approach, the EU could seek to de-regulate the European labour market for players thus ensuring greater cultural penetration into protected national markets or even liberalise the football product market by encouraging the formation of pan-European leagues.

A Eurobarometer survey in 2004 indicated generally favourable responses to a series of sports related propositions on the EU's involvement in sport. 51% of EU25 *tended to agree* that '[t]he EU should be able to intervene more in European sport issues', a figure highest in Cyprus (81%) and lowest in Denmark (22%). 62% of EU25 tended to agree that '[i]t is useful that sport is included in the project of the European Constitution'.[109] Nevertheless, evidence of shifting societal loyalties and expectations is scarce and even if they can be identified, they are not a consequence of a genuine shift in the cultural values of the public, but rather as a result of venue shopping on the part of litigants who see the EU as another venue through which they can seek redress. Despite the increasing interaction between citizens of the Member States, the sense of a common European cultural identity has not emerged and it is, to say the least, optimistic that sport can bridge the deficit between the EU and its citizens particularly given that sporting loyalties are deeply embedded nationally rather than supranationally. As Szamuley remarked, 'athletes will not run or jump, footballers will not play, swimmers will not swim for Europe. And if they do, they will not stand to attention when the flag with the ring of stars is raised or the last movement of Beethoven's Ninth is played. Audiences will not cheer. Sport is too deep-seated for that'.[110]

2.3.   RECONCILING SPORTING RULES WITH COMMUNITY LAW

Although attempts to support European integration through sport have been largely unsuccessful, there remains political will in the EU to continue with this agenda. The 1995 *Bosman* judgment may have changed the focus of EU sports policy to one concerned with the need to protect the specificity of sport from the application of Community law, but the judgment offered the EU another route into its traditional socio-cultural concern for sport. Advocates of EU involvement in sport as means of promoting European integration feared the ruling would hamper their cause as the EU could not simultaneously treat sport as a business and also as a vehicle of Europeanisation. *Bosman* also brought new actors into the debate such as the sports governing

---

[108] M. Roche, *The EU and TV Sport: Perspectives on Cultural Europeanisation With Particular Reference to Football,* paper presented at the European sport roundtable, University Association for Contemporary European Studies Annual Conference (Newcastle United Football Club, August 2003) p. 5.

[109] Commission of the European Communities, *The Citizens of the European Union and Sport*, special Eurobarometer survey (2004).

[110] H. Szamuley, 'The Golf Ball as a Symbol of Integration', see at <www.brugesgroup.com>.

bodies who lobbied intensively for sport to be exempt from Community law. Whilst these actors wanted a total removal of sport from the EU's legal framework, the EU institutions debated whether a more broad-based approach to sport could reconnect the EU with the spirit of Adonnino.

These questions were debated in a number of sports policy papers at the time of *Bosman*. In the 1994 'Larive Report' on the European Community and Sport, the 1997 'Pack Report' on the Role of the European Union in the Field of Sport and the 2000 'Mennea Report', the European Parliament articulate a desire to balance the economic regulation of sport with the promotion of sport's social, cultural, educational and integrationist qualities.[111] For example, the Pack Report claimed that 'although the European Union has taken an interest in professional sport as an activity, it has, to date, only taken account in a very marginal fashion of the cultural, educational and social dimension of sport, and whereas such neglect stems basically from the fact that there is no explicit reference to sport in the Treaty'.[112] Pack argued for sport's inclusion in the Treaty as a means of strengthening the position of sport in other EU policies, heightening awareness of the role of sport in European society and crucially, placing a legal obligation on the EU's judicial bodies to refer to the Treaty Article when disposing of sports related cases. Sports governing bodies welcomed this initiative as a potential vehicle through which sport could be exempt from EC law. Consequently, the Parliament emerged as a focal point for lobbyists from sports organisations seeking the same goal.

2.3.1.   The Amsterdam Declaration on Sport 1997

Despite the strength of support, the Heads of State and Government meeting in Amsterdam in June 1997 decided only to attach a non-binding Declaration on sport to the Amsterdam Treaty. The Declaration read,

> '[t]he conference emphasises the social significance of sport, in particular its role in forging identity and bringing people together. The conference therefore calls on the bodies of the European Union to listen to sports associations when important questions affecting sport are at issue. In this connection, special consideration should be given to the particular characteristics of amateur sport'.[113]

The wording of the Declaration is bland and displays a tendency on the part of the European Council to merely be seen to be 'doing something'.[114] It clearly repre-

---

[111] European Parliament, rapporteur: J. Larive, *Report on the European Community and Sport* (1994); European Parliament, rapporteur: D. Pack, *Report on the Role of the European Union in the Field of Sport* (1997); European Parliament, *Report on the Commission Report to the European Council With a view to Safeguarding Current Sports Structures and Maintaining the Social Function of Sport Within the Community Framework - The Helsinki Report on Sport* (2000).

[112] European Parliament, rapporteur: D. Pack, *Report on the Role of the European Union in the Field of Sport* (1997) Para. 1.

[113] Declaration 29 to the Treaty of Amsterdam.

[114] S. Weatherill, 'Fair Play Please! Recent Developments in the Application of EC Law to Sport', 40 *Common Market Law Review* (2003) p. 88.

sents only a limited victory for the sports governing bodies and it does not amount to an endorsement for sport to be exempt from Community law. Nevertheless, even though sport did not find its way into the legal passages of the Treaty, the impact of the Declaration should not be dismissed. The phrase 'forging identity and bringing people together' revives the traditional preoccupation for using sport for socio-cultural purposes. Elsewhere, the wording looks more towards the post *Bosman* agenda. The phrases 'social significance of sport' and the request for the 'European Union to listen to sports associations when important questions affecting sport are at issue' implies that the governing bodies perform a public function in that sport is imbued with important social characteristics. Whilst the Declaration does not endorse granting an exemption from EC law for the governing bodies in recognition for carrying this public service burden, the European Council does stress the importance of dialogue with them. In that sense, the Declaration provided soft political mandate for the EU to pursue a broad-based approach to sport which tackles not only the question of how EC law applies to sport, but also the political uses of sport to achieve integrationist goals.

As a consequence of the Declaration, sport is now more routinely discussed at high level intergovernmental meetings in the EU adding further impetus to the nascent sports policy. Conclusions on sport are occasionally released following European Council meetings and sport is also discussed in Council meetings, albeit under the auspices of Councils in which sport is a secondary concern. Sports ministers meet on an informal basis. In short, the Declaration has contributed to a more formalised discussion of sport within the Community in which EU institutions are granted a political mandate to discuss sport and sectoral stakeholders are consulted. The experience of European integration reveals that soft initiatives tend to harden over time.[115] At the December 1998 Vienna European Council the Member States added political impetus to the Amsterdam Declaration by requesting the Commission to submit a report to the forthcoming Helsinki European Council on 'safeguarding current sports structures and maintaining the social function of sport within the Community framework'.[116] The Amsterdam and Vienna Declarations provided the Commission with the political mandate to embark on a further review of sports policy. In 1998, the Commission published a working paper, 'The Development and Prospects for Community Activity in the Field of Sport'[117] which identified sport as performing an educational, public health, social, cultural and recreational function and that sport could be used as a vehicle through which policy objectives in these fields could be pursued. However, the paper also noted that sport plays a significant economic role in Europe and that no general exemption from EC law could be permitted. As a follow up, the Commission published the more influential consultation document, 'The European

---

[115] M. Pollack, 'Creeping Competence: The Expanding Agenda of the European Community', 14(2) *Journal of Public Policy* (1994).

[116] Presidency Conclusions, *The Vienna European Council* (December 1998).

[117] Commission of the European Communities, *Developments and Prospects for Community Activity in the Field of Sport*, Commission Staff Working Paper (1998), Directorate General X.

Model of Sport'.[118] The document implied political support for the maintenance of the European model and encouraged dialogue between the EU and sports bodies. The findings of the consultation exercise were used by the Commission to prepare the first EU conference on sport held in Greece in May 1999, the conclusions of which unsurprisingly expressed strong support for the maintenance of the European model. These conclusions were then used by the Commission to prepare the Helsinki Report on safeguarding current sports structures and maintaining the social function of sport within the Community framework. The report was submitted to the December 1999 Helsinki European Council.

2.3.2.   The Helsinki Report on Sport 1999

The introduction to the Helsinki Report suggests that the aim of the report is to give 'pointers for reconciling the economic dimension of sport with its popular, educational, social and cultural dimensions'.[119] At the heart of the so-called 'new approach' embodied in the Helsinki Report is a framework for applying EC law to sport. The report claims that 'this new approach involves preserving the traditional values of sport, while at the same time assimilating a changing economic and legal environment'.[120] In this connection, the report builds on a previous Commission press release published in February 1999 on the application of competition rules to sport.[121] In that paper, the Competition Policy DG made a distinction between purely sporting situations which are immune from EC law and wholly commercial situations to which Treaty provisions will apply. For those rules which are both sporting and economic in nature, the Commission indicated that the Article 81(3) exemption criteria could be employed. The European Council responded to the Helsinki Report in its June 2000 Santa Maria da Feira Presidency Conclusions. It requested that 'the Commission and the Council to take account of the specific characteristics of sport in Europe and its social function in managing common policies'.[122] The Helsinki Report and the Santa Maria da Feira Presidency Conclusions added further impetus to those calling for a specific reference to sport in the Treaty. The intergovernmental conference preparing for what would become the December 2000 Nice Treaty became the focus of further lobbying for such a sports Article. Again, the sports governing bodies hoped that an Article could act as a vehicle for a general exemption for sport from EC law despite the prevailing political and legal view that this would not be the case. At Nice, sport once again failed to se-

---

[118] Commission of the European Communities, *The European Model of Sport*, Consultation Document of DG X, 1998.

[119] Commission of the European Communities, *Report from the Commission to the European Council With a View to Safeguarding Sports Structures and Maintaining the Social Significance of Sport Within the Community Framework: The Helsinki Report on Sport*, COM (1999) 644, p. 3.

[120] Ibid. p. 7.

[121] Commission of the European Communities, *Commission Debates Application of Its Competition Rules to Sport*, 24 February 1999, Commission Press Release IP/99/133.

[122] Presidency Conclusions, *Santa Maria da Feira European Council* (June 2000) Para. 50.

cure a Treaty Article. For Weatherill, 'the refusal to exempt sport, but the temptation to garland it with laurel ... marks the negotiations at Nice'.[123]

2.3.3. The Nice Declaration on Sport 2000

The laurel was another political Declaration on sport, this time published as a Presidency conclusion. The 'Declaration on the Specific Characteristics of Sport and its Social Function in Europe, of which Account Should be Taken in Implementing Common Policies' was released as a Presidency Conclusion following the Nice European Council Meeting of 7, 8 and 9 of December 2000. In an unusually long Declaration which entered into specific debates, the Member States noted in Paragraph 1 that

> '[s]porting organisations and the Member States have a primary responsibility in the conduct of sporting affairs. Even though not having any direct powers in this area, the Community must, in its action under the various Treaty provisions, take account of the social, educational and cultural functions inherent in sport and making it special, in order that the code of ethics and the solidarity essential to the preservation of its social role may be respected and nurtured'.

In its second paragraph the Declaration attached particular importance to the preservation of solidarity and fairness in sport and of protecting 'both the moral and material interests and the physical integrity of those involved in the practice of sport, especially minors. In the seventh paragraph, on the role of sports federations, the Member States lent their support to the conditional autonomy of such bodies by stating

> '[t]he European Council stresses its support for the independence of sports organisations and their right to organise themselves through appropriate associative structures. It recognises that, with due regard for national and Community legislation and on the basis of a democratic and transparent method of operation, it is the task of sporting organisations to organise and promote their particular sports, particularly as regards the specifically sporting rules applicable and the make-up of national teams, in the way which they think best reflects their objectives.'

The theme underpinning the Nice Declaration was that the grant of autonomy was conditional on the governing bodies operating democratically and transparently. The commercialisation of sport had increased the demands of stakeholders to be afforded a greater say in how decisions were made and the Member States recognised that litigation was often borne out of a lack of representation. The Declaration continued by stressing its support for the preservation of sports training policies (Para. 11), the need to protect young sportsmen and women, particularly from commercial transactions targeting minors (Paras. 12 and 13), the important role governing bodies play in ensuring the integrity of competitions, particularly in relation to the ownership and control of clubs (Para. 14) and the important role that the collective sale of television

---

[123] S. Weatherill, 'Fair Play Please! Recent Developments in the Application of EC Law to Sport', 40 *Common Market Law Review* (2003) p. 89.

rights play in ensuring solidarity between all levels of sport (Para. 15). The Declaration also indicated support for the maintenance of the transfer system, which was at the time being investigated by the Commission for a potential breach of Community law. Paragraph 16 stated that 'the specific requirements of sport, subject to compliance with Community law' should be taken into account by the Commission.

2.3.4. Sport and constitutional reform

The convening of the European Convention on the Future of Europe presented proponents of a Treaty base for sport another opportunity to continue their lobbying. The Convention was established by the December 2001 Laeken European Council with a mandate to conduct a review of the activities of the EU with a view to proposing a new Constitutional Treaty for the Union. The Convention's final report of 18th July 2003 proposed the incorporation of sport into the legal framework of the new Treaty Establishing a Constitution for Europe.[124] Article III-282 of the Constitutional Treaty proposed a change in the legal status of sport by defining it as an area for 'supporting, co-ordinating or complimentary action' within the context of education, youth, sport and vocational training policy. Ultimately, the Constitutional Treaty was not ratified following its rejection in referendums in France and the Netherlands in 2005. In June 2007, the European Council agreed on the convening of an intergovernmental conference (IGC) to draw up a Reform Treaty which would replace, but be largely based on, the Constitutional Treaty. The IGC is due to complete its work before the end of 2007 so as to allow for ratification before the European Parliament elections in June 2009.

The draft Reform Treaty proposes to insert sport as an area of supporting, coordinating or complementary action with a legal basis modelled on the current Article 149 EC, presently located in the chapter on 'Education, Vocational Training and Youth'. The new chapter title will simply include sport following the reference to youth in a similar Article, renumbered within the draft Reform Treaty as Article 176b.[125] Union action shall be aimed at Paragraph 2, 'developing the European dimension in sport, by promoting fairness and openness in sporting competitions and cooperation between bodies responsible for sports, and by protecting the physical and moral integrity of sportsmen and sportswomen, especially young sportsmen and sportswomen'. Within areas of 'supporting, coordinating or complementary action', the Reform Treaty retains the Constitutional Treaty's prohibition on the harmonisation of the laws and regulations of Member States on that legal basis.[126] The provisions of the Reform Treaty are therefore identical to those found in Article III-282 of the Constitutional Treaty, which explicitly recognised the specific nature of sport and required this to be taken into account in the Union's supporting action contributing to the 'promotion of European sporting issues'. The inclusion of sport in the proposed amendment resolves the consequences of the *UK* v. *Commission* litigation on the legality of budget-

---

[124] Treaty establishing a Constitution for Europe *OJ* 2004 C 310 16. December 2004.

[125] Presidency Conclusions CIG 1/07, 23 July 2007, p. 90.

[126] Ibid. p. 45.

ary appropriations for measures with no legal base, since the promotion of European sporting issues is now an express competence.[127] This enables the establishment of a formal rolling Presidency agenda to replace the informal meetings of sports officials of the Member States. The formalisation of that agenda is likely to lead to increasing coherence and continuity in European sports policy.

The Reform Treaty's Article would require EU bodies to take account of the 'specific nature of sport' when considering the Union's supporting action contributing to the promotion of European sporting issues. Community institutions are therefore under no horizontal constitutional obligation to take this into account in the context of legislation under other competences, as is the case with horizontal provisions currently found for example in the field of environmental protection.[128] Nevertheless, as the experience of the Amsterdam Declaration has shown, political recognition of the 'specific nature of sport', even though merely in the context of positive action in the field, may infiltrate the legal reasoning of the Court and Commission in other fields with impacts on sport. It is also not inconceivable that sporting policy action could be invoked in other fields in the context of justifying measures otherwise contrary to one policy field, for example free movement or competition law, with reference to the pursuit of another policy. This reasoning is discussed in greater detail in the context of objective justification in free movement law and the notion of what constitutes a 'restriction' of competition in Chapters 3 and 5 respectively.

The impact of the Treaty Article should not be overstated. The *Walrave* sporting exception and the *Meca-Medina* inherency test were established without the guidance offered by a Treaty Article. Furthermore, in applying free movement and competition law to sport, the Court and the Commission have already recognised the specificity of sport and have, in fact, rather generously enshrined it in their jurisprudence.[129] Far from enshrining a neo-liberal approach to sport, the Court already in *Bosman* recognised 'the considerable social importance of sport'.[130] In the 2001 transfer system settlement, the Commission interpreted this as justifying the imposition of restrictions imposed on clubs and players which would not be witnessed in normal industries.[131]

For those completely opposed to EU involvement in sport, the Treaty Article represents a further unwelcome incursion on the part of the EU into sporting matters and a breach of the principle of subsidiarity. Many of the major governing bodies of sport such as the IOC, the National Olympic Committees (NOC) of the 27 Member States, the European Non Governmental Sports Organisations (ENGSO) and the UEFA hold the view that an Article for sport in the Treaty would place a legal obligation on the EU's judicial bodies to respect the specificity and autonomy of sport when disposing

---

[127] Case C-106/96 *UK* v. *Commission* [1998] *ECR* I-2729.

[128] Art. 6 EC Treaty.

[129] S. Weatherill, 'Fair Play Please! Recent Developments in the Application of EC Law to Sport', 40 *Common Market Law Review* (2003); R. Parrish, 'The EU's Draft Constitutional Treaty and the Future of EU Sports Policy', 3 *International Sports Law Journal* (2003).

[130] *Bosman* Para. 106.

[131] Commission Press Release IP/02/824, 'Commission Closes Investigations Into FIFA Regulations on International Football Transfers', 5 June 2002.

of sports related cases. This expectation is not supported by the context in which that specificity is recognised, namely the active pursuit of 'the promotion of European sporting issues'.

2.3.5. The Independent European Sports Review 2006

In 2005 the UK Presidency of the EU initiated a review of European football with a mandate 'to produce a report, independent of the Football Authorities, but commissioned by UEFA, on how the European football authorities, EU institutions and Member States can best implement the Nice Declaration on European and national level'. The central message of Nice, found in Paragraph 7, was that granting sport autonomy from Community law was conditional on sport operating 'with due regard for national and Community legislation and on the basis of a democratic and transparent method of operation'. The terms of the review were agreed at a meeting in Leipzig in December 2005 between the sports ministers of the UK, France, Germany, Italy and Spain and members of the European Commission and relevant football authorities. A reference group, including observers, was established thereafter in order to oversee the conduct of the work. In February 2006, José Luís Arnaut was appointed Chairman of the Review and 12 experts were invited to contribute to the work of three study groups examining legal, economic and political issues. Additional experts' reports were also commissioned. A public hearing was held in March 2006 at which a number of interested stakeholders contributed opinions. The Chairman also held a series of meetings with stakeholders and written contributions were invited. In its final title the scope of the report was widened to cover sport generally although the focus was still very much on football.

The final report took as its starting point acknowledgment that sport possesses characteristics distinct from other sectors, a theme developed in the Nice Declaration. In this connection, the Report concludes that sports governing bodies should enjoy a wide margin of discretion when performing their duties. This places the governing bodies in a powerful position with regards stakeholders and in order to satisfy the Nice Declaration's focus on participatory democracy in sport, the report argues that the governing bodies should ensure that the various stakeholders in sport are properly represented at both European and national association level. Consequently, the report focuses on both substantive and procedural issues relating to the decision making capabilities of governing bodies. In terms of substantive rules, the report identified three types of sports rules commonly adopted by sports governing bodies. These are rules designed to maintain regularity and proper functioning of competitions, rules on the integrity of sport and rules on competitive balance. On these matters, the Report's conclusions strongly recommend a wide margin of discretion for the governing bodies.

Concerning 'Regularity and Proper Functioning of Competitions', the report argued that the following rules of the governing bodies should be deemed compatible with Community law: field of play rules and rules on the structure of championships and calendars, rules concerning the composition of national teams, rules relating to the national organisation of sport in Europe (home and away rule), rules concerning organisation of sporting competitions in the European sports pyramid structure, rules relating to transfer 'deadlines', rules concerning the transfer of players in general, rules to encourage the attendance of spectators at sporting events, rules concerning the release of players for national teams and rules concerning doping. The report drew the same conclusions with the following rules designed to maintain the integrity of sport, rules relating to good governance of clubs (club licensing), rules related to the ownership/ control/ influence of clubs and rules concerning players' agents. Finally, the following rules of governing bodies designed to ensure competitive balance in sport were also compatible with Community law; rules concerning home-grown players, rules concerning the central marketing of commercial rights and rules concerning salary caps.

Clearly the Report's substantive findings were welcomed by governing bodies such as UEFA as it recommends a considerable widening of their territory of autonomy. However, the Independent Football Review report also stressed that as a corollary to this 'both UEFA and its national associations must ensure that they are sufficiently representative and democratic and that they also respect appropriate governance standards'.[132] The Report reviewed these current structures. In organisational terms the European model of sport places governing bodies in monopoly positions concerning issues of regulatory and commercial governance. The report did not identify this as a problem given two particular features of the organisation of football in Europe. The first feature concerns 'one of the fundamental features of a democracy',[133] namely the doctrine of the separation of powers. Within UEFA, the Congress acts as the legislative body, the Executive Committee, Chief Executive and President act as the executive and the disciplinary bodies and role of CAS act as the judicial bodies. The second feature concerns the pattern of stakeholder representation in UEFA. This comprises the Professional Football Committee, representing national professional leagues, the European Club Forum representing clubs, although with no separate recognition of G14, the Clubs Competitions Committee which engages in discussions with clubs on UEFA competitions, bi-lateral discussions with FIFPro, the players' union, and tripartite dialogue between the UEFA, Leagues and FIFPro Panel. The Report notes that as key stakeholders, supporters are not formally represented within UEFA and that financial redistribution between the stakeholders based on a principle of solidarity between the stakeholders should be strengthened.

Yet, these stakeholder committees and panels are not formally part of UEFA's decision making procedures. Whilst these flaws are acknowledged in the Report, the danger is that the Report pre-judges the democratic dialogue that should be taking place in sport by sweeping many of the most contentious issues in sport into an expanding territory of sporting autonomy whilst merely inviting UEFA to 'examine its

---

[132] J. Arnaut, *Independent European Sport Review* (2006), see at <www.independentfootballreview. com> p. 56.

[133] Ibid. p. 58.

own structures'.[134] Critics will argue that this concedes too much ground to the governing body. In fact, partly due to the Arnaut Report, in June 2007 UEFA approved the establishment of the Professional Football Strategy Council which includes amongst its membership representatives of the EPFL, representatives of the European Club Forum, and representatives of FIFPro.

In Chapter 6 on 'Instruments' the Report warned against a 'blind and insensitive application of EU law to sport', instead of favouring the Helsinki Report's call for a new approach to sports regulation at EU level which involves 'preserving the traditional values of sport, while at the same time assimilating a changing economic and legal environment'.[135] Having concluded that the substantive rules discussed above are required to preserve the traditional values of sport, the Report then discussed the most appropriate legal instruments which could be adopted to protect these rules. Despite arguing that '("sports and politics don't mix"), which is undoubtedly a principle that should be preserved for the future',[136] the Report then recommend a long list of political interventions the EU should adopt in sports including; the establishment of a European Sports Agency, the issuing of guidelines to the application of free movement and competition rules to sport, the amendment of EU legislation to allow for certain categories of state aids to sport and to recognise as compatible with the common market certain state aids in the field of sport, the EU to facilitate a European bargaining contract for each sport discipline, the EU to promote the idea that sport organisations fulfil a task of relevant general economic interest, recognised in Articles 16 and 86 EC, the EU to adopt several soft law instruments on the specificity of sport, the EU to adopt block exemption regulations on certain categories of agreements and concerted practices in sport, the EU to adopt a Directive on Minors in Sport, the EU to adopt a Directive on Betting in Sport and the EU to adopt a Directive on Agents in Sport. The report concluded by urging EU Governments to commit to enforce the review.

2.3.6. The White Paper on Sport

In the Impact Assessment document which accompanied the White Paper, the Commission described the range of options open to as it prepared to respond to the political initiatives developed at Member State level.[137] The Commission rejected the option of taking no action as it felt there was sufficient political support for a broad initiative on sport and that sporting stakeholders had expressed a need for legal clarity at EU level. Accordingly, the Commission also rejected a second option of consulting further with sporting stakeholders by way of a Green Paper, noting that this option

---

[134] Ibid. p. 134.

[135] Ibid. p. 99.

[136] Ibid. pp. 29-30.

[137] Commission of the European Communities, *Commission staff working document. Impact Assessment Accompanying the White Paper on Sport*, SEC 932, 11/07/2007, p. 20.

would not add value to the consultations that had already taken place. The choice fell between adopting a White Paper on sport or intervening in sport by way of regulation or specific legislative proposals as recommended in the Arnaut Report. This latter option was also rejected as the Commission favoured a comprehensive approach to sport rather than narrow targeted interventions in certain problem areas such as the regulation of players' agents. In July 2007, following a consultation exercise, the Commission's Directorate General for Education and Culture published a White Paper on Sport. The White Paper was not designed to act as the basis for legislative proposals but to state the Commission's current policy position on sport. In doing so the White Paper acts as another communication with sports organisations and also as an orientation document sensitising the other Commission DG's and EU institutions to the current debates within sport. The White Paper is structured around three themes: the societal role of sport, its economic dimension and its organisation in Europe.

The chapter on the societal role of sport discussed sport and public health, doping in sport, the role of sport in education and training, volunteering in sport, sport and social inclusion, combating racism and violence, sport's connection with the EU's external policies and sport and sustainable development and outlined ways in which the Commission would seek to mainstream these sporting issues. The chapter on the economic dimension in sport stressed the importance of conducting further research in order to determine the actual economic importance of sport so that policy actions at European level are underpinned by a sound knowledge base. There is a need for sound economic justifications for *prima facie* restrictive rules of sports governing bodies. Under EC competition law, contested rules of sports governing bodies can fail to constitute restrictions of competition and can thus be removed from the scope of competition law if the rule in question derives from a need inherent in the operation and organisation of sport. Similar supporting evidence is required for the exemption criteria contained in Article 81(3) to be applied to sporting contexts. In terms of free movement law, the process of objective justification requires similar evidence based justification.

It is within the chapter on the organisation of sport that the importance of these evidence based justifications is most evident. In that chapter, the Commission notes that certain values and traditions of the European model of sport should be promoted but that it is unrealistic to attempt to define a unified model.[138] Rules of the governing bodies designed to protect certain features of the European model may therefore be considered as legitimate even though they may impose restrictions on individuals and undertakings. Nevertheless, the Commission correctly acknowledges that the commercialisation of sport has attracted new stakeholders who may be dissatisfied with certain features of the European model, particularly regarding its standards of governance. The pending litigation in the *Charleroi/Oulmers* case amply illustrates this tension.[139] The Commission suggests that it can play a role in helping to de-

---

[138] Commission of the European Communities, *White Paper on Sport*, COM(2007) 391 Final, p. 12.
[139] Case C-243/06 *Charleroi/Oulmers*, *OJ* C 212, 2 September 2006, p. 11.

velop a common set of principles for good governance in sport such as transparency, democracy, accountability and representation of stakeholders.[140] In this connection, parallels between the White Paper and the Arnaut Report can be drawn. In the White Paper, the Commission argues that governance issues in sport should fall within a territory of autonomy and that most challenges can be addressed through self-regulation which must however be 'respectful of good governance principles'.[141] The Arnaut report drew a similar conclusion. At the heart of this analysis lies a willingness to accept that sport is characterised by unique features. Whilst the Paper stresses that sport is subject to EU law, it recognises two dimensions to the specificity of sport. The first is the specificity of sporting activities and rules. This includes traditional rules of the game and the legitimate objectives of ensuring outcome uncertainty and competitive balance. The second is the specificity of the sport structure which refers to the autonomy of sports organisations, the pyramid structure of competitions, solidarity mechanisms, the organisation of sport on a national basis and the principle of a single federation per sport. These, too, are recognised to warrant special treatment within any legal analysis.

In a passage which disappointed the governing bodies,[142] the Commission argues that whilst this specificity will continue to be recognised, it does not justify a general exemption from the application of Community law. Citing the principles deriving from *Meca-Medina* the Commission repeats that inherent and proportionate rules will escape the scope of the Treaty's competition provisions, but 'in respect of the regulatory aspect of sport, the assessment whether a certain sporting rule is compatible with EU competition law can only be made on a case-by-case basis'.[143] This is because applying the test of proportionality requires an assessment of the individual circumstances of each case which precludes the formulation of general guidelines on the application of competition law to sport. Clearly, this rules out a policy promoting general exemptions. A joint statement of the European sports teams including UEFA expressed disappointment 'that the EU has not reached firmer conclusions with regard to some of the key issues facing sport today'.[144] In this regard, it was unrealistic to expect the Commission to endorse exemptions from Community law in matters pending before the Court and Commission. The Commission is not competent to authorise the adoption of an alternative legal analysis to the one explicitly recognised by the Court in the recent *Meca-Medina* judgment.

The disappointment expressed by the governing bodies on the White Paper is somewhat misplaced. The Commission's approach is no more than a re-statement of the *Meca-Medina* principles and these do not provide for an automatic contraction in the autonomy afforded to sport. Rules which are inherent in the organisation of

---

[140] Commission of the European Communities, *White Paper on Sport*, COM(2007) 391 Final, p. 12.

[141] Id.

[142] G. Infantino, 'Meca-Medina: A Step Backwords for the European Sports Model and the Specificity of Sport?', *INF* (2 October 2006), see at <www.uefa.com>.

[143] Commission of the European Communities, *White Paper on Sport*, COM(2007) 391 Final, p. 14.

[144] *EU White Paper on Sport: Much Work Remains to be Done*, Statement of the European team sports, Media Release No. 093 (11 July 2007), see at <www.uefa.com>.

sport and which can be demonstrated as not going beyond what is necessary for the achievement of legitimate objectives will actually be removed from the scope of EU competition law. As is discussed in Chapter 8, many rules concerning the organisational structure of the European model of sport may therefore escape condemnation as a restriction under Article 81(1) without even having to undergo an analysis under Article 81(3) on the application of the exemption criteria. The Commission's approach to regulatory questions of governance can be contrasted with their approach to national segmentation in the players' market as discussed in the White Paper's sections on free movement as in relation to nationality and transfers. Here, the Commission remained firmly committed to the principle of non-discrimination and was only prepared to accept limited exemptions to the principle with respect to national eligibility criteria, limiting the number of participants in a competition and in relation to the revised transfer system agreed between the Commission and FIFA and UEFA in 2001. Consequently, whilst the White Paper promotes a liberalisation in the European player market, it also offers implicit support for the maintenance of national segmentation in the product markets relevant to national sports. As is discussed in Chapter 8, this differential approach may have significant consequences for the sports market.

The remainder of the section on the organisation of sport addresses some specific issues in sport. On the question of player agent regulation, the Commission proposes carrying out an impact assessment to provide a clear overview of the activities of players' agents in the EU and evaluate whether action at EU level is necessary.[145] Continuing a theme of the Nice Declaration, the White Paper also expressed a concern for the protection of minors in sport. In particular, although not explicitly mentioned in this context, UEFA's rule on home-grown players rule may promote the trade in young players, an issue highlighted in the European Parliament's Belet Report.[146] On the question of club licensing, the Commission acknowledged the 'usefulness of robust licensing systems for professional clubs at European and national levels as a tool for promoting good governance in sport'.[147] In the section on the role of the media in sport, the Commission continues to argue for the public's right to information, a reference to the provisions of the pending Audio-Visual Media Services Directive which contains reference to national lists of sport on free-to-air television and a right to short sports clips in news reports. The section also stresses the Commission's support for solidarity mechanisms in sport to be secured through safeguards in the manner in which media rights are sold.

The final section of the White Paper concerns dialogue within the sports sector. The Commission proposes to re-launch the dormant European Sports Forum as a means of promoting dialogue and strengthen existing channels of political co-operation within the EU. The final section is however most notable for the statement of political support for social dialogue within sport. Following the experience of the transfer system dispute in 2001, the Commission has funded a number of projects ex-

---

[145] Commission of the European Communities, *White Paper on Sport*, COM(2007) 391 Final, p. 16.

[146] European Parliament, rapporteur: Ivo Belet, *Much Work Remains to be Done,* European Parliament Committee on Culture and Education, 2006/2130(INI), point 18.

[147] Commission of the European Communities, *White Paper on Sport*, COM(2007) 391 Final, p. 17.

ploring the viability of social dialogue between representatives of clubs and players. As many issues pertaining to the employment relationship between these two social partners have contributed to litigation, the Commission proposes that social dialogue could lead to greater legal certainty within the sector. This can take place under the legal framework established by Articles 138 and 139 of the EC Treaty.

2.3.7. Social dialogue

Social dialogue can be conceptualised from both a constitutional and labour law perspective. From the constitutional perspective, it is a regulatory technique which empowers private actors to regulate a sector and conclude legislation outside the normal EU method of involving the democratic involvement of the European Parliament. From a labour law perspective is stressed the autonomous dimension of social dialogue based on the traditions of industrial relations.[148] These perspectives are evident within the European professional sports sector. Whilst in this context, social dialogue concerns the potential for clubs and players to conclude an agreement on labour conditions, it also implies a new form of regulation outside the traditional governing body structure.

Article 137 envisages the possibility of Community action to improve a number of employment conditions. Article 138 provides representatives of employers and employees the right of consultation and opinion over new Commission proposals in the field of social policy with these opinions potentially affecting the content of future legislation. Article 139 also grants these 'social partners' the right to intervene in the legislative process initiated by the Commission. If they are able to conclude a Community-wide agreement, the social partners can directly affect the subject of the Commission proposal. Finally, Article 139 also allows the social partners to initiate their own Community-wide agreement independent of a Commission proposal. Such agreements can be implemented in accordance with national practice or by way of a Council Decision.

The content of a collective agreement is potentially wide but it must pertain to the employment relationship between clubs and players. This could include contractual terms, transfer windows, the transfer system, salary capping, image rights, pension funds and doping rules. As a regulatory tool, social dialogue is limited in its capacity to establish wide-spread legal certainty within the professional football sector. Many of the disputes within sport stem from restraints imposed on players. As the issues to be discussed within a social dialogue committee must relate to improving the working conditions of labour, a collective agreement cannot be used as a mask for clubs to impose restrictions on players. Even if the players' union were to acquiesce, those elements falling outside the scope of Article 137 are not enforceable. The Commission makes this assessment before an agreement is presented to the Council for implementation. A measure of legal protection is afforded to agreements legitimately

---

[148] S. Smismans, 'The European Social Dialogue Between Constitutional and Labour Law', 32(3) *European Law Review* (2007) p. 342.

conducted within the Treaty framework. In *Brentjens* the Court of Justice established that the social policy objectives of collective agreements would be undermined if agreements seeking to improve conditions of work and employment where subject to competition law.[149] Should the collective agreement be subject to a free movement challenge, the court would examine the clause which restricts free movement and consider questions of objective justification. These questions are discussed in detail in Chapters 3 and 5.

Before a social dialogue committee can be established, the social partners must satisfy participation criteria established by the European Commission. Commenting on the establishment of sectoral dialogue committees, the Commission stated that they are to be established in those sectors where the social partners make a joint request to take part in a dialogue at European level and where organizations representing both sides of industry are cross-industry or relate to specific sectors or categories and be organised at European level and consist of organisations which are themselves an integral and recognised part of member States' social partner structures and have the capacity to negotiate agreements and which are representative of several Member States. They must also have adequate structures to ensure their effective participation in the work of the committees.[150] A concern raised with regards to the powers of a social dialogue committee concerns the deviation from the traditional EU legislative method which is based on the democratic involvement of the European Parliament. Legislation conducted via a social dialogue committee is a break from this method and raises some concerns as to the democratic legitimacy of the agreements concluded by way of social dialogue. These fears should not be overstated for as long as essential criteria on the collectively representative nature of the social partners can be guaranteed, the input of those affected by the decision can be assured.

The employees are represented by the FIFPro which was established in the mid 1960's as a mechanism to coordinate the activities of national players' associations and represent players' interests. A 2006 study on labour representation in European professional football found that in eight out of twenty eight countries surveyed professional footballers were not represented by any organisation. In other countries, more than one organisation represents players. In terms of the coverage rate of the representative organisations, in the countries which have one or several organisations, the affiliation rate of professional footballers is less than 50% in 4 countries (22%), between 50% and 80% in 6 countries (23%) and equal to or greater than 80% in 8 countries (45%). The affiliation rate for professional footballers within the 28 countries is estimated at 52%.[151] In some new EU states football players are not is-

---

[149] Joined Cases C-115/97, C-116/97 and C-117/97 *Brentjens Handelsonderneming BV* v. *Stichting Bedrijfspensioenfonds voor de Handel in Bouwmaterialen* [1999] *ECR* I-6025. Hereafter referred to as *Brentjens*.

[150] Commission of the European Communities, *Promoting and Adapting the Social Dialogue*, COM(98) 322 Final (1998), Para. 1.2.

[151] Commission of the European Communities, *Université Catholique de Louvain Study on the Representativeness of the Social Partner Organisations in the Professional Football Players Sector*, project No. VC/2004/0547 (February 2006), research project conducted on behalf of the Employment and Social Affairs DG of the European Commission, Para. 1.2.

sued with a contract of employment, and their treatment as self-employed persons in national law has impeded the development of collective bargaining bodies.[152] Whilst the definition of this employment status is not relevant to the EC Treaty definition of workers, that players are not considered employees under national law reduces their ability to organise themselves collectively and thus invoke the Treaty social dialogue provisions.[153]

On the employers' side a number of bodies cannot lay claim to represent management. This includes UEFA, which is not an employers' body, and G14 who only represent eighteen European clubs in Europe. The EPFL is the most representative employers' body. The EPFL is a grouping of major European leagues formed in 1998 to represent the interests of clubs throughout Europe. Of the 28 countries studied in the 2006 survey, the EPFL was present in 14 countries (50%). The study also found that of nine countries in which collective agreements were concluded, in seven these were done so by the organisation affiliated to the EPFL.[154] This experience of social dialogue on a national basis provides the EPFL with limited grounds to claim a representative nature. Furthermore, the structure and role of leagues throughout Europe can result in conflicts of interest. For example, some leagues have jurisdiction to decide cases involving employment-related disputes between players and clubs. This clearly conflicts with the leagues' role as a member of a representative employer organisation in social dialogue negotiations. Also, leagues have a close relationship with governing bodies. In a national context, the league is part of the governing body structure and at European level, the EPFL operates within UEFA's committee structure. This raises a concern that the governing bodies, who cannot be considered a social partner, could have access to the social dialogue legislative process. In addition, the recent enlargement of the EU from 15 to 27 has impacted on EPFL's representativeness as labour relations in the professional football sectors of the new states are underdeveloped.[155] Only such a collective organisation has standing under Articles 137-139 to conclude such an agreement at Community level. As the EPFL only represents the top leagues in each country, its role may assume added importance as a potential vehicle for a breakaway super-league in which questions of employer representativeness would be assured.

UEFA has a vested interest in opposing social dialogue taking place within the EU Treaty framework. Their preference is for the social partners to discuss matters

---

[152] Report for the Commission of the European Communities, *Promoting the Social Dialogue in European Professional Football (Candidate EU Member States)* (The Hague: T.M.C. Asser Institute November 2004), pp. 129-133.

[153] R. Siekmann, 'Labour Law, the Provision of Services, Transfer Rights and Social Dialogue in Professional Football in Europe', 1-2 *The International Sports Law Journal* (2006) p. 117.

[154] Commission of the European Communities, *Université Catholique de Louvain Study on the Representativeness of the Social Partner Organisations in the Professional Football Players Sector*, Project No.VC/2004/0547 (February 2006), research project conducted on behalf of the Employment and Social Affairs DG of the European Commission, Para. 2.3.1.

[155] European Parliament, *Professional Sport in the Internal Market*, Commissioned by the Committee on the Internal Market and Consumer Protection of the European Parliament on the initiative of Toine Manders, project No: IP/A/IMCO/ST/2005-004 (2005), p. 320.

via their committee structure which would retain their regulatory authority. In June, UEFA approved the establishment of the Professional Football Strategy Council which includes amongst its membership representatives of FIFPro and EPFL. UEFA hopes that this new committee will satisfy the demands of these two major stakeholders for more influence in governance questions in football. UEFA's tactical opposition to social dialogue conducted within the EU framework are that social dialogue is unrepresentative and undemocratic. Potentially, social dialogue provides the social partners with a means of agreeing legislation. By its definition, such agreements can only be conducted between representatives of management and labour. This only represents the professional game and leaves other stakeholders, who are affected by collective agreements, without representation. The narrow employment related concerns of management and labour are not necessarily in accordance with the concerns of all stakeholders within the European model. As such, issues of employment relations should not be confused with wider issues of sports governance in which only a governing body is able to take a holistic approach. This concern reveals a deeper strategic objection based on a suspicion of the motives of the social partners. The implication is that the social partners are not so concerned with improving the employment conditions of an already cosseted category of worker, but are motivated by a desire to exercise greater influence within football in order to control the wealth generated from it. This contrasts with the role of a governing body which exercises commercial functions in order to redistribute wealth for 'the good of the game'. In this connection, the European model of sport invests considerable regulatory authority in governing bodies. If social partners are able to assume a legislative competence within this model, this will substantially alter the vertical channels of authority which have traditionally been a feature of the European model.

2.4. CONCLUSIONS

In framing a policy on sport, the EU is caught between two powerful forces. The governing bodies and some Member States argue that sport is special as it carries with it important social and cultural functions. Penetration of market principles into sport would undermine the essential character of sport and create welfare losses for society. However, sport accounts for 3.7% of EU GDP and 5.4% of the European labour market.[156] Stakeholders in sport are autonomous economic actors whose commercial interests can be seriously undermined by the decisions of governing bodies. A central theme for the EU is which set of interests should prevail. In reality, the choice for the EU is not the endorsement of one model over another, but the creation of a stable and relatively predictable legal environment for the stakeholders to operate within. The Court's contribution to the creation of this environment has come by way of its major judgments. In *Bosman*, *Deliège*, *Lehtonen* and *Meca-Medina*, the Court acknowledged the specificity of sport with reference to the features that distinguish sport from normal industries. Thus, the need to ensure competitive balance, encour-

---

[156] Commission of the European Communities, *White Paper on Sport*, COM(2007) 391 Final, p. 11.

age the education and training of young players, maintain the integrity of sport and the need to protect national teams are recognised as legitimate objectives. The EU's policy on sport could have been confined to establishing guidelines and encouraging dialogue on how these objectives could be legitimately pursued within the framework of EC law. Instead, the EU has adopted a wide-ranging policy as articulated in the White Paper. This broad-based approach risks attack from those fearing the EU is not abiding by its commitments to subsidiarity and the Lisbon Agenda's focus on better regulation. In particular, by engaging with the debate on how EC law should apply to sport, the EU has entered into much broader policy considerations concerning the use of sport to achieve wider pro-integration goals and there are concerns that the EU is not competent to advance this agenda. Nevertheless, in terms of the debate on legal certainty in sport, this more broad-based approach can be defended on the grounds that the intellectual origins of specificity arguments lie in a range of socio-cultural considerations with which the EU needs to engage. For example, questions concerning the use of the transfer system and the home-grown player rule, which are justified with reference to the need to promote the education and training of young players, cannot be separated from deeper grassroots issues concerning educational and training matters. In other words, the European model of sport requires a holistic approach as it is impossible to separate the vertical and horizontal channels connecting the European model.

This argument may have its merits, but through a plethora of policy documents on sport, the EU has in fact moved beyond an approach to sport which merely recognises the structural characteristics of the European model. Its modern approach is one in which the Union has pledged political allegiance to that European model. In doing so, the EU needs to exercise caution. In Paragraph 77 *Bosman* the Court held that whilst the practical consequences of a judicial decision on the organisation of sport must be weighed carefully, this cannot go so far as to diminish the objective character of the law and compromise its application.[157] In 'weighing carefully' the consequences, the increasingly illusory nature of the European model of sport must be considered in which a greater disconnection between elite professional sport and the rest of the pyramid is evident, as must the impact of the European model on sports stakeholders who are increasingly engaging in significant economic activity. In this sense, sporting rules which purport to safeguard the European model may in fact simply reinforce the commercial position of those imposing the rule whilst affording interested stakeholders little or no influence in the decision making process. Whilst the Court's approach has been to recognise specificity arguments by constructing a growing list of sporting justifications, such as the need to maintain competitive balance, the Commission's reference to the 'specificity of the sport structure' in the White Paper may risk raising stakeholder expectations by implying that adherence to the European model generally is a defence for the maintenance of restrictive rules. Admittedly, in the White Paper the Commission somewhat dampened such inflated expectations by wisely choosing to endorse the case-by-case method favoured by the Court in *Meca-Medina*.

---

[157] *Bosman* Para. 77.

The Commission's White Paper endorsement of the organisation of sport on a national basis illustrates one of the potential dangers of the Commission's approach. At the heart of the European model lies a system of regulatory control designed to segment the European sports market along national lines. In *Bosman*, the Court significantly liberalised the European player's market and support for the prohibition of nationality discrimination was forcefully repeated in the White Paper. Yet, the White Paper then seems to endorse national segmentation in product markets. Consequently, whilst players are able to migrate freely, clubs remain nationally tied. This may have consequences on competitive balance in European sport as players migrate from smaller markets to the larger markets leaving the larger clubs in smaller markets seriously disadvantaged. This in turn leads to the prospect of some uncomfortable political choices. Either the EU allows for the player market to be re-regulated so that player mobility is constrained, or it promotes greater deregulation in the product market by challenging rules designed to maintain national segmentation. Whilst the latter may require less constitutional gymnastics given the present Treaty lack of competence, both of these options run contrary to principles expressed in the EU's policy on sport.

Perhaps in recognition that deeper engagement with sport will ultimately lead the EU into some very contentious disputes, the Commission has wisely endorsed two strategies in the White Paper. First, it has made the case for more research to be conducted on some of the issues on which the Commission and Court are, and will, be asked to adjudicate. This is sensible for the justificatory processes inherent in EU free movement and competition law require the elaboration of an evidence base. Second, the Commission is encouraging dialogue within the sports sector, a request made to it by the European Council at Amsterdam in 1997. In addition to the various consultation exercises promoted by the Commission, its advocacy of structured social dialogue taking place within the Treaty framework has the potential for social partners to negotiate collectively thus partly removing the EU from some potential future sources of conflict. Yet this policy option is also contentious. Encouraging horizontal channels of stakeholder dialogue disturbs the vertical pattern of governing body authority which has traditionally been a feature of the European model.

Chapter 3
EC Free Movement Law

European integration is explained with a mix of economic and political considerations. In free movement, as in other areas of Community law, these can be seen side by side in the Treaty text. The principle of non-discrimination on the basis of nationality is found in all Treaty titles on free movement and through the application of Article 12 to citizenship rights also operates within rights derived from Union citizenship. That principle could be characterised as a manifestation of the political drive towards integration. However, the Treaty as it has been subsequently interpreted by the European Court of Justice requires more than the abolition of nationality discrimination against citizens. Free movement rules often require even indirectly discriminatory or entirely non-discriminatory obstacles to trade to be justified. This ventures beyond political ideals and demonstrates a drive towards the Article 2 EC goal of a '... high degree of competitiveness and convergence of economic performance ...'. The present chapter considers the legal framework of these Community free movement rules, while the next outlines the evolution of the sporting exception and its impact on the development of those free movement rules.

3.1.   GENERAL ASPECTS OF THE FUNDAMENTAL FREEDOMS

3.1.1.   Non-discrimination

The free movement of goods under Articles 23-31 and 90, persons under Articles 39-42 (workers) and 43-48 (the self-employed and legal persons), services under Articles 49-55 and capital under Articles 56-60 of the EC Treaty, all establish legal regimes which aim to eliminate obstacles to free movement between the Member States in the spirit of Article 3(1)(c) and thus indirectly strive to approximate economic conditions within the Union. At the core of the free movement rules is the idea that nationality, all other things being equal, is not a legitimate basis for differentiation in the internal market. This stark contrast with one of the foundational premises of the European Model of Sport is reflected in specific prohibitions on nationality discrimination in Article 39(2), Article 43, and Article 50 in relation to workers, establishment and services respectively. The Community Treaty also incorporates a general prohibition on nationality discrimination in Article 12. This principle, combined with the notion of Union citizenship in Article 18(1), as has been interpreted by the European Court of Justice and reinforced by the recent Directive 2004/38/EC on Citizens' Rights, extends the right to equality between citizens of Member States beyond the economically active to whom protection was initially extended through the legal provisions of the fundamental freedoms. As the Court has observed in *Grzelzyck* and later cases, at least in so far as social rights in Member States are concerned, Union citizenship precludes those States from discriminating on the grounds of nationality.[158] However, Article 12 is relevant only to those cases where the activity is not covered by a more specific principle of non-discrimination and therefore the general rule against nationality discrimination in Article 12 only applies in the absence of specific regimes protecting free movement.[159] The same is true of the relationship between free movement rights derived from citizenship and economic activity: the latter take precedence and are mutually exclusive with citizens' rights.[160] Such specific contexts exist within all of the fundamental freedoms.

3.1.2. Direct effect

The European Court of Justice has progressively declared Articles 28, 29, 39, 43, 49, and 56, on which the freedoms are based to be directly effective. It has also concluded that the same is true of Article 18(1) which provides for similar rights based on Union citizenship.[161] However, only recently has it ventured to suggest that these articles might be capable of horizontal direct effect rather than merely an extended form of vertical direct effect applicable to bodies with state-like qualities or with powers derived from the state. In *Angonese* the ECJ confirmed that Article 39 applied to purely private organisations,[162] and whilst the Court has yet to rule on the matter in respect of other free movement provisions, Advocate General Maduro has suggested in his 2007 opinion in *Viking* that Treaty rules on '... freedom of movement apply to private action that, by virtue of its general effect on the holders of rights to freedom of movement, is capable of restricting them from exercising those rights, by raising an obstacle that they cannot reasonably circumvent'.[163] Even though the Treaty articles on services, establishment and capital have so far been denied horizontal direct effect, the Court has recognised their application to situations where public law powers have been exercised and in *Walrave* to situations where the rules amount to collective

---

[158] Case C-184/99 *Grzelczyk* [2001] *ECR* I-6193, Paras. 30 and 31, Case C-148/02 *Garcia Avello* [2003] *ECR* I-11613, Paras. 22 and 23, and Case C-209/03 *Bidar* [2005] *ECR* I-2119, Para. 31and Case C-403/03 *Schempp ECR* I-6421 Para. 15.

[159] See, *inter alia*, Case C-179/90 *Merci Convenzionali Porto di Genova* v. *Siderurgica Gabrielli* [1991] *ECR* I-5889, Para. 11; Case C-379/92 Peralta [1994] *ECR* I-3453, Para. 18; Case C-176/96 *Lehtonen ECR* [2000] *ECR* I-2681 Para. 37, Case C-262/96 *Sürül* [1999] *ECR* I-2685, Para. 64; Case C-55/98 *Vestergaard* [1999] *ECR* I-7641, Para. 16; Case C-422/01 *Skandia and Ramstedt* [2003] *ECR* I-6817, Para. 61; and Case C-185/04 *Öberg* [2006] *ECR* I-1453, Para. 25.

[160] Case C-345/05 *Commission* v. *Portugal* [2006] *ECR* I-10633 Para. 13.

[161] Arts. 28 and 29: Case 74/76 *Ianelli and Volpi* v. *Meroni* [1977] *ECR* 557 Para. 13; Art. 39 Case 167/73 *Commission* v. *France (French Merchant Seamen)* [1974] *ECR* 359 Para. 41; Art. 43: Case 2/74 *Reyners* [1974] *ECR* 631 Para. 32; Art. 49 Case 33/74 *Van Binsbergen* [1974] *ECR* 1299 Para. 27; Art. 56: Joined Cases C-163/94, 165/94 and 250/94 *Sanz de Lera* [1995] *ECR* I-4830 Para. 41; Art. 90(1) Case 57/65 *Lütticke* [1966] *ECR* I-205; Art. 90(2) Case 28/67 *Fink-Frucht* [1968] *ECR* 223; Art. 18 *Baumbast* Case C-413/99 [2002] *ECR* I-7091.

[162] Case C-281/98 *Angonese* [2000] *ECR* I-4139.

[163] Case C-438/05 *International Transport Workers*, Opinion of Advocate General Maduro, May 23, 2007 point 48. Hereafter referred to as *Viking*.

regulation, even when this is undertaken by actors unconnected with the State.[164] In that same case, the Court also suggested more broadly that the prohibition on nationality discrimination was horizontally directly effective at least within the context of Articles 12, 39 and 49.[165] As a consequence, the rules of sports governing bodies and other collective regulators are subject to free movement law regardless of whether the bodies are linked to the State as such.

3.1.3. Direct effect and directives

Even if the Court was to eventually recognise the horizontal direct effect of all Treaty articles relevant to free movement, it has in *Marshall* and subsequent case law denied the horizontal effects of directives.[166] As a consequence, many of those instruments that lay down detailed Community rules in the field apply only to bodies analogous to the state. While in *Mangold* the Court accepted the possibility that a directive might be a manifestation of 'general principles of Community law' and that its rules could therefore apply to private parties within the scope of Community law, the general rule remains that in the absence of domestic transposition, directives bind only Member States and their organs.[167] This will often be somewhat mitigated by many directives' close correlation to established, Treaty-derived case law. For example, the rules on entry and access to social benefits in the Citizens' Rights Directive mirror closely the Court's case law including its recognition of more fully developed social rights for the economically active than for citizens not exercising economic activity. The recent Professional Qualifications Directive 2005/36 and its predecessors are also substantially modelled on the Court's rulings on the equivalence of qualifications under Articles 43 and 49.[168] If an applicant cannot rely on the Directive because the rules fall outside its scope or because it is contesting purely private rules to which a directive does not apply, they may rely on the general scheme enunciated in the case law of the Court and derived from the Treaty articles and applicable to all forms of collective regulation. In the event that the horizontal direct effect of the articles on establishment and services were to be recognised, the 'collective regulation' criterion would also cease to be of relevance. However, where a directive introduces substantial innovations, it raises serious questions in sectors such as sport which are in some Member States regulated by the national legislature and in others by private bodies. This could lead to the prospect that EC-derived rules apply in some, but not all, of those states. Although the Court has long recognised an obligation of sympathetic interpretation derived from *von Colson* and *Marleasing,* it can only be of use where the national

---

[164] *Walrave* Para. 17.

[165] Ibid. Paras. 21-25.

[166] Case 152/84 *Marshall* [1986] *ECR* 723, Para. 48; Case C-188/89 *Foster* v. *British Gas* [1990] *ECR* I-3313, Para. 20. See for case law, A. Arnull, *The European Union and Its Court of Justice*, 2nd edn. (Oxford, Oxford University Press 2006) pp. 198-209.

[167] Case C-144/04 *Mangold* v. *Helm* [2005] *ECR* I-9981 Para. 75.

[168] R. White, *Workers, Services and Establishment* (Oxford, Oxford University Press 2004) p. 75-76.

provision is ambiguous so as to facilitate recourse to the directive.[169] In a State where
the sector is regulated by public rules, those rules are subject to directives upon which
any aggrieved individual may rely in the absence of compatible national legislation.
Where the State merely permits equivalent private restrictions, for example by way
of national-level collective bargains, an individual may not rely on the directive or
rights enumerated within it against that private body but must instead begin an action against the State for damages arising from its failure to properly transpose those
rules.[170] This does not leave the potential applicant entirely without a remedy, but
does prevent reliance on the free movement rights in the form of a challenge to the
validity of domestic private rules.

3.1.4. The economic test

Not all activity falls within the scope of the fundamental freedoms in the EC Treaty.
Before the substance of the rule is considered, two key conditions must be satisfied. The activity must have a sufficient economic dimension. It must also have some
Community dimension beyond the borders of a single Member State. In the context
of workers under Article 39, the economic test applied since *Lawrie-Blum* is that '...
for a certain period of time a person performs services for and under the direction of
another person in return for ... remuneration'.[171] The work performed must be 'genuine and effective' and not 'purely marginal and ancillary'.[172] It need not, however, be
in itself adequate for supporting the worker and in *Levin* amounted to less than the
national minimum wage. In relation to services under Article 49, the Court has found
a similarly low threshold of remuneration. '... [T]he essential characteristic of remuneration lies in the fact that it constitutes consideration for the services in question
and is normally agreed upon between the provider and the recipient of a service.'[173]
In *Deliège*, the ECJ had cause to revisit the implications of its judgment in *Bond van
Adverteerders*,[174] where it had noted that services need not be directly paid for by
the consumer to constitute services under the Treaty and therefore to be economic
activity within the meaning attributed to the phrase in the sporting-related case law.
The Court noted that '... a high-ranking athlete's participation in an international competition [is] capable of involving the provision of a number of separate, but closely
related, services which may fall within the scope of Article [49] of the Treaty even

---

[169] Case 14/83 *von Colson and Kamann* v. *Land Nordrhein-Westfalen* [1984] *ECR* 1891, Para. 26;
Case C-106/89 *Marleasing* [1990] *ECR* I-4135, Para. 8. Most recently, see Case C-212/04 *Adeneler*
[2006] *ECR* I-6057, Paras. 108-111. See for case law, A. Arnull, *The European Union and its Court of
Justice*, 2nd edn. (Oxford, Oxford University Press 2006) p. 214.

[170] Case C-212/04 *Adeneler* [2006] *ECR* I-6057 Para. 112.

[171] Case 66/85 *Lawrie-Blum* [1986] *ECR* 2121 Para. 17, confirmed recently in Case C-392/05 *Alevi-
zos* Judgment of the Fourth Chamber of 26 April 2007, Para. 67.

[172] Case 53/81 *Levin* [1982] *ECR* 1035 Para. 17, cited recently in Case C-213/05 *Geven* Judgment
of the Grand Chamber of 18 July, 2007, Para. 16.

[173] Case C-109/92 *Wirth* [1993] *ECR* I-6447 Para. 15.

[174] Case 352/85 *Bond van Adverteerders* [1988] *ECR* 2085, Para. 16.

if some of those services are not paid for by those for whom they are performed'.[175] Article 50 itself recognises that while services must normally be remunerated, they may also occasionally be provided for free. Establishment under Article 43 has been defined as 'the actual pursuit of an economic activity through a fixed establishment in another Member State for an indefinite period',[176] and is distinguished from services primarily by the criterion of permanence. However, the economic threshold does not require any great business success for free movement rights to be invoked since unlike within the field of competition law, there is no *de minimis* rule in the field of free movement.[177] All that is required is an attempt at what could constitute economic activity.

3.1.5. The territorial test

The application of Community free movement rules also requires a territorial dimension beyond the borders of an individual Member State. In the seminal *Dassonville* case, the ECJ considered the free movement of goods to be impeded even where a potential indirect effect on trade between Member States could be demonstrated. The limits of the Community territorial dimension can be illustrated in rules relating to reverse discrimination. The 'wholly internal situation', where an individual's activity has no Community dimension and occurs purely within the person's Member State of nationality, falls outside the scope of Community law as there is no attempt to move freely and therefore no justifiable restriction.[178] However, where a citizen has exercised rights of free movement, their situation may be governed by Community law even in their Member State of nationality and residence,[179] and Member States of origin are prohibited from restricting the rights of their nationals to establish in other Member States.[180] The Court of Justice can be seen to use the economic and territorial criteria in cases where the application of EC law would create a high level of tension between the principles of a national system and Community law. The facts of these cases have in the past included abortion in Ireland, where the rights of the unborn child are constitutionally protected,[181] the impact of a penal sentence for murder on free movement rights,[182] and where a constitutional ban on communist symbols was argued to be contrary to freedom of movement.[183] This is not to say that the Court seeks to give precedence to national rules. Nevertheless, the questions of whether an activity has a sufficient economic dimension and whether a Community-level territo-

---

[175] *Deliège* Para. 56.
[176] Case C-221/89 *Factortame II* [1991] *ECR* I-2433 Para. 20.
[177] Joined Cases 177/82 and 178/82, *Van den Haar* [1984] *ECR* 1797 Para. 13.
[178] Case 175/78 *Saunders* [1975] *ECR* 1129 Para. 11.
[179] Case 115/78 *Knoors* [1979] *ECR* 399 Paras. 20 and 24. *Knoors* predated Union citizenship by 15 years, but the relevant provisions require nationality of a Member State.
[180] Case 81/87 *Daily Mail* [1988] *ECR* 5483, Para. 16.
[181] Case C-59/90 *Grogan* [1991] *ECR* I-4685.
[182] Case C-299/95, *Kremzow*, [1997] *ECR* I-2629 Para. 16.
[183] Case C-328/04 *Vajnai* [2005] *ECR* I-8577 Paras. 13 and 14.

rial, rather than a 'purely internal situation' exists, seem to arise mainly in such cases. Where the case involves no sensitive public policy dimension, the Court rarely refuses to consider the compatibility of a practice with Community law on these grounds, and has even accepted preliminary references in cases without a Community dimension where national law recognises the applicability of Community-derived rules in purely internal situations if its reply 'might provide useful' to a national court.[184]

3.2.   FROM DISCRIMINATION TO OBSTACLES

3.2.1.   'Discrimination' in the Treaty text

The text of the Treaty does not recognise discrimination as the only legal basis for Community intervention in the field of free movement. Article 3(c) of the Treaty, which enunciates the ambitions of the internal market, refers to the objective of 'an internal market characterised by the abolition, as between Member States, of obstacles to the free movement of goods, persons, services and capital', but omits any reference to discrimination. This supports the proposition that restrictions and obstacles, not merely discriminatory practices, are to be abolished and has given rise to a number of detailed legal models for the application of free movement rules to private, non-discriminatory provisions.[185] Nevertheless, the notion of discrimination remains a prominent consideration in the Treaty texts relevant to free movement. Community rules prohibiting discriminatory taxation of goods under Article 90, customs and equivalent charges under Article 25, quantitative restrictions of exports or imports and measures of equivalent effect under Articles 28 and 29 are all manifestations of the discrimination model, either expressly as in Article 90, because only foreign goods can be subject to such rules, or because those rules result in a greater burden on imported goods than that which is placed on domestic goods. Article 39(1) requires the free movement of workers to be secured within the Community. Article 39(2) requires that this must '... entail the abolition of any discrimination based on nationality ...'.

> 'The list of free movement rights in Article 39(3) offers no basis for suggesting that non-discriminatory restrictions of those rights are beyond judicial scrutiny. Article 43, providing for the freedom of establishment, is at least as equivocal on the question of discrimination. Whilst including a specific provision requiring equal treatment within the host state, it requires more generally that all ... restrictions on the freedom of establishment on the nationals of a Member State in the territory of another ... shall be prohibited'.

In relation to services the Treaty offers another dichotomous treatment of the freedom, prohibiting in Article 49 'restrictions on the freedom to provide services' but

---

[184] Case C-448/98 *Guimont* [2000] *ECR* I-10663 Paras. 22 and 23.

[185] C. Barnard, *The Substantive Law of the EU: The Four Freedoms*, 2nd edn. (Oxford, Oxford University Press 2007) pp. 273-283.

elaborating in the subsequent Article a principle of non-discrimination: Article 50 prescribes'...the same conditions [upon Community service providers] as are imposed by that State on its own nationals'. Since the *Vlassopoulou* case, the Court of Justice has read this as permitting the requirement of substantively similar qualifications but precluding formal requirements for exclusively national qualifications or authorisations.[186] The exception to the general trend within the freedoms for discrimination to feature within the analytical framework can be found in the title on capital. The Treaty provision on the free movement of capital was originally modelled on non-discrimination on the basis of nationality, residence, or the location of the investment. The revised free movement of capital provisions found in Articles 56 et seq. post-Maastricht apply to restrictions, rather than discriminatory restrictions. The Court requires all 'obstacles and 'restrictions' to be justified with reference to either express Treaty derogations or objective justifications recognised in its case law.[187]

3.2.2.   'Restrictions', 'obstacles' and 'hindrances'

It is clear from the modern case law of the Court that all measures which place non-nationals at a disadvantage to nationals are prohibited by the free movement provisions in the EC Treaty.[188] The Court also developed in the 1990s the notion of obstacles to free movement as 'provisions which preclude or deter a national of a Member State from leaving his country of origin' in the context of social security and free movement.[189] In *Säger*, the Court noted that the freedom to provide services under Article 49 required 'not only the elimination of all discrimination ... but also the abolition of any restriction ... when it is liable to prohibit or otherwise impede the activities of a provider [lawfully established in its home state]'.[190] In *Bosman,* the Court applied this in the sporting context and identified as 'obstacles' all 'provisions which preclude or deter a national ... from leaving his country of origin in order to exercise his right to freedom of movement ... even if they apply without regard to the nationality ...'.[191] The jurisprudence of the Court now routinely ventures beyond discrimination and notions of formal equality to suggest that substantial[192] restrictions to the free movement that are not 'too uncertain and indirect'[193] and those which 'preclude or deter' a national from exercising his free movement rights[194] must be justified even in the absence of discriminatory intent or effects. In relation to workers, 'it is settled

---

[186] Case C-340/89 *Vlassopoulou* [1991] *ECR* I-2357 Paras. 16 and 17.

[187] Joined cases C-282/04 and C-283/04 *Commission* v. *Netherlands* [2006] *ECR* I-9141 Para. 20.

[188] Case C-345/05 *Commission* v. *Portugal* [2006] *ECR* I-10633 Para. 15 and Case C-464/02 *Commission* v. *Denmark (Danish Company Cars)* [2005] *ECR* I-7929 Para. 34.

[189] Case C-10/90 *Masgio* v. *Bundesknappschaft* [1991] *ECR* I-1119, Paras. 18 and 19; Case C-228/88 *Bronzino* v. *Kindergeldkassse* [1990] *ECR* I-531, Para. 12.

[190] Case C-76/90 *Säger* v. *Dennemeyer* [1991] *ECR* I-4221 Para. 12.

[191] *Bosman* Para. 96.

[192] Ibid. Para. 103.

[193] Case C-190/98 *Graf* [2000] *ECR* I-493 Para. 25.

[194] Case C-209/01 *Schilling and Fleck-Schilling* [2003] *ECR* I-13389 Para. 25, confirmed recently in Case C-104/06 *Commission* v. *Sweden* judgment of 18 January 2007 Para. 18.

case-law that Article 39 EC prohibits not only all discrimination, direct or indirect, based on nationality, but also national rules which are applicable irrespective of the nationality of the workers concerned but impede freedom of movement'.[195] While the Court has not always been consistent in its classification of rules as 'hindrances', 'obstacles', or 'restrictions',[196] in *Gebhard*, the Court suggested that the analytical framework was similar for all of the economic freedoms, and that all measures which hindered the exercise of the fundamental freedoms could be treated as restrictions that required justification.[197] Where a rule restricts market access and either constitutes an 'obstacle to the freedom of movement'[198] or is likely to '... hinder or render less attractive the exercise of the rights ...',[199] it restricts free movement to a degree that requires justification. As it falls within Community law, the scrutiny of the rule also entails application of the general principles of Community law including the require-ments of proportionality and respect for fundamental human rights. The consequence of the movement towards market access and 'restriction' tests, rather than discrimina-tion, as thresholds is a partial transfer of regulatory competence and judicial oversight from Member States to the Community even in those situations where the single market ideal as such is not threatened, but where for more nuanced reasons a common regulatory approach is seen as desirable. The early cases that developed the sporting exception in the context of workers also highlight the gradual shift in focus from dis-crimination to free movement[200] and when read together present a coherent sectoral case study of this process in the evolution of EC free movement law.[201]

3.2.3. 'Substantial hindrance'

Not all non-discriminatory rules are capable of constituting restrictions, obstacles or hindrances to free movement. As a consequence, not all such rules must be objec-tively justified. In the field of goods, the Court recognised in *Keck* that non-discrimi-natory rules on 'certain selling arrangements' did not 'hinder trade between Member States' within the meaning of the *Dassonville* test and thus did not constitute mea-sures equivalent to quantitative restrictions under Article 28 provided that they were non-discriminatory in law and in fact.[202] The Court recognised in *Graf* that where an

---

[195] Case C-464/02 *Commission* v. *Denmark (Danish Company Cars)* [2005] *ECR* I-7929 Para. 45; Case C-470/04 *N* [2006] *ECR* I-7409 Para. 40.

[196] Compare for example Case C-464/02 *Commission* v. *Denmark (Danish Company Cars)* [2005] *ECR* I-7929 Paras. 35-37 and 52.

[197] Case C-55/94 *Gebhard* [1995] *ECR* I-4165 Para. 37.

[198] Case C-150/04 *Commission* v. *Denmark* judgment of the Grand Chamber 30 January 2007 Para. 35.

[199] Case C-514/03 *Commission* v. *Spain* [2006] *ECR* I-963 Para. 26, tracing this form of words to Case C-19/92 *Kraus* [1003] *ECR* I-1663 Para. 32.

[200] E. Johnson and D. O'Keeffe, 'From Discrimination to Free Movement: Recent Developments Concerning the Free Movement of Workers 1989-1994', 31(6) *Common Market Law Review* (1994).

[201] C. Barnard, *The Substantive Law of the EU: The Four Freedoms*, 2nd edn. (Oxford, Oxford Uni-versity Press 2007) pp. 246-252.

[202] Joined Cases C-267/91 and 268/91 *Keck and Mithouard* [1993] *ECR* I-6097 Para. 16.

event was '... too uncertain and indirect a possibility for legislation to be capable of ... hinder[ing] free movement for workers',[203] it did not constitute a restriction to the free movement of workers. In *Deliège*, decided on the basis of Article 49, the Court recognised that limitations 'inherent in the organisation of a sporting competition' based on considerations such as 'the nature, the organization and the financing of the sport'[204] could not constitute restrictions even if they indirectly favoured a category of athletes.[205] In *Alpine Investments,* the Court rejected pleas of an analogy to *Keck* selling arrangements, noting that contested rules prohibiting cold calling 'directly affect[ed] access to the markets in services in the other Member States'.[206] This ruling was subsequently transposed to the *Bosman* and *Deliège* cases. The question of whether a direct effect on market access, rather than the mere exercise of a profession within the confines of another Member State is required for a rule to constitute a restriction is still subject to debate. Barnard interprets the Court as now retreating from its broad notion of what can constitute a 'restriction' or 'obstacle' and returning towards recognition of a distinction between 'rules which merely structure the market ..., [such as] the rules of the game ...', which are not justifiable as restrictions or obstacles, and those which 'substantially hinder access to the market' and therefore require justification.[207] She cites three recent cases on taxation and *Innoventif,*[208] concerning a charge linked to secondary establishment under Article 48 that, read together, indicate a limited retreat from the broad notion of 'restriction', and a return to a model of Treaty rules based on non-discrimination and market access.[209] Despite these preliminary indications of the Court's willingness to restrict the notion of what constitutes a 'restriction', Advocate General Tizzano's concerns in *Caixa-Bank*, that the Treaty was increasingly invoked '... not in order to create an internal market ... where operators can move freely, but in order to establish a market ... in which [all] rules are prohibited as a matter of principle, except for those necessary and proportionate to meeting imperative requirements in the public interest' remain largely unanswered.[210]

3.2.4. Citizenship and economic activity

Union citizenship differs materially from the fundamental freedoms in that Article 18(1) provides for a right to 'move and reside freely' within the Union which ap-

---

[203] Case C-190/98 *Graf* [2000] *ECR* I-493 Para. 25.

[204] *Deliège* Para. 65.

[205] Ibid. Paras. 64, 66 and 69.

[206] Case C-384/93 *Alpine Investments* [1995] *ECR* I-1141 Para. 38.

[207] C. Barnard, *The Substantive Law of the EU: The Four Freedoms*, 2nd edn. (Oxford, Oxford University Press 2007) pp. 265-266.

[208] Joined Cases C-544/03 and C-545/03 *Mobistar* [2005] *ECR* I-7723, Case C-387/01 *Weigel* case [2004] *ECR* I-4981, Case C-134/03 *Viacom II* [2005] *ECR* I-1167, Case C-453/04 *Innoventif* [2006] *ECR* I-4929.

[209] C. Barnard, *The Substantive Law of the EU: The Four Freedoms*, 2nd edn. (Oxford, Oxford University Press 2007) pp. 279-282.

[210] Case C-442/02 *Caixa Bank* [2004] *ECR* I-8961, Opinion of Advocate General Tizzano, point 68.

plies not only to the economically active but is derived from citizenship, rather than economic activity.[211] Like the provisions on capital, Union citizenship under Article 18(1) also entitles to a right to free movement which itself makes no express reference to non-discrimination. Nevertheless, citizenship-derived free movement rights were until the 2006 judgment in *Tas-Hagen* at a stage of development that corresponded to the economic freedoms in early Community law. Citizenship required equal treatment but did not subject all obstacles to a justificatory analysis irrespective of their non-discriminatory nature. Whilst the Court has recognised the direct effect of Article 18(1) and had read this in conjunction with Article 12 to prohibit the discriminatory treatment of non-nationals,[212] rights under Article 18(1) to '... move and reside freely within the territory of the Member States' are subject to 'limitations and conditions laid down by the Treaty and by measures adopted to give it effect'. These limits, found also in older secondary instruments, are codified in Directive 2004/38, referred to as the Citizens' Rights Directive. This provides procedural safeguards to protect against limits to entry and residence. Article 7(1)(b) of the Directive also permits Member States to require citizens exercising their rights of movement and residence to avoid excessive reliance on the public purse of the host state for support. Citizens entering and residing in the host state who are not economically active are entitled to equal treatment under Article 24(1) of the Directive. This right to equality may be derogated from on the basis of public policy, public security, and public health. Employment in the public service does not fall within the scope of the freedom. However, the Directive also entitles Member States to restrict citizens' rights where conditions of sufficient resources are not met. Once lawfully resident, nationals are entitled to non-discriminatory treatment even though a Member State could in principle revoke their lawful residence for failure to possess sufficient means.[213] The presence of direct discrimination can only be justified with reference to these express derogations.[214]

3.2.5. Citizenship rights in context

The conditions for non-discriminatory treatment in respect of social rights may for the economically active in some cases be more advantageous than those for citizens not pursuing economic activity. Those citizens that would fall within the economic categories under the fundamental freedoms are afforded more favourable treatment under Article 24 of the Directive's rules on equal access to social assistance and student grants. In *Tas-Hagen,* the ECJ confirmed that citizenship rights extended beyond non-discriminatory treatment and required every 'restriction' of free movement rights conferred to Citizens to be objectively justified. The ECJ recognised in that instance as restrictions '[n]ational legislation which places at a disadvantage certain of the nationals (sic) of the Member State concerned simply because they have exercised their

---

[211] Case C-184/99 *Grzelczyk* [2001] *ECR* I-6193 Para. 31.

[212] Case C-274/96 *Bickel and Franz* [1998] *ECR* I-7673.

[213] Case C-456/02 *Trojani* [2004] *ECR* I-7573 Para. 45.

[214] Case C-85/96 *Martinez Sala* [1998] *ECR* I-2691 Para. 64.

freedom to move and to reside in another Member State ...'.[215] Union Citizenship has therefore critically lowered the threshold for the application of the classic justificatory analysis found in the fundamental economic freedoms, since after the Court's ruling in *Tas-Hagen* it is clear that non-discriminatory restrictions to free movement are within the scope of the Treaty even where they do not concern the restriction of economic activity recognised as work, the provision of a service or the transfer of capital.

3.3. JUSTIFYING RESTRICTIONS TO FREE MOVEMENT

3.3.1. Treaty derogations

If a rule constitutes a 'restriction' or an 'obstacle', it must be objectively justified. Whilst directly discriminatory rules must generally be justified with reference to an express Treaty derogation,[216] other restrictions may be justified on the basis of either Treaty grounds or recognised additional grounds of objective justification based on the case law of the Court. The Treaty contains grounds for derogation on the grounds of '... public policy, public security or public health'[217] and excludes altogether work in the public service from the free movement of workers and services and the freedom of establishment.[218] In the field of goods, further bases for derogation include 'public morality ..., the protection of health and life of humans, animals or plants, the protection of national treasures possessing artistic, historic or archaeological value, [and] the protection of industrial and commercial property'.[219] For capital, the list also includes 'tax law which distinguish[es] between taxpayers who are not in the same situation with regard to their place of residence or with regard to the place where their capital is invested' and

> '... measures to prevent infringements of national law and regulations, in particular in the field of taxation and the prudential supervision of financial institutions ... procedures for the declaration of capital movements for purposes of administrative or statistical information [and] measures which are justified on grounds of public policy or public security.'[220]

The Treaty provides that if a rule is permissible as a restriction on establishment, it also satisfies the test for capital.[221] Despite historical doubts about the horizontal

---

[215] Case C-192/05 *Tas-Hagen* [2006] *ECR* I-10451 Para. 31.

[216] For example Case C-288/89 *Gouda* [1991] *ECR* I-4007 Para. 11; Case C-388/01 *Commission* v. *Italy* [2003] *ECR* I-721 Para. 19.

[217] Art. 39(3) EC, Art. 46(1) EC, applicable to services per Art. 55 EC; Art. 58(b) EC Capital, omitting the reference to public health. Art. 18 EC refers to derogations in secondary legislation; these can be found in Art. 27 of Directive 2004/38.

[218] Art. 45 EC on establishment, which also applies to services by virtue of Art. 55 EC; Art. 39(4) EC workers.

[219] Art. 30 EC Treaty.

[220] Arts. 58(1)(a) and (b) EC Treaty.

[221] Art. 58(2) EC Treaty.

invocation of the Treaty derogations,[222] the Court recognised in *Bosman* that these grounds are capable of being invoked by both private and public parties.[223]

3.3.2. Limits to derogations

Treaty derogations may not be invoked for purely economic or administrative reasons.[224] Historically, the Community law has also required parties invoking derogations to demonstrate that they are applied to the specific, relevant circumstances of an individual's case[225] rather than as blanket bans that do not take into account the real risks posed by individuals[226] or trade in particular goods.[227] Public health grounds have been curtailed significantly by the Citizens' Rights Directive, which enables the imposition of restrictions on free movement of persons only in relation to communicable, epidemic diseases or those that would also result in restrictions of domestic nationals' rights within their own country.[228] The Citizens' Rights Directive establishes further gradations on the use of public policy derogations based on the length of a Community citizen's residence in another Member State. Under its regime in Article 28, the public policy, security and health grounds are progressively reduced according to the amount of time the individual has spent within the State, until after ten years and in the case of minors only 'imperative grounds of public security' may be invoked to justify derogations. The Treaty also treats evidence of a discriminatory intent severely, and expressly disallows reliance on its grounds in the fields of goods and capital for derogation if the restrictions '... constitute a means of arbitrary discrimination or a disguised restriction on trade between Member States'.[229] Therefore those rules that are justified on the basis of Treaty derogation may not have as their primary aim discrimination on the grounds of nationality even if they are framed in terms of nationality. It is interesting to note that despite the Court's recognition in *Bosman* that public policy requirements could be relied upon by collective regulators as well as Member States, this argument has yet to be put forward in subsequent cases. Although the regulation of players' agents and doping could in principle give rise to such arguments in the context of free movement, the *Piau*[230] and *Meca-Medina* cases where these questions might otherwise have been raised were limited to ques-

---

[222] S. Weatherill, 'Discrimination on Grounds of Nationality in Sport', 9 *Yearbook of European Law* (Oxford, Oxford University Press 1989) pp. 66-67.

[223] *Bosman* Para. 85.

[224] Case C-388/01 *Commission* v. *Italy* [2003] *ECR* I-721 Para. 22; the principle can be traced to Case C-120/95 *Decker* [1998] *ECR* I-1831 Para. 39.

[225] C. Barnard, *EC Employment Law*, 3rd edn. (Oxford, Oxford University Press 2006) pp. 249-257.

[226] Directive 64/221 Art. 3a, now enshrined in Art. 27 Directive 2004/38.

[227] Case 40/82 *Commission* v. *United Kingdom (Poultry)* [1982] *ECR* 2793.

[228] Art. 29(1) Directive 2004/38.

[229] Arts. 30 and 58(3) EC Treaty. Compare Case 34/79 *R* v. *Henn and Darby* [1979] *ECR* 3795 and Case 121/85 *Conegate* [1986] *ECR* 1007.

[230] Case C-171/05P *Laurent Piau* v. *Commission of the European Communities* [2006] *ECR* I-37. Hereafter referred to as *Piau*.

tions of competition law. This is not a limitation applicable to the *Charleroi/Oulmers* case which the Court of Justice is expected to hear in 2008.

3.3.3. Objective justification

Following its recognition of non-discriminatory 'restrictions' as subject to judicial scrutiny, the European Court of Justice has recognised additional categories of 'objective justification',[231] also referred to as 'mandatory requirements' in the field of goods[232] and 'public', 'general interest' or 'imperative requirements related to the public interest' in the field of services and establishment.[233] These may be invoked to justify rules that are not directly discriminatory.[234] In *Gebhard*, the European Court of Justice considered that all measures that hindered the exercise of fundamental freedoms had to 'be applied in a non-discriminatory manner', justified by 'imperative requirements in the general interest', 'suitable for securing' the objectives pursued and 'not go beyond what is necessary' to attain those objectives in order to be considered justifiable.[235] The dual test of proportionality requires the suitability of the measure and that no less restrictive measure would satisfy those ends.[236] This is supplemented by the requirement to respect the fundamental rights of individuals who are subjected to restrictions of their free movement rights,[237] in particular the procedural requirements that are also codified in the Citizens' Rights Directive. From these considerations it follows that a rule which places unequal burdens on domestic and foreign factors of production is capable of objective justification. There is a considerable body of case law that recognises Treaty grounds of derogation as the only permissible grounds for direct nationality discrimination.[238] However, as will be demonstrated in the following chapter, although the Court has not on the facts of any decided case as yet found nationality discrimination objectively justifiable in the sporting context, it has implied in some of its recent case law that the sector may offer an exception to this general rule.

3.3.4. Categories of objective justification

The Court has been careful to place the burden of demonstrating the merits and the proportionality of objectives on those who seek to rely on them.[239] It is therefore

---

[231] Case C-237/94 *O'Flynn* [1996] *ECR* I-2617 Para. 19.

[232] Case 120/78 *Cassis de Dijon* [1979] *ECR* 649 Para. 8. Hereafter referred to as *Cassis de Dijon*.

[233] Case C-76/90 *Säger* [1991] *ECR* I-4221 Para. 15.

[234] Case 352/85 *Bond van Adverteerders* [1988] *ECR* 2085 Paras. 32-33.

[235] Case C-55/94 *Gebhard* [1996] *ECR* I-4165 Para. 37. Following the recognition of horizontal direct effect in relation to Art. 39, the reference to 'national measures' appears redundant.

[236] Case C-288/89 *Gouda* [1991] *ECR* I-4007 Para. 15; Case C-17/00 *De Coster* [2001] *ECR* I-9445 Para. 37. For a recent application see Case C-433/04 *Commission* v. *Belgium* [2006] *ECR* I-10653 Paras. 35-42.

[237] Case C-260/89 *ERT* [1991] *ECR* I-2925 Para. 43.

[238] For example Case C-288/89 *Gouda* [1991] *ECR* I-4007 Para. 11; Case C-388/01 *Commission* v. *Italy* [2003] *ECR* I-721 Para. 19.

[239] Case C-370/05 *Festersen,* Judgment of January 25, 2007, Para. 39.

for sporting organisations to demonstrate that their rules pursue legitimate objectives and that no less restrictive method could secure those objectives. The categories of objective justification are not closed, but have in the past included professional rules governing service providers,[240] and 'maintaining a balance between clubs by preserving a certain degree of equality and uncertainty as to results and of encouraging the recruitment and training of young players'.[241] The Court tests restrictions on a case-by-case basis, and the Commission's recent White Paper on Sport concludes that the current sporting case law is not sufficiently established to enable any wider conclusions to be drawn as to the legality of particular justifications that have yet to be tested. The Court has never accepted that a directly discriminatory sporting rule has escaped condemnation under Community law beyond those rules recognised in the original *Walrave* Paragraph 8 exception as clarified in Paragraphs 14 and 15 of *Donà*. However, its judgments in *Bosman, Kolpak* and *Simutenkov* suggest that in the field of sport, this might in some very limited circumstances be in principle possible, notwithstanding the failure of the rule to constitute 'rules or practices justified on non-economic grounds which relate to the particular nature and context of certain sporting events'. As the Commission observes in its White Paper, '[i]n line with established case law, the specificity of sport will continue to be recognised, but it cannot be construed so as to justify a general exemption from the application of EU law'.[242] The legal framework for nationality rules in sport is interrogated in detail in the following chapter.

3.4.   MODERN TRENDS IN FREE MOVEMENT

3.4.1.   **Better regulation?**

From the point of view of the Community's broader interests in maximising welfare, the increasing judicial scrutiny of even non-discriminatory 'obstacles' demonstrates the Court's acceptance of the modern European legislative paradigm that consumers, rather than regulators themselves, are best placed to determine the boundaries of acceptable regulation.[243] Although those rules that fall outside the scope of one of the Treaty provisions may still be justifiable in respect of compatibility with others as the *Meca-Medina* judgment makes clear, the removal of a rule from the scope of the Treaty can potentially restrict or preclude the application of Community rules on proportionality and leave the rule subject to only national law and thus potentially divergent interpretations of legality that vary between Member States depending on national legislation. This could create particular difficulties for sports that are organ-

---

[240] Case C-3/95 *Reisbüro Broede* v. *Sandker* [1996] *ECR* I-6511 Paras. 38-39.

[241] *Bosman* Para. 106.

[242] Commission of the European Communities, *Commission staff working document. The EU and Sport: Background and Context*, SEC (2007) 935, p. 13.

[243] S. Weatherill, 'The Challenge of Better Regulation' in S. Weatherill (ed.), *Better Regulation* (Oxford, Hart 2007) pp. 4-7.

ised on an international basis, because the legality of the national rules of similar governing bodies might in the absence of the application of a Treaty framework for justification vary within the Community. In this sense, a treatment of rules as 'restrictions' or 'obstacles' coupled with uniform Community-wide application of the system of objective justification may serve to increase, rather than minimise the sensitive application of legal rules to the specific features that distinguish of sport from other economic activity.

3.4.2. Mutual recognition and home state regulation

From the varied Treaty requirements and their reading by the Court of Justice emerges a broader principle commonly attributed to *Cassis de Dijon* but which pervades the entire regulatory ethos of the Community, and today, even many Union instruments.[244] The case law of the Court affirms the applicability of the general principle of mutual recognition, namely that where a service or product is lawfully provided in one Member State, it may be provided in another without being subject to substantial additional regulation. More broadly, the principle involves the validity within the entire Union of acts the validity of which is acknowledged by the law of the home state. Mutual recognition has some Treaty-based limits in the context of the fundamental freedoms. The temporary provision of services is regulated under Articles 49 et seq., which require restrictions to be evaluated for compatibility with the Treaty freedom to provide services. However, when a person wishes to establish themselves permanently under Article 43, the standard is one of non-discrimination. Under the rules on establishment, the rules of the state of establishment apply. Although prior experience and qualifications must be considered where they are equivalent, the new host state may apply the substantial requirements provided in its national rules for establishment. The liberal doctrines of the Court are not always confirmed by the Community legislature, as is highlighted by the problematic passage of the Services Directive, Directive 2006/123. Parliamentary revision of the 'country of origin' principle in Article 16 of the Directive offers an example of the reluctance to accept the full extent of the developments towards mutual recognition enunciated by the European Court of Justice.[245] Whilst the precise relationship between the Directive and preceding case law remains to be established, it is unlikely that the 'freedom to provide services' enshrined in Article 16 will restrict the more expansive interpretation given to the freedom by the European Court of Justice. For sport, the consequences of the emerging legislative provisions on mutual recognition are more profound following the gradual restriction of the sporting exception. Three developments raise concerns in this respect. The expansion of the categories of 'restrictions' that must be justified, renewed emphasis on objective justification following the curtailment of the 'sporting exception', and the legislative abolition of many objective justifications in general instru-

---

[244] Case 120/78 *Cassis de Dijon* [1979] *ECR* 649.
[245] Compare the original proposal COM (2004) 002 Final and COM (2006)160 Final.

ments such as the Services Directive[246] may present difficulties for sports governing bodies. As sporting objective justifications are also under threat, these developments may leave sporting bodies without the legal means to structure those appeals to the specificities of sport in cases where a justification is not found in the express Treaty derogations on free movement.

3.4.3. Convergence within free movement

There is reason to believe a modern interpretation of the fundamental freedoms often requires similar principles to be applied throughout the freedoms[247] and between the economic freedoms and citizenship rights.[248] The analytical frameworks of all four fundamental freedoms involve a strict treatment of discriminatory practices. These may generally only be justified with reference to express Treaty provisions, many of which are common to the freedoms even though some, notably the free movement of goods and the free movement of capital, refer to more grounds than the free movement of workers under Article 39, the self-employed under Article 43 and services under Article 49. In these fields, only the public policy, public security and public health derogations and the public services exception apply. Derogations to economic freedoms must be justified with reference to the circumstances of the affected individual. A similar, strict approach to Treaty derogations is taken by the court in relation to Citizenship rights under Article 18(1). Nevertheless, the Treaty frameworks, for the freedoms are separate and encompass key differences for example in terms of the Treaty justifications available, and in the case of services and establishment, the general approach towards the legitimacy of regulation in the State of operation. It has been forcefully argued that the philosophy of regulation, namely that of market liberalisation, is the same for goods and services,[249] but that services and establishment must *a priori* involve different principles since the difference between the Treaty articles is founded on the legitimacy of requirements imposed by secondary and primary regulators, respectively.[250] The definitions accorded to workers, services, and establishment by the Court of Justice are also mutually exclusive, since work involves a relationship of subordination not present in services or establishment, and establishment and services are distinguished by the degree of permanence involved. Despite the Court's inclination, demonstrated in the following chapter, to consider many aspects of the freedoms identical, its continued reference to specific freedoms suggests that it, too, considers that material differences remain. In practice, the Court never considers restrictions to free movement in the abstract, but when several cat-

---

[246] G. Davies, 'The Services Directive: Extending the Country of Origin Principle and Reforming Public Administration', 32(2) *European Law Review* (2007) p. 235.

[247] A. Arnull, *The European Union and Its Court of Justice*, 2nd edn. (Oxford, Oxford University Press 2006) pp. 498-500.

[248] E. Spaventa, 'From Gebhard to Carpenter: Towards a (non-)Economic European Constitution', 41(3) *Common Market Law Review* (2004).

[249] J. Snell, *Goods and Services in EC Law* (Oxford, Oxford University Press 2001).

[250] R. White, *Workers, Services and Establishment* (Oxford, Oxford University Press 2004) pp. 264-265.

egories of freedoms are presented in a preliminary reference, it invariably addresses these separately.[251] Citizenship has a residual status in relation to the fundamental freedoms,[252] and it is clear that the legal framework permits some restrictions to social benefits in the context of Citizens' rights that would not be justifiable in the context of the economic freedoms. If differences did not remain, it would be unnecessary for the Court to maintain the inferior status of non-economic citizenship rights. Key differences also remain between the freedoms in terms of their personal scope of application. The horizontal direct effect of the free movement of workers has been recognised by the ECJ, but the free movement of goods and capital remain relevant primarily to State-imposed rules and those rules that can be treated as deriving from collective regulation, where the result would otherwise be an incoherency between different national models of economic regulation. Although recent inroads have been made by Advocates General towards the horizontal application of the freedoms to the provision of services and of establishment, the ECJ has yet to confirm these.

3.4.4. Convergence between free movement and competition

The Court's ruling in *Meca-Medina* demonstrates that it is not prepared to conflate the systems of justification in competition law and in the fundamental freedoms even though its treatment of objective justification across the freedoms may be converging.[253] Mortelmans notes that the rules all pursue the same broad objective, the realisation of the single market, and that some categories of rules such as 'inherent' rules receive similar treatment within both sets of rules.[254] Nevertheless, competition law by its nature is aimed at private undertakings, and the prohibitions in Articles 81(1) and 82 have long been recognised as directly effective. This is not yet established in relation to the fundamental freedoms, and even if the Treaty articles themselves were to be recognised as such, the personal scope of application of directives has not expanded in tandem.[255] There have been suggestions that competition law and the fundamental freedoms should[256] and in some cases do employ similar analytical frameworks,[257] and in particular that where a practice is justifiable under one regime, it should be permitted under both.[258] However, the Court has historically been clear

---

[251] Case C-522/04 *Commission* v. *Belgium* Judgment of the Second Chamber, 5 July 2007.

[252] Case C-193/94 *Skanavi* [1996] *ECR* I-929 Para. 22; Case C-348/96 *Calfa* [1999] *ECR* I-11 Paras. 29-30.

[253] *Meca-Medina* Paras. 31-33, overruling the CFI on precisely this point.

[254] K. Mortelmans, 'Towards Convergence in the Application of the Rules on Free Movement and on Competition?', 38 *Common Market Law Review* (2001) p. 645.

[255] S. Prechal, *Directives in EC Law*, 2nd edn. (Oxford, Oxford University Press 2005) pp. 55-57.

[256] S. Weatherill, 'Discrimination on Grounds of Nationality in Sport', 9 *Yearbook of European Law* (Oxford, Oxford University Press 1989) pp. 88-92.

[257] R. O'Loughlin, 'EC Competition Rules and Free Movement Rules: An Examination of the Parallels and Their Furtherance by the ECJ Wouters Decision', 24(2) *European Competition Law Review* (2003).

[258] S. Weatherill, 'Discrimination on Grounds of Nationality in Sport', 9 *Yearbook of European Law* (Oxford, Oxford University Press 1989). See also S. Weatherill, *European Sports Law: Collected Papers* (The Hague, T.M.C. Asser Press 2007).

in applying the rules to a particular area, demonstrated in detail in the context of its case law on sport in the following chapter. Similarities may exist between grounds of objective justification and also reasons why a rule may not fall within the notion of a 'restriction' in free movement or under Article 81(1), in particular the 'inherency' of a rule recognised in the context of free movement in *Deliège* and later in relation to Article 81(1) in *Meca-Medina*. However, differences remain which preclude any wholesale conflation of the analytical frameworks for free movement and for competition law. This is particularly clear following the *Meca-Medina* judgment, where the Court declared that the compatibility with the Treaty of a given act must be considered independently in relation to free movement and to competition law.[259] A key question sometimes left unconsidered by proponents of the convergence theories is why, if the rules were intended to work towards the same ends, the Treaty did not simply prohibit, subject to justification, 'restrictions' in a general Treaty title addressed to all persons. Even if historical considerations may be argued in relation to the original Treaty texts, proponents of convergence theories must question why such a development is not presented in either the Constitutional Treaty or the draft Reform Treaty.

3.5. CONCLUSIONS

The development of market access reasoning and the notion of 'restrictions' which must be justified despite a lack of discriminatory effects, combined with the gradual extension of horizontal and extended vertical direct effect to the Treaty articles that concern free movement potentially has extended the Community regulatory framework beyond its original scope of application. Rules that originally constrained Member States' discriminatory market regulation now apply to situations where the restriction on trade is neither perpetuated nor influenced by a Member State, but where the extent of its complicity is a failure to vigorously police the application of Community principles in the private law domain. In relation to sport, this is recognised in the Commission's 2007 White Paper package, in which the Commission undertakes to scrutinise with some intensity whether Member States permit private parties to restrict free movement rights in conflict with their Article 10 duties of loyal cooperation.[260] Nevertheless, even without the prospect of meticulous transposition and enforcement of free movement rules by the Member States, the distinction between the private and the public fields is not often of interest in the regulation of sport because collective regulation itself is sufficient evidence of state-like powers to fall within the modern personal scope of application of free movement law. Where such a rule concerns market activity rather than market access, it remains to be settled how far non-discriminatory rules require justification. While it is established that non-discriminatory restrictions to taking up an activity may constitute 'obstacles' or 'restrictions' and that discriminatory rules are always caught by the free movement

---

[259] *Meca-Medina* Paras. 31-33.

[260] Commission of the European Communities, *Action Plan 'Pierre de Coubertin'*, SEC (2007) 934, point 37.

provisions, the frontiers of Community competence remain less defined as to the possibility of Community judicial oversight over non-discriminatory restrictions on the pursuit of economic activity. This is unproblematic where rules are harmonised by Community secondary legislation. Recent examples of the broad approach of the Community legislature include in the field of professional qualifications, Directive 2005/36/EC, Citizens' rights of entry and residence under Directive 2004/38/EC, and the provision of services and rules on establishment under Directive 2006/123/EC. However, competence questions raise concerns when directly effective general Treaty provisions are relied upon to establish that competence. Under those circumstances, private parties unconnected to the State, particularly sporting organisations, may need under the case law of the fundamental freedoms to objectively justify even non-discriminatory rules and practices. The Court is then required to fashion detailed rules where no legislative will to establish Community-wide standards can be identified. This explains in part the troubled judicial past of the sporting exception. Calls for the assessment of those rules in relation to legitimacy and the policy aims of the Community are not unreasonable considering the combined effects of the absence of Treaty references to horizontal effects and the substantial disquiet over the extension of the fundamental freedoms to non-discriminatory obstacles.

Chapter 4
The Sporting Exception: Form and Substance

The 'sporting exception' in European Community law has been used to describe both the removal of rules from the scope of the Treaty and the sensitive application of EC law to the sports sector. At one extreme, the removal of rules from the scope of the Treaty is the pure 'exception' from the scope of Community law developed in Paragraphs 4, 8 and 9 of *Walrave*. At the other, the term simply refers to the sensitive consideration of the specific features of sport within the ordinary framework of EC economic law. The exception developed by the European Court of Justice in *Walrave* and subsequent cases is not only significant for the sport sector. Its consideration also sheds light on the development of the analytical framework of free movement, and on reasons why restrictions of free movement might be considered acceptable despite their diametric opposition to the single market ideal and its trends towards liberalisation. In the broader context, analogous reasoning might be applied to explain why other rules integral to Community law might not apply to a particular sector. This chapter outlines the historical development of the 'sporting exception' strictly so called, namely that area of sporting activity which has been considered beyond the scope of Community rules, and places that 'sporting exception' in the broader historical context. The progressive curtailment of the notion of a 'sporting exception' and the expansion of Treaty scrutiny to non-discriminatory restrictions led to other routes of analysis that placed sporting activity within the scope of the Treaty but nevertheless resulted in the condonement of practices on justificatory grounds based on the specific features of sport. This chapter concludes with an outline of the present analytical framework of free movement in relation to sport, and considers the extent to which the original distinction between non-economic and economic sporting activity in Paragraph 4 of the *Walrave* judgment might take on a new dimension following the development of rights of free movement derived from citizenship rather than economic activity.

4.1.   The *WALRAVE* Analytical Framework

4.1.1.   Non-economic activity and national team sports

In his opinion in the *Bosman* case, Advocate General Lenz suggested that '[n]either basis of the 'exception' nor its extent can be deduced with certainty from the judgments [in *Walrave* and *Donà*]'.[261] There are nevertheless two distinct facets of the *Walrave* case that require scrutiny in the context of the relationship between sport

---

[261] *Bosman,* Opinion of Advocate General Lenz, point 139.

and Community law. In Paragraph 4, the European Court of Justice considered that '[h]aving regard to the objectives of the Community, sport is subject to Community law only in so far as it constitutes an economic activity within the meaning of Article 2 of the Treaty'. In other words, Community law only applied to economic activity. When sporting activity was not economic, it was entirely beyond the reach of Community law. In Paragraph 8 of *Walrave*, the Court of Justice laid down an exception from the principle of non-discrimination on the basis of nationality for '... sports teams, in particular national teams, the formation of which is a question of purely sporting interest and as such has nothing to do with economic activity' and therefore was beyond the scope of the free movement rules. As a consequence, sport was excluded where it was not economic, and even where sporting activity was also economic activity, the prohibition on nationality discrimination was in Paragraph 8 declared not relevant to 'the composition of sports teams, in particular national teams ...'.

4.1.2. 'Purely sporting rules' with 'nothing to do with economic activity'

However, the Court seemed to signal a willingness to go further than these two exceptions, and continued that the prohibition on nationality discrimination was inapplicable because the motives for such nationality rules were non-economic: '... the formation of [sports teams, in particular national teams] is a question of purely sporting interest and as such has nothing to do with economic activity'. On a literal reading of the Court's judgment, national teams were listed as an example but not as an exhaustive list of the rules relating to composition of sports teams. As a consequence it could be argued that where the team was not a national team in a competition structured exclusively on the basis of nationality, its rules of composition might still fall outside the prohibition if the motives for such rules had 'nothing to do with economic activity'. The Paragraph 8 reference to 'questions of purely sporting interest' and the Paragraph 9 constraint that the restriction on the scope of the prohibition must be 'limited to its proper objective' also raised questions as to whether the 'purely sporting' motives underlying sporting rules other than nationality restrictions governing team composition might be relied upon to exempt those rules from the scope of the Treaty. This question was even more problematic when read together with the Court's vague reference in Paragraph 9 to 'proper objective[s]', because that limit raised the inference that a proper objective could justify a restriction to the scope of the Treaty but did not give indications of what such objectives might be.

4.1.3. A narrow exception: the representative character of national teams

There are strong principled reasons for considering the sporting exception even as enunciated in *Walrave* to be extremely narrow in scope. Advocate General Warner's view of the sporting exception was a narrow and tightly worded one. In his view, 'an exception [should] be made, from the provisions of the Treaty against discrimination on the grounds of nationality, for rules of organisations concerned with sport that are designed to secure that a national team shall consist only of nationals of the country that that team is intended to represent'.[262] Following Advocate General Warner, the 'proper objective' reference could be construed as a requirement that the motive for the sporting rule to which the prohibition on discrimination does not apply must be limited to ensuring the representative nature of national teams. The Advocate General was clear that the exception from the rule against nationality discrimination pertained only to national teams, and that where there was no such national team, the exception could not apply.[263] 'The crucial test is whether the provision in the rules is aimed at the constitution of the national teams ..., [not] the nature of the event in which they are to compete ...'. Following his opinion, the modern economic nature of national team sports should not prevent the application of the Paragraph 8 limb of the *Walrave* sporting exception. Support for this view can also be gleaned by implication from Paragraph 4. If all non-economic sporting activity fell outside the scope of the Treaty, then conversely the Paragraph 8 exemption from equal treatment on the basis of nationality is only necessary in relation to economic sporting activity.

4.1.4. 'Purely sporting' motives as proportionality limits

Contrary to Advocate General Warner's view of the applicability of the Paragraph 8 exception to national team competitions which constitute economic activity, the references to limiting an exception to its proper objective and 'purely sporting' motivations can also be read as a reference to proportionality, namely that a rule which goes beyond the regulation of sport for the sake of sport itself cannot be exempted on the basis of the sporting exception. The operative part of the *Walrave* judgment follows this line of reasoning, and separates two distinct strands of reasoning in relation to sport. The first is the distinction between the economic practice of sport, subject to Community law, and non-economic activity, including non-economic sport, which does not constitute 'economic activity within the meaning of Article 2 of the Treaty'. The second is the limitation on the prohibition on discrimination, namely that where activity is economic and thus falls within the scope of Community law, the prohibitions on nationality discrimination in Articles 12, 39 and 49 'do not affect the composition of sports teams, in particular national teams, the formation of which is a question of purely sporting interest and as such has nothing to do with economic activity'. Non-economic motives that led to rules on composition were therefore simply not caught by the prohibition on nationality discrimination even where the activity itself was economic, so long as the motive was 'purely sporting'. Conscious of the difficulties determining whether the pacer and stayer could constitute a 'national team', Advocate General Warner advised the Court not to attempt to give the national court 'an indication of what is involved in the concept of a national team'.[264] In following his opinion on this point, the Court created uncertainties that have plagued the application of EC rules to sport ever since.

---

[262] *Walrave,* Opinion of Advocate General Warner, p. 1426 first column.
[263] Ibid. p. 1427 first column.
[264] Ibid. p. 1426 second column.

4.1.5. *Walrave* distinguished from *Keck*

The 'sporting exception' from the prohibition on nationality discrimination is distinguishable from some later case law such as *Keck*[265] in which the contours of Community regulatory competence were considered, for two reasons. Unlike much case law that serves merely to distinguish Community areas of regulation from those that are not pervaded by a particular provision of EC law the exempted rules may be directly discriminatory when they are justified with reference to non-economic reasons. The reasoning of the Court implied the exemption of the entire sector, rather than a particular rule or practice that did not have an effect on inter-state trade.[266] Rather than rely on pre-existing economic criteria for the application of the Treaty, as in *Keck*, the ECJ created a judicial gloss on the prohibition itself. The recognition of the possibility of 'purely sporting rules' that have nothing to do with economic activity in *Walrave* was followed by intense speculation as to how purely sporting such rules must be. Paragraph 4 is still interpreted more broadly by some who suggest that sport normatively ought not to be subject to ordinary market regulation because it possesses characteristics that fit poorly into a generalised commercial regulatory framework,[267] and that regulation of these 'special' aspects with no due concern for their integral nature to creating or structuring sports markets is alleged to create market failures.

4.1.6. *Walrave* as objective justification

Rules that benefited from the 'sporting exception' in *Walrave* were not merely objectively justified, but were entirely outside the reach of the relevant Treaty provision. However, despite its typology of restricting the scope of Treaty prohibitions on discrimination, the Court's judgment in *Walrave* might be seen as introducing the more circumscribed possibility of justifying a directly discriminatory rule, unmotivated by economic considerations and intimately linked with national team sports, rather than as grounds for the wholesale exclusion of sporting activity from the scope of the Treaty. The language of the court is not helpful. It may be tempting to remove the specific rule, that a prohibition against nationality discrimination 'does not affect the composition of sports teams',[268] out of the context of the broader analytical framework posited by the Court. As a consequence one might conclude from its letter that this is a novel exemption from the Treaty, rather than a particular interpretation of pre-existing Treaty rules. However, the use of sporting grounds to demonstrate that a rule was not caught by the prohibitions required a process not unlike that of objective justification introduced in the context of the free movement of goods some years later in the *Cassis de Dijon* mandatory requirements.[269] For the prohibition not to

---

[265] Case C-267/91 *Keck and Mithouard* [1993] *ECR* I-6097.

[266] *Bosman* Para. 103.

[267] J. Arnaut, *Independent European Sport Review* (2006), see at <www.independentfootballreview. com>.

[268] *Walrave* Para. 8.

[269] Case 120/78 *Cassis de Dijon* [1979] *ECR* 649.

apply, the rule must be justified with reference to its 'purely sporting' nature and an absence of economic motives, but limited to its proper objectives. This is not unlike the analytical framework of objective justification, which requires some recognised public interest requirement, the lack of economic motives, and an examination of the proportionality of the restriction.

4.1.7. *Walrave* as a derogation

The view of the *Walrave* 'purely sporting rule' as objective justification is not entirely unproblematic because the orthodox modern position in relation to objective justification is that grounds other than the Treaty grounds of public policy, public health and public security are unavailable where express nationality discrimination is in question.[270] However, it should be noted that at the time *Walrave* was decided and for a decade afterwards until the *Bond van Adverteerders* case, the exhaustive nature of the Treaty derogations lists was not well established, with parties regularly asking the Court to recognise further grounds of derogation.[271] The Court's modern case law, notably *Bosman, Kolpak* and *Simutenkov*, also suggests that even it is unsure where in the analytical framework of free movement sporting justifications belong. As is considered in greater detail below, in those cases it implied that direct nationality discrimination may be objectively justified with reference to sporting-related grounds not found in the Treaty derogations. Whilst it is true that it has yet to decide a case on precisely this point, often preferring to find directly discriminatory rules disproportionately restrictive, that possibility cannot be altogether excluded despite the outcomes on the facts of *Donà* and *Bosman*.

4.1.8. Objective justification and personal attributes

AG Warner was also less than enthusiastic about the Commission's pleas that such differences were 'a proper case of objective differences between the situations of different workers', derived from *Sotgiu*[272] from which the notion of objective justification developed in the context of EC equal treatment principles. In the context of objective justification as it then was, found only in Community equality law, this characterisation is awkward because the justificatory grounds related not to some objective differences between players of different nationalities, but to broader reasons why even in the absence of some distinguishing personal characteristic that correlated with nationality, nationality rules should not apply to national team sports. The previous chapter demonstrates that reliance on Treaty derogations also required, and still requires, reference to tangible threats to policy interests posed by identified individuals, rather than by categories of persons identified only with reference to nationality.

---

[270] Case C-288/89 *Gouda* [1991] *ECR* I-4007 Para. 11; Case C-388/01 *Commission* v. *Italy* [2003] *ECR* I-721 Para. 19.

[271] Case 352/85 *Bond van Adverteerders* [1988] *ECR* 2085.

[272] *Walrave,* Opinion of Advocate General Warner, p. 1426. Case 152/73 *Sotgiu* v. *Deutsche Bundespost* [1974] *ECR* 153.

4.1.9.   Consequences of *Walrave* on competences

The Community competence to regulate sport is not derived from a discrete Treaty base, but relies on rules that pertain to economic activity practiced by both natural and legal persons. In the event that the 'sporting exception' is an exception rather than a justification, the risk is that it not only prevents the regulation of sport through these economic provisions but that sport in all its manifestations enjoys exemption from those non-economic principles that have been incorporated into the Treaty since *Walrave*. However, if the 'sporting exception' is in fact objective justification, not only is the activity indirectly within the scope of Community regulation but the interpretation of the restriction becomes a matter of Community law subject to its canons of interpretation. It could be argued that the ECJ clearly intended to demarcate a broader sporting exception, since the Court proclaimed fearlessly on the status of nationality discrimination in sport throughout Articles 12, 39, and 49 despite the apparent judicial economy of disposing of the reference in the context of only one of those provisions of non-discrimination. This argument is further strengthened by the Court's failure in case law decided after the Maastricht Treaty to curtail the Paragraph 4 distinction between non-economic and economic sporting activity, which leads by analogy to a robust sporting exception in the field of citizens' rights under Article 18(1).

4.2.   THE EVOLUTIONARY CONTEXT OF THE SPORTING EXCEPTION

4.2.1.   Direct effect

The 'sporting exception' derived from Paragraphs 4, 8 and 9 of the ECJ judgment has, despite its immense impact on the current debates on the relationship between EC law and sport, rarely been placed in the evolutionary context of Community law. When the Court decided *Walrave,* its doctrines on vertical direct effect and supremacy were a mere decade established,[273] and Member States were still regularly attempting to argue the primacy of their internal constitutional orders in front of the European Court of Justice.[274] *Walrave* was among the first judgments to recognise the vertical direct effect of Article 49. The first cases to expressly consider the vertical direct effect of Articles 39, 43 and 49 were all decided within the preceding year.[275] The horizontal direct effect of Treaty articles was first tested a year before *Walrave*, and then only in the context of competition law which 'by [its] very nature produce[d] direct effects in relations between individuals ...'[276] unlike those of the four freedoms that were addressed expressly to Member States. *Walrave* also represented the Court's

---

[273] Case 26/62 *Van Gend en Loos* [1963] *ECR* 1, Case 6/64 *Costa* v. *ENEL* [1964] *ECR* 585.

[274] For example Case 11/70 *Internationale Handelsgesellschaft* [1970] *ECR* 1125.

[275] Art. 39: Case 167/73 *Commission* v. *France (French Merchant Seamen)* [1974] *ECR* 359 Para. 41; Art. 43: Case 2/74 *Reyners* [1974] *ECR* 631 Para. 32; Art. 49: Case 33/74 *Van Binsbergen* [1974] *ECR* 1299 Para. 27.

[276] Case 127/73 *BRT* v. *SABAM* [1974] *ECR* 51 Para. 16.

first move towards establishing horizontal direct effect in the four freedoms.[277] The Court made this leap by analogy between collective regulation and state measures[278] on the basis that the Article 39 prohibition on nationality discrimination '... .extends ... to agreements and rules which do not emanate from public authorities',[279] and that in this respect there was no material difference between services and work,[280] the only (immaterial) distinction being a contract of employment.[281] Within a few years of *Walrave*, it went further to conclude in *Defrenne* v. *Sabena* that even those articles that were addressed directly to the Member States could produce horizontal direct effects,[282] and furthermore that those effects extended to private contracts that did not constitute collective regulation.[283]

4.2.2.   Substantive scope of free movement

Citizenship and the early case law that recognised the direct effect of Article 12 in conjunction with Article 18(1) was more than two decades away,[284] and in this context, the awkward choice of words in *Walrave* that blurred the distinction between the economic motives behind sporting rules and the economic nature of the activity itself seems less problematic than in the context of its modern reiteration in *Meca-Medina*.[285] In the context of a Union without rights derived from citizenship, and a Community that had as its tasks only the regulation of economic activity, the distinction could be considered purely academic since only economic activity would be governed by the Treaty free movement regime. The scope of the Treaty prohibitions on restrictions to free movement originally appeared limited to nationality discrimination and analogous situations. At the time *Walrave* was decided, the modern line of cases emphasising market access that required all restrictions, as opposed to discriminatory restrictions, to be justified was to be decided some twenty years later. Finally, it was not until the *Bosman* case that the Court expressly recognised that private parties could rely on the public policy derogations in the Treaty text.[286] In the context of extending the application of free movement rules to private parties, the development of a 'sporting exception' may seem less radical an approach than the wholesale devolution of public policy derogations to private parties.

---

[277] A. Arnull, *The European Union and its Court of Justice*, 2nd edn. (Oxford, Oxford University Press 2006) p. 173.

[278] *Walrave* Paras. 17 and 18.

[279] Ibid. Para. 21.

[280] Ibid. Paras. 23-24.

[281] Ibid. Para. 23.

[282] Case 43/75 *Defrenne* v. *Sabena* [1976] *ECR* 455 Para. 33. Hereafter referred to as *Defrenne*.

[283] *Defrenne* Para. 39. See also A. Arnull, *The European Union and its Court of Justice*, 2nd edn. (Oxford, Oxford University Press 2006) pp. 536-540

[284] Case C-413/99 *Baumbast* [2002] *ECR* I-7091 Para. 84.

[285] *Meca-Medina* Para. 22.

[286] *Bosman* Para. 86.

4.2.3. Historical community competences and 'economic activity'

The broadest statement exempting sport in Paragraph 4 of *Walrave,* where the Court considered that '[h]aving regard to the objectives of the Community, the practice of sport is subject to Community law only in so far as it constitutes an economic activity within the meaning of Article 2 of the Treaty', is partly explained by the Community's constitutional state of development at the time of the judgment. In arriving at his opinion, AG Warner employed the officious bystander test found in the English law of contract to arrive at the conclusion that 'at the time of the signing of the EEC Treaty ...' the officious bystander would have conceded that the framers did not intend to prohibit 'a requirement that, in a particular sport, a national team should consist only of nationals of the country it represented'.[287] Indeed, even then Warner's officious bystander is likely to have come to the same conclusion based on the Treaty text in force at the time. The list of the Community's objectives in 1974 is not identical with that of the Union in either form or interpretation well over thirty years later. Today, it is recognised that even non-economic activity is subject to Community law where the rights of Union citizens are concerned, and that a lack of a Treaty competence in a particular field does not preclude the application of Article 12 so long as the situation falls within the substantive scope of other Treaty provisions. The list of objectives in the Treaty as it was in 1974 has been substantially added to by subsequent amendments. Treaty provisions alluded to in Article 2, the article upon which the broader exception in *Walrave* was founded, now regulate some activities even when they clearly have no direct economic dimension. The original Treaty text recognised as the tasks of the Community only

> '... establishing a common market and progressively approximating ... economic poli-
> cies..., promot[ing] ... a harmonious development of economic activities, a continuous and
> balanced expansion, an increase in stability, accelerated raising of the standard of living
> and closer relations between the States ...'.[288]

The modern revision of this Article also refers to 'the promotion of social protection, gender equality, protecting the environment, and social cohesion', all tasks that could plausibly involve, and today do involve, the regulation of activity other than purely economic activity.[289] The activities of the Community in Article 3, which in previous revisions alludes to those activities as necessary for the fulfilment of the Article 2 tasks further accent this contrast. Whilst Article 3 originally referred to ten activities of which only the European Social Fund and the association of overseas countries[290] expressly referred to non-economic considerations, the current version refers to no less than 21,[291] all of which also require the furtherance of gender equal-

---

[287] AG Warner at 1426 first col.

[288] Art. 2 EC Treaty (1957 original, unamended).

[289] Art. 2 EC Treaty (Consolidated Treaties *OJ* C 321/44 29.11.2006).

[290] Arts. 3(i) and 3(k) EC Treaty (1957 original, unamended).

[291] Art. 3(1)(a)-(u) EC Treaty (consolidated version 2006).

ity.[292] The modern list of activities in Article 3 includes 'measures concerning the entry and movement of persons ...', 'the strengthening of economic and social cohesion'; 'a policy in the sphere of the environment', 'the promotion of research and technological development', 'a contribution to the attainment of a high level of health protection', 'a contribution to education and training of quality and to the flowering of the cultures of the Member States', 'a contribution to the strengthening of consumer protection' and 'measures in the spheres of energy, civil protection and tourism'. The exclusion of a rule on the basis that it related to non-economic activities could therefore be deduced at the time *Walrave* was decided from the formal list of conferred Community competences.

4.2.4. *Walrave* and modern competences

Excluding an activity on the basis that it involves non-economic activity decades later would circumscribe Community competence in non-economic fields where it has since *Walrave* developed, a conclusion further strengthened in the context of the proposed Reform Treaty. The notion of a 'sporting exception' also raises the question of whether exclusion from the scope of one of the fundamental freedoms, or even of both the freedoms and competition law provisions of the Treaty precludes regulatory competence. Whilst it may be tempting to suggest that an exception precludes Community regulatory competence, the absence of a competence in one area has not historically precluded the Community from legislating on a substantially similar point using the legal basis of another. On page 1346 of his opinion in *Donà*, Advocate General Trabucchi raised this spectre of Community lack of sectoral competence in sport, and suggested that whilst sporting rules may not 'fall within the field subject to the Community's legislative powers ... the Commission could, within the limits ... in Article [94] of the Treaty, encourage the harmonization and approximation of national legislation'. Although this facet of EC sports policy is likely to become of historical interest only following a successful ratification of the proposed Reform Treaty which includes an express sports competence, it helps to explain the awkward development of the legislative framework relevant to sport in EC law.

4.2.5. *Walrave* as an expansion of EC competence

It must be recalled that the very judgment that gave sporting bodies cause to argue a 'sporting exception' from Community law also in many respects extended the ambit of ordinary economic regulation to sporting bodies. In *Walrave*, the ECJ for the first time expressly recognised that sport could be subject to the Community Treaty in so far as sport was an economic activity. It also noted in Paragraph 17 that the prohibition on nationality discrimination applied to rules '... aimed at regulating in a collective manner gainful employment and the provision of services' and clarified in Paragraph 21 that this was even if those rules were created by private persons rather than public

---

[292] Art. 3(2) EC Treaty (consolidated version 2006).

authority derived directly from the Member State. In Paragraph 24 of its judgment, the Court furthered the convergence of the freedoms and declared that the prohibition on nationality discrimination was identical in scope within the fields of workers and services because the 'single distinction [of a contract of employment] cannot justify a more restrictive interpretation of the freedom [to provide services]'. For the same reasons, in Paragraph 22 of the judgment, the Court judicially extended the application of Regulation 1612/68 to working conditions also in relation to services.[293] The Regulation was adopted only on the legal basis of ensuring the free movement of workers. After *Walrave*, all discriminatory rules that restricted the free movement of workers or the freedom to provide services in a collective manner were clearly within the scope of the prohibition on nationality discrimination, not merely those that were directly attributable to Member States.

4.2.6. Economic motives of purely sporting rules?

Many subsequent proposals to broaden the 'sporting exception' in *Walrave* to rules with economic impact overlook the distinction between the economic threshold required for the application of Community rules and the justification for a restriction that falls within those rules but escapes infringing them on some excusatory basis. The basis for exempting 'the composition of sports teams, in particular national teams', from the prohibition on nationality discrimination is not that the activity in itself is uneconomic, but that the motives for the rule on team composition are '... of purely sporting interest and as such has nothing to do with economic activity'.[294] As the consideration of derogations and objective justification in Chapter 3 demonstrates, this could be assimilated with the Treaty text tests for derogations and the Court's case law, which often employs reasoning that precludes objective justification in cases where that justification is in fact masking *de facto* economic protectionism. Although the Treaty generally precludes discrimination on the grounds of nationality, it also provides for derogations from this rule so long as the discrimination is genuinely based on such public policy reasons and is not purely arbitrary. Even when a Treaty derogation such as public policy, public health or public security is put forward for behaviour that might otherwise constitute unlawful discrimination, it must have discrimination not as its object and therefore must pursue some other lawful purpose. It could be argued that the choice of words used by the Court implied a similar process, rather than an exclusion of sport from the EC Treaty independent of the motives for such rules. National team sports even at the time of *Walrave* had an economic dimension. Therefore the Court could hardly be argued to have intended that a discriminatory rule had no economic impact at all. The question would therefore be not whether any economic impact was foreseeable, but whether any economic motive was present for the discriminatory rule. It is interesting to consider this reasoning in the light of those rules which are sought to be justified on the grounds that they pursue some

---

[293] *Walrave* Para. 22 applying Art. 7(4) of Regulation 1612/68/EEC (nullity of discriminatory clauses) to services.

[294] *Walrave* Para. 8.

economic benefit to sport. In relation to restrictions on lotteries, the Court had been invited to accept the financing of sporting activity as a justification for restricting fundamental freedoms. In *Schindler*, the Court declined to extend the sporting-related objective justification to direct restrictions on economic activity,[295] demonstrating that where its rationale had something to do with economic activity, it could not form a ground of objective justification. In *Meca-Medina*, the Court recognised in that secondary economic motives did not preclude the sporting nature of anti-doping rules so long as the primary motive was not economic. Weatherill interprets this as a signal that the court has rejected the notion of purely sporting rules with nothing to do with economic activity, in favour of a balanced consideration of the primary motives of sporting rules.[296]

4.3. THE SPORTING EXCEPTION IN *DONÀ*

Eighteen months after its seminal judgment in *Walrave*, the ECJ delivered its judgment in the *Donà* case[297] and revisited the nature of the sporting exception that it had developed in *Walrave*. In *Walrave* the Court declared that the economic activity, rather than the sporting context of economic activity, was the criterion for the application of the EC Treaty. Despite this distinction, the national court in *Donà* asked for confirmation of whether Treaty prohibitions on nationality discrimination conferred the same rights to football players '... where their services [were] in the nature of a gainful occupation'.[298] The national court was also unsure whether sporting associations were subjects of the Treaty, and whether the Treaty prohibitions had direct effect, despite the Court's unequivocal statement in *Walrave* that the origin of discriminatory rules was irrelevant from the point of view of the Treaty prohibition. Finally, the national court was uncertain as to whether the prohibition had direct effect.[299] As with many of its other questions, it could be argued that this, too, was a point already settled in *Walrave*.

The Court stood by its reasoning in *Walrave* and, having repeated its determination of the functional equivalence between the prohibitions against nationality discrimination in the field of workers and services, noted that 'any national provision which limits an activity covered by [the Treaty titles on workers and services] to the nationals of one Member State alone is incompatible with the Community rule'.[300] In the context of the facts of the case, which involved the limitation of national federation membership and therefore also playing in the national professional league, to nationals of that Member State, no further elaboration was required. Despite this and in

---

[295] Case C-275/92 *Schindler* [1994] *ECR* I-1039 Para. 60.
[296] S. Weatherill, 'Anti-Doping Revisited: The Femise of the Rule of Purely Sporting Interest', 27(12) *European Competition Law Review* (2006) pp. 656-657.
[297] Case 13/76 *Donà and Mantero* [1976] *ECR* 1333. Hereafter referred to as *Donà*.
[298] Ibid. Para. 2 questions 1 and 2 put to the court.
[299] Ibid. Para. 4, fourth question by the national court.
[300] Ibid. Para. 11.

retrospect the wisdom of an exercise of judicial economy, the Court considered the relationship between sport and EC law in further detail. The relationship between sport and Community law in *Walrave* was restated word for word in *Donà*. '[T]he practice of sport is subject to Community law only in so far as it constitutes an economic activity ...'.[301] The Court went on to reiterate that Community freedoms apply to all players who pursue gainful employment or provide services and are nationals of a Member State.[302] In *Donà,* as in *Walrave,* the Court proceeded beyond the general application of the rules prohibiting discrimination and raised the possibility that certain specific rules could constitute 'purely sporting' rules that were not contrary to the Treaty freedoms and their requirement of non-discrimination. Community law did not '... prevent the adoption of ... a practice excluding foreign players from participation in certain matches for reasons which are not of an economic nature ...'[303] when these non-economic rules 'relate to the particular nature and context of such matches and are thus of purely sporting interest only'.[304]

4.3.1.   **Retreat from *Walrave*?**

As examples of non-economic rules, the Court went no further than in *Walrave* and offered only '... matches between national teams from different countries'.[305] As in *Walrave,* the Court's choice of words suggested that other examples of 'rules ... which relate to the particular nature and context of such matches and are thus of sporting interest only' might later be divined.[306] However, in its application of the rule in *Donà,* the ECJ suggested that the rule might be limited not to the composition of teams as such, but merely the exclusion of players from certain matches. The prohibition was not infringed if foreign players were excluded 'from participation in certain [but presumably not all] matches for reasons which are not of an economic nature, which relate to the particular nature and context of such matches and are thus of sporting interest only, such as, for example, matches between national teams from different countries'.[307] As Advocate General Lenz noted in *Bosman,* if the formulation in *Walrave* was correct, 'the Court could have contented itself in *Donà* with a simple reference to that judgment. It rightly did not do so, since it was presumably not unaware that the question of the composition of teams may very well be dominated by non-sporting motives'.[308] AG Lenz concluded from this that '[w]hile in *Walrave* the question of the formation of teams in competitions is still exempt from the prohibition, in *Donà* the Court restricted the exception to the exclusion of foreign players from certain matches'.[309]

---

[301] Ibid. Para. 12.
[302] Ibid. Paras. 12 and 13.
[303] Ibid. Para. 14.
[304] Id.
[305] Id.
[306] Id.
[307] *Bosman,* Opinion of Advocate General Lenz, points 137 and 138.
[308] Ibid. point 138.
[309] Ibid. point 5.

4.3.2.   Advocate General Trabucchi in *Donà*: a broad 'sporting exception'?

Advocate General Trabucchi's opinion in *Donà* is in many ways more illuminating than the Court's reiteration of *Walrave* principles. The Advocate General developed in greater detail the possibility of a sporting exception that related to greater categories than merely nationality discrimination in the context of national teams – and expressly put forward suggestions that even economic activities and motives could be justified on sporting grounds. It is equally instructive that the Court did not follow this line of reasoning, and rather than adopting Advocate General Trabucchi's expansive notion of the exception in Paragraphs 8 and 9 of *Walrave*, the Court adopted a more restrictive reading that applied only to the exclusion of foreign players from 'certain matches'. Whilst he conceded briefly that 'gloss on the general principle', namely the exemption from nationality discrimination, must be strictly interpreted, Advocate General Trabucchi made much of the Court's open-ended reference to nationality rules in the composition of national teams and interpreted 'in particular' in Paragraph 8 of *Walrave* as implying that this was merely an example of one, but not the sole exception to the rule of non-discrimination on the basis of nationality.[310] In his view 'the composition of sports teams which compete for the national championship' could also be regarded as a consideration 'of purely sporting interest ... justifying the imposition of some restriction on the signing ... or participation [of foreign players] in official championship matches so as to ensure that the winning team will be representative of the State of which it is the champion team'.[311] This is the first elaboration of the rationale for the sporting exception, namely that nationality may be a legitimate consideration when there is some representative national honour involved. Furthermore, Advocate General Trabucchi also considered the nationality rules justified, because of the links between the national champions and their representation of the state in international competitions.[312] He was equally permissive of more specific, domestic locality rules in relation to local teams.[313] Several limbs of the subsequent analytical framework for objective justification are expressly referred to here for the first time, namely the suitability of the rule for the objectives pursued, and its proportionality. The sum of these parts was a sporting exception that began to appear more as an objective justification in line with the framework developed some two decades later, rather than an exception properly so called, because of the requirement of proportionality expressly introduced by the Advocate General.

> 'Even sporting activities run on a business basis may ... fall outside the application of the fundamental rules of the Treaty against discrimination in cases where [nationality restrictions] are based on purely sporting considerations *provided that such restrictions are appropriate and proportionate to the end pursued.*'[314]

---

[310] *Donà*, Opinion of Advocate General Trabucchi, p. 1344 first column.
[311] Id.
[312] Id.
[313] Id.
[314] *Donà*, Opinion of Advocate General Trabucchi, p. 1344 second column.

Any requirement of proportionality despite references to exclusion from the scope of the Treaty must imply that the disputed rule is in principle subject to judicial scrutiny. The Advocate General also considered in detail the distinction in free movement between access to professional activity and its pursuit, and came to the conclusion that the right to non-discrimination existed not in the context of access to a professional activity but only in the context of its actual pursuit.[315] This is reminiscent of earlier case law where the Court expanded the notion of 'restriction' in free movement, where not all restrictions but merely those restrictions that affected market access required objective justification.[316]

4.4. BOSMAN

In *Bosman*, the question decided by the Court of Justice concerned whether nationality restrictions and transfer rules in professional football contravened Article 39. The Court expressly denied consideration of the national court's question in so far as it referred to Articles 81 and 82, perhaps recognising the difficulties involved with the application of competition law to sporting competitions.[317] Two legally distinct rules were called into question. One of these, the so-called 3+2 rule, involved direct nationality discrimination in the rules on fielding players. The other concerned highly restrictive but entirely non-discriminatory transfer rules which essentially enabled a club to prevent a player from transferring subsequent to completing their contract of employment.

4.4.1. The analytical framework in *Bosman*

In *Bosman*, the Court reiterated its earlier distinction between economic activity and non-economic activity in the sporting context, and noted in Paragraph 73 that sport was subject to Community law only in so far as it constituted '... an economic activity within the meaning of Article 2 EC'. If it did, it was subject in principle to EC law. However, within that context of economic sporting activity, the Court recognised a category of rules or practices 'justified on non-economic grounds related to the particular nature and context of certain matches' and limited to their proper objectives. In Paragraph 76 of *Bosman*, the Court noted that 'the provisions of Community law concerning the free movement of person and the provision of services did not preclude such rules'. Despite the language of 'justification', such rules did not constitute 'restrictions' within the scope of the Treaty rules on free movement. It should also be noted that this aspect of the Court's reasoning was in the context of non-discriminatory transfer rules, and as such the restriction on the scope of the free movement rules was therefore applied not only to nationality discrimination, but to non-discrimina-

---

[315] Ibid. p. 1344 second column and p. 1345 first column.
[316] C. Barnard, *The Substantive Law of the EU: The Four Freedoms*, 2nd edn. (Oxford, Oxford University Press 2007) pp. 267-277.
[317] *Bosman* Para. 138.

tory restrictions. As such, the sporting exception derived from Paragraphs 8 and 9 of *Walrave* was in *Bosman* extended beyond the examples of nationality rules in national team sports that was recognised in *Walrave* and *Donà*. Once rules failed these tests, they were subject to the established analytical framework related to restrictions. In Paragraph 96, the Court noted that '[p]rovisions which preclude or deter a national of a Member State from leaving his country of origin in order to exercise his right to freedom of movement therefore constitute an obstacle to that freedom even if they apply without regard to the nationality of the workers concerned'. They therefore constituted 'an obstacle to freedom of movement', unless they 'pursued a legitimate aim compatible with the Treaty ..., were justified by pressing reasons of public interest ..., [and] ensure[d] achievement of the aim in question [without] [going] what [was] necessary for that purpose'. In Paragraph 104, the Court expressly referred to the analytical framework for objective justification found in Paragraph 37 of *Gebhard*. This framework is discussed above in Chapter 3. The Court also introduced a notion of the relationship between economic activity and the sporting rule into the *Walrave* Paragraphs 8 and 9 test for rules that did not fall within the Treaty prohibition. In Paragraphs 14 and 15 of *Donà*, the Court referred to 'rules or practices excluding foreign players from certain matches for reasons which are not of an economic nature, which relate to the particular nature and context of such matches and are thus of sporting interest only, such as, for example, matches between national teams from different countries'. In Paragraph 128 of *Bosman*, the Court referred to this but noted that '... the nationality clauses do not concern specific matches between teams representing their countries but apply to all official matches between clubs and thus to the essence of the activity of professional players'. Thus, the sporting exception in the context of economic activity could not apply where the rules related to 'the essence of the activity of professional players'.

4.4.2. From 'exception' to justification

In the context of discussing the slim likelihood of divining 'purely sporting' rules that could be entirely severed from the economic aspects of sport, the Court clearly restated its previous rule that the free movement provisions 'do not preclude ... practices justified on non-economic grounds which relate to the particular nature and context of certain matches'.[318] However, in *Bosman* the analytical process of the Court contained a distinction between 'purely sporting' rules removed from the scope of the Treaty, and those rules that could be justified 'on non-economic grounds'. The latter is an example of the process of objective justification based on 'mandatory requirements'-type grounds developed in the Court's case law in the nearly two decades between *Donà* and *Bosman*. Whilst not in the text of the Treaty, these can be relied upon to justify restrictions that are not directly discriminatory. The Court noted that the restriction of the exception to its proper scope[319] precluded the exclusion of '... the

---

[318] Ibid. Para. 76.
[319] *Donà* Paras. 14 and 15.

whole of a sporting activity from the scope of the Treaty'.[320] It could be argued that the broader 'sporting exception', namely that the sporting nature of a rule resulted in restricting the scope of the entire Treaty, was therefore effectively extinguished. The Court also limited the more defined 'sporting exception' from Paragraphs 8 and 9 of *Walrave* to the one example originally given in *Walrave* and *Donà*, that of nationality rules in the organisation of competitions between national teams. Its reasoning in dismissing arguments that nationality restrictions could be justified turned on the fact that '... the nationality clauses [did] not concern specific matches between teams representing their countries...'[321] and that therefore they could not be compatible with Article 39.[322] Implicit in this reasoning is the principle that the free movement of workers takes precedence over nationality rules except when the competition is structured around competition between national teams.

4.4.3. *Bosman* objective justification

Another contribution of the *Bosman* reasoning is the development of a relatively coherent system of objective justification expressly recognised as such from the smouldering ashes of the 'purely sporting rule'. By the time *Bosman* came to be decided, free movement rules were evolving beyond notions of discrimination and equality of treatment to require obstacles irrespective of their non-discriminatory nature to be justified. The non-discriminatory transfer rules were enacted in the context of economic activity within the meaning of Article 2 EC and were therefore in principle within the scope of the Treaty under the first limb of the *Walrave* test in Paragraph 4 of that case. They were not deemed rules justified on non-economic grounds which related the particular nature and context of certain matches limited to their proper objectives as per Paragraphs 8 and 9 of *Walrave* and thus the Article 39 prohibition applied to those rules. As a consequence, they were declared capable of justification only if they '... pursued a legitimate aim compatible with the Treaty and were justified by pressing reasons of public interest'.[323] The Court applied this system of objective justification to rules that were expressly discriminatory, even though it concluded in Paragraphs 131-135 that none of the justificatory grounds put forward were both suitable for achieving those aims and the least restrictive measures possible, and that the nationality rules were therefore disproportionate. Weatherill points out that this is a shift from the orthodox position that nationality discrimination when subject to the Treaty can only be justified on the basis of the Treaty exceptions.[324] The general principle of Community law, proportionality, also found a specific expression in this context: the restrictive rules must in order to be justifiable '... ensure achievement of the aim ... and not go beyond what is necessary for that purpose'.[325] In addition to

---

[320] *Bosman* Para. 76.

[321] Ibid. Para. 128.

[322] Ibid. Para. 129.

[323] Ibid. Para. 104.

[324] S. Weatherill, 'Fair Play Please! Recent Developments in the Application of EC Law to Sport', 40 *Common Market Law Review* (2003) p. 59.

[325] *Bosman* Para. 104.

expressly adding that third tier of analysis, the process of objective justification, to sporting rules, the Court in *Bosman* contributed to doctrinal discourse by expressly listing two objectives that were capable of constituting objective justification: 'the aims of maintaining a balance between clubs by preserving a certain degree of equality and uncertainty as to results and of encouraging the recruitment and training of young players ...'.[326]

4.4.4. Conclusions on *Bosman*

In *Bosman*, the Court recognised that the notion of a 'purely sporting' rule that had nothing to do with economic activity within the context of economic sporting activity was difficult to divine, but that even rules with some economic implications could be exempted from the free movement provisions where they constituted 'practices justified on non-economic grounds which relate to the particular nature and context of certain matches', in other words where those rules fell within the more circumscribed sporting exception in Paragraphs 8 and 9 of *Walrave*.[327] In Paragraph 128 the Court effectively restricted the sporting exception within economic activity to nationality rules 'concern[ing] specific matches between teams representing their countries ...'. Following the development of a broad notion of 'restrictions' and 'obstacles' to free movement that went beyond nationality rules, the Court compensated for this expansion of the scope of free movement jurisdiction by developing the analytical framework of objective justification in the sporting context. In applying the *Gebhard* framework to sporting rules, it recognised novel categories of objective justification relevant to sport and furthermore, appeared to accept in principle their application even to directly discriminatory rules in the context of professional sport despite finding that they failed to be compatible in that instance for other reasons, namely their disproportionate application.

4.5. *Deliège*

The Court of Justice passed judgment in *Deliège* on 11 April 2000, 2 days before *Lehtonen*.[328] In *Deliège*, the Court's answer did not turn on whether discriminatory rules could be excluded from the scope of the Treaty or justified.[329] Instead, the Court was asked to explore the frontiers of what constituted 'economic activity' and thus the application of the Treaty free movement rules. The Court did not develop the *Walrave* 'sporting exception' further, but instead offered an expansive interpretation of 'economic activity'. It also introduced a notion, subsequently considered in *Meca-Medina* in the context of competition law, of rules that are 'inherent' to sport and

---

[326] Ibid. Para. 106. The other limbs of the test were not met for either justification to be valid in relation to transfer fees.

[327] *Bosman* Para. 76.

[328] Joined Cases C-51/96 and C-191/97 *Deliège v. Ligue francophone de Judo et disciplines Associeés Asb* [2000] *ECR* I-2549.

[329] *Deliège* Para. 62.

therefore are not capable of constituting 'restrictions'. The Court noted that for sport to constitute economic activity, it need not be directly remunerated. Sponsorship and other income outside the sporting structure may therefore serve to qualify the sport as economic. 'Leading sports personalities could receive, in addition to grants and other assistance, higher levels of income because of their celebrity status, with the result that they provided services of an economic nature'.[330] The economic significance of the sport to the participant was integral to determining whether sport was 'economic activity'. In Paragraph 46 the Court observed that '... the mere fact that a sports association or federation unilaterally classifies its members as amateur athletes does not in itself mean that those members do not engage in economic activities within the meaning of Article 2 of the Treaty'. Whether activity was in fact economic and constituted a service under the Treaty was left to the national courts[331] in the light of Community guidance on what might constitute 'economic',[332] namely that the notion must not be given a restrictive interpretation.[333] Referring to its earlier case law, the Court reiterated in Paragraph 54 the requirements that the economic dimension of the work or service must be 'genuine and effective'[334] as opposed to 'purely marginal and ancillary'[335] and that the economic relationship must not constitute a 'purely internal situation'.[336]

4.5.1. 'Restriction'

In *Deliège*, the rule called into question was not discriminatory, but did restrict the number of contestants entered into competitions. Under the developing doctrine of market access, this could in principle constitute an obstacle that required justification: '[t]he systematic requirement of a quota and selection at national level would appear to constitute a barrier to the freedom to pursue an activity of an economic nature'.[337] Since the ECJ accepted that there was a sufficient Community dimension and the rule could in principle constitute a restriction, its reasoning represents the second sports-related case in which clearly non-discriminatory rules are called into question in the context of the fundamental freedoms.[338]

4.5.2. 'Inherency'

However, the Court added a new tier to the analytical framework. Whilst observing in Paragraphs 60-63 that the rules could not fall within either Paragraph 4 or Para-

---

[330] Ibid. Para. 13.
[331] Ibid. Para. 59.
[332] Ibid. Para. 50.
[333] Ibid. Para. 52.
[334] Ibid. Para. 54.
[335] Id.
[336] *Deliège* Para. 58.
[337] Ibid. Para. 14.
[338] Ibid. Paras. 61-63.

graphs 8-9 of *Walrave,* the Court then introduced the possibility that the rule did not constitute a 'restriction', implicitly even though it was capable of forming a barrier to free movement. Rules that were 'inherent in the conduct of an international high-level sporting event' could not constitute obstacles or restrictions: '... such a limitation is inherent in the conduct of an international high-level sports event, which necessarily involves certain selection rules or criteria being adopted'.[339] Despite some need to develop uniform rules in the area, the Court left rather unclear how directly connected the economic activity must be for the sporting rule to be capable of constituting a restriction on the freedom to provide services.

4.5.3. Economic dimension

In *Deliège*, athletes were formally classified as 'amateur' and not directly paid for their participation. Although the Court recognised that the classification was a matter for Community law and that sponsorship deals could constitute the required economic dimension,[340] it suggested that at least some of the services must be paid for by those for whom they are performed.[341] This begs the question, so far unanswered, of whether services can possibly constitute an economic activity where none of the services are paid for by those for whom they are performed.[342] Given the facts of *Deliège* involving the Olympics, an international competition based on nationality, it is interesting to note that the Court did not follow Advocate General Cosmas who in point 74 of his opinion considered the related qualification process carried out by the national federation to constitute 'rules or practices excluding foreign players from certain matches for reasons which are not of an economic nature ...'.[343] This was because the rule in *Deliège* did not merely involve the structuring of an international competition along national lines, but '... reserve[d] participation, by the national federation, in certain other international events of a high level to athletes who are affiliated to the federation in question, regardless of their nationality'.[344] As with *Bosman,* the Court noted that because the rule was employed outside the justifiable context of nationality-based competition, it fell in principle within the Treaty.[345] After *Deliège,* it was clear that the decisions of national amateur associations could be subject to EC law even where the sport itself had no direct economic dimension and the rule in question was non-discriminatory.

---

[339] Ibid. Para. 64. This was reiterated in the final formulation in Para. 69.

[340] *Deliège* Para. 51.

[341] Ibid. Para. 56 referring to Case 352/85 *Bond van Adverteerders* [1988] *ECR* 2085, Para. 16.

[342] See *Deliège*, Opinion of Advocate General Cosmas, points 58 and 59, and Case 352/85 *Bond van Adverteerders* [1988] *ECR* 2085, Opinion of Advocate General Mancini, point 8.

[343] *Deliège* Para. 43.

[344] Ibid. Para. 44.

[345] Id.

4.6. *LEHTONEN*

In *Lehtonen*,[346] decided two days after *Deliège*, the ECJ was asked whether transfer rules that were uniform for all Community players were contrary to Articles 12, 39, 81 and 82 and whether the need to prevent distortion of sporting competitions was capable of justifying those rules.[347] The Court refused to consider issues of competition law because it considered the information presented insufficient[348] and noted that Article 12 could not apply where a more specific application of the principle of equality existed, as did in the context of Article 39. After a reiteration of the inapplicability of Treaty prohibitions on discrimination to nationality rules in national team matches with the traditional form of words,[349] the Court applied a market access analysis rather than focusing on whether the rules were discriminatory, confirming the analytical framework followed in *Bosman* and *Deliège*.[350]

4.6.1. The 'essential purpose' test

As in previous case law, the Court rejected arguments that because the rules bound clubs, rather than players, they could not restrict the players' freedom to work. Its reasoning, however, went beyond the collective regulation rationale presented in earlier cases and reiterated the 'essential purpose' test originally introduced in Paragraph 128 of the *Bosman* judgment: 'In so far as participation in such matches is the essential purpose of a professional player's activity, a rule which restricts that participation obviously also restricts the chances of employment of the player concerned.'[351] The new threshold for the application of Community market access requirements was whether a rule restricted something which was the 'essential purpose of a professional player's activity', not the legal status of the person enforcing the rule or how remote the source of the restriction on free movement was to a Community national.

4.6.2. Objective justification

Having recognized the rule constituted a restriction, the Court considered the possibility of objective justification. '[T]he objective of ensuring the regularity of sporting competitions',[352] recognized in *Bosman* to ensure that the competitive balance between teams did not shift during the playing season, was considered. However, whilst leaving the final determination to the national court, the Court thought the rule disproportionate and therefore incapable of constituting objective justification for

---

[346] Case C-176/96 *Lehtonen and Castors Braine* [2000] *ECR* I-2681. Hereafter referred to as *Lehtonen*.

[347] Ibid. Para. 18.

[348] Ibid. Paras. 28 and 29.

[349] Ibid. Para. 34.

[350] Ibid. Para. 49, referring to *Bosman* Paras. 99 and 100.

[351] Ibid. Para. 50, referring to *Bosman* Para. 120.

[352] *Lehtonen* Para. 53.

what prima facie amounted to a restriction on free movement because international transfer windows, equally capable of distorting competitive balance, were longer than those within the European zone.[353] In the final paragraph of its judgment, the Court of Justice raised the possibility that objective justification for this disparity could exist under EC law but that on the facts that argument had not been presented. However, the Court did not offer any examples of what might constitute objective justification for discriminating against Community players in favour of international transfers. In his opinion, Advocate General Alber noted that discriminatory rules might be capable of objective justification, and discerned two additional grounds put forward by the parties in *Lehtonen*: 'sporting competition ... under the rubric "sporting ethics",' and the danger of 'an actual risk of distortion of competition between different teams within a competition'.[354] That success in a sporting competition should reflect the performance of the participants over the entire duration of the event 'should admittedly be recognised by Community law, since sport differs from most other spheres of application of the fundamental freedoms in that it cannot exist without defining rules ... . Sport can exist only within fixed rules.'[355] The decisive question in Advocate General Alber's view was the reasonableness of organisational rules. '[O]vert or covert barriers to access ... interfere so radically with fundamental freedoms that they require a more weighty justification than the sporting associations' necessary organisational authority.'[356] A consequence of the Court's failure to expand upon the grounds for objective justification in its *Lehtonen* judgment was the deeper incursion of Community law into the autonomy of sports governing bodies with no advances in grounds of objective justification, much less a more general 'sporting exception'.

4.7.   *KOLPAK AND SIMUTENKOV*

4.7.1.   **Direct effect of Accession Agreements**

The *Kolpak* case involved the extension of free movement to relationships governed by Accession Agreements but did not provide significant advances as to the scope of the purported sporting exception. In *Kolpak*, the Court made explicit that Accession Agreements granted rights of non-discrimination similar to free movement within the EC Treaty but did not advance the thesis of the sporting exception in detail except for noting its previous rules that the prohibition on discrimination existed and applied to rules of sporting organisations regardless of their legal status.[357] As with the preceding cases of *Lehtonen, Deliège* and *Bosman,* the Court employed the language and formula of objective justification rather than Treaty exemption to determine whether disputed rules were in fact contrary to Community law.

---

[353] Ibid. Paras. 58-59.

[354] *Lehtonen*, Opinion of Advocate General Alber, point 66.

[355] Ibid. point 68.

[356] Ibid. point 70.

[357] Case C-438/00 *Deutscher Handballbund* v. *Kolpak* [2003] *ECR* I-4135 Paras. 31 and 32. Hereafter referred to as *Kolpak*.

4.7.2.   Proportionality and objective justification

In *Kolpak*, the court struck down arguments that a quota of foreign players was '... justified on exclusively sporting grounds, as its purpose is to safeguard training organised for the benefit of young players of German nationality and to promote the German national team' because this objective was defeated by the possibility that clubs were free to field an unlimited number of nationals of European Economic Area (EEA) Member States.[358] In particular, the Court noted that it did not 'concern specific matches between teams representing their countries ...', and reiterated the bar developed in *Bosman,* namely that where a rule restricted 'the essence of the activity of professional players', it could not be excluded from the application of the Treaty on purely sporting grounds.[359] However, the discriminatory nature of the rule was not seen by either Advocate General Stix-Hackl[360] or the ECJ to preclude objective justification as such. Since no other objective justification had been claimed, the rule was deemed contrary to the Accession agreement with Slovakia, the relevant provisions of which closely resemble the Treaty rules on the free movement of workers.[361]

4.7.3.   Direct discrimination and objective justification

Although used to extend free movement rights on the facts of the case, the reasoning of the Court implied that objective justification on the grounds of promoting the training of young players could be considered where the league was organised purely on the basis of nationality, namely where all EEA nationals other than of the Member State in question were excluded. It is difficult to reconcile this with its established rules requiring market access to economic activity without concluding that sport may, after all, be special in one aspect of the Treaty freedoms: While these generally preclude non-Treaty objective justification of rules that restrict market access, *Kolpak* develops further the possibility implicitly raised by the court in *Bosman* that directly discriminatory rules are capable of objective justification even when they apply to economic activity so long as the motives for those rules are not primarily economic.[362] The reasoning of the Court in *Kolpak* also seemed to imply that objective justification must, as in the context of EC equality law, be based on some objective distinction between nationals and non-nationals that was not itself nationality.[363] This seems to signal a retreat towards closer analogies between objective justification in free movement and in other areas of EC equality law.

---

[358] *Kolpak* Paras. 52 and 56.
[359] Ibid. Para. 54.
[360] *Kolpak*, Opinion of Advocate General Stix-Hackl, points 67 and 68.
[361] *Kolpak* Para. 57.
[362] *Walrave* Para. 8.
[363] *Kolpak* Para. 57.

4.7.4. *Simutenkov*

Simutenkov concerned a situation analogous to *Kolpak* in that the Court of Justice recognised the direct effect of provisions in the Association Agreement with Russia concerning the abolition of nationality discrimination. The case does not significantly add to the discourse on the sporting exception; the brief statement that the rule could not fall within the category of rules outside the scope of the free movement rules was based on the fact that the 'limitation based on nationality does not relate to specific matches between teams representing their respective countries but applies to official matches between clubs and thus to the essence of the activity performed by professional players'.[364] This could be seen as a further restatement of the very strict limits of the sporting exception from Paragraphs 8 and 9 of *Walrave*: 'purely sporting' rules outside the scope of the Treaty prohibitions could only exist where they concerned specific matches between national teams and where the rules did not restrict 'the essence of the activity performed by professional players'. The Court recognised the possibility of objective justification beyond the 'sporting exception', which implied the possibility of objectively justifying nationality discrimination if there were objective differences between the characteristics of players that were linked to nationality but did not find evidence that required further examination under that analytical framework on the facts of the case.[365]

4.7.5. Modern free movement and sporting rules

The contribution of *Kolpak* and *Simutenkov* is to further cement the distinction between purely sporting rules, restricted to 'specific matches between teams representing their countries', which could restrict 'the essence of the activity of professional players', and the objective justification of sporting rules under a *Gebhard*-like framework. The Court also seemed to imply in its reasoning that under the *Gebhard* framework, objective justification must relate to the personal characteristics of players. If confirmed by the Court in subsequent cases, this would herald a reversion from a general public-interest objective justification regime to the traditional *Sotgiu* approach that requires an individually applied rule sensitive not only of public interest considerations but some genuine objective differences between nationals and non-nationals. Under such a system, it might be suggested that mere sporting autonomy is insufficient to justify rules that constitute restrictions, and that the borders between sporting autonomy and restrictions will be policed instead with reference to the 'inherency' test developed in *Deliège* and confirmed in *Meca-Medina*.

---

[364] Ibid. Para. 38, referring to 'justification' on those grounds.
[365] Case C-265/03 *Simutenkov* [2005] *ECR* I-2579 Para. 39. Hereafter referred to as *Simutenkov*.

4.8.   *MECA-MEDINA*

The judgment of the European Court of Justice in *Meca-Medina* could reasonably be thought of as striking a final blow against the notion of a broader sporting exception from the application of EC law.[366] In line with its earlier observations in *Bosman* that an activity could not in its entirely be exempted from the Treaty simply because it was sporting activity,[367] the ECJ declared '... the mere fact that a rule is purely sporting in nature does not have the effect of removing from the scope of the Treaty the person engaging in the activity governed by that rule or the body which has laid it down'.[368] As with its earlier judgment in *Piau*,[369] the appeal concerned the legality of a Commission decision under the Regulation empowering competition enforcement. In dismissing the original appeal against the decision, the Court of First Instance had employed logic that suggested the sporting exception was to be interpreted broadly, contrary to established jurisprudence that had failed to recognise any great breadth of sporting autonomy within economic activity but yet entirely beyond the reach of Community law.[370] As in *Piau*, the applicants had included grounds under Article 49. The Commission had only examined those under the competition rules which it was empowered to enforce and found that there was no infringement of Articles 81 or 82. Despite this, in *Meca-Medina* the Court of First Instance (CFI) saw fit to examine the question of the anti-doping rules' compatibility with Article 49 because the question was thought to have a bearing on the compatibility of the rules with the competition rules at issue in the main proceedings.[371] The ECJ expressly rejected any consideration of the merits of a claim under Article 49 rules on the grounds that it went beyond the scope of the appeal from the Commission's decision under Regulation 17/62.[372] Nevertheless, its reasoning for striking down the Court of First Instance's decision is illuminating also with respect to the fundamental freedoms.

4.8.1.   The Court of First Instance

In its earlier judgment in the case, the CFI rehearsed the *Walrave* rule that sport was subject to the EC Treaty only where it constituted economic activity[373] and recounted instances where the ECJ had recognised sport as an economic activity subject to the rules enabling free movement.[374] 'Where a sporting activity takes the form of paid

---

[366] S. Weatherill, 'Anti-Doping Revisited: The Femise of the Rule of Purely Sporting Interest', 27(12) *European Competition Law Review* (2006).

[367] *Bosman* Para. 76, discussed above in that context.

[368] *Meca-Medina* Para. 27.

[369] Case C-171/05 P *Piau* [2006] *ECR* I-37. Hereafter *Piau*.

[370] Case T-193/02 *Piau* v. *Commission* [2005] *ECR* II- 209 CFI Paras. 41 and 42. Hereafter referred to as *Piau* CFI.

[371] *Piau* CFI Paras. 35 and 36.

[372] *Meca-Medina* Para. 58.

[373] Case T-313/02 *Meca-Medina* [2004] *ECR* II-3291 Para. 37. Hereafter referred to as *Meca-Medina* CFI.

[374] *Meca-Medina* CFI Paras. 40 and 41.

employment or a provision of remunerated service, it falls, more particularly, within the scope of [workers or services].'[375] However, it continued to make a distinction between these and 'rules concerning questions of purely sporting interest [which have] nothing to do with economic activity'.[376] As has been noted above, under the *Walrave* Paragraph 8 formula the sporting activity that constituted economic activity within the meaning of Article 2 EC was not exempt from the Treaty, but if it could be explained with reference to reasons that had nothing to do with economic activity, the prohibition on discrimination would not apply to those rules. The CFI concluded that the judicial recognition of the specificity of sport in the form of rules of 'purely sporting interest', although developed in the context of the fundamental freedoms, was '... equally valid as regards the Treaty provisions relating to competition'.[377] If rules did not constitute a restriction on the free movement of workers or services, according to the CFI they also had '... nothing to do with the economic relationships of competition, with the result that they also do not fall within the scope of Articles 81 EC and 82 EC'.[378] Anti-doping rules were not seen to pursue an economic objective but were instead aimed at preserving the competitive nature of sport.[379] Doping rules concerned an exclusively '... non-economic aspect of that sporting action, which constitutes its very essence'.[380] Because of the uneconomic aims, the CFI declared that anti-doping rules '... cannot, any more than the rules considered by the Court of Justice in *Walrave*, *Donà* and *Deliège*, come within the scope of the Treaty provisions on the economic freedoms and, in particular, of Articles 49 EC, 81 EC and 82 EC'.[381]

Despite its unfortunate depiction of purely sporting rules as outside the scope of the Treaty, the CFI treated those rules in some respects as if they were justified restrictions rather than excluded from the scope of the Treaty. In the same passage it suggested that nationality discrimination could not ever constitute a 'properly limited' exception in the context of the *Walrave* Paragraph 9 requirement: '... if there were such discrimination, the restriction of the scope of the Treaty ... could not, it is clear, apply with regard to the rules concerned'[382] because the rules would be inappropriate for the aims and therefore fail to be limited to their proper objectives as required in Paragraph 9 of *Walrave*. This raises the interesting question of whether, following the reasoning of the CFI, the sporting exception has any function beyond that which can be performed by the process of objective justification. If discriminatory application precludes satisfaction of the 'proper objective' limit, the 'sporting exception' incorporating a 'proper objective' limit so construed is substantially similar to the

---

[375] *Meca-Medina* CFI Para. 39, referring to *Walrave*, Para. 5, *Donà*, Paras. 12 and 13 and *Bosman*, Para. 73.

[376] *Meca-Medina* CFI referring to *Walrave* Para. 8.

[377] *Meca-Medina* CFI Para. 42.

[378] Id.

[379] *Meca-Medina* CFI Para. 44. The CFI also noted the protection of the health of athletes might constitute justification

[380] *Meca-Medina* CFI Para. 45.

[381] Ibid. Para. 47.

[382] Ibid. Para. 49.

conventionally accepted general regime of objective justification under *Gebhard*-type reasoning, save for the fact that the assessment of proportionality is recognised to be within the discretion of sports governing bodies rather than the courts. The CFI noted that such rules would not be justifiable in relation to proportionality even where the rules were excessive: '... the allegedly excessive nature of those rules, were it to be established, would not result in them ceasing to be purely sporting rules ... provided that they remain limited to their proper object ...'.[383] The conclusion from the CFI's reasoning must therefore be that a justificatory analysis at least in so far as discriminatory intent or effects would need to be carried out before a court could find that the rules were within the purported sporting exception and therefore outside the scope of the Treaty. At the very least the suitability of sporting rules for the aims pursued by 'sporting' rules would require consideration before a rule could be accepted as 'purely sporting'. Its express recognition of discrimination as a bar to the 'purely sporting' plea also supported the move towards dismantling any absolute exemption from the Treaty rules.

4.8.2. Sport is subject to community law

The Court of Justice quashed the CFI's reasoning that erroneously equated the sports-related reasoning applied to the fundamental freedoms and competition law. '... [T]he mere fact that a rule is purely sporting in nature does not have the effect of removing from the scope of the Treaty the person engaging in the activity governed by that rule or the body which has laid it down.'[384] The fundamental freedoms and competition provisions were to be considered separately, and satisfaction of the rules for free movement because the restriction was intrinsic to sporting activity did not automatically lead to satisfaction of competition provisions.[385] 'If the sporting activity in question falls within the scope of the Treaty, the conditions for engaging in it are then subject to all the obligations which result from the various provisions of the Treaty.'[386] The Court of Justice therefore set aside the CFI's judgment and proceeded to re-examine the merits of the case under competition law. Because the appeal was based on a Commission competition decision, the Court refused to consider issues of free movement[387] beyond noting in Paragraph 31 that the notion of a 'restriction' within competition law and within free movement was not necessarily identical in scope. The grounds re-examined by the Court were limited to Articles 81 and 82 and will be discussed in detail in the next chapter.

It is interesting to note that Advocate General Leger proposed in his opinion a resurrection of the broader sporting exception: in his view, the Court identified in *Donà, Bosman and Lehtonen* 'an exception of general application which cannot be restricted

---

[383] *Meca-Medina* CFI Para. 55. The CFI nevertheless did examine the proportionality of the limits against scientific criteria in Paras. 58 and 59.

[384] *Meca-Medina* Para. 27 (European Court of Justice).

[385] *Meca-Medina* Para. 31.

[386] Ibid. Para. 28.

[387] Ibid. Para. 58.

... to the composition and formation of sports teams'.[388] Without great elaboration, Advocate General Leger considered the restrictive reading of the sporting exception (that it applied to only the composition of sports teams) unfounded and 'an artificial distinction between the rules [on national team composition] considered in those cases' and anti-doping rules.[389] Because of the Court's acceptance of those restrictions to the scope of the free movement provisions, he considered the CFI's conclusions proper in so far as the CFI considered that the prohibitions in Articles 39 and 49 applied to rules concerning economic aspects of sport but 'do not affect purely sporting rules, that is to say concerning questions of purely sporting interest and, as such have nothing to do with economic activity'.[390] In relation to the plea that anti-doping rules had something to do with economic activity and therefore fell within the Treaty, Advocate General Leger considered the partial economic motives of the International Olympic Committee in safeguarding the ethical values, and thus the attractiveness to consumers of sport, were not enough 'to prove a contradiction' in the CFI's reasoning in Paragraphs 44 and 47, that anti-doping rules do not pursue an economic objective, and Paragraph 57, where the CFI recognised the possible economic rationale for the IOC's pursuit of sporting ethics.[391] This was because whilst 'it may be impossible for purely sporting rules ... to possess no economic interests.., that interest is purely secondary ...'.[392] In practice, a secondary economic consideration could not preclude the purely sporting nature of the rules where they were primarily motivated by purely sporting considerations.

4.8.3. Conclusions on *Meca-Medina*

Meca-Medina goes some way towards dismantling the notion of a broad sporting exception that removes rules *a priori* from the scope of the Treaty, and Paragraphs 27 and 28 are good authority for the proposition that the compatibility of allegedly 'sporting rules' in the context of one Treaty title will not necessarily lead to a similar conclusion in respect of others. As the Court did not give judgment on the substance of the free movement questions, the analytical framework of free movement in relation to sport was not further developed. In this sense, *Meca-Medina* is not in itself sufficient authority for the proposition that the *Walrave* sporting exception has also ceased to exist in the context of free movement. The ECJ reiterated in Paragraph 22, without critique, its *Walrave*-derived notion of a distinction between economic activity, to which the Treaty applies, and sporting activity which is outside the scope of the Treaty because it does not constitute 'economic activity within the meaning of Article 2 EC'. This is increasingly awkward given the recent extension of citizenship rights, because it implies that where citizenship rights are concerned, all non-economic sporting activity is excluded from the scope of the Treaty rules. As a consequence,

---

[388] *Meca-Medina*, Opinion of Advocate General Leger, point 19.

[389] Ibid. point 29.

[390] Ibid. point 20 quoting Para. 41 *Meca-Medina* CFI.

[391] *Meca-Medina*, Opinion of Advocate General Leger, point 27.

[392] Ibid. point 28.

nationality rules in genuinely amateur sports would seem to be within the broader sporting exception based on Paragraph 4 of *Walrave* so long as the athlete does not become a provider of services within the meaning developed in *Deliège*. In the event that no economic links can be found between the sporting organisation or club and the athlete, the Court can be expected to receive a preliminary reference requesting clarification for whether any of the services must be paid for by those whom receive them. The Court has also not as yet received a reference regarding the compatibility of such sporting rules with citizenship rights that it has not been able to respond to on the basis of the economic Treaty freedoms. Whilst its unaltered reiteration of Paragraph 4 of *Walrave* suggests that the Court might entertain a notion of a sporting exception in the context of non-economic citizenship rights, its acceptance of this is not a foregone conclusion. It is difficult to reconcile such a result with the drive towards the abolition of nationality rules in other sensitive contexts, and with the overall trends in European political integration.

4.9.   PROSPECTS FOR THE SPORTING EXCEPTION

4.9.1.   Economic activity and 'purely sporting' motives

The present state of free movement law in relation to sport demonstrates a multi-tiered approach to the analysis of sporting activity and its relationship with free movement law. In the first tier, the Court's demarcation between economic and non-economic sporting activity, originally found in Paragraph 4 of the *Walrave* judgment, remains valid today. Despite questions about its application in relation to non-economic Treaty provisions, on the basis of the present case law, non-economic sporting activity remains outside the scope of the Treaty, and there is considerable modern authority that suggests an absence of citizenship-derived rights in relation to amateur sport. The second tier of analysis can be traced back to Paragraphs 8 and 9 of *Walrave*, where the Court originally restricted the scope of the Treaty prohibitions against nationality discrimination even in areas that constituted economic activity and thus failed the first tier exclusion. Read together with subsequent refinements, and the Paragraph 9 reference to 'proper objectives', it now appears that the exception for '… sports teams, in particular national teams, the formation of which is a question of purely sporting interest and as such has nothing to do with economic activity' does not apply to sports teams, or to general rules on team composition, but only to nationality rules in national team sports. The reference to motives of 'purely sporting interest' in this context can be read as an indication of the Court's refusal to countenance nationality rules based on primarily economic motives, rather than as authority for the proposition that rules of a 'purely sporting' nature other than nationality rules in national team sports might be beyond the scope of the Treaty prohibition. This view is strengthened by the later developments, especially in *Bosman*, of recognising that whenever rules restrict the essence of a professional's activity, they cannot be 'purely sporting' within the meaning of Paragraphs 8 and 9 of *Walrave*, and by the tendency of the Court since *Bosman* to consider all other rules in the context of a *Gebhard*-type framework of objective justification.

4.9.2. Objective justification and inherency

The third tier of sporting-specific analysis applies to rules that despite falling within the notion of Article 2 economic activity and outside the scope of the exception in the second tier, do not constitute 'obstacles' or 'restrictions' because they are 'inherent' to the organisation of sport as such within the meaning accorded to this category in *Deliège*. Although 'inherent' rules do not constitute restrictions within the meaning of free movement law, the process of analysis involves an examination of the proportionality of the rule and of the relationship between fundamental rights and the rule purported to be 'inherent'. As a consequence, the distinction between objective justification and the process of determining whether a rule is 'inherent' is limited to the Court's treatment of the proportionality of 'inherent' rules: the Court appears less inclined to examine the proportionality of 'inherent' rules and more inclined to require that the applicants demonstrate its disproportionality, whereas in the context of objective justification the party purporting to objectively justify a rule is required to demonstrate that no less restrictive means will achieve the same, justified, ends. The fourth tier of analysis is for economic sporting rules that are not inherent but constitute an 'obstacle' or 'restriction' of free movement. Such rules can be objectively justified under the *Gebhard* criteria, and in the sporting-related case law the ECJ has listed some justificatory rationales that might be relied upon. These are distinguished from classic notions of objective justification in free movement, and in this sense some vestige of the sporting exception still remains even in the context of objective justification, because the analytical process has in the sporting context been applied to rules that are directly discriminatory, not only in *Bosman* but also in *Kolpak* and *Simutenkov*.

4.9.3. Sport as a citizen's right

It could be argued, more so today than in the time period of *Walrave* and *Donà*, that Community law has expanded its influence so far beyond economic activity as to make an exception from economic law meaningless. In the field of the fundamental freedoms, the Court of Justice has recognised that the social advantages of residents who travel with migrant workers should be identical to those of citizens of the Member State. As a consequence, the families of workers may be entitled to non-discrimination even in the field of activity that is not economic. The Court of Justice has also developed the legal implications of Union Citizenship beyond the scope of equal treatment offered to the economically active. Articles 12 and 18 have been read in conjunction with each other to offer, irrespective of economic status, Union Citizens equal social rights within the Member States of the Union. In this respect, even though the 'sporting exception' within the field of economic sport seems confined to its original facts, in the absence of a relevant test case before the ECJ, the exception seems alive and well within the scope of non-economic activity that falls within the scope of a Community rule applicable to non-economic activity.

Chapter 5
EC Competition Law and Sport

The second keystone of the European internal market is its competition law, of which Articles 81 and 82 form the main focus of this chapter. These provisions prohibit anti-competitive collusion between market actors and abuses of a dominant position. The EC Treaty regulates the relationship between state action and other provisions of the Treaty in Articles 86 which concerns state action in competitive markets and Article 87, which governs the compatibility of state aids to targeted undertakings within the internal market. The insertion into the EC Treaty by the Maastricht Treaty of Article 4 EC signals a clear policy shift towards 'the adoption of an economic policy ... conducted in accordance with the principle of an open market economy' even in areas traditionally run, directly or indirectly, by the state. Prosser cites its insertion as a milestone in the increasing application of competition law to even those areas, and notes that it has led '... to a form of presumption that the values associated with competition law and liberalized markets are the most appropriate ones unless a very strong reason exists otherwise'.[393] A key question examined within the chapter is whether sporting justifications constitute such very strong reasons, and if so, which legal mechanisms are capable of softening the application of the market values of undistorted competition to sport.

5.1.   THE SCOPE OF COMPETITION LAW

5.1.1.   **Sectoral exemptions**

Certain sectors enjoy exemption from the scope of competition law because they are governed entirely by different provisions of the EC Treaty. Agriculture is governed by its own title in the Treaty and agricultural undertakings fall within competition law only in so far set out by the Council in secondary legislation. Services of general economic interest, national security, and nuclear energy, also receive exemptions. It is significant in this context that sport possesses neither a Treaty-based exemption nor one recognised within the secondary legislation in the field of competition. Following the Helsinki Report on Sport, the Commission has distinguished between two levels of sporting activity: that '... which fulfils a social, integrating and cultural role that must be preserved and to which in theory the competition rules of the EC Treaty do not apply', and 'economic activities generated by the sporting activity', to which the rules apply but where 'the specific requirements of this sector' will be

---

[393] T. Prosser, *The Limits of Competition Law: Markets and Public Services* (Oxford, Oxford University Press 2005).

taken into account.[394] Despite the absence of a Treaty legal base for sport, the Commission's views are significant because it plays a key role in the enforcement of EC competition law. In addition to Treaty exemptions, the question of whether collective employment agreements are also subject to some exceptional analysis continues to receive considerable judicial attention.[395] The reasoning behind the exemption of collective employment agreements is significant, since it recognises that the objectives of competition law may give way to other Treaty objectives even though such an effect on competition law is not foreseen in the Article itself. According to the ECJ in *Brentjens*, '... certain restrictions of competition are inherent in collective agreements between organisations representing employers and workers ... the social policy objectives pursued by such agreements would be seriously undermined if management and labour were subject to Article [81(1)] ...'.[396] The 'European social model' and its protection take precedence over the maintenance of competition, and have not in the past required consideration of the proportionality of the measures taken in pursuit of those social objectives.[397]

5.1.2. Inherent rules

In *Meca-Medina,* the ECJ transposed the reasoning found in the context of professional regulation in the *Wouters* case to the organisation of sport. It noted that rules that were 'inherent' in the proper organisation of sport did not constitute restrictions of competition. 'Inherent rules' did not have the object, but merely an ancillary effect of restricting competition that was the inevitable consequence of that 'inherent' rule. There are also plausible arguments to the effect that the paradigm of open and unrestrained competition simply does not apply to competitive sport, because of the interdependence of sporting clubs and the pronounced detrimental effects of market exit. These issues are discussed in detail in Chapter 1. Bell, Lewis and Taylor argue that '[t]he fundamental economic principle that the public interest is best served by unrestrained competition in a completely free market environment simply *does not apply* in the sports sector'.[398] It will be demonstrated that many of these concerns can be accommodated within the pre-existing framework of competition law without recourse to a *Walrave*-like 'sporting exception'.

---

[394] Commission Press Release IP/99/133 24 February 1999 'Commission Debates Application of Its Competition Rules to Sports'.

[395] Case C-219/97 *Maatschappij Drijvende Bokken BV* [1999] *ECR* I-6121 Para. 47. See for example *Viking*, Opinion of Advocate General Maduro.

[396] *Brentjens* Para. 56.

[397] D. Chalmers et al., *EU Law* (Cambridge: Cambridge University Press 2006) pp. 985-986.

[398] A. Bell, A. Lewis and J. Taylor, 'EC and UK Competition Rules and Sport', in A. Lewis and J. Taylor, *Sport: Law and Practice* (London, Butterworths Lexis Nexis 2003) p. 353.

5.2.   THE SPORTING EXCEPTION AND COMPETITION LAW

5.2.1.   **Fitting sport into the ordinary framework**

Despite the demise of the notional sporting exception in the field of competition following the ECJ *Meca-Medina* judgment, analogies can be drawn between the *Walrave* rules and facets of the ordinary EC competition law framework. Whatever one
might consider ought to be the competitive policy aims of EC competition law, and
the relationship between competition aims and other tasks in Articles 2 and 3, it is
clear that the legal framework of competition law posited in Articles 81 and 82 enable
the consideration of some 'special' features of sports markets that distinguish the economic aspects of sport from other economic activity. These considerations have been
regularly applied by the Commission in its investigatory role despite the steadfast
refusal of the ECJ to address the question of the sporting exception in the context of
competition law until the 2006 *Meca-Medina* case. It will be recalled from Chapter 4
that the *Walrave* Paragraph 4 dictum distinguished between 'economic activity within
the meaning of Article 2 EC' and in Paragraph 8 the Court laid down an exception to
the prohibition on nationality discrimination where the reasons for such nationality
discrimination had 'nothing to do with economic activity'. In the context of competition law, it could be argued that the former has been a feature of EC competition law
since its inception due to the distinction between undertakings engaged in economic
activity, subject to Articles 81 and 82, and those which are not, and therefore not
undertakings for the purposes of competition law. The Court is reluctant to accept
territorial protection in competition law. However, it is increasingly tolerant towards
ancillary restraints of competition that result from the pursuit of legitimate objectives.
When applied to sport, it will be demonstrated that this jurisprudence can achieve effects similar to the *Walrave* 'sporting exceptions' in free movement.

5.2.2.   *Meca-Medina*

In its 2006 *Meca-Medina* judgment, the Court finally heeded decades-long calls by
its Advocates General that it considers the relationship between competition law and
sport, perhaps in part because as an appeal from the CFI it could only adjudicate on
that basis as was demonstrated in the *Piau* appeal.[399] In contrast to the field of free
movement where the original exception has yet to be expressly overruled, the Court
noted in Paragraph 27 of *Meca-Medina* that 'the mere fact that a rule is purely sporting in nature does not have the effect of removing from the scope of the Treaty the
person engaging in the activity governed by that rule or the body which has laid it
down'. In Paragraph 31, the Court observed that an exemption in the context of free
movement did not preclude an analysis under competition law, demoting the 'sporting exception' in the context of competition law to a sporting justification not capable
of removing the rule from the scope of competition provisions, but one capable of

---

[399]   Case C-171/05P *Laurent Piau* v. *Commission of the European Communities* [2006] *ECR* I-37.

precluding the rule from constituting a 'restriction' of competition. Where a sporting activity is governed by the Treaty, its rules must now be considered in the light of relevant Treaty provisions on competition law. Such rules cannot be excluded from the scope of competition law simply because they are excluded in the context of free movement. Paragraph 8 of *Walrave*, which identified rules of 'purely sporting interest which have nothing to do with economic activity', can no longer be relied upon to exempt restrictions of competition. As demonstrated in Chapters 3 and 4, the scope of free movement rules has expanded since *Walrave* to govern private relationships and also restrictions that are non-discriminatory. Curtailing the 'sporting exception' therefore has the consequence of subjecting almost any sporting rule to both EC free movement and competition law.

5.2.3. Case-by-case analysis

The Commission's reading of *Meca-Medina* in the White Paper package is that 'the ECJ has unequivocally rejected' the notion of purely sporting rules in the context of competition rules, and that as a consequence there is a 'need to determine, on a case-by-case basis and irrespective of the nature of the rule, whether the specific require-ments of Articles 81 and 82 EC are met'.[400] The practical effects are not to rule all previously 'purely sporting' rules as contrary to competition law, but simply that '... this cannot be done by way of declaring certain categories of rules *a priori* exempt from the application of the competition rules ... but it has to be included as an element of legal significance within the context of analyzing the conformity of such rules with EC competition law'.[401]

5.2.4. 'Purely sporting rules'

This second category of the *Walrave* sporting exception in free movement is also capable of transposition into the competition law framework without recourse to a sporting-specific rule. In *Walrave,* this concerned rules which *de facto* restricted free movement but nevertheless which did not fall within the Treaty provision because they were exempted with reference to their 'purely sporting' nature. In the context of competition law, that less pronounced area of sporting autonomy is comprised of the 'special' features of economic sport. Despite concerns as to their effect on competi-tion, these are treated as ancillary restraints within competition law but are incapable of constituting restrictions. This is because the primary aims pursued are recognised as mitigating any possible resulting restrictions on competition, or in the language of the Court, 'inherent' in the pursuit of legitimate objectives. The *Wouters* case, also discussed below, is instructive in distinguishing the scope of competition regulation from areas motivated by non-economic considerations. These areas include public

---

[400] Commission of the European Communities, *Commission staff working document. The EU and Sport: Background and Context*, SEC (2007) 935, p. 36.

[401] Ibid. p. 37.

law rules, public social security and professional regulation by states or devolved legislative power, all of which fall outside the ambit of competition law.

5.2.5. State intervention

The relationship between EC competition law and the actions of the State is further governed by Articles 86 and 87. Article 86(1) prohibits undertakings controlled by the state and those to which the state grants public law powers or other special status from infringing competition law. Article 86(2) nevertheless grants special dispensation to '[u]ndertakings entrusted with the operation of services of general economic interest or having the character of a revenue-producing monopoly' in cases where the application of competition law could obstruct the performance of those State tasks assigned to them. However, the 'development of trade [must not be] affected to such an extent as would be contrary to the interests of the Community'. This raises the very topical questions of what constitutes such 'services of general economic interest', and who the ultimate arbiter of Community interests is in such a case, both of which are discussed in detail below. Article 87(1) prohibits State aid which 'distorts or threatens to distort competition by favouring certain undertakings or the production of certain goods'. However, Article 87(2) lists direct social aid to consumers, disaster aid and structural aid to the areas of the former German Democratic Republic as *a priori* acceptable, and Article 87(3) provides a further list of aids which may be considered compatible on a case by case basis. These include structural aid to deprived areas, projects of common European interest or those which remedy 'a serious disturbance in the economy of a Member State', aid related to the development of specific activities or economic areas subject to a rule of reason-type balancing exercise, culture and heritage conservation aid is also subject to a balancing exercise, and those categories of aid recognised by separate Council Decisions on permissible aids. As the legal analysis accompanying the White Paper on Sport observes, the Council has not as yet identified sport as such an area.[402] Nevertheless, the Commission has in some recent decisions found infrastructure and training aids relevant to sport capable of justification within the ordinary state aid framework.

5.3. THE FRAMEWORK OF EC COMPETITION LAW

5.3.1. Objectives of competition law

There is considerable agreement that allocative efficiency and overall consumer welfare are best served by competition between producers of goods and services, and that the main function of competition law is therefore to promote and maintain a process of effective competition. However, the notion of what constitutes 'competition' is difficult to define with precision. As Odudu points out, 'what competition is, and hence

---

[402] Ibid. p. 28.

what a restriction entails, is undefined'.[403] Articles 81 and 82 are founded on the prohibitions on 'anticompetitive' private behaviour. However, the wording of those Treaty provisions, their interpretation by the Court and the decisional practice of the Commission all indicate that the policy aims pursued by competition law extend beyond competition. At the very least that competition law must have due regard to non-competition aims within the scope of its application. There is also a clear separation between private market activity, governed by competition law, and state action in discharging its duties. This has been deemed to fall outside the scope of competition law and in the case of 'services of general economic interest', enjoys special privileges under Article 86 when it falls within competition law. The notion of 'undertaking' presumes some economic purposes pursued by the entity, as a consequence of which direct state action would not often fall within the prohibitions in Articles 81(1) and 82. Somewhere in between lie Community rules on state aid under Article 87, which govern the conditions under which private undertakings may be given special assistance by the State despite the *de facto* distortions in competition this may cause. The Commission's State Aid Action Plan for 2005-2009 is tellingly subtitled 'Less and Better Targeted State Aid: A Roadmap for State Aid Reform 2005–2009'.[404] Whilst its state aid reform policy has simplified and hardened legal rules into block exemption regulations, the boundaries of improper state aids are now policed even in the field of sport with increasing vigour by the Commission.

5.3.2. Exemptions: Article 81(3)

Private agreements that are anticompetitive and include 'restrictions' within the meaning of Article 81(1) may be excused if they pursue a recognised aim that improves competition, or if they are otherwise necessary for the functioning of the single market or some Community public policy interest. Under Article 10 of Regulation 1/2003, the Commission may take a decision that an arrangement is not prohibited under Article 81 or 82 because it is in the Community's public interest. In relation to Article 81, this may be '... either because the conditions of Article 81(1) are not fulfilled, or because the conditions of Article 81(3) of the Treaty are satisfied'. Agreements that satisfy the criteria of Article 81(3) and that are therefore not prohibited no longer need any form of prior negative clearance since national courts may also apply Article 81(3), which following the reform of its application by Article 1(2) of Regulation 1/2003 is directly effective.[405] State aids, however, must generally still be notified under Article 88 to the Commission despite the existence of exceptions for some small amounts for example under the Commission's 2006 *de minimis* Regulation.[406]

---

[403] O. Odudu, The Boundaries of EC Competition Law: The Scope of Article 81 (Oxford, Oxford University Press 2006) p. 175.

[404] Commission of the European Communities, *State Aid Action Plan*, COM(2005)107 Final.

[405] Regulation 1/2003 Art. 1(2).

[406] Commission Regulation (EC) No. 1998/2006 of 15 December 2006 on the application of Arts. 87 and 88 of the Treaty to *de minimis* aid *OJ* L 379 of 28 December 2006.

5.3.3. Rules of reason?

US competition law is founded on a balancing exercise between the anti-competitive and pro-competitive effects of agreements. Despite some similarities, the ECJ has consistently denied that a similar doctrine exists in Community competition law. Three key questions on the role of 'rules of reason' in EC competition law remain unanswered. The extent to which the Treaty grounds in Article 81(3) are supplemented by additional grounds, whether these affect the definition of 'restriction' under Article 81(1) or constitute a justification of a restriction under Article 81(3), and whether these amount to the introduction of a rule of reason have all been subject to intense debate since *Wouters*.[407] What is certain is that the grounds other than those in Article 81(3) may be invoked with the ultimate effect that collusive arrangements between separate firms or acts of dominant firms do not fall foul of EC competition rules. Article 82 is not infringed where conduct does not constitute an 'abuse'. In *Hoffman-La Roche,* the Court noted that anti-competitive 'abuse' is behaviour which '... is such as to influence the structure of a market where ... the degree of competition is weakened and ... has the effect of hindering the maintenance of the degree of competition still existing in the market ...'.[408] Exclusionary abuse is also prohibited, and Article 82 itself lists a number of prohibited exclusionary abuses. The finding of an abuse under Article 82 implies similar public interest tests as those in Article 81: where an act is in the public interest, it does not constitute an abuse. Both competition law articles consequently place some emphasis on whether the conduct, even if restrictive of competition, serves a recognised non-competition aim. In sport, the specific question of competition organisation raises many questions in this respect, since some restriction of the sporting competition is by definition necessary for a structured competition.

5.3.4. Enforcement

The Community competition law framework is enforced at both Community and national level. Regulation 1/2003 governs the enforcement of EC competition law. Under its provisions, breaches of competition law may result in Commission investigations leading to injunctions and fines. In proceedings before national bodies, the ECJ recognised in *Eco Swiss* that anti-competitive features may lead to the unenforceability of agreements,[409] and in *Courage* developed rules for compensation claims for damage suffered due to anti-competitive practices.[410] Community competition rules take precedence over national rules and have direct effect.[411] Where an agreement with effects on trade between Member States does not restrict competition or pur-

---

[407] E. Szyszczak, 'Competition and Sport', 32(1) *European Law Review* (2007) pp. 100-106.

[408] Case 85/76 *Hoffmann-La Roche* v. *Commission* [1976] *ECR* 461.

[409] Case C-126/97 *Eco Swiss China Time Ltd.* [1999] *ECR* I-3055.

[410] Case C-453/99 *Courage* v. *Creehan* [2001] *ECR* I-6297 where a party to an anticompetitive agreement was entitled to damages.

[411] Case 127/73 *BRT* v. *SABAM* [1974] *ECR* 51 Para. 16 (Art. 81(1)); Case 155/73 *Sacchi* [1974] *ECR* 409 Para. 18 (Art. 82). Regulation 1/2003 gives direct effect to Art. 81(3).

sues a recognised policy aim, Article 3(2) of the Regulation recognises that national competition provisions may not interfere. In this sense, the regulation of interstate competition in the EC is an exclusive competence of the Community, regulated by the Community rules. Of some sporting interest is the provision in Article 10 of the Regulation, under which the Commission may issue a decision exempting a particular practice on the basis that it does not restrict competition, or that where it does so, it is justified. Recital 14 of the Regulation envisages the possibility of doing so 'with a view to clarifying the law and ensuring its consistent application throughout the Community, in particular with regard to new types of agreements or practices that have not been settled in the existing case-law and administrative practice'. Although the Commission has declined to do so, citing in its White Paper package a lack of case law on the topic, it is in principle open to it to revisit this assessment. However, in relation to Article 82, Member States may impose more stringent standards on the behaviour of dominant undertakings acting unilaterally. They may also apply more restrictive national merger control laws. Article 3(2) of the Regulation recognises that they may intervene against undertakings when the policy grounds of the national rules '... pursue an objective different from that pursued by Articles 81 and 82'. The relationship between national and EC competition policy and enforcement remains problematic. Considerable questions still exist as to the practical effects of decisions of national and EC competition regulators in relation to each other. In the context of sport, this uncertainty is aggravated whenever sports are governed on a national, rather than an international level, because the rules relating to appreciable effects on trade between Member States rarely offer a clear result as to which regimes should be applied to those national sporting rules.

5.4.   DEFINING COMPETITION

Following *Meca-Medina,* it is clear that the analytical process of determining whether a particular rule constitutes a restriction under free movement or under competition law is not identical in relation to sporting rules. Compatibility under one does not *a priori* lead to a similar conclusion under the other. This is discussed in greater detail above in Chapter 4. The ECJ has only recently for the first time considered the relationship between sport and EC competition law. Despite having dismantled the sporting exception in that context, it is likely that both analytical frameworks will produce similar results. For example in many cases, it is likely that a rule that falls within the *Walrave* Paragraph 8 exception will constitute an 'inherent' restriction under the *Wouters*-type analysis conducted in *Meca-Medina.*

5.4.1.   'Undertakings' and *Walrave* Paragraph 4

EC Competition law is primarily aimed at regulating private economic activity. Articles 81 and 82 apply to every 'undertaking', defined in *Höfner and Elser* as 'every entity engaged in an economic activity regardless of the legal status of the entity or the way in which it is financed'.[412] In this respect, the competition provisions contain within their letter a function similar to that performed by the *Walrave* Paragraph 4 limb of the sporting exception since organisations pursuing uneconomic sporting activity fail to fall within the scope of that concept. Individuals not acting on behalf of an employer, sports bodies, and professional bodies have for example all been found capable of falling under this definition.[413] The meaning of 'undertaking' is identical under both Articles.[414] Where an activity is not economic, an undertaking is not an 'undertaking' within the meaning of Articles 81 and 82.[415] The frontiers of the notion of 'undertaking' in competition law lie in the distinction between public functions and economic activity,[416] and between directly controlled activity,[417] not within the meaning of an 'undertaking' and independent entrepreneurial activity, which is. Thus an organisation carrying out regulatory functions and economic functions will be subject to competition law in so far as its economic functions are concerned, but not where that regulatory function is being carried out. This is recognised in both the *Piau* judgment of the Court of First Instance as well as the Commission's decisional practice in the sporting field. In its White Paper package the Commission listed as undertakings individual athletes performing services, sports clubs carrying out economic activities such as selling tickets, broadcasting or advertising rights, and national and international sports associations that commercially exploit a sports event as capable of constituting undertakings.[418]

5.4.2. Collective bargaining

The Independent European Sport Review and the White Paper on Sport both endorse social dialogue between collective bodies as a vehicle for mitigating some legal issues raised by professional sport.[419] A number of sport-specific projects on social dialogue

---

[412] Case C-41/90 *Höfner and Elser* [1991] *ECR* I-1979 Para. 21.

[413] A. Jones and B. Sufrin, *EC Competition Law: Text, Cases and Materials*, 2nd edn. (Oxford, Oxford University Press 2004) pp. 108-110.

[414] Joined Cases T-68, 77 and 78/89 *Societa Italiana Vetro* v. *Commission* [1992] *ECR* II-1403 Paras. 358 and 359.

[415] Case C-475/99 *Ambulanz Glöckner* [2001] *ECR* I-8089 Opinion of Advocate General Jacobs point 72.

[416] See for example Case C-218/00 *Casal di Battistello Veneziano* [2002] *ECR* I-691 Paras. 31-46 and Case C-364/92 *Eurocontrol* [1994] *ECR* I-43. In the sporting context, see Case C-49/07 *MOT.O.E.* Reference lodged on 5 February 2007.

[417] Case C-73/95 P *Viho* [1996] *ECR* I-5457, Case 48/69 *ICI* v. *Commission (Dyestuffs)* [1972] *ECR* I-619.

[418] See also *Bosman*, Opinion of Advocate General Lenz, points 255 et seq.; Commission decision 27 June 2002 *ENIC* v. *UEFA* COMP/37.806 Paras. 25 and 26; Commission of the European Communities, *Commission staff working document. The EU and Sport: Background and Context*, SEC (2007) 935, pp. 66-67.

[419] J. Arnaut, *Independent European Sport Review* (2006), see at <www.independentfootballreview. com>, p. 90 and Commission of the European Communities, *White Paper on Sport*, COM(2007) 391 Final, p. 19.

have also been funded by the Commission.[420] These are discussed in some detail in Chapter 2. In *Albany,* the Court recognised that 'agreements concluded in the context of collective negotiations between management and labour in pursuit of [recognised objectives] must, by virtue of their nature and purpose, be regarded as falling outside the scope' of Article 81(1) because the restrictions on competition were 'inherent' in the pursuit of those objectives.[421] As Advocate General Maduro points out in his opinion in the 2007 *Viking Case,* collective agreements must enjoy a 'limited antitrust immunity' because '[t]he Treaty encourages social dialogue leading to the conclusion of collective agreements on working conditions and wages [and] this objective would be seriously undermined if the Treaty were, at the same time, to prohibit such agreements by reason of their inherent effects on competition'.[422] This is indicative of the broader debates on the relationship between undistorted competition and other aims in Article 3 of the EC Treaty, and of the possibility that non-competition concerns may influence the application and scope of competition law. In Paragraph 25 of the same opinion, he considers that social policy considerations are in the context of freedom of movement 'justifications', but do not exempt 'restrictions' so as to place them altogether outside the scope of the relevant Treaty provisions.

5.4.3.   'Purely sporting' motives

The altruistic motives of sporting organisations might be invoked in an effort to challenge the existence of the requisite economic dimension for the application of EC competition law. The Court has consistently held in the context of free movement law that the use of some, or even all, of the proceeds of an economic activity conducted by a private party does not lead to a conclusion that the activity itself is uneconomic.[423] The result will however differ if a State is able to rely on Article 31 or 86 exceptions, discussed in detail below. If a state function is being performed, competition law does not apply, and competition law does not apply to state legislation as such. Where legislation merely permits anti-competitive behaviour, rather than mandating such behaviour, an undertaking will be liable for the infringement, together with the Member State.[424] Whilst self-employed persons[425] and companies may be subject to competition law, employees,[426] agents[427] and subsidiaries[428] acting under the direction of another are not independent of the undertakings which they serve. As such, whilst

---

[420] Report for the Commission of the European Communities, *Promoting the Social Dialogue in European Professional Football* (EFFC/T.M.C. Asser Institute, September 2004); Report for the Commission of the European Communities, *Promoting the Social Dialogue in European Professional Football (candidate EU Member States)* (The Hague, T.M.C. Asser Institute November 2004).

[421] Case C-67/96 *Albany* [1999] *ECR* I-5751 Paras. 59 and 60.

[422] *Viking,* Opinion of Advocate General Maduro, 23 May 2007, point 27.

[423] Case C-275/92 *Schindler* [1994] *ECR* I-1039 Para. 60.

[424] Case C-198/01 *CIF* [2003] *ECR* I-8055.

[425] Case C-309/99 *Wouters* [2002] *ECR* I-1577. Hereafter referred to as *Wouters.*

[426] Case C-22/98 *Becu* [1999] *ECR* I-5665 Paras. 26 and 27.

[427] Commission Notice on Guidelines on Vertical Restraints *OJ* 2000 C291/1 Para. 13.

[428] Case C-73/95 P *Viho Europe BV* [1996] *ECR* I-5457 Para. 16.

those undertakings are subject to competition rules, their agents are not independently responsible for infringements committed by those undertakings. When professional associations that regulate economic units are themselves engaged in economic activity, they may constitute undertakings for the purposes of Article 82.

5.4.4. Public and private regulators

As the CFI recognised in *Piau,*

> '[t]he very principle of regulation of an economic activity concerning neither the specific nature of sport nor the freedom of internal organisation of sports associations by a private-law body, like FIFA, which has not been delegated any such power by a public authority, cannot from the outset be regarded as compatible with Community law, in particular with regard to respect for civil and economic liberties'.[429]

A professional association regulating undertakings may make a 'decision of an association of undertakings' for the purposes of Article 81(1).[430] In order to constitute a group of undertakings exercising a collective dominant position under Article 82, they must be 'sufficiently linked to each other to adopt the same conduct on the market with the result that competition between them is eliminated'.[431] European and international federations are recognised by Commission decisional practice to be linked in such a way, and it is difficult to imagine a situation where joint regulation of economic activity would not in the sporting context be susceptible to a challenge based on either Article 81 or 82, depending on the strength of the links between the organisations.

5.5. SCOPE OF COMPETITION LAW: EFFECT ON TRADE

EC competition law applies only to acts implemented in the European Union that have an effect on trade between Member States, required under both Articles 81 and 82.[432] This test has been interpreted broadly, and in *STM* was considered to require only probable foresight of '... influence, direct or indirect, actual or potential, on the pattern of trade between Member States'[433] which can be either detrimental or beneficial.[434] Where a practice does not restrict, but instead facilitates competition, it satisfies this test and is in principle within the scope of the prohibition. However, it will be unlikely to fall foul of the requirement for an 'object or effect' of restricting

---

[429] *Piau*, CFI Para. 77.

[430] *Wouters* Paras. 44-71.

[431] Ibid. Para. 113, tracing this to Case C-96/94 *Centro Servizi Spediporto* [1995] *ECR* I-2883, Paras. 33 and 34.

[432] Joined Cases 89, 104, 114, 116, 117 and 125 to 129/85 *Wood Pulp* [1988] *ECR* I-1307.

[433] Case 56/65 *STM* [1965] *ECR* 337.

[434] Case 56/64 *Consten and Grundig* [1966] *ECR* 429.

competition.[435] Anti-competitive effects must under Article 3 of Regulation 1/2003 be 'appreciable'[436] to fall within EC, rather than national competition law. According to Commission guidance based on the case law of the Court of Justice, where the parties to an agreement or abuse control less than 5% of the relevant market and the turnover of the products in question is less than EUR 40 million an agreement fails the appreciability test implied by the 'effect on trade' criterion.[437] Similar guidance is offered in the Commission Notice on agreements of minor importance.[438] Market definition may thus be of the utmost importance in determining whether EC competition rules apply. Where an appreciable effect is not found on the Community level, a practice may still fall within the scope of national competition law.

5.5.1. Market definition

The question of what constitutes the relevant market is instrumental in determining whether products are sufficiently similar activity to be competitors. If they do not operate in the same market, they are not in competition and therefore are incapable of engaging in anticompetitive agreements. If they do operate on the same market, it will be necessary to consider market shares for the purpose of *de minimis* rules. Market definition is particularly important in the context of Article 82, because the existence of a dominant position must be demonstrated before the notion of an abuse of that position can be considered. It can also be used to determine the relevance of the various exemptions under the *de minimis* rule and practices in determining market power for block exemptions in relation to Article 81. The Commission does not always expressly consider market definition in its decisional practice, as can be seen in the sporting context in the 1990 *World Cup* decision and the *M6/Metropole* case.[439] When it does, the Commission has considerable discretion in its appreciations of fact which are not often revisited by the Community courts except where this leads to a 'manifest error' of judgment.[440] Its decisions are not always particularly nuanced when they do consider sporting questions. For example in the *Mouscron* decision it considered that Lille was active in the 'market for renting stadiums', and in *Piau*, the CFI and the Commission entertained notions of FIFA's activities in the 'football market'.

---

[435] Commission Decision 27 June 2002 *ENIC* v. *UEFA* COMP/37.806 Commission Decision Para. 27.

[436] Case 5/69 *Völk* v. *Vervaecke* [1996] *ECR* 295.

[437] Commission Notice, Guidelines on the Effect of Trade Concept Contained in Arts. 81 and 82 of the Treaty, *OJ* 2004 C101/81 Para. 52.

[438] Commission Notice on agreements of minor importance which do not appreciably restrict competition under Art. 81(1), *OJ* 2001 C368/13.

[439] Commission Decision IV/33.384 and IV/33.378 *Distribution of package tours during the 1990 World Cup* 27 October 1992; Case T-185/00 *M6/Metropole* [2002] *ECR* II-3085 Paras. 51-57, appeal C-470/02 P dismissed by order, *OJ* 2004 C 314 18. December 2004 p. 2.

[440] *Piau* CFI Para. 80.

5.5.2. Defining product markets

If the Commission fails to consider market definition questions in detail, this is certainly not because objectively defined criteria do not exist. The Commission has issued a notice on outlining its practice in defining the relevant market which generally reflects the case law of the Court of Justice.[441] Three facets of the market definition must be considered: the product, the geographical market, and its temporal dimension. Its approach begins '... from the type of products that the undertakings involved sell and the area in which they sell them in ... 'and other products that affect the pricing policy of the undertakings.[442] If customers would switch to other products given a hypothetical small but significant non-transitory increase in price, the substitutes constitute part of that product market; if the price increase could be sustained and remain profitable because consumers do not switch, they do not.[443] The Commission takes account of economic evidence including demand substitutability, namely whether consumers consider other products as substitutes, and the cross-elasticity of demand, the tendency of consumers to switch to those products. In the *Ticketing Arrangements* decisions, the Commission considered that the relevant market is generally 'the market for the sale of tickets for the sport event in question',[444] in particular because consumers do not consider other events substitutable.[445] Although this is the focus of the Commission's substitutability analysis, it also sometimes considers supply substitutability, namely whether other producers can easily switch to producing in the relevant product market. Where quantifiable objective evidence in the form of market studies is available, it considers this. However, it often resorts to the use of more subjective evidence. This includes notions of 'reasonable interchangeability' also called 'functional interchangeability' based on the subjective conditions of the consumer. The classic example of this reasoning can be found in the *United Brands* judgment of the ECJ, where the Court confirmed the Commission's consideration of the age and infirmity of customers material in determining the relevant product market.[446] An analogy of this transposed to the sporting context might be found in ticketing arrangements targeted at enhancing the availability of tickets to major competitions to grassroots supporters. 'The key criteria [for functional interchangeability] are the properties, prices and intended use of the products' from the point of view of the consumer.[447]

---

[441] Commission Notice on the definition of relevant market for the purposes of Community competition law *OJ* 1997 C372/5 pp. 5-11. Hereafter referred to as Market Definition Notice.

[442] Market Definition Notice Para. 16.

[443] Ibid. Para. 17.

[444] Commission of the European Communities, *Commission staff working document. The EU and Sport: Background and Context*, SEC (2007) 935, p. 90.

[445] Case 36888 *1998 World Cup* Commission Decision of July 20, 1999 Case *OJ* 2000 L 5/55 Para. 74.

[446] Case 27/76 *United Brands* [1978] *ECR* 207 Para. 31.

[447] Case M 580ABB/Daimler Benz *OJ* 1997 L11/1 Para. 13.

5.5.3. Product market segmentation

Firms intentionally segment product markets through advertising. In the context of sporting markets one need only look towards the brand loyalty of football supporters to note that for many consumers, tickets to matches are not part of a market larger than those involving the local matches for a team that the consumer supports. In Paragraph 43 of its Market Definition Notice, the Commission treats this as a special case that applies only when '[a] distinct group of customers ... could be subject to price discrimination' and occurs when '... it is possible to identify clearly which group an individual belongs to ... 'and at the same time parallel trade or resale between customers is not feasible. This might be demonstrated in sports ticketing with reference to price discrimination aimed at encouraging young supporters to attend through discounted pricing. In that context, the Commission has also demonstrated its preparedness to identify very specific product markets. Narrow market definitions reduce the likelihood of avoiding appreciability thresholds. The Commission avoids precise market definition where it can dispose of the case by other means. For example, in the *1998 World Cup* decision it found that 'blind pass' tickets which entitled spectators to view first-round matches and one of the last sixteen constituted separate products from 'blind individual tickets' that related to the three matches at different stages of the competition.[448] Conversely, point 42 of the decision considered that as there were no appreciable restrictions, it was not necessary to define the relevant product market. The decisional practice of the Commission is particularly well nuanced in relation to media rights. In relation to upstream broadcasting rights, namely the purchase of those rights by broadcasters, it has in *Bertelsmann* and *TPS+7* distinguished between sports and other programming.[449] It regularly considers '... brand image, the ability to attract a particular audience, the configuration of that audience and advertising/sponsoring revenues'.[450] Individual sports events have been recognised in *Eurovision I* as independent markets,[451] and the Commission has recognised new media rights for football events and out-of-season matches as separate markets from ordinary fixtures shown on the traditional media of television broadcasting.[452] In relation to downstream product markets, in other words those on which the ultimate consumers and broadcasters participate, the Commission has distinguished between subscription-based and free-to-air television[453] on the basis of limited substitutabil-

---

[448] Case 36.888 Commission Decision of 20 July 1999 *1998 World Cup OJ* 2000 L 5/55 Para. 74.

[449] Commission Decision of 7 October 1996, Case M.779 *Bertelsmann/CLT OJ* 1996 C 364/3 Para. 19; Commission Decision of 3 March 1999, Case 36237 *TPS+7, OJ* 1999 L 90/6 Para. 34.

[450] Commission of the European Communities, *Commission staff working document. The EU and Sport: Background and Context*, SEC (2007) 935, p. 79.

[451] Commission Decision of 11 June 1993, Case 32150 *EBU/Eurovision System OJ* 1993 L 179/23, Case T-528/93 *Eurovision I ECR* 1996 II-649 Para. 45.

[452] Case 37.398 *Joint selling of the commercial rights of the UEFA Champions League, OJ* 2003 L 291/25 Para. 67 separate fixtures, Para. 85 new media; Case M.2876 *Newscorp OJ* 2004 L 110/73 Para. 66 for non-regular season fixtures.

[453] Case M.2876 *Newscorp/Telepiu, OJ* 2004 L 110/73, Para. 43.

ity,[454] and between television and new media such as wireless mobile networks and the internet.[455]

5.5.4. Geographic market

The geographical market is the area where the objective conditions of competition applying to the product in question are the same for all traders. Factors considered include the impact of transportation costs on product prices, national technical standards, national retailer preferences and national purchasing patterns. Some sectors are recognised to be special in this respect: national languages and cultures serve to naturally segment the geographical markets for media.[456] It has been argued that sport, too, is special because of national preferences. The Commission Notice defines the relevant geographic market as '... the area in which the undertakings concerned are involved in the supply and demand of products or services, in which the conditions of competition are sufficiently homogenous and which can be distinguished from neighbouring areas because the conditions of competition are appreciably different in those areas'.[457] In this respect, sports markets are unlike many markets for goods that are considered Community-wide, capable of more limited geographic scope. This is not because sport is recognised as intrinsically special in the 'sporting exception' sense, but because the objective features of those markets are capable of influencing the outcome of the conventional geographic market analysis. For example in relation to media rights, the Commission has considered that downstream markets may be national or based on linguistic regions, and that the upstream markets may also be segmented due to the national organisation of sport within the European model.[458] However, whilst the Commission has demonstrated its preparedness to consider regional market segmentation that results from pre-existing objective conditions, its practice in the *Ticketing Cases* demonstrates that it is not inclined to countenance artificial market segmentation in the context of sport any more than in the product market and for example considered in the *1998 World Cup* case that that the geographic market for

---

[454] Commission Decision of 9 November 1994, Case M.469 *MSG Media Service, OJ* 1994 L 364/1, Paras. 32 and 48; Commission Decision of 7 October 1996, Case M.779 *Bertelsmann/CLT OJ* 1996 C 364/3 Para.. 16; Commission Decision of 27 May 1998, Case M.993 *Bertelsmann/Kirch/Premiere, OJ* 1999 L 53/1, Para. 18; Case M.2876 *Newscorp/Telepiu, OJ* 2004 L 110/73, Para. 34. Interdependencies were also stressed in the ruling of the CFI in Case T-158/00 *ARD v. Commission*, [2003] *ECR* II-3825, Paras. 80 et seq.

[455] Case 37.398 *Joint selling of the commercial rights of the UEFA Champions League, OJ* 2003 L 291/25 Para. 82; and Commission Decision of 19 January 2005, Case 37.214 *Joint selling of the media rights to the German Bundesliga, OJ* 2005 L 134/46, Para. 18. Premier league collective selling of 3G and internet rights: IP/04/134.

[456] Case M553 *OJ* 1996 L134/21 *RTL/Veronica/Endemol*.

[457] Commission Notice on the definition of the relevant market for the purposes of Community competition law *OJ* C 372 9/12/1997.

[458] Case 37.398 *Joint selling of the commercial rights of the UEFA Champions League, OJ* 2003 L 291/25 Paras. 88-90 and for the downstream question, also Commission Decision of 27 May 1998, Case M.993 *Bertelsmnann/Kirch/Premiere, OJ* 1999 L 53/1 Para. 22.

the sale of tickets to international events will generally be at least EU-wide.[459] In the sporting context, the question of geographic market definition raises the question of whether the Commission is inclined to accept consumer preferences for national sport, or whether it is rather inclined to consider whether there are other objective criteria that naturally segment markets. It could be that no objective criteria relate to some areas where consumers demonstrate national or local preferences.

5.5.5. Temporal markets

Market definition may also have a temporal element. In the context of goods, this often relates to seasonal goods such as agricultural produce.[460] This has two immediately apparent consequences in the classification of markets relevant to sport. Firstly, where the Commission has considered joint selling of rights, its practice in settling has demonstrated that it has balanced the restrictive effects with the temporal effects of the agreement, and accepted restrictions where their exclusivity was limited.[461] Secondly, as demonstrated in the *1998 World Cup Ticketing* case, the time-span of rights sold to consumers may be instrumental in determining the product market itself.

5.6. 'RESTRICTIONS' OF COMPETITION

Once the threshold questions for the application of EC competition law are satisfied the analytical framework under Articles 81 and 82 requires some restriction on competition. In Article 81, this is expressly stated as such. In the case of Article 82, the notion of 'restriction' is intrinsic in the concept of what constitutes 'abuse' of a dominant position. While the case law on what constitutes a 'restriction' focuses on Article 81(1) for this reason, what follows is equally applicable in that respect to Article 82. Article 81(1) prohibits '... all agreements between undertakings, decisions by associations of undertakings and concerted practices which may affect trade between Member States and which have as their object or effect the prevention, restriction or distortion of competition within the common market ...'. Article 81(1) seeks to ensure that market coordination is effected by market forces and competition rather than collusion between firms.[462] What constitutes an agreement, decision, or concerted practice is broader than the idea of express agreements in contractual form[463] and has in the *Wood Pulp* been inferred from market activity.[464] 'The only

---

[459] Case 36.888 *1998 World Cup* Commission Decision of July 20, 1999 Case *OJ* 2000 L 5/55 Para. 77.

[460] Case 27/76 *United Brands* [1978] *ECR* 207.

[461] Case M.2876 *Newscorp/Telepiu*, *OJ* 2004 L 110/73 Para. 233.

[462] Case C-49/92 P *Commission* v. *Anic* [1999] *ECR* I-4125 Para. 116.

[463] Ibid. Paras. 115-6 (concerted practice) and 130-131 (agreement).

[464] Joined Cases 89, 104, 114, 116, 117 and 125 to 129 /85 *Wood Pulp* [1988] *ECR* I-1307

essential [factor] is the distinction between independent conduct, which is allowed, and collusion, which is not ...'.[465] In fields where there are few competitors and entry costs are high, independent decisions may result in tacit collusion. This independently achieved coordination is not prohibited by Article 81(1) so long as there is no agreement to exchange information that assists in coordinating activity.[466] In relation to sporting activity, such oligopolies may exist in relation to broadcasting rights and the ticketing practices of major clubs. 'Restrictions' of competition recognised in the sport-related decisional practice of the Commission include exclusive distribution rights under contracts,[467] discriminatory ticketing practices on the basis of territorial limits[468] and credit card exclusivity.[469]

5.6.1. 'Object or effect'

Article 81(1) requires either an object or effect of adverse impacts on competition. Where the objective of coordination is to reduce competition or to partition the single market, no effects must be proven.[470] The Commission's investigation strategy has focused heavily on such agreements, rather than those with other objects but which nevertheless have restrictive effects. However, where '... a rule which at first sight appears to contain a restriction of competition is necessary in order to make that competition possible in the first place, it must indeed be assumed that such a rule does not infringe Article [81(1)]'.[471] This dictum from Advocate General Lenz's opinion in *Bosman* has since developed in the jurisprudence of the Court as something akin to a rule of reason. The precise legal form, however, is not a balancing exercise between pro- and anti-competitive effects as such but recognition that such *de facto* restrictions do not constitute 'restrictions' of competition within the meaning of Article 81(1). They therefore fall outside the scope of the prohibition. An analogy could be made between this analysis and that conducted under the Paragraph 8 *Walrave* limb of the 'sporting exception' in the context of free movement.

5.6.2. Contextual approach: defining 'restrictions'

In *Wouters*, the ECJ confirmed that even where the effect of an agreement is to restrict competition, it might not constitute a 'restriction of competition' within the meaning of Article 81(1) if its object is recognised as legitimate and the resulting restriction of competition is an unavoidable secondary consequence of pursuing that legitimate aim.

---

[465] Case C-49/92 P *Commission* v. *Anic* [1999] *ECR* I-4125 Para. 108.

[466] Case C-7/95 P *John Deere* [1998] *ECR* I-3111.

[467] Cases 33.378 and 33.384 Commission Decision of 27 October 1992 *1990 World Cup package tours*.

[468] Case 36.888 *1998 World Cup* Commission Decision of 20 July 1999 Case *OJ* 2000 L 5/55.

[469] Case 38.703 *2004 Athens Olympic Games*, Commission press release IP/03/738 of 23 May 2003.

[470] Case 56/65 *STM* [1965] *ECR* 337.

[471] *Bosman*, Opinion of Advocate General Lenz, point 265.

'[N]ot every agreement between undertakings ... which restricts the freedom of action of the parties or of one of them necessarily falls within the prohibition laid down in Article [81(1)] ... . [A]ccount must first of all be taken of the overall context in which the decision of the association of undertakings was taken or produces its effects [and] of its objectives [whilst not expressly recognised by the Treaty, that consumers] are provided with the necessary guarantees ... . It has then to be considered whether the consequential effects restrictive of competition are inherent in the pursuit of those objectives.'[472]

In other words, when the restriction of competition is 'inherent' in the pursuit of other legitimate objectives, that restriction does not fall within the scope of the prohibition in Article 81(1). In *Wouters,* the ECJ recognised a large margin of appreciation in this respect, noting that it is generally for the body creating the restrictive rule to determine whether in its reasonable consideration that rule is 'necessary'.[473] This could be seen as recognition of the conditional autonomy of non-statutory regulatory bodies such as sports governing bodies.

5.6.3. Incidental restrictive effects

This distinction, developed in *Wouters* in the context of regulating professional legal services, can be used to preclude the application of Article 81(1) to rules that pursue non-economic aims but have restrictive effects. By analogy, if in the reasonable contemplation of a sports governing body a restrictive rule is necessary to secure the attainment of a 'legitimate' sporting objective, then that rule does not contravene Article 81(1). *Meca-Medina* is at the time of writing the only subsequent ECJ ruling to consider in detail the notion, introduced in *Wouters*, of what constitutes an inherent restriction in the pursuit of other objectives and thus not a restriction of competition within the meaning of Article 81(1), despite the frequent references to the case in respect of procedural questions. In Paragraph 42 of *Meca-Medina,* the Court established an analytical framework:

'For the purposes of application of that provision to a particular case, account must first of all be taken of the overall context in which the decision of the association of undertakings was taken or produces its effects and, more specifically, of its objectives. It has then to be considered whether the consequential effects restrictive of competition are inherent in the pursuit of those objectives and are proportionate to them.'

In *Meca-Medina*, the objective of ensuring fair competitions, the protection of athletes' health, the integrity and objectivity of competitive sport and ethical values were all considered to contribute to the 'inherency' of anti-doping rules in protecting the 'organisation and proper conduct of sport'.

---

[472] *Wouters* Para. 97.
[473] Ibid. Paras. 107 and 110.

5.6.4. Rules of reason

US competition law distinguishes between agreements that are prohibited because they are prima facie anticompetitive and those that require detailed economic assessment to determine whether the cumulative effects of the agreement promote, rather than diminish, consumer welfare. In Community competition law, the Court of Justice has rejected attempts to introduce it since *Consten and Grundig*,[474] perhaps motivated to safeguard the exclusivity of the grounds in Article 81(3). Neither the ECJ nor the CFI have consistently applied a single analytical approach to the application and relationship between Articles 81(1) and 81(3).[475] Whilst Regulation 1/2003 eliminates the two-stage regulatory approach of notification and Commission responses by enabling judicial authorities courts to consider both limbs at once, legal uncertainty remains because the parties must determine the justifiability of their agreement, often without receiving legal guidance much less a binding decision from either the Commission or national competition authorities. Chalmers observes that '... *some* economic analysis must be performed before determining that an agreement has anti-competitive effects, but we are still uncertain as to how much is needed before the burden shifts to the defendant to justify the practice under Article 81(3)'.[476] The prospect of the Commission resorting to Article 10 of Regulation 1/2003 seems remote in the field of sport. However, it may be that it empowers a rule of reason type approach, and that consequently despite the failure of the ECJ to recognise these in the analytical approach of Article 81(3) as expounded by the Court, the Commission has within its reach the legal means with which to impose this through express legislation empowered by the enforcement Regulation.

5.6.5. *Wouters* national policy requirements and 'inherency'

In *Wouters*, the ECJ recognised that proportionate national policy requirements, in that case ensuring 'the proper practice of the legal profession', could also result in a finding that Article 81(1) was not infringed.[477] It has been argued that this amounts to a category of 'mandatory requirements' in competition law that go beyond the Treaty exceptions in Article 81(3).[478] Where the recognised policy aims pursued result in restrictions on competition, those restrictions are not prohibited by Article 81(1) if they

---

[474] Case 56/64 *Consten and Grundig* [1966] *ECR* 429.

[475] G. Monti, 'Article 81 EC and Public Policy', 39(5) *Common Market Law Review* (2002); O. Odudu, 'Article 81(3), Discretion and Direct Effect', 23(1) *European Competition Law Review* (2002); O. Odudu, 'A New Economic Approach to Article 81(1)?', 27(1) *European Law Review* (2002); O. Odudu, *The Boundaries of EC Competition Law: The Scope of Article 81* (Oxford, Oxford University Press 2006).

[476] D. Chalmers et al., *EU Law* (Cambridge, Cambridge University Press 2006) p. 1006.

[477] *Wouters* Para. 109.

[478] G. Monti, 'Article 81 EC and Public Policy', 39(5) *Common Market Law Review* (2002) pp. 1086-1090; A. Komninos, *Non-competition Concerns: Resolution of Conflicts in the Integrated Article 81*, Oxford Centre for Competition Law and Policy Working Paper (L) 08/05 part IV (2005), see at <www.competitionlaw.ox.ac.uk/competition/portal.php>.

are 'inherent' to the pursuit of the objective and proportional. This policy aim need not be economic, and as Goyder notes *Wouters* therefore does not represent an example of a 'rule of reason' approach involving the balance of pro- and anti-competitive effects of an agreement.[479] While Weatherill considers these to lead to substantially identical outcomes in relation to sports governing bodies, *Wouters* shifts focus from the sporting/economic rule analysis towards the necessity of rules to pursue legitimate objectives.[480] The analytical distinction between justified restrictions and those that are not restrictions within the meaning of Article 81(1) may be significant. The margin of appreciation which the Court has been prepared to extend to rules resulting in ancillary restraints of competition appears greater than that which it affords to justified restrictions. Nevertheless, under either system, rules with economic effects must be justified. As Weatherill has observed, *Wouters* as read in *Meca-Medina* provides a framework for doing this without recourse to the artificial notion of 'purely sporting' rules which somehow have nothing whatsoever to do with economic activity.[481] Mash has observed that the *Wouters* formula involves a determination which in the reasonable consideration of a professional body is 'necessary to ensure' the public policy objective.[482] The autonomy of sports governing bodies in making agreements that fall outside Article 81(1) for these reasons is limited in that although they in the first instance are at liberty to determine whether a rule is necessary, the acts taken in pursuit of those rules must be proportionate.[483] The Commission has in *ENIC* recognised that UEFA's restrictions on the common ownership of clubs are subject to a similar analysis despite the absence of a statutory delegation of power.[484] Whilst *Wouters* involved statutory power, the ECJ in *Meca-Medina* applied a similar analysis to rules of sports governing bodies with no public law powers. This constitutes a further move in the modern trend towards the abolition of the public/private divide in Community law. The source of the rule is therefore not an essential element for consideration as an inherent ancillary restraint. However, it should be noted that despite its foundational effect on Article 81 analysis, only *Meca-Medina* cites this aspect of *Wouters*. It is unlikely that *Wouters* and *Meca-Medina* represent the final refinement of the Court's case law in this respect.

5.6.6.   'Inherency' as objective justification

'Inherency' in *Wouters* and *Meca-Medina* is in some senses not unlike objective justification under free movement law, but differs in that inherent rules do not constitute restrictions within the meaning of competition law, whereas objectively justified rules

---

[479] D.G. Goyder, *EC Competition Law*, 4th edn. (Oxford, Oxford University Press 2003) pp. 94-95.

[480] S. Weatherill, 'Anti-doping Rules and EC Law', 26(7) *European Competition Law Review* (2005) pp. 416-421.

[481] S. Weatherill, 'Anti-Doping Revisited: The Femise of the Rule of Purely Sporting Interest', 27(12) *European Competition Law Review* (2006).

[482] J. Mash, 'Is There an EU "Sporting Exception"', 13(2) *Sport and the Law Journal* (2005) p. 28.

[483] Case C-309/99 *Wouters* [2002] *ECR* I-1577.

[484] Case COMP/37 806, *ENIC/UEFA*, Commission Decision of 22 July 2002.

under free movement are within the meaning of 'restriction', but nevertheless justified. The practical differences are limited, since the analytical criteria applied to both are similar: to be 'inherent', sporting rules must pursue legitimate objectives and be proportionate to those objectives. It might be therefore concluded that an aim which is recognised within free movement is also recognised within the field of competition law. However, the Commission has noted in its White Paper package that legitimate objectives of sporting rules in the context of competition 'will normally relate to the "organisation and proper conduct of competitive sport", as recognised by the ECJ in Paragraphs 45 and 46 of *Meca-Medina*'. The only sporting-related legitimate objective so far recognised as 'inherent' is the 'organisation and proper conduct of competitive sport'. This has been recognised to include the ensuring of fair sport competitions with equal chances for all athletes, ensuring the uncertainty of results, protecting athletes' health, ensuring the financial stability of sports clubs or teams, and ensuring consistency in the rules of the game.[485] There is no reason to believe this constitutes an exhaustive list.

5.6.7. 'Inherency' and *Walrave* Paragraph 8.

Since 'inherent' rules do not constitute 'restrictions' within the meaning of Article 81(1), it bears a remarkable similarity to the *Walrave* Paragraph 8 purely sporting rule, which precludes a rule from constituting a restriction of free movement. In this sense, even though the ECJ dismissed the notion of 'purely sporting' rules in the context of competition law, it is submitted that 'inherency' is in this respect a new manifestation of that notion, albeit in nominally different form. In relation to professional regulations, the subjects of *Wouters* and *Meca-Medina*, it should be noted that the Commission continues to investigate the legitimacy of professional rules in other contexts. It has recently studied the restrictive effects of professional regulations, and has published Communications in 2004 and 2005 highlighting the widespread enforcement of anti-competitive national professional regulatory schemes.[486] In its efforts to liberalise professional activity, it has achieved the passage of the new Professional Qualifications Directive and a general directive on the provision of services and establishment. Together these instruments impose strict justificatory regimes in relation to the compatibility of professional rules and practices with principles of free movement. Whilst the competitive effects of such rules are not the focus of the modern directives, it is likely that forthcoming preliminary references will explore in greater detail the extent to which a restriction on free movement under those regimes also constitutes a restriction within the meaning of competition law.

---

[485] Commission of the European Communities, *Commission staff working document. The EU and Sport: Background and Context*, SEC (2007) 935, p. 68.

[486] Commission of the European Communities, *Report on Competition in Professional Services*, Commission Communication COM(2004) 83 Final; Commission of the European Communities, *Professional Services-scope for More Reform Commission Communication* COM(2005) 405 Final.

5.6.8. Justificatory regime under Article 81(3)

Article 81(3) exempts those agreements, decisions or concerted practices which contribute '... to improving the production or distribution of goods or to promoting technical or economic progress ...' that allow '... consumers a fair share of the resulting benefit ...' so long as they do not either impose '... restrictions which are not indispensable to the attainment of these objectives ...'[487] or enable '... eliminating competition in respect of a substantial part of the products in question'.[488] Although often drafted in terms of goods, the provisions are equally applicable to services. All of the conditions must be satisfied before an agreement can be exempted under Article 81(3).[489] Promoting '... technical or economic progress' can be interpreted as broader policy considerations beyond economic efficiencies.[490] Although the Commission considers only agreements that enhance economic efficiency can be exempted[491] and therefore influences national authorities in this direction, it has been argued that its own practice has been to consider non-efficiency considerations such as environmental benefits, employment policy, environmental goals, creation of pan-European champions, which have all been considered as satisfying Article 81(3).[492] Within this framework it would appear open to the Commission to also consider sporting reasons as legitimate aims. This could be facilitated by the insertion of an express sporting competence into the Treaties following a successful ratification of the principles of the Reform Treaty agreed at the June 2007 intergovernmental conference. Jones and Sufrin observe that the debate surrounding the modernisation of the EC Merger Regulation involved precisely this question, and that the absence of broader rules of reason in this instrument would make it '... bizarre to allow non-competition factors to trump adverse effects on competition in the sphere of Article 81 but not in the sphere of the [modernised Merger Regulation]'. Nevertheless, they conclude that the ECJ's willingness to adopt teleological interpretations makes it '... entirely conceivable that the four criteria ... might be interpreted broadly against the backdrop of the wider Community aims and objectives ...'.[493] The notion of consumer benefit is also subject to criticism. While it might appear thatthe consumers of the products must be the primary beneficiaries of such an agreement, for example in *CEDED* the Commission considered 'collective benefits to society' as 'consumer benefits'.[494] It can therefore be credibly argued that an Article 81(3) analysis has in the past, despite considerable

---

[487] Art. 81(3)(a) EC Treaty.

[488] Art. 81(3)(b) EC Treaty.

[489] Case T-528/93 *Metropole* [1996] *ECR* II-649 Para. 86.

[490] R. Whish, *Competition Law*, 5th edn. (London, Butterworths Lexis Nexis 2003) pp. 151-156.

[491] Commission Notice, Guidelines on the Application of Art. 81(3) of the Treaty *OJ* C 101, 27 April 2004.

[492] Case IV.F.1/36.718 *CEDED* Commission Decision 2000/475/EC *OJ* 2000 L187/47 Para. 52 re: environment; Case IV/30/810 *Synthetic Fibers* Commission Decision 84/380/EEC *OJ* 1984 L207/17 Para. 37 re: sectoral crisis; D. Chalmers et al., *EU Law* (Cambridge, Cambridge University Press 2006) pp. 1007-1008.

[493] A. Jones and B. Sufrin, *EC Competition Law: Text, Cases and Materials*, 2nd edn. (Oxford, Oxford University Press 2004) p. 233.

[494] Case IV.F.1/36.718 *CEDED* Commission Decision 2000/475/EC *OJ* 2000 L187/47.

objections from an economic point of view, involved considerations clearly beyond economic efficiency.[495]

5.7.   'ABUSE OF A DOMINANT POSITION'

5.7.1. **Dominance**

Article 82 prohibits '[a]ny abuse by one or more undertakings of a dominant position within the common market or in a substantial part of it ... in so far as it may affect trade between Member States'. Four abuses are listed in the Article itself: imposing unfair prices or other unfair trading conditions, 'limiting production, markets or technical development to the prejudice of consumers', 'applying dissimilar conditions to equivalent transactions with other trading parties ...' and requiring contractual terms unconnected to the subject matter of those contracts. The list is not exhaustive. As the Court recognised in *Continental Can,* where a practice detracts from other Community aims, it may also constitute an abuse.[496] There are no statutory exceptions as in relation to Article 81(3), but similar factors can be cited to argue that conduct is not an abuse. The assessment of dominance involves consideration of the relevant market, outlined above in the context of Article 81, and the extent to which undertakings dominate that market.[497] Dominance does not require a monopoly position, but merely an ability to restrict competition through unilateral action. '[A]lthough the importance of the market shares may vary ... very large shares are in themselves ... evidence of the existence of a dominant position.'[498] When that market share is 50% or above, a presumption of dominance exists.[499] A market share over 40% can also signify dominance when there are significant barriers to entry, as can the relative power of a larger firm in a fragmented market.[500]

5.7.2. **'Abuse'**

The notion of 'abuse' can be illustrated with reference to the process of 'objective justification', developed by the ECJ also in the context of Article 82 to distinguish between abusive conduct and that which does not fall within the scope of Article 82. As Jones and Sufrin observe, neither the Court nor the Commission have '... developed any theoretical framework for identifying conduct which is objectively justified'.[501] Dominant undertakings have responsibilities both to consumers directly, and in rela-

---

[495] O. Odudu, *The Boundaries of EC Competition Law: The Scope of Article 81* (Oxford, Oxford University Press 2006) pp. 164-174.

[496] Case 6/72 *Continental Can* [1973] *ECR* 215 Para. 26.

[497] Case 322/81 *Michelin* [1983] *ECR* 3461 Para. 31.

[498] Case 85/76 *Hoffmann-La Roche* [1979] *ECR* 461 Para. 41.

[499] Case 62/86 *AKZO* v. *Commission* [1991] *ECR* I-3359 Para. 60.

[500] Case 27/76 *United Brands* [1978] *ECR* 207.

[501] A. Jones and B. Sufrin, *EC Competition Law: Text, Cases and Materials*, 2nd edn. (Oxford, Oxford University Press 2004) p. 282.

tion to the healthy maintenance of competition. As the Court observed in *Michelin*, dominant firms have '... a special responsibility not to allow [their] conduct to impair genuine undistorted competition on the common market'.[502] Abuse is determined by effects of the unilateral acts of the dominant party. When they harm consumers or competitors, for example by raising prices or by undercutting competition, it is possible to find that an abuse has occurred. Criticisms have been levelled against the Community's approach to dominance, and particularly that Article 82 has been applied too strictly to restrict the market freedom of dominant undertakings even where their actions do not restrict competition.[503] The Commission is reviewing its approach to Article 82 and was expected to publish some findings in Early 2007, although none have as of August 2007 been published.

5.7.3. Sports governing bodies as dominant undertakings

A number of distinct issues arise in relation to the operation of Article 82 and its relationship to undertakings engaged in economic sporting activity. Sports governing bodies tend by even the most permissive definitions constitute dominant undertakings where they engage in economic activity. The crucial question therefore becomes the extent to which their acts constitute 'abuses'. In *Piau*, the Court of First Instance made clear that this could be reviewed even where the undertaking was engaged in a regulatory function and not directly active in the economic aspect itself, although in that context the CFI considered FIFA as an association of economic undertakings which themselves engaged in the market for professional agents.[504] Nevertheless, it is instructive that the CFI considered, as a matter of principle, that

> '[t]he very principle of regulation of an economic activity concerning neither the specific nature of sport nor the freedom of internal organisation of sports associations by a private-law body, like FIFA, which has not been delegated any such power by a public authority, cannot from the outset be regarded as compatible with Community law...'.[505]

This implies that professional regulation itself could constitute an abuse where an undertaking was unilaterally engaging in such activity. Since what constitutes an abuse is less clearly defined than agreements which restrict competition under Article 81 and no clear indication of exemption criteria exists, the legitimacy of professional regulation under an Article 82 analysis is currently under strain. The Commission's review of professional services has indicated that in this field, the Commission is committed to intensely scrutinise the prospects of further liberalisation, and is unlikely to accept the justifiability of regulation where no public mandate exists.[506]

---

[502] Case 322/81 *Michelin* [1983] *ECR* 3461 Para. 57.

[503] B. Sher, 'The Last of the Steam Powered Trains: Modernising Article 82', 25(5) *European Competition Law Review* (2004).

[504] *Piau* CFI Para. 72. Upheld by ECJ Order 23 January 2006, Case C-171/05 P *ECR* [2006] I-37.

[505] *Piau* CFI Para. 77.

[506] Commission of the European Communities, *Report on Competition in Professional Services*, Commission Communication COM(2004) 83 Final; Commission of the European Communities, *Professional Services-scope for More Reform Commission Communication* COM(2005) 405 Final.

5.8. COMMISSION ASSESSMENT OF COMPETITION ISSUES IN SPORT

5.8.1. Significance of dominance

The documents accompanying the White Paper on Sport highlight a number of rules which the Commission considers may infringe Articles 81(1) and 82, without specifying the analytical processes underlying that reasoning. This implies that in its view, the outcome of the analysis is similar regardless of whether the offence is an agreement between independent undertakings or the unilateral action of a single, dominant undertaking. Rules shielding sports associations from competition, rules prohibiting recourse to national courts, nationality clauses for sports clubs, transfer rules for expired contracts, disproportionate transfer rules for valid contracts, and excessively restrictive licencing rules for agents were all identified as raising competition concerns.[507] Prohibitions on new leagues structures may also raise concerns, and would require careful consideration of whether an analogy to *Gottrup-Klim* collective arrangements for purchasing is possible.[508]

5.8.2. Essential facilities

In relation to shipping, the Commission has in *Sealink* recognised that the refusal to allow competitors access to expensive facilities that are essential for the pursuit of a business can constitute an abuse of a dominant position.[509] In *Oscar Bronner* the essential facilities doctrine was considered by the ECJ in the context of distribution channels, albeit not using that form of words.[510] Hornsby considers that closed leagues would constitute such 'essential facilities only where it could be demonstrated that parallel league structures could not co-exist', and notes that examples of such leagues in other markets suggest this would not be the case with many pan-European sports organised on an international basis.[511] Analogies to the use of stadia might also be entertained in the sporting context. Predatory pricing, namely selling a product at a price that does not reflect its production costs in order to drive competition from markets, may also raise sporting-specific concerns. Intellectual property rights, on the other hand, have been recognised in *Magill* not to give rise to any obligations towards competitors.[512] There is generally no duty to licence intellectual property except where four conditions related to the creation of new products are satisfied. The new product must be essential for carrying out business. Refusal to licence must

---

[507] Commission of the European Communities, *Commission staff working document. The EU and Sport: Background and Context*, SEC (2007) 935, pp. 75-76.

[508] Case C-250/92 *Gøttrup-Klim and others* [1994] *ECR* I-5641.

[509] Commission Decision in *Sea Containers/Stena Sealink*, *OJ* 1994 L15/8 232.

[510] Case C-7/97 *Oscar Bronner* [1998] *ECR* I-7791; See recently Case C-533/03 P *Unilever Bestfoods* [2006] *ECR* I-9091 and Case C-12/03 P *Tetra Laval* [2005] *ECR* I-987 where the ECJ again avoided expressly recognizing 'essential facilities' in EC competition law.

[511] S. Hornsby, '"Closed Leagues": A Prime Candidate for the "Sporting Exception" in European Competition Law', 2 *International Sports Law Review* (June 2001).

[512] Case C-7/97 *Oscar Bronner* [1998] *ECR* I-7791 Para. 40.

effectively prevent the creation of a new product with potential consumer demand. Refusal must not be objectively justifiable. Finally, the refusal to licence must be likely to exclude all competition in a secondary market.

5.9.   PROMOTING LEGAL CERTAINTY

Sports governing bodies have historically argued against the application of Community competition law to sport on the grounds that competition law contains many legal uncertainties. One form of legal certainty is the wholesale of exclusion of sport from the scope of competition law. More nuanced modern approaches raise concerns regarding the absence of the formal notification process under Article 81(3) subsequent to its devolution to national authorities under Regulation 1/2003. In the context of small and medium-sized enterprises, the Commission's block exemption regulations provide some mitigation to this, facilitating the *a priori* exemption from detailed scrutiny competition law of agreements and practices that fall within those rules. The Commission is empowered under Regulation 2821/71 to create exemptions for agreements that fulfil the criteria of Article 81(3).[513] These could in principle include areas relevant to sport, although in this context it should be noted many of the current questions in the field fall within Community sectoral harmonisation initiatives, such as the recent rules on professional qualifications in Directive 2005/36 and on service provision in Directive 2006/123. Where harmonising provisions exist, the compatibility with competition law of rules within the range permitted by harmonised rules is rarely tested. The key instruments of the current block exemption regime are the Vertical Agreements Regulation 2790/99,[514] the Specialisation Agreement Regulation 2658/2000,[515] the Research and Development Regulation 2659/2000,[516] and the Licencing Agreements Regulation 772/2004.[517] All of these are based on a notional recognition of the satisfaction by such agreements of Article 81(3). The Commission has also permitted 'crisis cartels' in twilight industries, based on reasoning beyond consumer benefit and economic efficiency.[518] There have been recent suggestions that professional sports and football in particular are experiencing such crises.[519] If such a situation were demonstrably the case, it may be a possibility, even if a remote one, that the Commission might consider that crisis to warrant special dispensation.

---

[513] Council Regulation (EEC) No. 2821/71 of 20 December 1971 on the application of Art. 81(3) *(formerly Article 85(3))* of the EC Treaty to categories of agreements, decisions and concerted practices.

[514] Commission Regulation (EC) No. 2790/1999 of 22 December 1999 on the application of Art. 81(3) of the Treaty to categories of vertical agreements and concerted practices.

[515] Commission Regulation (EC) No. 2658/2000 of 29 November 2000 on the application of Art. 81(3) of the Treaty to categories of specialisation agreements.

[516] Commission Regulation (EC) No. 2659/2000 of 29 November 2000 on the application of Art. 81(3) of the Treaty to categories of research and development agreements.

[517] Commission Regulation (EC) No. 772/2004 of 27 April 2004 on the application of Art. 81(3) of the Treaty to categories of technology transfer agreements.

[518] Commission Decision 84/380/EEC *Synthetic Fibres OJ* 1984 L207/17.

[519] J. Arnaut, *Independent European Sport Review* (2006), see at <www.independentfootballreview. com>.

5.9.1. Block exemption

The Independent European Sport Review has called on the Commission to adopt block exemption regulations to increase legal certainty regarding questions on central marketing of media rights and issues pertaining to the players' market.[520] These are discussed in detail in Chapters 6 and 7. An examination of the block exemption Regulation on the Application of Article 81(3) of the Treaty to Categories of Vertical Agreements and Concerted Practices demonstrates the mechanics of block exemption from competition law. The Regulation is phrased in terms of goods, but could in principle apply to services. In general terms, it seeks to exempt agreements which, whilst restricting competition, pursue objectives that offer consumers benefits that cannot be ensured without such restrictions, for example after-sales care. The vertical agreement can contain only one party on each level. Agreements that bind several actors on the same level of distribution fail this test. Market share is a factor. Powerful actors controlling over 30% of supplies or 30% of the market for buyers cannot benefit and so here, as with Article 81 and 82 analyses, market definition may be of the utmost importance.

5.9.2. Hard-core restrictions

The Regulation does not apply to agreements which have as their object the imposition of restrictions on competition, rather than the achievement of efficiencies. The agreement may not contain certain types of restrictions. It must not have as its objective setting minimum resale prices. Territorial restrictions that limit sales based on the residence of the customer, rather than the location where the sale is concluded, are prohibited. Restrictions on resale to end customers are likewise incapable of exemption. Agreements that restrict supplying distributors that are members of the same selective distribution system but which are based on factors other than whether their establishment is authorised under the system, are prohibited. So are those which restrict repairs in the context of agreements between the seller of components and a buyer who incorporates them. Territorial restrictions are only permitted if they do not 'limit sales by the customers of the buyer', restrict sales to end-users by a wholesale buyer, restrict sales to unauthorised distributors by members of a selective distribution system or restrict the resale of components intended for incorporation into a final product, rather than components to be used as replacements. Offending any of the Article 4 grounds renders the entire agreement incapable of block exemption. A second list of prohibited grounds is contained in Article 5. If these can be severed from the agreement, they are void but the remaining agreement can fall within the block exemption. These severable terms include a tie-in lasting over five years, an enduring restriction beyond the time frame of the agreement, and a clause in a selective distribution agreement that prohibits the sale of competing goods. An automatic

---

[520] Ibid. pp. 102-103.

block exemption may be withdrawn if the Commission finds it is anti-competitive, or declares that more than 50% of the relevant market is restricted by vertical restraints. A national competition authority may also withdraw the block exemption within its territory if it has local anti-competitive effects. It should be recalled that in order for the Verticals regulation to be of relevance, the acts in question must constitute 're-strictions' of competition. This is not the case with those rules that are recognised as outside Article 81(1) under the emerging case law on ancillary restraints.

5.9.3. Categories of block exemption

In relation to horizontal agreements, two key instruments exist: the Specialisation Agreement Regulation 2658/2000,[521] and the Research and Development Regulation 2659/2000.[522] These are supplemented by a detailed Commission Notice on the Applicability of Article 81 to Horizontal Agreements.[523] Both of these Regulations are based on the presumption that such agreements create efficiencies by eliminating the duplication of processes in firms, and that these efficiencies outweigh the possible restrictions of competition which result from those agreements. The thresholds for joint market share are relatively low, at 20% for specialisation agreements and 25% for research and development agreements. Block exemptions also exist in relation to licensing agreements for technology transfer, under Regulation 772/2004[524] and a number of other, specific fields with less immediate impacts on economic sporting activity. All of these instruments are general, and none involve express recognition of sport beyond that afforded to all activity relevant to the exemption regulations.

5.9.4. No imminent block exemption

The Commission is in principle capable of adopting block exemption Regulations that apply to competition law issues relevant to sport. However, from the list of those presently in force it is clear that it has done so in the past only where a considerable body of formal Decisions have established clear principles in a particular field. Since sports bodies have often sought informal means of settlement, a comparable body of formal Decisions does not exist in the sporting sector. As a consequence of this under-development, in the context of state aid block exemptions the Commission's White Paper package dismisses the possibility of block exemptions relevant to sport.[525] Whilst block exemptions have also existed in some isolated sectors, these have all

---

[521] Commission Regulation (EC) No. 2658/2000 of 29 November 2000 on the application of Art. 81(3) of the Treaty to categories of specialisation agreements.

[522] Commission Regulation (EC) No. 2659/2000 of 29 November 2000 on the application of Art. 81(3) of the Treaty to categories of research and development agreements.

[523] Commission Notice of 6 January 2001 Guidelines on the Applicability of Art. 81 of the EC Treaty to horizontal cooperation agreements.

[524] Commission Regulation (EC) No. 772/2004 of 27 April 2004 on the application of Art. 81(3) of the Treaty to categories of technology transfer agreements.

[525] Commission of the European Communities, *Commission staff working document. The EU and Sport: Background and Context*, SEC (2007) 935, p. 28.

been based on a Community competence in those fields. The Commission observes that it does not have the power to adopt block exemption regulations in the state aid sector because the Council has yet to empower it to do so by way of a Decision under Article 87.[526] The White Paper on Sport does not address this aspect of the present lack of a sports competence, perhaps in anticipation of its inclusion in the forthcoming Reform Treaty.

5.10. MERGERS

The EC Treaty does not expressly regulate mergers. In *Continental Can*,[527] the ECJ recognised that it could constitute an abuse where it strengthened a dominant position. In *BAT and Reynolds* v. *Commission*, it recognised certain circumstances where a merger could constitute an agreement to restrict competition under Article 81.[528] Regulation 4064/89 finally provided for an independent regime to govern mergers, based on the paradigm of protecting competition rather than other flanking policies employed in other areas of competition law. The merger regulation was modernised by Regulation 139/2004 but its policy emphases remain unaltered. It requires all mergers which create concentrations with a significant Community dimension to be notified in advance to the Commission, which then considers the permissibility of the merger with a view to its compatibility with the common market. The organisational issues related to sport are generally not whether mergers are permitted under EC competition rules, but rather whether mergers can be permitted under the organisational rules which see multiple club ownership as a risk to the integrity of sport. Furthermore, if one considers that sporting clubs' services are not generally interchangeable for consumers, these form different product markets and as such, their merger would have no effect on this aspect of their economic activity.

5.11. THE STATE AND COMPETITION

5.11.1. Anticompetitive state action

One limb to the Community competition policy is the prohibition of private anticompetitive behaviour. Apart from some generally well-defined sectoral exceptions, states are also prohibited from legitimating anticompetitive behaviour either by means of legislation permitting such activity or by way of direct interference in competition through state aids. The ECJ has consistently recognised that states may not legitimate anticompetitive behaviour by legislation that is inconsistent with Articles 81 or 82 and is required by Article 10 read together with Articles 81 and 82 not to keep in force

---

[526] Id.
[527] Case 6/72 *Continental Can* [1973] *ECR* 215 Paras. 22 et seq.
[528] Joined Cases 142 and 156/84 *BAT* and *Reynolds* v. *Commission* [1986] *ECR* 1899.

or introduce such measures.[529] However, competition law does not apply as such to those State measures and the ECJ has recognised for example in *Meng* that 'read in isolation, [competition law] relates only to the conduct of undertakings and does not cover measures adopted by Member States by legislation or regulations'.[530]

5.11.2. Article 86 and 'Services of General Economic Interest'

Article 86(1) provides that public undertakings and those to which Member States grant exclusive rights are equally bound to the Treaty, in particular the Article 12 prohibition on nationality discrimination and competition law. However, Article 86(2) provides that 'services of general economic interest or [undertakings] having the character of a revenue-producing [State] monopoly' are subject to Treaty rules '... in so far as the application of such rules does not obstruct the performance ... of the particular tasks assigned to them'. This special treatment is not unqualified: 'The development of trade must not be affected ... contrary to the interests of the Community.' The prohibition is directly effective in the sense that where the state infringes some directly effective Treaty rule, a private individual can rely on the direct effect of that rule. The Treaty of Amsterdam introduced a new Article 16 into the EC Treaty. This new Article reflected Member States' anxieties to ensure that certain state actions in the market would receive special dispensation when performed in the context of 'Services of General Economic Interest' (hereafter referred to as 'SGEIs'). This despite the modern trend towards the application of competition law even in fields where the state is a participant in economic activity. What constitutes 'services of a general economic interest' is ultimately a Community concept defined in a number of ECJ Judgments,[531] but involves the use of an 'undertaking' within its meaning under competition law as an instrument of economic, fiscal[532] or social[533] policy. Article 86(2) requires that the State 'entrusts' undertakings with that public serviced obligation. This must be a positive obligation on the undertaking.[534] The term has also been defined by the Commission as '... market services which the Member States or the Community subject to specific public service obligations ... such as transport networks, energy and communication'.[535] Common features of SGEIs include that the State imposes some requirements on the service provider even if it does not control the provider by way of direct ownership,[536] by way of for example '... universal

---

[529] Case 311/85 *Van Vlaamse* [1987] *ECR* 3801; Case 267/86 *Van Eycke* v. *ASPA* [1988] *ECR* 4769, Para. 16; Case 13/77 *GB-INNO-BM* [1977] *ECR* 2115.

[530] Case C-2/91 *Meng* [1993] *ECR* I-5751.

[531] Case 10/71 *Muller* [1971] *ECR* 723 Paras. 14-15.

[532] Case C-202/88 *Telecommunications equipment* [1991] *ECR* I-1223 Para. 12.

[533] Case C-67/96 *Albany International* [1999] *ECR* I-5751 Paras. 103-105.

[534] Case C-203/06 *Dusseldorp* [1998] *ECR* I-4075 Opinion of Advocate General Jacobs point 103.

[535] Commission of the European Communities, Commission Communication on Services of General Economic Interest *OJ* 2001 C 17/4 Annex II.

[536] Commission of the European Communities (2004c), *White Paper on Services of General Economic Interest* COM(2004) 374 Final.

service, continuity, service quality, affordability ..., user and consumer protection requirements'.[537]

5.11.3. Defining 'Services of General Economic Interest'

Whether an activity constitutes a SGEI is determined by national courts on the basis of the Community rules,[538] as is that of whether the application of competition rules would obstruct the public task.[539] The question of whether the interests of the Community are adversely affected would appear to be a question for the Commission, but has as yet to be ruled upon by the ECJ. As Jones and Sufrin observe, the cases in which the ECJ considers the meaning of 'services of general economic interest' usually also involve consideration of whether non-compliance with Treaty rules is essential to the fulfilment of those tasks. Since *Corbeau*, the ECJ has recognised that Article 86(2) contains in essence a proportionality requirement, and that the key question in that respect is '... the extent to which a restriction on competition or even the exclusion of all competition from other economic operators is necessary in order to allow the holder of the exclusive right to perform its task of general interest ... [under] economically acceptable conditions'.[540] In the *Altmark* judgment, the ECJ noted that compensation for the provision of services of general economic interest does not constitute State Aid.[541] This required the consideration of four criteria. The public service obligation must be clearly defined. The parameters for the compensation must be objective, transparent, and established in advance. Compensation should not exceed the costs of providing the public service and a reasonable profit. Finally, the compensation must be determined either through a public procurement process or on the basis of the costs of a typical well-run company. The Commission has in 2005 adopted a Decision which specified the relationship between state aid rules and services of general economic interest for the purposes of Article 86(2), largely following these *Altmark* criteria.[542]

5.11.4. Sport as a 'Service of General Economic Interest'

The Independent European Sport Review has argued that sports federations fulfil tasks of relevant general economic interest.[543] This argument has not been forcefully promoted by the sports governing bodies themselves. Establishing a particular activ-

---

[537] Commission of the European Communities, *Green Paper on Services of General Economic Interest*, COM(2003) 270, Para. 49.

[538] Case 127/73 *BRT* v. *SABAM* [1974] *ECR* 313.

[539] Case C-260/89 *ERT/DEP* [1991] *ECR* I-29 Para. 34.

[540] Case C-320/91 *Corbeau* [1993] *ECR* I-2533 Para. 16.

[541] Case C-280/00 *Altmark* [2003] *ECR* I-7747.

[542] Commission Decision 2005/842/EC of 28 November 2005 on the application of Art. 86(2) of the EC Treaty to State aid in the form of public service compensation granted to certain undertakings entrusted with the operation of services of general economic interest.

[543] J. Arnaut, *Independent European Sport Review* (2006), see at <www.independentfootballreview. com>, pp. 109-111.

ity as a 'service of general economic interest' requires more than an interested private organisation simply attaching that label to it. Article 86(2) requires that the State expressly imposes a specific legal obligation for that particular undertaking to perform a defined public service. This type of intervention runs counter to sports governing bodies' pleas for greater autonomy and self-regulation. Achieving SGEI status is not therefore likely to provide benefits that outweigh the inevitable state supervision which it requires. The case has also as yet not been articulated why sports federations provide public services that could not be provided by the market in the absence of state intervention or precisely what those services might constitute. In some Member States, sport is identified as a constitutional right which the state would therefore be required to provide were the sports governing bodies to cease providing it. This does not, however, amount to the 'entrusting' of a specific undertaking with its provision as per Article 86(2).

Even given acceptance by the Member State of SGEI status, the *Altmark* criteria would have to be satisfied for aid not to constitute state aid contrary to the Treaty. In the absence of constitutional entitlements, some public service obligations could probably also be identified in sport, for example obligations related to training, education or to the promotion of public health. However, it is not a foregone conclusion funding for that any such obligations, even if adequately defined, fulfil the other three *Altmark* criteria. The parameters for the compensation must be objective, transparent, and established in advance. Since compensation should not exceed the costs of providing the public service and a reasonable profit, it is clear that some relationship between the service and the relevant compensation must also be demonstrated. Potentially most difficult is the requirement that compensation must be determined either through a public procurement process or on the basis of the costs of a typical well-run company. In principle, it is difficult to accept that any given sport is better placed than another to for example promote public health through involving citizens.

Finally, as discussed above, the Commission's preference is for competition to exist even in fields identified as constituting SGEIs. Only where competition would seriously undermine the possibility of fulfilling that objective, could the prospect of a limitation on competition law even be considered. If the objective of the exercise for sports governing bodies is to exclude competition provisions on this basis, they may find that even where national governments designate aspects of sport as SGEIs, competition in these fields will be the policy objective of the Commission. It is noteworthy that the White Paper package contains no discussion of the prospect of sport as a Service of General Economic Interest.

5.11.5. State aid

Aid granted by state resources '... in any form whatsoever which distorts or threatens to distort competition by favouring certain undertakings or the production of certain goods ...' is prohibited if that aid affects trade between Member States.[544] Certain types of state aid are expressly permitted under Article 87(2): aid granted directly

---

[544] Art. 87(1) EC Treaty.

to individual consumers, disaster assistance, and structural aid to the former German Democratic Republic. Article 87(3) also provides a list of aids which may be considered compatible, but which are not *a priori* deemed compatible: regional aid to deprived areas, aid to 'an important project of Common European interest', aid to 'remedy a serious disturbance in the economy of a Member State', 'facilitate the development of certain economic activities' or areas, and aid promoting in cultural heritage. All of these require the Article 87(3)(e) empowers the Council to add to this list by way of Council decisions, but no such decision in relation to sport has as yet been made. Nevertheless, the existing criteria and block exemptions for state aid have facilitated a soft approach to sporting issues, illustrated by the consideration of sporting questions in the Commission decision on state aid related to training and its formal letter issuing guidance on the infrastructure aid issues relevant to stadia.[545] Commission notices may be persuasive, but will not bind national authorities. However, national courts are prohibited from taking decisions contrary to a Commission decision.[546] Therefore a decision on the compatibility of a practice with competition law is more satisfactory. There is also a clear separation between private market activity, governed by competition law, and state action in discharging its duties, which has been deemed to fall outside the scope of competition law and therefore also of the state aid rules.[547] Where the state competes with private markets but demonstrates solidarity through subsidization, such as in the fields of health care services, the Court has considered this proof of its non-economic nature. Similar arguments might be raised in relation to sport.[548]

5.11.6. Block exemptions for state aid

A number of block exemptions apply to state aid in all sectors, and as such could apply to state aids given to sport. The most important is the *de minimis* block exemption, granted to aid of up to EUR 200,000 over any three-year fiscal period.[549] Under Article 2(1) of the Regulation, such aid is deemed not to constitute aid within the Meaning of Article 87(1) and therefore is not subject to the notification requirement. Aid to small and medium-sized enterprises is until June 30, 2008 governed by the 2001 Block Exemption Regulation, after which time the Commission hopes to have in place a replacement.[550] Under these rules, states may assist SMEs in areas where

---

[545] Commission of the European Communities, *Commission staff working document. The EU and Sport: Background and Context*, SEC (2007) 935, p. 28.

[546] Art. 16 Regulation 1/2003.

[547] Case C-364/92 *Eurocontrol* [1994] *ECR* I-43 (air traffic control); Case C-343/95 *Diego Cali* [1997] *ECR* I-1547 (pollution control surveillance).

[548] Joined cases C-159/91 and C-160/91 *Poucet and Pistre* [1993] *ECR* I-637 Paras. 15 and 18. See for example Case C-218/00 *INAIL* [2002] *ECR* I-691.

[549] Commission Regulation (EC) No. 1998/2006 of 15 December 2006 on the application of Arts. 87 and 88 of the Treaty to *de minimis* aid. This is applicable between 1 January 2007 until 31 December 2013.

[550] Commission Regulation (EC) No. 1976/2006 of 20 December 2006 amending Regulations (EC) No. 2204/2002, (EC) No. 70/2001 and (EC) No. 68/2001 as regards the extension of the periods of application.

they are typically under-resourced due to their size, such as research and development, or infrastructure projects. State aid may also be granted to facilitate training,[551] the generation of employment,[552] or assist deprived regions under the terms of those Regulations, which tend to offer preferential treatment to SMEs and projects involving a concurrence of Community objectives, for example the employment or training of disadvantaged workers.[553] The Commission has also adopted a number of general positions in relation to aid targeted at legitimate purposes, generally in the form of Commission communications. For example, rescue and restructuring aid is interpreted by the Commission in some cases to fall within Article 87(3)(c).[554] Sector-specific treatment exists in the context of broadcasting, audiovisual works, steel, shipbuilding, and certain universal services such as telecommunications and postal services. Although no sport-specific rules exist as yet, it is open to the Commission to develop informal guidelines based on particular readings of the Treaty provisions, for example analogous to those on rescue and restructuring aid.

5.11.7. State aid and sport

State aid and other Member State interference with markets is only prohibited where there is a market, namely economic activity. The Commission White Paper Package suggests that amateur clubs '... are generally not considered as undertakings within the meaning of Article 87(1) EC, to the extent that they do not pursue economic activities'.[555] This raises the very topical question of the extent to which it is possible to police the cross-subsidization of leagues within the European model. It will be recalled that the European model is dependent on the interplay between amateur and professional levels, and that the amateur level tends to graduate its most proficient players to higher professional leagues. Where these are locally connected, as for example under the regime envisaged by UEFA's home-grown player rules, questions of cross-subsidy between amateur activity supported by the state and the economic practice of sport may arise. Professional clubs, on the other hand, are recognised as engaged in economic activities, and the White Paper package observes that '... there is no compelling argument why they should be exempted from the State aid rules'.[556] The question of appreciability may also arise, and the Commission has noted in its decisional practice that aid for local infrastructure is rarely likely to carry inter-state implications.[557]

---

[551] Commission Regulation No. 68/2001 of 12 January 2001 on the application of Arts. 87 and 88 of the EC Treaty to training aid *OJ* L 10, 13.01.2001, pp. 20-29.

[552] Commission Regulation No. 2204/2002 of 12 December 2002 on the application of Arts. 87 and 88 of the EC Treaty to State aid for employment.

[553] Commission Regulation (EC) No. 1628/2006 of 24 October 2006 on the application of Arts. 87 and 88 of the Treaty to national regional investment aid.

[554] Communication from the Commission–Community guidelines on State aid for rescuing and restructuring firms in difficulty Paras. 19 and 20.

[555] Commission of the European Communities, *Commission staff working document. The EU and Sport: Background and Context*, SEC (2007) 935, p. 29.

[556] Id.

[557] SG (2001) D/ 285046 *Local Swimming Pools* Letter of 12.01.2001 from Commissioner Monti.

5.11.8. Commission practice in state aid

When a sporting club is performing a function recognised as a state function under the EC Treaty, the Commission does not intervene. This was the case in relation to French aid to sports clubs that had established approved youth centres. The work was considered to fall within the Member States' competence in the field of education, and therefore outside Community law.[558] Conversely, Italian aid given to clubs in the form of tax exemptions did not relate to the fulfilment of state functions and was prohibited.[559] The Commission considers that most state aids that assist with the development of local infrastructure are unlikely to have an effect on trade between Member States and therefore escape the application of Community law.[560] It also considers that so long as assistance for sporting facilities is concerned with a project that the market would not be able to provide because of the risks or size of the project, and that facility does not benefit any particular firm, Community state aid rules will not prohibit aid. This calls into question whether Member States may provide aid to facilities that are designed to benefit, even if not exclusively, a particular firm such as a football club, particularly if they do not pay for the privileges at market rates. Nevertheless, as with competition policy under Articles 81 and 82, the Commission has demonstrated its capacity to recognise the specificities of sport without recourse to a sectoral exemption where the purpose of the special consideration is not linked to economic, anti-competitive motives.

5.12. COMMISSION ENFORCEMENT PRACTICE

5.12.1. Permissible rules

The EC law dossier in the Commission White Paper package provides a comprehensive coverage of Commission practice in enforcing competition law.[561] The Commission Staff Working Document 'The EU And Sport: Background and Context' accompanying the White Paper on Sport provides a digest of the existing case law and decision-making practice on the Community level, and identifies sporting rules which in the Commission's view are unlikely to infringe Articles 81(1) and 82 EC. Non-discriminatory rules concerning the participation of athletes in sporting competitions were considered in *Deliège* to be 'inherent' in the organisation of those events.[562] So, too, is the organisation of sport on a territorial basis, namely the Home and Away rule which the Commission in its *Mouscron* Decision considered 'was not called into

---

[558] SG (2001) D/ 288165 *French Subsidies for Youth Training* N118/00, 24.5.2001. IP/01/599.

[559] *Measures in favour of sports clubs in Italy* Commission Decision of 22 June 2006, *OJ* 2006 L/353.

[560] SG (2001) D/ 285046 *Local Swimming Pools* Letter of 12.01.2001 from Commissioner Monti.

[561] Commission of the European Communities, *Commission staff working document. The EU and Sport: Background and Context*, SEC (2007) 935.

[562] *Deliège* Paras. 62, 64 and 69.

question by Community law'.[563] In the White Paper package, the Commission considered it

> 'likely that the rule would not constitute a violation of Article 82 EC ... (assuming that the rule restricts competition) since the rule pursues a legitimate objective (equality of chances in club competitions), possible restrictions caused by the rule are inherent in the organisation of club competitions and the rule is not disproportionate'.[564]

Rules on multiple club ownership were posited to be 'inherent' under the *Wouters* criteria, which the Commission applied in the *ENIC* case with that effect,[565] as were transfer deadlines. Nationality rules for national teams, acknowledged since *Walrave* as purely sporting rules outside of the scope of the Article 39 and 49 prohibitions, are considered 'likely [to] meet the *Meca-Medina* test for Articles 81 and 82 as it pursued a legitimate objective for which it was inherent'.[566] Anti-doping rules were recognised in *Meca-Medina* as inherent rules, the restrictive effects of which did not constitute restrictions within the meaning of Article 81(1). Although press releases in particular herald a Commission application of the 'specificities of sport', the reasoning in published decisions discussed in detail in the following chapters, demonstrates that this is often done within the existing framework of competition law, rather than through the deployment of an identifiable 'sporting exception'.

5.12.2. **Prohibited rules and remaining uncertainties**

The White Paper background document also highlights a number of undecided legal issues for which Commission investigations are open or cases pending before the ECJ, and those which the Commission considered suspect from the point of view of competition law. 'Licensing requirements, such as rules on financial management and financial stability ... and the availability of proper and safe sport facilities ... would have to be reviewed very carefully'[567] in view of the diversity of licensing requirements, indicative that some are disproportionate, and their frequent inclusion of rules that clearly interfere with economic aspects relevant to sport. So, too, would transfer rules in the context of valid contracts, which were investigated by the Commission in the context of FIFA's and UEFA's transfer regulations but settled in 2002 on the basis of guarantees on the support of young players' training, specified transfer periods, minimum/maximum durations for contracts and specified penalties

---

[563] Case 36.851, *Mouscron/Home and away rule*, unpublished decision. Press release: IP/99/965.

[564] Commission of the European Communities, *Commission staff working document. The EU and Sport: Background and Context*, SEC (2007) 935, p. 71.

[565] Case COMP/37 806, *ENIC/UEFA*, OJ 2001 C/169, Commission Decision of 13 June 2001 Paras. 31 et seq.

[566] Commission of the European Communities, *Commission staff working document. The EU and Sport: Background and Context*, SEC (2007) 935, p. 72.

[567] Id.

for breaches, and the abolition of jurisdiction ouster clauses.[568] Rules which shield sports associations from competition such as the commercial arrangements tied into the regulatory aspects of the Fédération Internationale de l'Automobile (FIA),[569] the ouster of the jurisdiction of ordinary courts in favour of mandatory arbitration or organs of the governing body,[570] nationality clauses in club sports[571] and transfer rules for expired contracts,[572] are all considered likely to constitute a violation of Articles 81 and/or 82. The regulation of players' agents was considered problematic by the CFI in *Piau*, which nevertheless recognised that in the absence of national statutory authority some regulation by professional bodies could be considered not to have anti-competitive effects under Article 81(1) and could thus be permissible where they did not have as their object the restriction of competition.[573] 'Inherent' rules listed by the commission include rules of the game, selection rules for competitions, home and away rules, multiple ownership rules, national team composition, anti-doping, and transfer window rules. Less likely to be 'inherent' but possibly justifiable under Article 81(3) or not an abuse for similar reasons are rules protecting sports associations from competition, ouster of jurisdiction rules, nationality rules for club sports, transfer rules other than windows, and rules regulating professional economic activities connected with sport.[574] Currently undecided questions highlighted by the White Paper but not commented upon therein include FIFA's player release rules, challenged in *Charleroi/Oulmers*, UEFA's home-grown players' rules, and salary caps in professional sports.[575]

5.12.3. Divergences between Commission practice and ECJ judgments

Competition law is, as has been demonstrated, a tool that can be employed in a number of contradictory ways and yet within the boundaries of the law itself. Given the subjective elements in relevant tests, many questions of fact exist upon which experts may disagree. The application of Community law requires consideration of market definition, how competitions must be structured in order to create markets, the relationship between consumer welfare, undistorted competition and other Treaty aims, and the appreciable impact on trade between Member States that is sufficient to bring an activity within the scope of Community competition law. When the Commission issues its decisions in competition investigations, it has considerable scope to employ these malleable definitions to the ends which it wishes to pursue. It could be argued

---

[568] Commission Press Release IP/02/824 of 5 June 2002.

[569] Commission Press Release IP/99/434 of 30 June 1999; Commission press release re: the settlement IP/01/1523 of 30 October 2001.

[570] Commission Press Release IP/02/284 of 6 June 2002.

[571] *Bosman*, although not decided on this point, is referred to on p. 74.

[572] *Bosman*.

[573] Case C-171/05P *Piau* [2006] *ECR* I-37.

[574] Commission of the European Communities, *Commission staff working document. The EU and Sport: Background and Context*, SEC (2007) 935, p. 77.

[575] Case C-243/06 *Charleroi/Oulmers, OJ* C 212, 2 September 2006, p. 11.

that the Commission has afforded sports governing bodies considerable autonomy at the expense of the application of strict economic tests and that it tends to recognise the precedence of sporting considerations linked to other Treaty objectives over undistorted competition within the meaning of competition law. The legal form of its policy has in the past emphasised the use of soft law instruments.[576] The Commission's approach to sports policy enables it, within the boundaries of competition law, to issue decisions rejecting complaints or approving practices that may not necessarily fit comfortably with orthodox notions of the purposes of competition law, namely the pursuit of economic efficiency and the maximisation of consumer welfare. It has also recognised the problems caused by legal uncertainty in its decisional practice on penalties, and has in the past imposed insubstantial penalties in such cases. Finally, the Commission does not always exercise its discretion within the bounds of the law. When it does not do so, interested parties may be able to appeal its decisions. The seminal example of this is *Bosman*, where the Commission had collaborated with sports governing bodies to draw up a rule that the Court of Justice in due course declared incompatible with the freedom of movement for workers, rebuking the Commission for its complicity in drawing up the disputed 3+2 rule.

5.13. CONCLUSIONS

5.13.1. Sport fits into the ordinary framework

EC competition law includes many qualitative criteria that are subject to some degree of subjective judgment. As such, it is a general tool of regulation but difficult to examine with a great degree of legal certainty when such criteria, particularly those outside the scope of what might conventionally be considered economic efficiency, invade the otherwise analytically clear provisions of the Treaty in Articles 81 and 82. The crucial questions in terms of the practical application of EC competition provisions are whether an area attracts regulatory attention and whether as a result the regulators consider that either the interests of the single market or consumers are infringed by the actions of undertakings. How this is done may vary on a case-by-case basis partly because of asymmetries in the scope of legal instruments, but also by the adjudicators' appreciation of variables such as market definition. In terms of satisfying the threshold of a notionally restrictive anti-competitive effect, there is often no need to show that unlawful action had any factual consequences. An agreement with an unfulfilled object of restricting competition and an abusive act that failed in its desired effects are both capable of leading to penalties. The Court has historically not considered partitioning the single market an acceptable objective, and in the context of competition law nationality discrimination is 'always a heinous offence'.[577] However, in its case law the ECJ has developed a legal distinction between a restrictive effect and a

---

[576] R. Parrish, *Sports Law and Policy in the European Union* (Manchester, Manchester University Press 2003) pp. 154-155.

[577] J. Mash, 'Is There an EU "Sporting Exception"', 13(2) *Sport and the Law Journal* (2005) p. 25.

restrictive object under Article 81. Restrictive objects are by definition incapable of forming justifications with reference to non-competition grounds. Restrictive effects that are intrinsic to the pursuit of a legitimate policy aim have not been deemed contrary to EC competition law.

5.13.2. Settlements cause uncertainty

After *Meca-Medina* it can be said that in relation to sport, this is not because sporting rules are without economic impacts, but because legitimate regulatory objectives requiring proportionate sporting rules are not deemed contrary to EC competition rules even when they have economic impacts. Mash has suggested that a reason for the survival and expansion of the notional 'sporting exception' before the *Meca-Medina* judgment was linked to the lack of ECJ jurisprudence 'caused to a large degree by the Commission's tendency to close investigations on the basis of an informal settlement, thereby precluding an appeal'.[578] Where governing bodies choose to informally settle cases rather than allow the Commission and ECJ to consider their merits, they are partly responsible for the resulting lack of formal decisional practice, and thus of the lack of legal certainty for which they call. The seminal example of this was the *Balog* case,[579] which was settled days before the Advocate General's opinion was due. Van Bogaert suggested that this was at least in part to protect the 2001 transfer rules settlement subsequently agreed with the Commission.[580]

5.13.3. EU action increases coherency

Many of the exceptions to market-liberalising rules require some consideration of common interest or the extent to which these rules hinder the aims of the common market. If sporting organisations are entitled to apply those rules for whatever reason, it seems courageous to also delegate to them on the Community level powers to make those determinations of whether their actions or rules hinder the aims of the common market. National courts relying on ECJ jurisprudence may legitimately take different views than the Commission, which relies on its notices and past practice. No study exists as yet of this in the context of economic sporting activity. The 'sporting exception' has an interesting structural dimension relevant to the division of regulatory competences between Member States and the Community. If a rule falls outside the scope of the Treaty, this leaves Member States free in principle to legislate as they wish so long as their rules do not breach other provisions of the Treaty. On the other hand, if a sporting activity falls within the area of competition law, then national rules may be more stringent only where they regulate abuses of dominant undertakings. Agreements, decisions and concerted practices that come within Community compe-

---

[578] A. Jones and B. Sufrin, *EC Competition Law: Text, Cases and Materials*, 2nd edn. (Oxford, Oxford University Press 2004) p. 520.

[579] Case C-264/98 *Balog*, reference removed from the register, 2 April 2001.

[580] S. Van den Bogaert, Practical Regulation of the Mobility of Sportsmen in the EU Post Bosman (The Hague, Kluwer 2005) p. 107.

tition law but which for reasons linked to the specific characteristics of sport do not infringe the Treaty may not be more restrictively controlled by national policies. As a result, if the Commission is inclined to view sporting practices favourably, it may be in the interests of undertakings to argue that rules or practices fall within the Treaty but are in fact compatible with it, rather than be subject to the vagaries of diverse national regulatory systems.

5.13.4. Typology of justification

In conclusion, there are a number of legal means with which sport can avoid conflicts with EC competition law. After *Meca-Medina*, it is clear that a *Walrave*-style broad sporting exception does not exist within the context of competition law. However, restrictive arrangements that pursue recognised objectives and are proportionate may not fall within the notion of what constitutes a 'restriction' under Article 81(1), and similarly may not constitute 'abuse' when found in the context of a practice by an undertaking in a dominant position. Sporting considerations outside Article 81(3) such as social factors and financial solidarity may constitute grounds for such a finding. A prima facie restriction on competition may be justified where it satisfies the Article 81(3) conditions. While this process may involve some legal uncertainty in so far as its application by national bodies is concerned, block exemption regulations will protect small market actors without significant market power. Those bodies charged with the enforcement of competition rules can also resort to broad market definitions to ensure, where desirable, that even significant market actors are not deemed to infringe competition rules. *Meca-Medina* cannot, however, be considered to have any impact on the classification of discriminatory rules in competition law. The true test of the Court's attitude towards nationality discrimination in the context of sport and competition law will come when, unlike on the facts of *Meca-Medina*, the Court is unable to avoid basing its judgment on the merits of that question.

Chapter 6
Sports Broadcasting in Community Law

The sale and purchase of broadcasting rights for sporting events has traditionally been negotiated between cartels. On the supply side, the governing bodies of sport such as FIFA, UEFA and National Associations have co-ordinated their activities and bundled rights together in order to establish a single point of sale. On the demand side, powerful cartels such as the European Broadcasting Union (EBU) acquired market strength through their collective purchasing arrangements. Similarly, in the UK the market for football rights was structured around two cartels, the Football League on the supply side and the BBC/ITV duopoly on the demand side. The BBC and ITV 'acted collusively' in order to act as the sole purchaser of sports rights thus deflating their value.[581] The lack of demand side competition, and the lack of platform space, restricted the value of rights. Live transmission of English league football began in 1983 when the BBC and ITV televised 20 live matches over two seasons at a cost of GBP 5.2 million.[582] A lack of investment in the game in the 1980's and the ongoing problem of public disorder at football matches further suppressed the value of rights. The League's policy of resisting wide television coverage for fear of the effect on stadium attendance also contributed to the relative low value. By 2007, the three year contract to broadcast live top flight English football until 2010 was valued at GBP 1.7 billion.

6.1. PRICING BROADCASTING RIGHTS

Two factors account for this development in the value of broadcasting rights. First, whilst the cartelisation of sports organisers remained strong, the broadcasting sector witnessed a decartelisation and this affected the dynamics of the market for sports rights.[583] At the beginning of the 1980's Collins noted that there were just four commercial television broadcasters in Europe.[584] Of critical importance was the emergence of cable and satellite broadcasting in the late 1980's, supported by de-regulatory media policies at national and EU level. Their presence heightened competition and expanded platform space. For example, the UK market was transformed by the emer-

---

[581] M. Cave and R. Crandall, 'Sports Rights and the Broadcast Industry', 111 *Economic Journal* (February 2001) F15.

[582] P. Massey, 'Are Sports Cartels Different? An Analysis of EU Commission Decisions Concerning the Collective Selling Arrangements for Football Broadcasting Rights', 30(1) *World Competition* (2007) p. 88.

[583] F. Bolotny and J-F. Bourg, 'The Demand for Media Coverage', in W. Andreff and S. Szymanski, *Handbook on the Economics of Sport* (Cheltenham, Edward Elgar 2006).

[584] R. Collins, *Broadcasting and Audio-Visual Policy in the European Single Market* (London, John Libby 1994) p. 146.

gence of British Sky Broadcasting (BSkyB), a company founded in 1990 following the merger of British Satellite Broadcasting and Sky Television. This added a competitor in the market for rights and their business model was based on the acquisition of football rights as a lead offering for their pay-TV services. Their presence led to the BBC and ITV cartel being dismantled as ITV pursued a policy of heading off their threat by securing the sole rights for the 1988 league season at a cost of GBP 44 million over four years. A similar pattern emerged across Europe with the rise of private networks upsetting traditional public service models of market organisation and undermining the EBU's market position. The value of rights continued to rise as digital technology took hold throughout the 1990's. Consumers are now able to follow sport on a much wider range of platforms including digital, internet and mobile phone and the rights holders continue to take advantage of a competitive market. Second, a more competitive market offered the leading English football clubs the opportunity to maximise revenue from rights.

6.1.1. Impediments to commercialisation

Two major obstacles impeded their more commercially aggressive vision. First, the football product was weak, suffering from a lack of investment, poor facilities and a serious public order problem. Second, the leading clubs were part of the Football League who ran football at all levels in England. A one member-one-vote constitution operated and all 92 members stood to benefit from a rise in the value of rights. The solution was for a re-branding of football and this required the old first division clubs to resign from the Football League and establish the Premier League in 1992. BSkyB acquired the rights to the new Premier League for 5 seasons at a cost of GBP 191.5 million, the revenues being shared between the 22 founding members, and not the entire Football League.[585] The contract ultimately secured the financial viability of both parties. It allowed the league and clubs to invest in the product thus making it more attractive and it attracted subscribers for BSkyB. The current three year contract from 2007 is valued at GBP 1.7 billion, although for the first time since the creation of the Premier League, BSkyB have lost their monopoly over the broadcasting of live games. The rights to major international events have witnessed similar increases. The European Broadcasting Union paid USD 240 million to acquire the rights to the 1990, 1994 and 1998 Football World Cups. The rights to the 2002, 2006 and 2010 events were purchased by the Kirch Group at a cost of USD 2.36 billion, a 900% increase.[586]

---

[585] P. Massey, 'Are Sports Cartels Different? An Analysis of EU Commission Decisions Concerning the Collective Selling Arrangements for Football Broadcasting Rights', 30(1) *World Competition* (2007) p. 88.

[586] T. Hoehn and D. Lancefield, 'Broadcasting and Sport', 19(4) *Oxford Review of Economic Policy* (2003) p. 555.

6.1.2. Consequences of broadcast rights pricing

A number of consequences have flowed from the commercialisation of sport. First, the business models of the sports governing bodies have changed to reflect modern commercial practice. The collective sale, on an exclusive basis, of rights became an industry norm and this method of sale has raised competition law concerns regarding market foreclosure to aspiring market entrants, the inability of individual commercial undertakings (clubs) to exploit rights and the impact on consumers. Possible justifications for *prima facie* restrictive commercial practices include the need to maintain competitive balance in sport as collective selling raises the value of rights and revenues are shared between league members. Thus the language of the specificity of sport still appears capable of expression in the context of very significant commercial transactions. Yet as Bolotny and Bourg argue, market reversal may be in process. Sport may be experiencing de-cartelisation as clubs, acting as powerful economic undertakings, explore strategies to exploit their own rights. Equally, the broadcasting sector may be experiencing a re-cartelisation following the mergers of cable and satellite networks.[587] Competition law must therefore be cognisant of these wider developments when considering what weight to attach to sports specificity arguments in relation to the manner in which rights are sold.

Second, commercialisation has placed a strain on the business models of the public service broadcasters. Public service broadcasters have been individually unable to compete with pay-TV operators in the market for rights and have instead relied on the joint acquisition arrangements of the European Broadcasting Union. Again, this raises competition law concerns. Whilst collective purchasing agreements are not necessarily incompatible with EC law *per se*, membership rules and sub-licensing arrangements have been subject to legal challenge, the outcome of which is discussed below. Third, with live sport accounting for an ever increasing percentage of television schedules, governing bodies have also needed to manage the balance between their commercial and regulatory functions. UEFA has introduced 'blocking rules' to ensure live television broadcasts of football matches do not conflict with stadium attendance and grassroots participation in the sport. Yet broadcasters complain that this interferes with their scheduling. The chapter examines the question of whether restrictions in the supply of services can be justified on these sporting grounds. Fourth, the drift towards pay-TV also has implications for consumers of sport. Sport, it is contended, plays an important social role and that the public has a right to information. Consequently, the Community has enacted the Television Without Frontiers Directive which enables Member States to enact domestic legislation guaranteeing the public has access to major events on free-to-air television. Within the framework of the Audiovisual Media Services Directive, the Community is also proposing to establish a right to short reporting for news items of major importance. Here we see specificity of sport arguments justifying greater Community intervention in the activities of the

---

[587] F. Bolotny and J-F. Bourg, 'The Demand for Media Coverage', in W. Andreff and S. Szymanski, *Handbook on the Economics of Sport* (Cheltenham, Edward Elgar 2006) pp. 126-127.

sports governing bodies, a reversal of the traditional arguments in which specificity arguments are used to justify the immunisation of sport from Community law. Each of the above four case studies are explored in turn.

6.2.   COLLECTIVE SELLING AND EXCLUSIVITY

Collective selling and the exclusive licensing of rights on a territorial basis are established commercial practices in the European sports sector. Collective selling refers to a requirement that clubs, often the owners of the rights, cede the broadcasting rights to their home matches to the governing body. The governing body then sell these rights in joint (bundled) form on their behalf and often on an exclusive basis to a broadcaster or broadcasters. Participation in the league is often conditional on the acceptance of this practice.

6.2.1. **Exclusivity**

The principle of exclusivity, the practice of selling sports rights on a territorial basis to one broadcaster, appears prima facie restrictive of competition as it segments the market on national lines and forecloses the market to those unable to access the content. Nevertheless, territorial exclusivity is a reflection of the national nature of the sports market and it is a protection much sought after by rights holders and purchasers. For the rights holder, exclusivity protects the value of rights thus allowing governing bodies to fulfil a wealth redistributive function. For the purchasers, exclusivity maximises profitability and allows broadcasters to invest with greater confidence in innovative programming. Exclusivity may therefore benefit the internal organisation of sport at all levels whilst allowing consumers to benefit. In examining whether an exclusive agreement breaches Article 81, the Commission would examine the duration of the contract in relation to the length of time required for the buyer to recoup their investment and the effect of the agreement on the possible foreclosure of the market. This requires the Commission to define the relevant market in order to establish whether competitors have access to comparable rights and assess whether sublicensing could mitigate foreclosure concerns.

Territorial exclusivity is not objectionable in itself, provided that it is not created but exists as the result of pre-existing market conditions. In *Coditel*, the court sanctioned its use provided that artificial or unjustifiable barriers to trade were not erected.[588] One such unjustifiable barrier would be the granting of a long period of exclusivity for one broadcaster. In the *British Satellite Broadcasting (BSB)* case, the Commission sanctioned an exclusive five year agreement for what is now BSkyB to broadcast certain live English football matches between 1988 and 1993 to a subscription audience.[589] The Commission exempted the long agreement on the grounds that as a new operator embracing new technology, BSB needed a long-term contract to

---

[588] Case 262/81 *Coditel SA* v. *Ciné-Vog Films SA* [1982] *ECR* 3381.
[589] Case No. IV/33.245 *BBC, BSB and Football Association OJ* 1993 C 94.

establish its operations. However, as former Commissioner Van Miert announced in a speech on 'Sport and Competition' on 27 November 1997, 'looking back...the five year period approved by the Commission was probably too long because the broadcasting technique in question became established more rapidly than had been expected'. In the *KNVB* decision, the Commission did not sanction a seven year agreement between the Dutch Football Association and Sport 7, a Dutch television channel.[590] The Commission objected to the length of the exclusive contract and to a contractual renewal clause that would have privileged Sport 7 in the tendering procedure at the end of the term.

6.2.2. Collective selling: the benefits

Discussions on exclusivity cannot be divorced from those on the collective sale of broadcasting rights. In defence of collective selling, governing bodies such as UEFA make a number of claims. First, collective selling allows for a single point of sale and this facilitates the efficient exploitation of the rights. Broadcasters' transaction costs are reduced as they only need to negotiate with one body rather than with football clubs throughout the 53 member associations of UEFA. Furthermore, collective selling avoids practical problems stemming from varying rights ownership structures across Europe. It also reduces uncertainty for broadcasters as clubs selling on an individual basis clearly cannot give assurances to broadcasters on how far they will progress in a competition. Broadcasters who have acquired a package of rights through a single point of sale have made efficiencies from this process and are more likely to invest in their programming, particularly as their risks are significantly reduced by collective sale. Collective selling also allows sponsors and suppliers to receive a uniform package for the duration of a tournament. This guarantees such undertakings exposure throughout the entire period of the event and allows them to structure their advertising budgets accordingly.[591] Collective selling also responds to consumer demand in that it allows broadcasters to provide live coverage and highlights to consumers of the entire tournament. In addition, collective selling removes the need for clubs to acquire expensive in-house expertise in order to exploit their rights on an individual basis. Finally, in some sports such as Formula 1 the individual sale of rights by teams is unworkable given the nature of the competition.

Second, collective selling purports to safeguard brand association by ensuring a uniform coverage, harmonised kick-off times, standardised 'dressing-up' of the stadium facilities, the use of standard logos and on-screen presentation and music. Brand protection is important as it ensures the value of the rights is maintained. Branding allows viewers to easily identify the product and broadcasters and sponsors find this attractive. In this connection, UEFA contend that collective selling leads to more objectivity in the media coverage of the Champions League in that the media reports the league as a whole rather than focussing on just one club to the detriment of other

---

[590] Case No. IV/36.033 *KNVB/Sport OJ* 1996 C 228
[591] Commission Decision 2003/778 *OJ* 2003 L291/25 Para. 140.

clubs and the Champions League brand. Public interest in the league is therefore maintained.[592]

The third benefit of collective selling is that it allows the governing bodies to maximise revenues from the rights. This is because those seeking to acquire the rights face a single supplier, the governing body. Given the importance of sports rights for attracting viewers, subscribers and advertisers, broadcasters are prepared to pay large sums to acquire these bundled rights. Maximising revenues in this way enhances the re-distributive capabilities of the governing bodies. This allows the governing body to ensure that all participants receive benefits from collective selling. Revenue sharing of this kind is defended on the grounds that it promotes horizontal competitive balance. The governing bodies argue that spectators, sponsors and broadcasters would show little interest in sport if the contest became predictable. If rights were to be exploited by individual clubs, the fear is that this would lead to a state of competitive imbalance as the value of the broadcasting rights for the larger clubs would easily outstrip that of the smaller clubs. This could undermine the viability of the league. In his opinion in *Bosman*, Advocate General Lenz recognised the need to maintain competitive balance in sport and suggested revenue sharing from the sale of collectively sold rights as an alternative to the disputed transfer system.[593] Revenue sharing also allows the governing bodies to redistribute revenues vertically so that lower leagues benefit and do not become too disconnected from the top flight. As the European model of sport is based on a system of promotion and relegation, a state of disconnection between leagues would undermine this philosophy by condemning to failure teams who secure promotion. Vertical revenue sharing also allows for the base of the European pyramid, amateur sport, to secure investment. As is discussed elsewhere in this book, sport at this level performs certain social and cultural functions, an argument used to justify the practice of central selling.

Finally, governing bodies argue that as they have invested the creativity and organisational effort into establishing the Championship product, they should be viewed as the owners or co-owners of the resultant rights.[594] As co-owners, clubs could not sell the rights without the co-owners consent. Furthermore, what is being offered, and what is attractive to broadcasters, is a league established by the governing body. As Bell, Lewis and Taylor point out, the Community is not competent to assess these ownership issues as this is a matter for national law.[595] In this connection, the authors identify varying national practice.

---

[592] Ibid. Para. 157.

[593] *Bosman*, Opinion of Advocate General Lenz, point 230.

[594] A. Bell, A. Lewis and J. Taylor, 'EC and UK Competition Rules and Sport', in A. Lewis and J. Taylor, *Sport: Law and Practice* (London, Butterworths Lexis Nexis 2003) p. 404.

[595] Ibid. pp. 405-406.

6.2.3. The European Commission's approach to central selling

The European Commission has investigated these practices and enquired into four key issues raised by central selling. The first of these is whether collective selling amounts to price fixing and whether the prevention of clubs from entering into individual agreements with broadcasters prevents, restricts or distorts competition within the single market. The second is whether collective selling affects competition between broadcasters by establishing a single source of supply thus reducing the number of available rights on offer and restricting consumer choice. This would impede the development of new technologies and the creation of a single market in broadcasting services. The third is whether the central marketing of broadcasting rights can qualify for an exemption under Article 81(3). The fourth is whether collective selling constitutes an abuse of a dominant position by the vendor. At the same time, the Commission has needed to be cognisant of wider debates within Community sports policy on the specificity of sport. For some, this has resulted in the Commission appreciating 'that there is a peculiar economic dynamic in sport that justifies a different, sui generis, application of the competition rules in the sports broadcasting context'.[596] The specificity of sport arguments and the Commission's general approach to the application of competition law to sport, particularly in relation to market definition, receive comprehensive attention in the previous chapter.

A number of these concerns were considered in the *UEFA Champions League* case.[597] UEFA notified their collective sales policy to the Commission in February 1999. In July 2001, the Commission issued a statement of objections relating to UEFA's policy of selling the Champions League rights on a collective and exclusive basis. In March 2002 UEFA submitted a revised selling policy based on an unbundling of rights presented in the form of a rights segmentation table for the exploitation of TV rights and other media rights including radio, internet, Universal Mobile Telecommunications System (UMTS) and physical media such as DVD, VHS and CD-ROM. Further amendments to the selling policy were made and the Commission exempted the agreement under Article 81(3) by concluding that the new collective selling regime improves production and distribution by creating a quality branded league focused product sold via a single point of sale which allows consumers to benefit. Collective selling, it concluded, is indispensable in terms of UEFA achieving these objectives and is unlikely to eliminate competition in respect of a substantial part of the media rights in question. The Commission was satisfied that the unbundling of the rights into packages should enhance the possibility for more broadcasters to acquire Champions League rights.

Collective selling was again at issue in the German *Bundesliga* case.[598] In a preliminary assessment, the Commission noted that the collective selling of the rights could restrict competition between the clubs and breach Article 81. The German

---

[596] Ibid. p. 400.
[597] Decision 2003/778 *OJ* 2003 L291/25.
[598] Decision 2005/396 *OJ* 2005 L134/46

Football League gave a number of commitments on its sales policy including the unbundling of the rights into packages which are offered in a transparent and non-discriminatory process with contracts limited to three years. The commitments also improved the accessibility of content for TV, radio and new media operators and enabled clubs to exploit some rights individually. The Commission found that these changes would promote innovation in broadcasting and safeguard against media concentration and as such the commitments were made legally binding by a Commission 'commitment' Decision, the first of its kind under the new procedures established by Regulation 1/2003. The decision stated that in light of the commitments given, there were no grounds for further action.

The Commission's approach to collective selling was further confirmed in the Football Association Premier League (FAPL) case.[599] Since the creation of the FAPL in 1992, the league has sold the rights on a collective basis exclusively to one broadcaster, BSkyB. The Commission's decision to exempt the five year 1993 agreement between the newly formed Premier League and BSkyB significantly strengthened BSkyB's monopoly of English sports rights (see above). After ten years of Premier League football, BSkyB had maintained its monopoly and the Commission revisited the issue. Following notification of the FAPL's selling arrangements, the Commission issued a 2002 statement of objections outlining potential incompatibilities between the collective selling arrangements and Article 81 EC.[600] In December 2003 the FAPL proposed a number of amendments to its selling policy known as the December 2003 commitments. These included increasing the number of matches available for live TV transmission, the sale of rights in packages, the terms of which would preclude one buyer acquiring all the packages, the separation of UK and Irish rights, easier access for mobile and internet rights, maximum contract length of three years, the sale of rights in a transparent and non-discriminatory tendering procedure and the ability of clubs to exploit unused or unexploited rights.[601] The commitments were strengthened further following their publication in a Commission Notice. Live rights would now be offered in six packages with no purchaser permitted to acquire all six. Additional commitments were given in relation to the availability of mobile rights and radio rights. The tendering process was also amended so that an open and competitive bidding process was initiated which is overseen by an independent Monitoring Trustee selected by the Commission. These commitments satisfied the Commission that its statement of objections had been satisfactorily addressed by the FAPL. Consequently, in 2006, the Commission closed its investigation.[602] The FAPL's commitments remain in force until June 2013. Commenting on the closure of the investigation, Competition Commissioner Neelie Kroes remarked, 'the solution we have reached will benefit football fans while allowing the Premier League to maintain its timetable for the sale of its rights'.[603] This assertion is questionable as for the 2004-2007 rights

---

[599] Decision C(2006)868. See also IP/06/356, 22 March 2006.

[600] IP/02/1951, 20 December 2002.

[601] IP/03/1748, 16 December 2003.

[602] Commission Decision C(2006)868. See also IP/06/356, 22 March 2006.

[603] IP/06/356, 22 March 2006, p. 1.

package, a single broadcaster (BSkyB) acquired four of the six packages with another pay-TV operator acquiring the other two.

6.2.4. Criticisms of the Commission's approach

In the *UEFA Champions League*, the German *Bundesliga* and the *FAPL* cases, the Commission has not condemned collective selling as such, but has insisted on ending exclusivity through an unbundling of rights so that a wider range of operators have the opportunity of acquiring rights. In this regard, the Commission's willingness to maintain the principle of collective selling has received critical attention. The Commission's insistence on unbundling with commitments on the wider accessibility of rights only partly addresses the issue of unexploited rights. Technological developments in broadcasting have not only enhanced competition for the acquisition of rights, but have also expanded platform space on which games can be broadcast. Unexploited rights are a consequence of collective selling and an issue not previously felt when cartels acted as both buyer and seller. In 2003 Harbord and Szymanski concluded that the lost viewership from the FA Premier League's collective selling arrangements was as much as 200 million over the year, equivalent to about nine matches per household per season, amounting to a welfare cost of approximately GBP 1 billion.[604] In an attempt to satisfy consumer demand, broadcasters have resorted to broadcasting games of secondary interest to fans such as friendly matches and matches from other national associations. From a consumer perspective, this is unsatisfactory as that demand could be met through greater unbundling or individual selling arrangements.[605] This would also have the result of lowering the subscription costs consumers must currently pay. As collective selling increases the value of rights, broadcasters' costs are passed on to consumers, and to advertisers who compete for air time during the screening of the matches.

Whilst the Commission has forced governing bodies to broaden the range of rights on offer, the governing bodies resist blanket availability in order to protect stadium attendance. The evidence on this is somewhat contradictory and is reviewed more fully below in the context of blocking rules. Reviewing the literature, Noll suggests that 'the effect of television on attendance at the same match is probably between small and non-existent, the effect on simultaneous matches at a lower quality level is negative and possibly large, and the effect on other simultaneous matches at the same quality is between slightly negative and zero'.[606] Nevertheless, if one were to accept that live coverage did negatively affect stadium attendance, under an individual selling system the vendor (the clubs) would need to form a judgment on how to balance these competing factors. Furthermore, dismantling collective selling arrangements

---

[604] D. Harbord and S. Szymanski, *Restricted View. The Rights and Wrongs of FA Premier League Broadcasting*, Report for the Consumers' Association (London 2003) p. 25.

[605] S. Parlasca, 'Collective Selling of Broadcast Rights in Team Sports', in W. Andreff and S. Szymanski, *Handbook on the Economics of Sport* (Cheltenham, Edward Elgar 2006) p. 722.

[606] R. Noll, 'Broadcasting and Team Sports', 54(3) *Scottish Journal of Political Economy* (2007) p. 411.

will expand the platforms on which sport is broadcast and this can expose a sport to a wider audience which would have a positive impact on the popularity of the sport. The US Supreme Court's prohibition of central selling in National Collegiate Athletics had such an effect.[607]

Maintaining collective selling, albeit with the conditions described above, has also been criticised on the grounds that it impedes market access to new and small broadcasters. Such broadcasters are unable to compete on price with larger undertakings. The acquisition of sports rights is an important commercial tool to establish broadcasters and a failure to acquire rights will hamper their growth and possibly contribute to media concentration in Europe. For Harbord and Szymanski, 'the source of BSkyB's market power lies in its stranglehold over the rights to broadcast key premium content such as Premier League football'.[608] Competitors including other Pay-TV operators, free-to-air broadcasters, internet and mobile phone operators will struggle to acquire rights under collective selling arrangements and regional broadcasters face the same impediments meaning that supporters of small to medium sized clubs with a strong regional following are denied the opportunity of following their team on television. Whilst the Commission has insisted that collective selling and exclusivity be de-coupled, in the FAPL case, this has simply resulted in the substitution of a duopoly for the existing monopoly.[609]

A central question concerning whether collective selling represents a justifiable restraint is its connection with revenue sharing and the maintenance of competitive balance in sport. Revenue sharing arrangements have received high level political support in the EU. For example, during the 2000 Nice European Council, the Heads of State and Government released a Declaration on the Specific Characteristics of Sport which read:

'[t]he sale of television broadcasting rights is one of the greatest sources of income today for certain sports. The European Council considered in Paragraph 15 of the Declaration that efforts to encourage the mutualisation of part of the revenue from such sales, at the appropriate levels, are beneficial to the principle of solidarity between all levels and areas of sport'.

This was endorsed by the Arnaut Report. Arnaut observed that 'there has been a significant decline in competitive balance' throughout some of Europe's leagues and that this could be remedied through greater revenue sharing based on collective selling.[610] Given the constitutional limits of Community action in sports policy, the Competition

[607] S. Parlasca, 'Collective Selling of Broadcast Rights in Team Sports', in W. Andreff and S. Szymanski, *Handbook on the Economics of Sport* (Cheltenham, Edward Elgar 2006) p. 725.

[608] D. Harbord and S. Szymanski, *Restricted View. The Rights and Wrongs of FA Premier League Broadcasting*, Report for the Consumers' Association (London 2003) p. 25.

[609] P. Massey, 'Are Sports Cartels Different? An Analysis of EU Commission Decisions Concerning the Collective Selling Arrangements for Football Broadcasting Rights', 30(1) *World Competition* (2007) p. 92.

[610] J. Arnaut, *Independent European Sport Review* (2006), see at <www.independentfootballreview.com>, p. 48.

DG has taken care to avoid reference to this policy guidance in its decisions. In the Champions League case, the Commission avoided entering the debate on whether collective selling promotes horizontal and vertical solidarity in sport. The case for exemption had already been made out on other grounds described and therefore the Commission did not need to decide upon this issue. Thus it has not yet been established in law that a connection exists between collective selling, solidarity and competitive balance.

Economists urge caution on making such a link and suggest that revenue sharing may in fact reinforce competitive imbalance. Parlasca argues that central selling strengthens the dominant position of the larger clubs as they are more likely to benefit from live coverage resulting in smaller clubs struggling to attract new supporters.[611] Szymanski and Késenne examined gate revenue sharing and discovered that competitive balance can be impaired as solidarity mechanisms reduce total investment in talent by teams in a league. They argue that '[t]his has important implications for competition authorities and legislators who have generally taken a permissive view of revenue sharing schemes on the grounds that they favour competitive balance'.[612] Szymanski also argues that 'even quite unbalanced matches, championships, and leagues can be attractive to consumers', and that the basis for arguing in favour of revenue sharing assumes that the supply of labour is fixed. In the USA, it is arguably axiomatic that all the best baseball or basketball players would prefer to play in the major leagues.[613] If the supply of talent is fixed, the acquisition of a talented player by one club results in one less player being available to others. In European football, the supply is not fixed with clubs being able to recruit globally.

Noll indicates that the actions of the governing bodies or leagues are not the best mechanism for correcting competitive imbalance as they face financial incentives to maintain the status quo.[614] Both national leagues and UEFA have a rational desire to maintain historical competitive imbalances as the clubs to which this applies to generate significant revenues for them. Furthermore, the larger clubs themselves resist greater revenue sharing and their increasing influence on the game, embodied in the G14 grouping, places pressure on the governing bodies not to extend revenue sharing further. Massey explores competitive balance in the FAPL and argues that collective selling by the FAPL cannot compensate for other factors which contribute to income disparities between clubs and which serve to undermine competitive balance.[615] Revenue from collective selling is not distributed evenly amongst participants with merit

---

[611] S. Parlasca, 'Collective Selling of Broadcast Rights in Team Sports', in W. Andreff and S. Szymanski, *Handbook on the Economics of Sport* (Cheltenham, Edward Elgar 2006) p. 723.

[612] S. Szymanski and S. Késenne, 'Competitive Balance and Gate Revenue Sharing in Team Sports', 52 *The Journal of Industrial Economics* (2004) p. 172.

[613] S. Szymanski, 'The Economic Design of Sporting Contests', 41 *Journal of Economic Literature* (2003) p. 1165.

[614] R. Noll, 'Broadcasting and Team Sports', 54(3) *Scottish Journal of Political Economy* (2007) p. 417.

[615] P. Massey, 'Are Sports Cartels Different? An Analysis of EU Commission Decisions Concerning the Collective Selling Arrangements for Football Broadcasting Rights', 30(1) *World Competition* (2007) p. 103.

based allocations being common throughout Europe. Furthermore, participation in European competitions such as the Champions League in football further compounds competitive imbalance as revenue disparities are increased. Therefore, even if a theoretical case for maintaining collective selling could be made out, current patterns of income redistribution appear to preclude a rebalancing of these disparities and alternative models of redistribution produce different effects.[616] The alternative to collective selling is for clubs to commercially exploit their own rights. Noll argues that the Arnaut assumption is flawed and that 'decentralization (sic) of television rights, because it gives historically weaker teams a relatively larger incremental incentive to improve team quality, can actually improve competitive balance'.[617] Parlasca argues that individual selling has much to offer smaller clubs as almost all home games would be commercially attractive to broadcasters.[618] Cave and Crandall argue that individual selling in the National Collegiate Athletic Association resulted in a sharp increase in the number of games broadcast in comparison to the previous collective selling arrangements, a large decline in the value of the rights per game, 'and an increase in competitive balance in college football.[619] Furthermore, the existence of individual selling in other leagues, such as in Italy, demonstrates that collective selling is not indispensable'.

Collective selling does offer smaller clubs the guarantee of revenue through solidarity payments but despite many assumptions to the contrary, it is far from certain that collective selling is indispensable in terms of maintaining competitive balance. Weatherill suggests that pleas for solidarity in sport are plausible and indeed rational, but solidarity mechanisms need not be located solely within the domain of collectively sold broadcasting rights.[620] A levy on individually sold rights or a levy in some other aspect of clubs activities could equally achieve solidarity goals. This could include a levy on compensation payments following a players' transfer or a levy on gate receipts although in the Restrictive Practices Court judgment in *FAPL/BSkyB* (see below) the court suggested that such alternatives would pose 'quite practical serious problems'.[621] Nevertheless, under an Article 81 analysis, the Commission would examine whether less restrictive means of achieving revenue sharing were available to the governing bodies. Alternative revenue sharing schemes operate successfully in US sports. The National Football League (NFL) operates a system whereby 40% of designated stadium income is paid to the visiting team and Major League baseball op-

---

[616] S. Szymanski, 'The Economic Design of Sporting Contests', 41 *Journal of Economic Literature* (2003).

[617] R. Noll, 'Broadcasting and Team Sports', 54(3) *Scottish Journal of Political Economy* (2007) p. 417.

[618] S. Parlasca, 'Collective Selling of Broadcast Rights in Team Sports', in W. Andreff and S. Szymanski, *Handbook on the Economics of Sport* (Cheltenham, Edward Elgar 2006) pp. 724-725.

[619] M. Cave and R. Crandall, 'Sports Rights and the Broadcast Industry', 111 *Economic Journal* (February 2001).

[620] S. Weatherill, 'The Sale of Rights to Broadcast Sporting Events under EC Law', 3-4 *International Sports Law Journal* (2006) p. 20.

[621] *Re the supply of services facilitating the broadcasting on television of Premier League football matches* [1999] UKCLR 258 Para. 158.

erates a luxury tax in which all teams contribute 34% of net local income to a sharing pool.[622] This raises the questions of whether such less restrictive means might satisfy solidarity concerns, and whether therefore the present arrangements are disproportionately restrictive.

Closely linked to the question of competitive balance is the need within sport for vertical solidarity mechanisms. Collective selling has been defended on the grounds that it allows for a redistribution of greater wealth to all levels, including amateur sport, and this fulfils important social and cultural functions that the state would need to provide in the absence of the governing bodies. Former Competition Commissioner Mario Monti suggested in his speech at the conference 'The Governance in Sport' in Brussels (26 February 2001) that 'arrangements that provide for a redistribution of financial resources to – for example – amateur levels of sport may be justified, if they are necessary to preserve sport's essential social and cultural benefits'. He added that when considering whether to exempt a practice, 'factors such as the possible link between the collective selling of rights and financial solidarity between clubs or between professional and amateur sport, as long as they are quantifiable and objectively defined, could be taken into consideration with all other relevant factors'. As a matter of law, Weatherill argues that the exemption criteria contained in Article 81(3) cannot be stretched to take account of the type of justifications for central selling articulated by Monti. In other words, 'if a practice is incapable of exemption pursuant to Article 81(3), it cannot be saved by reference to horizontal provisions ... 'such as the social and cultural concerns articulated by Commissioner Monti.[623]

6.2.5. Collective selling in national law

The Commission's approach to collective selling can be contrasted with the situation in the USA and with that of some Member States where collective selling has been prohibited. For example, in 2002, the Dutch competition authority, the Nederlandse Mededingingsautoriteit, prohibited the collective selling of live rights for Dutch Premier League games.[624] In Italy, the government introduced legislation seeking to prevent rights being monopolised by a single broadcaster. Clubs can also exploit their own rights to domestic games. Furthermore, in Germany, the German Bundeskartellamt, and ultimately the German Supreme Court, the Bundesgerichtshof, prohibited the collective sale of European Cup matches by the Deutscher Fußball-Bund. Fearful of the impact of these judgments on national competition (the Bundesliga), Parliament added a block exemption under the German Cartel Act for the collective selling of sports rights. The exemption appeared to contradict EC competition law and was ultimately removed, Bundesliga rights eventually being investigated by the Commis-

---

[622] S. Szymanski, 'Baseball Economics', in W. Andreff and S. Szymanski, *Handbook on the Economics of Sport* (Cheltenham, Edward Elgar 2006) p. 616.

[623] S. Weatherill, 'The Sale of Rights to Broadcast Sporting Events under EC Law', 3-4 *International Sports Law Journal* (2006) p. 20.

[624] S. Parlasca, 'Collective Selling of Broadcast Rights in Team Sports', in W. Andreff and S. Szymanski, *Handbook on the Economics of Sport* (Cheltenham, Edward Elgar 2006) p. 725.

sion.[625] In the UK the Office of Fair Trading (OFT) challenged the collective sale of the 1997-2001 Premier League rights. The value of these rights had risen sharply from the previous agreement in 1992 and was now valued at GBP 670 million over four years as opposed to GBP 191.5 million for a five year contract in 1992.[626] The Restricted Practices Court found that the system of collective selling did operate in the public interest as under the law at the time, the Restrictive Trade Practices Act 1976, the relevant test was whether the public benefited compared to a free market system.[627] Under this test, collective selling is defensible as less restrictive means of achieving the stated objectives cannot be considered. However, the judgment of the Court is not considered a reliable predictor of how an investigation under the UK Competition Act 1998 would proceed. The 1998 Act replaced the Restrictive Trade Practices Act and brings UK competition law more into line with Articles 81 and 82 EC under which proportionality criteria find expression.

6.3.   THE PURCHASE OF BROADCASTING RIGHTS

Established in 1950, the EBU was formed to improve the collective bidding power of the public service broadcasters in Europe, although its membership has subsequently expanded to include commercial operators. The EBU operates the Eurovision network of programme exchanges and acts as a collective purchasing agent for its members. This role has assumed heightened significance for its members given the advent of commercially aggressive pay-TV operators who are better able to secure rights to sporting events. Collective purchasing agreements for public service broadcasters may therefore promote competition for rights by adding a competitor to the market that would otherwise be absent. Nevertheless, having used this competitive advantage to secure rights, concern was raised that competitors were refused access to sub-licences and this placed non-EBU competitors at a commercial disadvantage in the market for sports rights. In 1987, 'Screensport', a commercial broadcaster, registered a complaint with the Commission to this effect. They also complained about the joint venture between a consortium of EBU members and News International/Sky Channel establishing a sports channel called Eurosport. This second complaint was subject to a Commission Decision which found the arrangement infringed Article 81(1) and was not suitable for exemption under 81(3).[628] The arrangements had as their effect the granting of direct access to the Eurovision system and consequently offered such

---

[625] C. Hatton, C. Wagner and H. Armengod, 'Fair Play: How Competition Authorities Have Regulated the Sale of Football Media Rights in Europe', 28(6) *European Competition Law Review* (2007) p. 6.

[626] P. Massey, 'Are Sports Cartels Different? An Analysis of EU Commission Decisions Concerning the Collective Selling Arrangements for Football Broadcasting Rights', 30(1) *World Competition* (2007) p. 88.

[627] *Re the supply of services facilitating the broadcasting on television of Premier League football matches* [1999] UKCLR 258.

[628] Commission Decision 91/130/EEC of 19 February 1991 *Screensport/Members of the EBU, OJ* L 63 of 9 March 1991.

parties an unfair competitive advantage in the market. Screensport merged with Eurosport in March 1993 and was subsequently closed down by its new owner. As a consequence, the appeal was removed from the register of pending cases in June 1993.

Although Screensport withdrew its initial complaint concerning access to sub-licences following agreement with Eurosport, the issue was considered in another context. Following notification in 1989 by the EBU of its joint acquisition regime, its programme sharing arrangements and its revised policy on sub-licensing, the Commission initiated separate proceedings on this question. The EBU requested negative clearance or an exemption pursuant to 81(3). In 1993 the Commission found that the collective purchasing agreement was restrictive of competition but could be exempt under Article 81(3) if strict conditions on sub-licensing were adopted.[629]

The decision was annulled by the Court of First Instance. The CFI examined the rules restricting membership of the EBU to non commercial operators and concluded that the Commission had failed to sufficiently consider whether these membership rules were objective and sufficiently determinate so as to enable them to be applied uniformly and in a non-discriminatory manner *vis-à-vis* all potential active members. Consequently, although the Commission had found that these rules were indispensable, the CFI annulled the decision because that view could not take place until the nature of the restrictions in question was correctly assessed.[630] The EBU adopted new sub-licensing rules and notified the Commission. The Commission exempted the EBU's joint acquisition policy for sport television rights, the sharing of the jointly acquired sport television rights, the exchange of the signal for sporting events and the sub-licensing scheme and rules.[631] The decision was once again annulled by the CFI who this time objected to the Commission's assessment of the operation of the sub-licensing rules.[632] The CFI disagreed with the Commission's assessment that the sub-licensing rules allowed for sufficient access to sports rights for non-EBU members. Since the Commission's decision to grant the individual exemption assumed that the Eurovision agreement satisfies all four of conditions contained within Article 81(3), the decision was set aside. Consequently, collective purchasing agreements are not necessarily incompatible with EC law *per se*, but the manner in which they are constructed, particularly in relation to membership rules and sub-licensing agreements, will be closely monitored by the courts.

6.4. BLOCKING RULES

Blackout (or blocking) rules have been used by sports governing bodies to shield stadium attendance from the impact of live television coverage of sport. A blocking rule prevents a game from being broadcast at the same time as the event is being staged. In

---

[629] Commission Decision 93/403/EC *Eurovision* [1993] *OJ* L179/23.

[630] Joined Cases T-528/93, T-542/93, T-543/93 and T-546/93 *Métropole Télévision and Others* v. *Commission* [1996] *ECR* II-649.

[631] Commission Decision 2000/400 *Eurovision* [2000] *OJ* L151/18.

[632] Cases T-185/00 *Métropole Télévision (SA) (M6) and Others* v. *Commission* [2002] *ECR* II-3805.

the USA the Sports Broadcasting Act 1961 justified the imposition of blackout rules by leagues. For example, the NFL operated blackout rules in the 1970's fearful that a live broadcast of a game would deter ticket holders from attending the game. This would have a consequential impact on secondary revenue streams such as parking and catering. Research found no connection between lived televised games and no-shows and in 1973 Congress intervened and placed restrictions on the use of blackouts.[633] UEFA also subscribe to the substitution theory which suggests that fans substitute stadium attendance for live television coverage. UEFA's broadcasting regulations allowed national associations to place restrictions on the cross border transmission of football matches.[634] In order to protect attendance at the stadium, only within designated 'slots' can live games be broadcast on television. This provision restricts the ability of broadcasters to transmit matches at times favourable to their schedules and it prevents national football federations, and potentially clubs, from freely marketing their transmission rights in the Single Market.

UEFA had operated such restrictions since 1988 but the regulations drew objection from a number of broadcasters and the Commission. In July 1998, the Commission issued a formal statement of objections to UEFA concerning a breach of Article 81. Following negotiations between UEFA and the European Commission, the 'blocking rules' were amended. In April 2001 the Commission found that allowing national associations to block the broadcasting of games during a two and a half hour slot on either Saturday or Sunday fell outside the scope of Article 81 as no appreciable restriction of competition could be identified.[635] In the opening paragraph of the press release which accompanied the formal Commission decision, the Commission noted that the decision is 'a good example of how to reconcile the competition rules and the specific characteristics of sport'.[636] This statement is troubling for it is not a view expressed in the formal decision.

In the formal Decision, the Commission did acknowledge that the object of the disputed restriction was to protect football attendance and participation from the distraction of live television. Yet, the decision to remove the rule from the scope of Article 81 was not a sporting exception decision. There was no separation of sport and the economy, nor was it argued that the rule was inherent in the operation of sport. The limited nature of the restriction was considered to have neither an appreciable effect on the upstream market for the acquisition of rights, nor the downstream market on which broadcasters compete for audience, advertising revenues and subscribers. The limited nature of the restriction, not the specificities of sport, removed the rule from the reach of Article 81. This assessment removed the need to question whether the blocking rules could be exempt under 81(3). Dissenting parties argued that UEFA had failed to show a connection between the televising of football and stadium at-

---

[633] B. Buraimo, 'The Demand for Sports Broadcasting', in W. Andreff and S. Szymanski, *Handbook on the Economics of Sport* (Cheltenham, Edward Elgar 2006) p. 109.

[634] UEFA, *Regulations governing the implementation of Article 47 of the UEFA statutes*, 2000 edition.

[635] Commission Decision 2001/478/EC UEFA broadcasting regulations [2001] *OJ* L 171/12.

[636] Commission Press Release IP/01/583, 20 March 2001.

tendance and participation in football generally. An examination of this issue would have required the specificities of sport to be considered and the party imposing the restriction to substantiate the link. Having established such a link, the case for removal from 81(1) or exemption under 81(3) might be strong. Consequently, the Decision is not a good example of how to reconcile EC law and the special characteristics of sport, beyond stressing the importance of ensuring restrictions have no appreciable effect – good advice for all undertakings. In that sense, the blocking rules case adds little to the legal framework of the sporting exception, but illuminates a political line of reasoning within the Commission. In this regard, Weatherill argues that 'it is not the Commission's business to embark on an assessment of sport's cultural and social function, except in so far as it may be relevant under Article 81(3)'.[637] Having chosen not to make an assessment under the exemption criteria, it would have been preferable for the Commission to avoid reference to the specificities of sport in its press release.

Although the Commission Decision does not endorse the substitution theory, the accompanying press release implies sympathy with it. The counter-argument is that live television compliments stadium attendance and has no adverse effect on it.[638] Buraimo reviews data from the USA and finds conflicting results as to the effect on lived televised sport on stadium attendance. A 1986 study into college football found that televising college football actually increases stadium attendance by 7.8% whilst a follow up study in 1989 by different authors found no effect on attendance.[639] In Europe, Kuypers's study on 'why people watch football' found no significant impact of live television coverage on stadium attendance.[640] Baimbridge and others found that during the FAPL 1993-94 season live matches broadcast by BSkyB on a Sunday had no impact on attendance whilst those on Monday evenings saw a 15% reduction in stadium attendance.[641] Similarly, Buraimo notes that Carmichael's study of English rugby league found attendances on workdays did suffer as a result of live television broadcasts, the explanation being self-evidently that supporters preferred to watch the game on television due to the higher opportunity costs of attending the game on workdays.[642] Allan's study of Aston Villa highlighted a significant negative impact on attendance of live satellite television coverage of 7.75% over the period 1995/96 to 2000/01.[643] Forrest and Simmons' study of attendance at Football League games in

---

[637] S. Weatherill, 'The Sale of Rights to Broadcast Sporting Events under EC Law', 3-4 *International Sports Law Journal* (2006) p. 22.

[638] B. Buraimo, 'The Demand for Sports Broadcasting', in W. Andreff and S. Szymanski, *Handbook on the Economics of Sport* (Cheltenham, Edward Elgar 2006) p. 108.

[639] Id.

[640] T. Kuypers, 'The Beautiful Game? An Econometric Study of Why People Watch Football', *University College London Discussion Paper in Economics* (1996).

[641] M. Baimbridge, S. Cameron and P. Dawson, 'Satellite Television and the Demand for Football: A Whole New Ball Game?', 43(3) *Scottish Journal of Political Economy* (1996).

[642] B. Buraimo, 'The Demand for Sports Broadcasting', in W. Andreff and S. Szymanski, *Handbook on the Economics of Sport* (Cheltenham, Edward Elgar 2006) p. 109.

[643] S. Allen, 'Satellite Television and Football Attendance: The Not so Super Effect', 11(2) *Applied Economics Letters* (2004) p. 123.

England did not find a general adverse effect of broadcasting on stadium attendance at the same match but televising Champions League games involving British teams did significantly affect attendance, between 15.8% and 21.4% for free-to-air broadcasts and 5.8% for pay-TV broadcasts.[644] Clearly the research findings from these studies vary and additional investigation is required. Whilst the variation of results may be interpreted as strengthening the case for the governing bodies to be afforded conditional autonomy in adopting proportionate rules designed to protect stadium attendance from the impact of live television, it must be stressed that this conditional autonomy has only been granted by the Commission in so far as blocking rules have no appreciable effect on competition. The Commission has not yet formed a judgment that the specificity arguments predominate over single market concerns relating to the impact of such rules on the broadcasting sector.

6.5.   ACCESS TO MAJOR SPORTING EVENTS ON TELEVISION

National broadcasting regulation, including measures designed to ensure public access to major events on free-to-air television, is prone to circumvention in the absence of a pan European regulatory regime. The legal basis for the creation of a single market in broadcasting services was provided for by the ECJ in *Sacchi* in which the court established that television signals were tradable services falling within the meaning of Articles 49 of the Treaty.[645] Member states could no longer restrict a broadcasting signal on the grounds of its national origin. At the same time, proponents of the 'People's Europe' project saw the prospect of a pan European broadcasting policy as a vehicle of achieving greater cultural and political integration, the 1982 Hahn Report being one such advocate.[646] By the time the Television Without Frontiers Directive was agreed in Council in 1989, the socio-cultural elements of the project had largely given way to single market imperatives.[647] Consequently, the Directive advanced market liberalisation in broadcasting, including minimum standards on advertising and sponsorship, although it did contain provisions on European programme content quotas, which excluded sport.

   The Directive came into effect in 1991 but contained a provision for a review within five years. The timing of the review allowed the European Parliament, a traditional advocate of cultural and political integration, to be influential. The 1992 Maastricht Treaty on European Union granted the Parliament co-legislative rights with the Council. In addition, the ECJ's decision in *Bosman* (1995) strengthened perceptions that market-based commercial forces were undermining the traditional values

---

[644] D. Forrest and R. Simmons, 'New Issues in Attendance Demand. The Case of the English Football League', 7(3) *Journal of Sports Economics* (2006) pp. 259-260.

[645] Case 155/73 *Sacchi* [1974] *ECR* 409.

[646] P. Humphreys, *Mass Media and Media Policy in Western Europe* (Manchester, Manchester University Press 1996) p. 258.

[647] R. Collins, *Broadcasting and Audio-Visual Policy in the European Single Market* (London, John Libby 1994) pp. 52-80.

of sport and that Community law was complicit. Commercialisation and technological developments within the broadcasting sector were contributing to a drift towards sports broadcasting being restricted to transmission on pay-TV platforms as free-to-air broadcasters struggled to keep pace with rapid increases in the prices of sports rights.

The European Parliament's response to the drift towards pay-TV was to insist on an amendment to the Directive designed to ensure the public had access to major events on free-to-air television. Article 3a(1) of the 1997 Directive established a voluntary regime in which Member States may take measures, in the form of protected lists, to ensure that broadcasters under its jurisdiction do not broadcast on an exclusive basis such listed events which are regarded by that Member State as being of major importance for society in such a way as to deprive a substantial proportion of the public in that Member State of the possibility of following such events via live coverage or deferred coverage on free television. Member states must then notify the list to the Commission which is obliged by Article 3a(2) to verify its legality. Article 3a(3) places the Member States under an obligation to ensure within the framework of their legislation that broadcasters under their jurisdiction do not exercise the exclusive rights purchased by those broadcasters in such a way that a substantial proportion of the public in another Member State is deprived of the possibility of following events which are listed by that other Member State.

The 1997 Directive underwent major review between 2001 and 2007. The Commission has proposed replacing the Directive with the Audiovisual Media Services Directive (AMSD) which should enter force at the end of 2007 and be transposed into domestic law by the end of 2009. The Directorate General for Information Society and Media drafted the proposed Directive, which at its heart seeks to adapt the regulatory framework based on the 1997 Directive in order to take account of the impact of structural change and technological developments on business models within the audiovisual industry. It does so by establishing a new graduated regulatory framework encompassing both traditional linear services and new non-linear (on demand) services which are currently regulated by the E-Commerce Directive. The AMSD provides for the express extension of the country of origin principle to both linear and non-linear services meaning that an audiovisual service provider is subject only to the rules of the home Member State. The text of the AMSD proposes to maintain the substance of Article 3a, although this will be renumbered Article 3i in the new Directive.[648]

6.5.1. Arguments in support of Article 3a

Advocates of Article 3a argue that access to major events on free-to-air television is a corollary of a wider 'right to information'. Information which has traditionally been made available 'freely' is now being commercialised and access to it restricted by profit making private bodies. Article 10 of the European Convention on Human

---

[648] Council's Political Agreement on Common Position of 24 May 2007.

Rights protects the right to 'receive and impart information without interference by public authorities and regardless of frontiers'. Helberger denies that Article 10 establishes such a right, 'the right of access to information is the right of an undefined public to receive information and ideas on matters of public interest that the media impart, not the right of individual viewers to have access to media content'.[649] It appears that the discourse of a 'right to information' which has accompanied the Article 3a debate, derives not from constitutional safeguards, but from an historical expectation in which free-to-air TV operators provided sport 'freely'. Furthermore, rights holders may regard the interference with their property as a breach of Article 10 and Article 1 Protocol 1 of the ECHR. These arguments are also flawed. As Craufurd Smith and Böttcher explain, 'state intervention in the market for sports rights may not seem so strange when we remember that the state is often willing to restrict the way in which individuals use their property in order to realise specific social benefits'.[650]

Second, regulation is defended on the grounds that sport performs important social functions. Framed in these terms, sport, and access to it, is analogous to a public good and the public should therefore be afforded reasonable access to it. Whilst being persuasive in terms of the public's access to sport in a participatory context, the act of watching sport on television, which is protected by Article 3a, performs few, if any, of the social functions sport is associated with. Watching sport on television is not 'sport', rather the provision of entertainment for which consumers in other sectors, such as premium films, purchase. Furthermore, sport plays no significant social function for many within society and they may object to having to contribute to the costs associated with free-to-air broadcasters acquiring the rights to events from their pay-TV competitors. Concentration of resources in this field may undermine other aspects of their public service mission.

Third, Article 3a remains an important symbol of political and cultural integration in Europe. As discussed elsewhere in this book, sport has become associated with the 'People's Europe' project and as a means of implementing policy goals in other fields. For example, the Amsterdam Declaration on Sport, Declaration 29 to the Treaty of Amsterdam 1997, referred to the role of sport in 'forging identity and bringing people closer together'. Yet justifying Article 3a in these terms brings with it constitutional dangers as the Community would be relying on arguments it is not yet competent to advance in support of the legislation prior to the entry into force of the proposed Reform Treaty.

Fourth, a number of proponents of Article 3a make reference to the dangers of commercialised sport and the need to safeguard consumer interests. In 'The Development and Prospects for Community Action in the Field of Sport', the Commission referred to the 'risk of excessive commercialisation'.[651] The Helsinki Report on Sport

---

[649] N. Helberger, 'The "Right to Information" and Digital Broadcasting – About Monsters, Invisible Men, and the Future of European Broadcasting Regulation', 17(2) *Entertainment Law Review* (2006) p. 72.

[650] B. Crauford Smith and B. Böttcher, 'Football and Fundamental Rights: Regulating Access to Major Sporting Events on Television', 8(1) *European Public Law* (2002) p. 115.

[651] Commission of the European Communities, *Developments and Prospects for Community Activity in the Field of Sport*, Commission Staff Working Paper (1998), Directorate General X, p. 8.

added that 'the increase in the number of lucrative sporting events, which may end up promoting the commercial approach, to the detriment of sporting principles and the social function of sport'.[652] Furthermore, the Independent European Sports Review recognised the danger that '... an overly commercial approach to sport will end up compromising important sporting values and undermining the social function of sport'.[653] On these grounds, regulation is justified as a counterweight to commercial forces in sport which are restricting consumer access to major events. Undoubtedly in the last decade consumers have faced a drift towards conditional access for sports events but they have also benefited from the levels of investment in sport which are attributable to the vibrancy of the market in which governing bodies are able to exploit their rights. In the UK, such investment is thought to have contributed to enhanced investment into squads, stadia and infrastructure, dedicated channels with specialist coverage, new technologies and wider consumer choice supported by contractual obligations imposed on the broadcasters to broadcast a wider choice of teams.

6.5.2.   Arguments against Article 3a

The governing bodies of sport argue that Article 3a diminishes the value of sports rights and that this has a negative impact on their ability to achieve re-investment (solidarity) goals within the sport through the redistribution of profits. The governing bodies recognise the public interest arguments of ensuring public access to major events, but assert that they are best placed to ensure a balance is struck between such arguments and the need to maximise revenues for solidarity purposes.[654] Furthermore, governing bodies are driven by the need to promote their sport to a wide audience so that its popularity is maintained and sponsors are attracted by large audiences. Statutory regulation is therefore not required because of these imperatives. A governing body which denies access to free-to-air viewers would be acting irrationally. For example, the EBU secured the 2000-08 Olympic Games rights for USD 1.44 billion despite being outbid by News Corporation, owner of pay-TV services, who bid USD 2 billion.[655] The argument is somewhat contradictory as it rests on the belief that Article 3a unduly interferes with the market's allocation of resources. Yet, on the question of collective selling arrangements and blocking rules, UEFA argues in favour of market restrictions on the grounds of the 'specificity of sport'.

In addition to denying income to governing bodies, Article 3a may also have consequences for the development of a vibrant and competitive market in broadcasting services. In October 1996 Rupert Murdoch, Chairman of News International and

---

[652] Commission of the European Communities, *Report from the Commission to the European Council With a View to Safeguarding Sports Structures and Maintaining the Social Significance of Sport Within the Community Framework: The Helsinki Report on Sport*, COM (1999) 644, p. 4.

[653] J. Arnaut, *Independent European Sport Review* (2006), see at <www.independentfootballreview. com> p. 19.

[654] UEFA, *Public Consultation on the Review of the Television Without Frontiers Directive* (15 July 2003).

[655] B. Crauford Smith and B. Böttcher, 'Football and Fundamental Rights: Regulating Access to Major Sporting Events on Television', 8(1) *European Public Law* (2002) p. 111.

leading pioneer of satellite television in Britain, addressed the *News Corporation Annual General Meeting (AGM)* in Adelaide and signalled his intention to 'use sports as a battering ram and a lead offering in all our pay television operations'. The acquisition of sports rights is still an important business model for broadcasters and placing restrictions on how rights are exercised may privilege free-to-air broadcasters at the expense of potential market entrants. Furthermore, Article 3a privileges free-to-air broadcasters over pay-TV operators thus affording the free-to-air broadcasters a competitive advantage. Regulation therefore has a pronounced public service television bias. Both the question of revenue streams and market access are valid but need to be balanced against the public interest arguments expressed by the advocates of 3a. Nevertheless, the actual impact of 3a appears limited. Currently Austria, Belgium, Finland, France, Italy, Ireland, Germany and the United Kingdom have adopted measures under Article 3a(1) of the Directive and have notified the Commission of the lists.[656] Some of these events were of national interest only. Of international sporting events of note, only the Olympics, the Football World Cup and the Football European Championships are regularly appearing.

A further objection to the 3a regime relates to the Directive regulating the exercise and not the acquisition of rights. The practical impact of the Directive is that a rights holder, who does not broadcast to a substantial proportion of viewers on a free-to-air basis, may be required to enter into negotiations with free-to-air operators interested in purchasing the rights. No mechanism exists for determining what constitutes a fair price in these negotiations and thus the regime favours free-to-air operators and further diminishes the revenue streams available to the governing bodies. Rather than regulating the exercise of the rights, an alternative would be to regulate the manner in which rights are acquired. In the initial TWF project, the Commission considered establishing a regime which specified that rights to certain events are only available to be purchased by free-to-air broadcasters. Fleming suggests that the Commission settled on the current regime of regulating the exercise of rights as this represented the least restrictive means of achieving the 3a objectives and because competition law was better equipped to deal with acquisition issues.[657] As is discussed above, Articles 81 and 82 can limit the length of exclusive contracts and can unbundle rights making it more likely, although not certain, that free-to-air broadcasters acquire some rights.

6.5.3. Judicial scrutiny of Article 3a

The *TV Danmark* litigation concerned the enforceability of the mutual recognition conditions contained in Article 3a(3) of the Directive. The applicant, TV Danmark, a satellite television company established in England, acquired the exclusive rights to televise five away football matches of the Danish national football team in the 2002 World Cup.[658] The rights were acquired following a competitive tender process,

---

[656] *OJ* L 180 10/07/07, *OJ* C 328 18/11/2000, *OJ* C 45 19/02/02.

[657] H. Fleming, 'Television Without Frontiers: The Broadcasting of Sporting Events in Europe', 8(8) *Entertainment Law Review* (1997) p. 284.

[658] *R.* v. *Independent Television Commission, ex parte TV Danmark 1* [2001] UKHL 42 [2001] 1 *WLR* 1604, HL.

TV Danmark having outbid two Danish public service broadcasters. TV Danmark's transmissions reached about 60% of the Danish population whereas the unsuccessful Danish broadcasters reached more than 90% of the population. As required by the UK legislation, TV Danmark applied to the Independent Television Commission (ITC) for consent to exercise the rights. All interested broadcasters had been given a genuine opportunity to acquire the rights on fair and reasonable terms at the auction and that the price paid for the exclusive rights had been fair and reasonable. Having satisfied the requirements of the code, TV Danmark considered they held a legitimate expectation that consent would be granted. The ITC nevertheless refused consent. The ITC's refusal goes to the heart of the mutual recognition requirements contained in Article 3a(3). It noted that it needed to have regard to Danish provisions, which required that a successful non-qualifying broadcaster should offer to share the rights with qualifying broadcasters at a reasonable price. TV Danmark had not done so and consequently, the Danish public service broadcasters had not had a genuine opportunity to acquire such non-exclusive rights on fair and reasonable terms. The subsequent exercise of the exclusive rights by TV Danmark would thus be contrary to the directive which seeks to ensure that a substantial proportion of the public are not denied access to major events.

TV Danmark applied for judicial review of the ITC's decision. The High Court rejected their claim on the grounds that the Directive regulated the exercise of the exclusive rights in such a way that a substantial proportion of the public was deprived of the possibility of following a listed event, and not the manner in which the rights were acquired. Consequently, TV Danmark could not have had a legitimate expectation that the ITC would exercise its discretion in a manner contrary to the terms of the directive. On appeal the Court of Appeal found in favour of TV Danmark by finding that the object of Article 3a(3) was not an unqualified object. Recitals to the Directive qualified this objective with reference to free market considerations and consequently, the UK was entitled to implement the Directive with due regard to these objects as well, thus justifying the focus on the acquisition, rather than the exercise, of rights. On appeal, the House of Lords restored the judgment of the High Court. The Lords regarded the objectives of Article 3a(1) as clear – preventing the exercise by broadcasters of exclusive rights in such a way that a substantial proportion of the public in another Member State was deprived of the possibility of watching on television a designated event. This obligation was not, according to the House of Lords, qualified by single market considerations.

In *Infront WM AG* v. *Commission*, a challenge was brought to the UK's listing of the 2002 Football World Cup Finals.[659] The applicant, formerly the Kirch Media Group, was in the market for the acquisition of broadcasting rights to major sporting events which they then marketed to interested broadcasters. In 1998 the company acquired, from FIFA, the European rights to the 2002 and 2006 World Cup Finals for a large sum. As required by Article 3a(2) of the directive, the United Kingdom

---

[659] Case T-33/01, *Infront WM (Formerly Kirchmedia)* v. *Commission* [2005] *ECR* II-5897. Appeal under consideration in C-125/06 P, *Commission* v. *Infront WM* Application of 1 March 2006, *OJ* 2006 C 108/7 6 May 2006.

notified the Commission on 25 September 1998 of the listing of all the matches at the Finals. The list was somewhat unusual in that it covered all matches, and not just those involving the England team. The applicant stood to suffer a serious commercial detriment because of this list. They complained that list was not drawn up pursuant to a clear and transparent procedure, that it included events which were not of major importance for United Kingdom society and that the national and Community consultation procedures were marred by serious deficiencies. It also criticised the retroactive nature of the UK Broadcasting Act, 1996 and raised the issue of interference with their property rights. The Commission did not object to the UK's list and notified the UK of this finding by letter. The applicant contested this finding and applied for its annulment.

In the proceedings before the Court of First Instance, the Commission claimed, *inter alia*, that the application was inadmissible because it did not adopt any measure on the basis of Article 3a(2) of the directive capable of being challenged. In other words Article 3a(2) makes no mention of a formal 'decision' which can be subject to judicial review. The Commission's role is to carry out a preliminary check of the compatibility with Community law of the national measures notified. The applicant contended that the directive confers upon the Commission a role which in fact produces legal effects open to challenge. The CFI agreed because the contested letter envisages the publication in the Official Journal of the national measures in question and the effect of that publication is to trigger the mechanism for mutual recognition laid down by Article 3a(3) of the directive. As the Directorate General for Education and Culture did not regard the approval of the notified list as a 'decision', it did not seek the consent of the College of Commissioners, a procedure required for acts producing legal effects. Consequently, the DG lacked the competence to make such a decision. Accordingly, the CFI annulled the Commission's decision to approve the UK's listing. The Commission has brought an appeal before the ECJ challenging the CFI's finding that the applicant possessed the necessary standing within the meaning of Article 230(4) EC in which it asserts that the contested letter to the UK authorities was not of direct concern to the applicant.[660]

Whilst *Infront* clarifies the status of the Commission's approval procedure it adds little to the overall framework of the enforceability of Article 3a. In particular, it does not clarify what is meant by an event of major importance for society. For instance, Recital 21 of the directive states that

> 'events of major importance for society should ... meet certain criteria, that is to say be outstanding events which are of interest to the general public in the European Union or in a given Member State or in an important component part of a given Member State and are organised in advance by an event organiser who is legally entitled to sell the rights pertaining to that event'.

The UK enabling legislation, the Broadcasting Act 1996 refers to the listed event having 'a special national resonance, not simply a significance to those who ordi-

---

[660] Case C-125/06 P, *Commission* v. *Infront WM OJ* 2006 C108/7.

narily follow the sport concerned; it is an event which serves to unite the nation; a shared point in the national calendar'. Appendix 2 recognises some categories of such events:

'... it is a pre-eminent national or international event in the sport, it involves the national team or national representatives in the sport concerned. An event which satisfies the essential criterion is likely to be considered for listing, but listing of such an event is not automatic. It is more likely to be listed if it exhibits particular characteristics making listing an apt response, such as: it is likely to command a large television audience, it has a history of being broadcast live on free-to-air services.'

The listing of every match of the World Cup Finals appears inconsistent with these definitions. Furthermore, the fact that the World Cup has a history of being broadcast on free-to-air television is not relevant as until relatively recently, all television channels in the UK have been freely available, subject to licensing fees and the cost of the equipment itself.

6.5.4. Right to short reporting

Article 3j of the AMSD proposes to establish a right to short reporting for linear services.[661] Article 3j requires Member States to ensure that for the purposes of short news reports, broadcasters established in other Member States are not deprived of access on a fair, reasonable and non-discriminatory basis to events of high interest to the public which are transmitted by a broadcaster under their jurisdiction. If agreed, broadcasters will be able to select short news reports from the transmitting broadcasters' signal and simply identify the source. The provisions on short reporting are defended as a corollary to the right to information. In the absence of a Community regulatory framework, the free movement of information programmes could be restricted thus limiting the exercise of the right to information and undermining media pluralism in Europe.[662] The submissions to the AMSD consultation exercise reflected the commercial considerations of the respondents rather than a wider concern for the public's right to information. Some broadcasters saw commercial value in being able to report on events of high interest to the public. Others, such as the printed press, wished to see Article 3j adopted as a means of securing access to events for the purpose of short reporting. For example, the European Publishers News Association (ENPA) detailed numerous examples of physical and financial restrictions placed on newspaper reporters and publishers by owners of rights keen to protect the exclusivity of their rights.[663]

Article 3j is opposed by rights owners fearful of the impact on the value of their property. This is a particular concern in relation to access to short reports by the new

---

[661] Council's Political Agreement on Common Position of 24 May 2007.

[662] Commission of the European Communities, *Issues paper for the audiovisual conference in Liverpool. Right to information and right to short reporting* (July 2005) p. 2.

[663] European Publishers News Association (ENPA), *ENPA response to the Issue Paper for the audiovisual conference in Liverpool. Right to information and right to short reporting* (August 2005).

media (internet and mobile phones). Their coverage is reliant on short clips because of the nature of the platform, namely the technical difficulties and expense of greater bandwidth. To grant a legal right to short reports to these operators could significantly affect the value of the rights sold to these operators. For example, in its submission to the AMSD consultation exercise, UEFA expressed concern that governing bodies themselves should be able to strike a balance between the right to information and the ability to maximise income from rights, particularly as the Commission and Court have recognised that the collective sale of sports broadcasting rights is a legitimate commercial practice. Furthermore, a number of submissions claim that the current news access regime precludes the need for further regulation. For example, the Copyright Directive already contains provisions concerning news access exceptions.[664] The Council of Europe Convention on Transfrontier Television enables signatories to enact access measures. Broadcasters may also be subject to contractual obligations on access arrangements and be signatories to voluntary codes such as the Sports News Access Code operating in the UK. These safeguards potentially offer less restrictive means of achieving the objectives and should be read in conjunction with the goals of Article 3a of the TWF Directive which enables Member States to take measures to ensure major events are broadcast on free-to-air television. In short, opponents of Article 3j argue that the case has not been made for a Community instrument within the AMSD on short reporting and that such a provision may well serve to further the commercial interests of secondary broadcasters rather than secure the public's right to information.

6.6. CONCLUSIONS

The application of the sporting exception is put to greatest work in the context of sports broadcasting rights. This is because in its original form the sporting exception rested on a separation between sporting and commercial rules. Revenue generated from broadcasting rights is a very significant source of income for sport and it has been at the heart of the transformation of the sports sector. Yet, watching sport is still of considerable social importance for fans and the revenue generated by broadcasting rights allows governing bodies to respond to social policy objectives in sport. Therefore, the balance between the imposition of regulatory burdens on sport and the justification for regulatory immunities is again at issue. In none of the cases explored above is the sporting exception applied to sport in a pure sense.

In relation to collective selling, the specificities of sport were not material, and the issues raised were disposed of in the context of a standard competition law analysis. The thorny issue of whether collective selling is indispensable in terms of ensuring revenue sharing and promoting competitive balance was avoided by the Commission. On the question of collective purchasing, the specificities of sport were not at issue

---

[664] Directive 2001/29/EC of the European Parliament and of the Council of 22 May 2001 on the harmonisation of certain aspects of copyright and related rights in the information society.

beyond the question of whether collective purchasing was pro-competitive given the escalating value of sports rights. This assessment is applicable to all forms of valuable property right including premium films. The case of UEFA's blocking rules raised the prospect of deeper engagement with specificity of sport arguments, yet the Commission avoided analysing whether such rules were required to protect stadium attendance by deciding the rules had no appreciable effect on competition. The special characteristics of sport did not form the basis of the Commission Decision despite the implication in the accompanying press release to the contrary. Finally, whilst it appears that specificity arguments underpinned Article 3a of the Television Without Frontiers Directive, such arguments were only used vicariously to justify the imposition of a regulatory burden on the holders of rights. The decision to adopt Article 3a rested on a choice between ensuring public access to sport on television, a corollary to the right to information, and the desire of the governing bodies to maximise revenues through the sale of broadcasting rights so that a policy of re-investment in sport could be pursued. In balancing these competing interests the Community legislature clearly favoured the former at the expense of the specificity arguments articulated by the governing bodies.

As Weatherill argues, the Community's approach to sports broadcasting 'reveals an emphasis on market analysis which is not blind to the particular characteristics of professional sport'.[665] Competition law has demonstrated itself to be sufficiently flexible to accommodate specificity arguments. Some consider it is too flexible in this respect. Commenting on the exemption decision in the *Champions League* case, Parlasca remarked that it 'seems to be rather based on intransparent political compromises than on sound economics'.[666] The EU's approach to sports broadcasting is therefore somewhat Janus-faced. It stares into the socio-cultural world of sport and articulates a case for the sensitive application of EC law to sport. Yet the strength of this stare is constitutionally constrained so the Court and the Commission, with an eye on the fundamentals of Community law, avoid reference to it in their sports related decisions. The outcome of their deliberations has not seen the widespread condemnation of sports rules as the Commission has arguably become sensitised to the specificity arguments.

---

[665] S. Weatherill, 'The Sale of Rights to Broadcast Sporting Events under EC Law', 3-4 *International Sports Law Journal* (2006) p. 25.

[666] S. Parlasca, 'Collective Selling of Broadcast Rights in Team Sports', in W. Andreff and S. Szymanski, *Handbook on the Economics of Sport* (Cheltenham, Edward Elgar 2006) p. 728.

Chapter 7
The European Labour Market for Professional Players

The European model of sport has traditionally segmented the European labour market for players along national lines. One of the founding goals of the European Union is the deconstruction of national segmentation in labour markets generally and the establishment of a single market for the benefit of those undertaking economic activity. The national segmentation of the labour market in sport has been promoted by three market interventions. First, national teams impose eligibility criteria based on nationality discrimination. Second, nationality restrictions were a common feature of club football. Third, a transfer system operated which, although applied without regard to nationality, acted to deter a Member State national from leaving his home state in order to exercise his right to freedom of movement. This third feature formed part of a wider pattern of player restraint which operated in Europe in which professional footballers were considered a distinct category of workers, justifying restrictions on their employment freedoms which were not tolerated in other sectors. This chapter explores the extent to which national segmentation in sport can be maintained in the context of the fundamental principles of European law. It questions whether the specific characteristics of sport have been taken into account in the decision-making of the ECJ and the European Commission. In doing so it highlights a liberalisation in the European players market and an extension of the non-discrimination principle to some non-EU nationals. It interrogates claims that these developments have had a negative impact on competitive balance, produced disincentives for clubs to educate and train young players and had a deleterious impact on national team sports. The chapter also explores attempts by FIFA and UEFA to re-regulate the players market by way of the home-grown player initiative and examines the consequences of pursuing a policy of labour market deregulation in the absence of deregulation in the product market, a theme explored in more depth in the next chapter.

7.1. THE TRANSFER OF PLAYERS

The transfer system, a long standing feature of the European model of sport, is discussed in detail in Chapter 1. It allows clubs to recruit players to improve their performance on the pitch and to sell players in order to improve their financial position. It also acts as a means through which players can seek alternative employment. Transfer systems have been defended on the grounds that they provide incentives for clubs to train young players and ensure an equal distribution of playing talent throughout leagues. In a system without rules limiting transfers the best players would simply migrate to the best teams leaving uncertainty of results and competitive balance seriously diminished and leaving smaller clubs uncompensated for the costs invested in training young players.

Transfer systems impose restraints on both clubs and players. Nevertheless, it is the impact on players which has received most attention because the transfer system is commonly perceived to be 'part of the control mechanism of management over players'.[667] Historically, the central component of the transfer system was the 'retain and transfer' system. Under this system a club retained a player's registration even though contractual relations between club and player had ended. At the end of the season the club either listed a player as 'retained' or placed him on the transfer list. By retaining a player, the club had an ongoing option to re-employ him on terms at least as favourable to the player as those contained in the final year of his expiring contract. A transferred player could seek alternative employment although the vendor could still demand a transfer fee as they retained the player's registration. If the transfer fee was not met, the player had no alternative but to stay with his club, often with the player's wages being reduced a minimum permitted threshold. If these terms were refused the player was not entitled to play, nor entitled to seek alternative employment until a club purchased his registration from the selling club. This system provided the club with a 'virtual monopoly over the player's services ... effectively tying him to his club until, and if, the club gave the player permission to move elsewhere'.[668]

This led to somewhat exaggerated claims that the transfer system was a form of modern day slavery. In *X* v. *Netherlands* the European Commission on Human Rights rejected a claim that the transfer system contravened Article 4 of the European Convention on Human Rights which provides that no-one shall be held in slavery or servitude, or be required to perform forced or compulsory labour.[669] The Commission found that the complainant had voluntarily entered into a contract with the club in full knowledge of the consequence. In other words, whilst he was being restrained in his work, he was not being forced into unjust or oppressive labour against his will. In England, the retain and transfer system was gradually modified following the 1963 *Eastham* case.[670] Players reaching the end of their contract could leave on a free transfer if the club failed to offer new terms at least as favourable as those contained in the final year of his expiring contract. A player intent on leaving could do so dependent on a transfer fee being payable by the purchasing club. In the absence of an agreed price, the fee would be fixed by arbitration. Whilst the English system did not normalise a player's contract *vis-à-vis* normal employees who benefited from freedom of contract, it compared favourably with the practice in some continental countries.

---

[667] A. Caiger and J. O'Leary, 'The End of the Affair: The Anelka Doctrine – the Problem of Contract Stability in English Professional Football', in A. Caiger and S. Gardiner, eds., *Professional Sport in the EU, Regulation and Re-regulation* (The Hague, T.M.C. Asser Press 2000) p. 198.

[668] D. Thomas, 'The Retain and Transfer System', in W. Andreff and S. Szymanski, *Handbook on the Economics of Sport* (Cheltenham, Edward Elgar 2006) p. 63.

[669] Case 9322/81, *X* v. *Netherlands*, 3 May 1983.

[670] *Eastham* v. *Newcastle United Football Club Ltd.* [1963] 3 *All ER* 139.

7.1.1. The *Bosman* judgment

In *Bosman*, a Belgian footballer challenged the legality of the international transfer system for players. Bosman objected to his former club retaining a decisive influence over his ability to seek alternative employment despite his contract with the club having ended. This was as a consequence of the club owning his registration. Bosman applied to the Tribunal de Première in Liège in August 1990 and requested the case to be referred to the ECJ for a preliminary ruling on the question of the compatibility of the international transfer system with Articles 39 and 81 and 82 of the EC Treaty. The request was, on appeal, granted. The Court heard a number of submissions concerning the application of Article 39 to the rules of sporting associations. These included that only the major European clubs could be regarded as economic undertakings and that transfer rules did not concern the employment relationship between club and player,[671] that the EU had always respected sporting autonomy, that it was difficult to distinguish between the economic and sporting aspects of football,[672] that sport is analogous with culture for which there exists Treaty protection and that the freedom of association and the principle of subsidiarity precludes intervention by the Court.[673]

In response, the Court held that the application of Article 39 was not affected by the transfer rules governing the business relationship between clubs rather than between clubs and players as the system affected the employment relationship.[674] On the question of the economic nature of the activity in question, the Court found that 'that the provisions of Community law concerning freedom of movement of persons and of provision of services do not preclude rules or practices justified on non-economic grounds which relate to the particular nature and context of certain matches'.[675] Here the Court referred to the non-economic arguments in terms of objective justification even though the discussion took place outside the analysis on the existence of justifications discussed in Paragraphs 105-114 of the judgment. A cultural analogy was also rejected since the question submitted by the referring court did not relate to Article 128 but to the rights contained in Article 39.[676] Finally, a subsidiarity argument was rejected on the grounds that its application should not lead to a situation in which the freedom of private associations to adopt rules restricts the exercise of rights conferred on individuals by the Treaty.[677] The Court also rejected arguments that the dispute before the national court concerned a purely internal Belgian situation which removes it from the scope of Article 39, finding that a cross border element was evident from the facts.

---

[671] *Bosman* Para. 70.
[672] Ibid. Para. 71.
[673] Ibid. Para. 72.
[674] Ibid. Paras. 74-75.
[675] Ibid. Para. 76.
[676] Ibid. Para. 78.
[677] Ibid. Para. 81.

Having established the application of Article 39 to the rules of sports governing bodies, the Court considered whether the disputed transfer rules constituted a restriction to the free movement of workers. In doing so the Court found that provisions, such as the disputed transfer system, which preclude or deter a Member State national from leaving his home state in order to exercise his right to freedom of movement constitutes a restriction to labour mobility even though the restriction is applied without regard to the nationality of the worker.[678] The Court arrived at this outcome despite the fact that the existence of the transfer rule did not make it more difficult for a player to move between clubs in different Member States than between clubs in the same state. As such, the Court held that the application of Article 39 went beyond a mere prohibition of discrimination, but extended to all restrictions. Even though the transfer rules applied equally to all clubs in all Member States and affected foreign and domestic transfers equally, the Court chose not to apply the principles of *Keck* in which the Court held that Article 28 EC does not apply to indistinctly applicable rules on certain selling arrangements, considered in detail in Chapter 3.[679] Instead, the Court relied on *Alpine Investments* which concerned restrictions within the host state affecting access to the market of another Member State.[680]

After establishing that the transfer system constituted a restriction prohibited by Article 39, the Court considered the question of objective justification. In the proceedings, the Union Royale Belge des Sociétés de Football Association (URBSFA), UEFA and the governments of France and Italy claimed that transfer rules are justified by reference to the need to maintain a financial and competitive balance between clubs and to support the search for talent and the training of young players.[681] The Court agreed that these two objectives were legitimate.[682] However, the Court agreed with the submission of Bosman that transfer rules were not an appropriate means of achieving these objectives. First, transfer rules do not prevent the richest clubs from securing the best players nor do they prevent the availability of financial resources from being a decisive factor in competitive sport, thus considerably altering the balance between clubs.[683] Second, whilst it was acknowledged that the prospect of receiving a transfer fee would encourage clubs to train young players, the uncertainty surrounding the progression of young talent into professional players, and the disconnection between transfer fees and the actual costs incurred in training young players, seriously limits the argument on the link between the two.[684] Consequently, the prospect of receiving a transfer fee could not be considered a decisive factor in encouraging the training of players. Furthermore, the Court agreed with Advocate General Lenz that less restrictive measures could achieve the same aims as the transfer system.[685]

---

[678] Ibid. Para. 96.

[679] Joined cases C-267 and 268/91 *Keck and Mithouard* [1993] *ECR* I-6097.

[680] Cases C-384/93, *Alpine Investments BV v. Minister van Financiën* [1995] *ECR* I-1141.

[681] *Bosman* Para. 105.

[682] Ibid. Para. 106.

[683] Ibid. Para. 107.

[684] Ibid. Paras. 108-109.

[685] Ibid. Para. 110, referring to point 226 of the Opinion of Advocate General Lenz.

On these grounds, the Court held that Article 39 precludes the application of transfer rules which required payment for the transfer of a player whose contract had expired and who wished to move between clubs in different Member States.

7.1.2. Remodeling the transfer system

FIFA amended the international transfer system in October 1997.[686] The new regulations allowed players to move to another club in a different EU/EEA state at the end of their contract without a transfer fee being payable. Furthermore, in UEFA competitions, clubs were no longer restricted to fielding foreign players within the terms of the 3+2 rule. This rule was adopted by UEFA in 1991 following discussions with the European Commission. From July 1992, national associations and UEFA could limit to three the number of foreign players whom a club may field in any first division match in their national championships and in UEFA competitions, plus two assimilated players who have played in the country in question for five years uninterruptedly, including three years in junior teams.

In December 1998, the Commission launched a formal investigation into the operation of the revised international transfer system objecting to certain provisions which amounted to a potential breach of Article 81. In particular, the new system prohibited players from transferring to another club following their unilateral termination of a contract, even if the player has complied with national law governing the penalties for breach of contract. Second, it allowed a club to receive payment for a player leaving a club if the contract had been terminated by mutual consent. Third, it encouraged high transfer fees which bore no relation to the training costs incurred by the club selling the player, a practice condemned by the Court in *Bosman* and one which limits the ability of small clubs to hire top players. Fourth, it allowed for a transfer fee to be demanded for the transfer of players, both under contract and out of contract, from a non-EU country to a Member State of the EU and vice versa. These features had as their object or effect the limitation of the source of supply of players for clubs.

The Commission issued FIFA with a deadline of October 31st 2000 to submit formal proposals to amend the international transfer system. Failure to do so would result in the Commission issuing a formal decision declaring the transfer system incompatible with Article 81. FIFA and UEFA established a joint transfer task force in order to explore possible amendments to the international transfer system and in doing so they received high level political support from the German Chancellor and British Prime Minister by way of a joint statement supporting the transfer system.[687] A 'Negotiation Document' was produced by the joint task force on a revised transfer system which was submitted to the Commission by the imposed October deadline. This document articulated the principles FIFA and UEFA wished to maintain which were that contract stability was maintained, that clubs were rewarded for the investment in the training of young players and that the new system must ensure the re-

---

[686] FIFA Regulations for the Status and Transfer of Players, October, 1997.

[687] German Government Press Release No. 425/00. 10. September 2000.

distribution of income which would help maintain a balance between the clubs.[688] The detailed proposals were rejected by the international players union FIFPro on the grounds that the desire to maintain contract stability imposed undue restraints on players because of their inability to unilaterally break a contract of employment with a club and move freely to another once compensation for breach had been paid in accordance with national labour law. Furthermore, the maintenance of the transfer system created incentives for clubs to sell players, in contradiction to the stated aim of maintaining contract stability. FIFPro also questioned the connection between the transfer system and the need to maintain a balance between clubs and the need to educate and train young players. FIFPro argued that transfer revenues to smaller clubs were in decline and that due to transfer fee inflation, most top clubs invest heavily in youth academies in order to develop their own young players.[689] FIFPro therefore held the view that the real agenda behind the Negotiation Document was a desire on the part of the clubs and governing bodies to continue to 'restrain players' earnings and bargaining power' whilst imposing further restraints on players than those which previously existed.[690]

At the December 2000 Nice European Council, the Member States released a Declaration on Sport in the form of a Presidency Conclusion. The provisions relating to the transfer dispute supported, 'dialogue on the transfer system between the sports movement, in particular the football authorities, organisations representing professional sportsmen and -women, the Community and the Member States, with due regard for the specific requirements of sport, subject to compliance with Community law'.[691] Despite the objections of FIFPro and an unseemly disagreement between FIFA and UEFA over the handling of the transfer negotiations with the Commission in January 2001, the Nice Declaration lent political support to a compromise solution. A remodelled transfer system was eventually agreed in March 2001 by way of an exchange of letters between the Commission and FIFA President Sepp Blatter. In the Commission letter to FIFA, Commissioner Monti considered that FIFA's 'undertaking contains sufficient elements ... to be able to confirm that [the Commissioner will] no longer ... propose that the Commission adopts a negative decision in the procedure that is open against FIFA as regards the international transfer rules'.[692] In July 2001 FIFA's Executive Committee adopted a new set of international transfer rules in line with the March 2001 principles.[693]

---

[688] Joint FIFA/UEFA Negotiation Document (International Transfer of Players). Available at <www.uefa.com> (October 2001).

[689] FIFPro, *Time for a New Approach. The International Player Transfer System*, FIFPRO Report to the European Commission (9 February 2001), Para. 3.3.

[690] Ibid. p. 6.

[691] Presidency Conclusions, *Declaration on the specific characteristics of sport and its social function in Europe, of which account should be taken in implementing common policies*, Nice European Council Meeting (December 2000), Para. 16.

[692] Letter from Mario Monti to Joseph S. Blatter, 5.03.01 D/000258.

[693] FIFA Regulations for the Status and Transfer of Players, July 2001.

The new regulations subjected the international transfer of players under the age of 18 to some conditions, including the establishment and enforcement of a code of conduct to guarantee the sporting, training and academic education of minors. In the case of players aged under 23, a system of training compensation was to be in place to encourage and reward the training effort of clubs, in particular small clubs. Contracts of employment would be protected for a period of 3 years up until the age of 28 and 2 years thereafter. Sporting sanctions can be applied to players unilaterally terminating their contract within this protected time. Financial compensation can be paid if a contract is breached unilaterally whether by the player or the club. The creation of solidarity mechanisms based on a proportion of compensation fees was designed to redistribute a significant proportion of income to clubs involved in the training and education of a player, including amateur clubs. One transfer period would be permitted per season, and a further limited mid-season window, with a limit of one transfer per player per season. A dispute resolution and arbitration body is established which does not prejudice the ability of players to seek other forms of legal redress.

The agreement deviated significantly from interests of FIFPro who wished to see professional footballers' contractual rights being brought into conformity with national laws thus placing footballers on an even legal footing with normal employees. In May 2001 FIFPro brought an action before a Belgian court seeking an injunction to prevent FIFA from implementing the new rules on the grounds that they remained incompatible with Articles 39 and 81 EC. FIFPro objected to several elements of the new regime including the proposed minimum length of contracts, the question of sanctions being imposed on players who breached their contracts and the operation of the sporting just cause clause which, given certain circumstances, allowed players to unilaterally terminate their contract without sanction.[694] However, FIFPro applied for an adjournment pending the outcome of the FIFA Congress at Buenos Aires in July 2001. In August FIFA and FIFPro reached an agreement on FIFPro's participation in the implementation of the new transfer regulations with FIFPro representatives being able to sit on FIFA's Dispute Resolution Chamber along with representatives of the clubs. FIFPro was also permitted to nominate representatives for the new Arbitration Tribunal for Football, to which decisions of the Dispute Resolution Chamber can be appealed.

Following the agreement between FIFA and FIFPro, the new transfer regulations came into force in September 2001.[695] In June 2002 the Commission released a press release in which it announced the formal closure of its investigations into FIFA's regulations on international football transfers.[696] In the press release then-Commissioner Monti stated that '[t]he new rules find a balance between the players' fundamental right to free movement and stability of contracts together with the

---

[694] M. Bennett, 'They Think It's All Over ... It Is Now! How Extra Time Was Required to Finally Settle Football's Transfer Saga', 9(3) *Sport and the Law Journal* (2001).

[695] FIFA Regulations for the Status and Transfer of Players, 2001.

[696] Commission Press Release IP/02/824, 'Commission Closes Investigations into FIFA Regulations on International Football Transfers', 5 June 2002.

legitimate objective of integrity of the sport and the stability of championships'.[697] In assessing the legality of the new international regime Weatherill refuted the suggestion that the agreement represents a collective agreement for which EU competition law offers some immunity.[698] In *Brentjens* the Court found that collective labour agreements can escape the reach of competition law although the social partners would need to demonstrate that the agreement improves the employment and labour conditions of those covered by the agreement.[699] On the 2001 regulations Weatherill answers that 'neither the method of its production nor its content brings the 2001 agreement on transfers within the sanctuary recognised by the Court. The level of collective involvement was inconsistent and fragmented; the effect is not to improve players' working conditions'.[700]

The Commission's decision not to issue an exemption decision covering the 2001 agreement, favouring instead an exchange of letters and a press release, precludes a firm legal foundation for its findings. Furthermore, even though the Commission sanctioned the new regime, questions on the application of competition law remain. As the Court held in *Bosman*, 'in no circumstances does it [the Commission] have the power to authorise practices which are contrary to the Treaty'.[701] In *Meca-Medina*, the Court stated the importance of taking into account the overall context in which the disputed rules were taken or produce their effects, assessing the objectives of the rules, examining whether the restrictive effects are inherent in the pursuit of those objectives, and whether the rule was proportionate in that it did not go beyond what is necessary to achieve the objectives. Following this method could result in the transfer rules being removed from the scope of the Treaty's competition provisions. Alternatively, should the transfer system not be considered inherent, it could still be issued with an exemption under Article 81(3) should it satisfy the exemption criteria. A decision to remove the transfer system from the reach of Article 81(1) or the issuance of an exemption decision would not preclude a challenge to the rules based on Article 39 as the transfer regulations would be assessed in light of the Court's decision in *Meca-Medina* and will need to satisfy both competition and free movement law under which restrictions on player mobility will require objective justification. In 2005 FIFA revised the rules governing international transfers, although a number of contentious issues remain including the rules protecting minors, the provisions on training compensation for young players, provisions on contractual stability and the provision for transfer windows.

---

[697] Commission Press Release IP/02/824, 'Commission Closes Investigations into FIFA Regulations on International Football Transfers', 5 June 2002·

[698] S. Weatherill, 'Sport as Culture in EC Law', in R. Craufurd Smith, *Culture and European Union Law* (Oxford, Oxford University Press 2004) p. 123.

[699] Case C-115/97 *Brentjens*, judgment of 21 September 1999 [1999] *ECR* I-6025.

[700] S. Weatherill, 'Sport as Culture in EC Law', in R. Craufurd Smith, *Culture and European Union Law* (Oxford, Oxford University Press 2004) p. 123.

[701] *Bosman* Para. 136.

7.1.3. The protection of minors

Article 19 of the 2005 FIFA Regulations for the Status and Transfer of Players provide that international transfers of players are only permitted if the player is over the age of 18. Three exceptions to this rule apply. First, if the player's parents move to the country in which the new club is located for reasons not linked to football. Second, the transfer takes place within the territory of the EU or EEA and the player is aged between 16 and 18, subject to the new club fulfilling a number of minimum obligations including the provision of education, training and accommodation. Third, the player lives no further than 50km from a national border, and the club for which the player wishes to be registered in the neighbouring Association is also within 50km of that border. The maximum distance between the player's domicile and the club's quarters shall be 100km. In such cases, the player must continue to live at home and the two Associations concerned must give their explicit consent.

The regulations therefore impose a restriction on the movement of minors even though in EC law a minor can still be considered a worker and seek the relevant protections offered by Article 39. The Nice Declaration on Sport expressed in Paragraph 13 its 'concern about commercial transactions targeting minors in sport'. Article 282(1) of the Constitutional Treaty also provides that 'Union action shall be aimed at ... protecting the physical and moral integrity of sportsmen and sportswomen, especially young sportsmen and sportswomen'. Commenting on UEFA's home-grown player rule, the Belet Report on the Future of Professional Sport argued that '... additional arrangements are necessary to ensure that the home-grown players initiative does not lead to child trafficking, with some clubs giving contracts to very young children'.[702] The sports competence in the proposed Reform Treaty makes express reference to the protection of 'young sportsmen and sportswomen' in the context of Union action in the field. On the basis of this support, it must be accepted that the protection of minors is a legitimate concern. Nevertheless, an outright ban on the international transfer of minors is unlikely to be considered proportionate. As Van den Bogaert explains, if the transfer of minors is permitted within a Member State, a young player could still be transferred within a Member State and face relocation of many hundreds of miles, whilst a short cross border move would be prohibited.[703] Such a prohibition is indirectly discriminatory as it imposes a disproportionate burden on non-nationals. If internal transfers are also prohibited, the ban on international transfers represents a non-discriminatory restriction as it deters a national of a Member State from leaving their country of origin in order to exercise their right to free movement.[704] As discussed above, Article 19 of the 2005 FIFA Regulations does not amount to an outright ban on international transfers but it still acts as an impediment to free movement and, if challenged, would need to be objectively justified. Given that the protection of

---

[702] European Parliament, rapporteur: Ivo Belet, *Much Work Remains to be Done,* European Parliament Committee on Culture and Education, 2006/2130(INI), Para. 18.

[703] S. Van den Bogaert, *Practical Regulation of the Mobility of Sportsmen in the EU Post Bosman* (The Hague, Kluwer 2005) p. 238.

[704] *Bosman* Para. 96.

minors will be considered a legitimate objective, the regulations arguably represent a proportionate pursuit of this objective in that they permit cross border movement subject to minimum standards being observed. For Van den Bogaert, these conditions satisfy the requirements of Directive 94/33 on the protection of young people at work and thus satisfy the standards required for objective justification in Article 39 EC.[705]

7.1.4. Training compensation for young players

In order to encourage and reward the training effort of clubs, in particular small clubs, Article 20 of the FIFA Regulations provides that training compensation shall be paid to a player's training club(s) when a player signs his first contract as a professional, and on each transfer of a professional until the end of the season of his 23rd birthday. Article 21 states that if a professional is transferred before the expiry of his contract, any club that has contributed to his education and training shall receive a solidarity payment amounting to a proportion of the compensation paid to his previous club.[706] The obligation to pay training compensation arises whether the transfer takes place during or at the end of the player's contract.[707] FIFA regards a player's training and education as taking place between the ages of 12 and 23. In order to calculate the compensation due for training and education costs, national associations divide their clubs into a maximum of four categories which correlate with the clubs' financial investment in training players. The training costs are set for each category and correspond to the amount needed to train one player for one year multiplied by an average 'player factor', which is the ratio between the number of players who need to be trained to produce one professional player. Special provisions apply to players moving within the EU/EEA. In particular, if a player moves from a lower to a higher category club, the calculation of training costs is based on the average of the training costs of the two clubs. If the player moves from a higher to a lower category, the calculation is based on the training costs of the lower category club.[708]

The maintenance of out-of-contract transfer payments for players under the age of 23 is a clear departure from the judgment in *Bosman* in which all out-of-contract payments were prohibited. It restricts the free movement of young players by deterring them from leaving their home state for the purposes of taking up employment in another Member State.[709] Nevertheless, as Article 20 is applied without reference to nationality, it can potentially be objectively justified in free movement law. It must be recalled that whilst the Court accepted as legitimate the need to maintain a financial and competitive balance between clubs and accepted the need within sport to educate and train young players, the Court found that the transfer rules were not an appropriate means of achieving these objectives. On these grounds, the Court held that Article

---

[705] S. Van den Bogaert, *Practical Regulation of the Mobility of Sportsmen in the EU Post Bosman* (The Hague, Kluwer 2005) p. 239-240.
[706] Art. 21, FIFA Regulations for the Status and Transfer of Players, July 2005.
[707] Ibid. Art. 20.
[708] Ibid. Annex 4, Art. 6.
[709] *Bosman* Para. 96.

39 precludes the application of transfer rules which permits payment for an out-of-contract player wishing to move between clubs in different Member States. The new regulations are less restrictive only in so far as they place a potential restraint on young players as opposed to those over the age of 23 and '[i]t is difficult to see, comprehend or understand how such rules would not fall foul of Article 39'[710] simply because of the additional discrimination on the basis of age included in the new rules.

Elements of the FIFA formula for calculating training costs may also be considered a deviation from *Bosman*. In *Bosman*, the Court found that transfer fees were contingent, uncertain and totally unrelated to the actual costs of training a player. As a consequence, the prospect of receiving a transfer fee could not be considered a decisive factor in encouraging the training of young players.[711] FIFA's formula for calculating the training compensation due to clubs is based on estimated training costs. The costs incurred do not therefore necessarily relate to the actual training costs incurred. In the discussions on the 2001 agreement FIFPro claimed that the formula for calculating compensation fees bore no relation to the actual cost incurred in the training of a player and that '[h]istory shows that such fees operate as a significant and sometimes definitive restraint that can not only seriously undermine player earnings but also put players out of the game'.[712] Furthermore, FIFPro claimed that given the larger clubs already invest heavily in youth programmes, the maintenance of transfer fees for young players would result in resources flowing to the large clubs and not from them. The dominant position of the top clubs would be reinforced and this contradicts the solidarity argument presented in support of these rules.

The disconnection between the training compensation and the training costs actually incurred is compounded by the multiplier effect built into the formula which bases training costs, not on the actual cost of training one player, but the costs of training a number of players required to progress just one to professional status. Whilst the estimated system can be defended on the grounds of administrative convenience for smaller clubs in that it would be an arduous task to calculate the actual costs incurred in training a specific player, larger clubs are professional undertakings who should be able to keep accurate records through normal accountancy systems.[713] Despite these concerns, the multiplier effect does not seem unreasonable nor a deviation from *Bosman* in which the Court referred to 'the actual cost borne by clubs of training both future professional players and those who will never play professionally'.[714] What would appear to suffice is demonstration that that the FIFA formula is a relatively accurate reflection of the actual costs incurred. In that connection, an additional safeguard is provided by the FIFA Dispute Resolution Chamber which hears cases of disagreement over training compensation amounts.

---

[710] B. Dabscheck, 'The Globe at the Feet: FIFA's New Employment Rules – II', 9(1) *Sport in Society* (January 2006) p. 5.

[711] *Bosman* Para. 109.

[712] FIFPro, *Time for a New Approach. The International Player Transfer System*, FIFPRO Report to the European Commission (9 February 2001), p. 15.

[713] S. Van den Bogaert, *Practical Regulation of the Mobility of Sportsmen in the EU Post Bosman* (The Hague, Kluwer 2005) p. 256-257.

[714] *Bosman* Para. 109.

Article 20 of the FIFA Regulations may also be questionable under Articles 81 and 82 EC in that the recruitment choices for clubs are curtailed by the requirement to compensate a club for an out-of-contract player under the age of 23. In this context, Article 20 may be interpreted as having as its object or effect the limitation of the source of supply of players for clubs. The *Bosman* arguments relating to the transfer system appear to seriously undermine the case for Article 20 to be removed from the scope of Articles 81 and 82 EC on the grounds that these restrictions imposed on clubs derive from a need inherent in sport. The Court's reasoning in *Bosman* also suggests that the transfer rules cannot be considered as amounting to a proportionate restriction.

In assessing the legality of the system of training compensation, it is necessary to enter into two analyses. FIFA will need to demonstrate a meaningful connection between training compensation and the provision of incentives for clubs to invest in youth development. FIFA will also need to demonstrate that less restrictive means of achieving the legitimate objective of encouraging the education and training of young players is not available. On the first issue, Dobson and Goddard argue that the transfer system created an element of cross subsidy which has been crucial in ensuring the survival of many smaller clubs.[715] Despite the changes introduced by the 2001/2005 regime, this cross subsidy function appears in decline. Under the pre-*Bosman* system a club could recoup its investment in a player as the club could demand a transfer fee for a player who was both under contract and out-of-contract. Although the *Bosman* judgment prohibited out-of–contract transfers, it left in-contract transfers untouched and so again an incentive for training was maintained. Furthermore, following *Bosman* many clubs employed a strategy of placing players on longer contracts in order to protect their investments in players. Average contract length increased by about six months (20%) following *Bosman*.[716] As the 2001/2005 system enhances player mobility and limits both contract length and the compensation payable to the training club, one would expect average contract length to fall.[717] Consequently the new system has the potential to diminish incentives to invest in the education and training of young players because a new club can benefit from the initial investment without contributing to it.[718] The new regime may not therefore be suitable for achieving its stated objectives.

From this analysis flow two policy considerations. The first is whether more restrictive means of achieving the training objective are required. The second is whether

---

[715] S. Dobson and J. Goddard, 'Performance, Revenue and Cross-subsidisation in the Football League, 1927-1994', LI 4 *Economic History Review* (1998) p. 782.

[716] B. Frick, 'The football Players' Labor Market: Empirical Evidence from the Major European Leagues', 54(3) *Scottish Journal of Political Economy* (2007) p. 437.

[717] Ibid. p. 442.

[718] E. Feess and G. Mühlheußer, 'Economic Consequences of Transfer Fee Regulations in European Football', 13 *European Journal of Law and Economics* (2002); E. Feess and G. Mühlheußer, 'Transfer Fee Regulations in European Football', 47 *European Economic Review* (2003); E. Feess and G. Mühlheußer, 'The Impact of Transfer Fees on Professional Sports: An Analysis of the New Transfer System for European Football, 105(1) *Scandinavian Journal of Economics* (2003).

as a matter of policy the training objective should be abandoned. Clearly, in all occupations the employers' incentive to train the employee is diminished the less binding the contractual relationship between the parties is. Consequently, one may struggle to differentiate sport from other sectors in this regard. In that connection, Weatherill regards the Court's acceptance of the training objective as a '... mistaken concession to the perceived special characteristics of professional sport and [takes] the view that the idea that this is a sport-specific issue would and should be demolished were it to be revisited by the European Court'.[719] If that were the case, Article 20 would be condemned.

On the second analytical question concerning less restrictive means, two potentially less restrictive means merit consideration.[720] First, under the French-style 'pattern contract' a player trained by a club is obliged to sign their first professional contract with that club. Any subsequent move by that player entitles the training club to receive compensation for training provided. This system was rejected by the Commission in the post-*Bosman* negotiations as representing a potential breach of both Articles 39 and 81. Indeed, by requiring a player to join the training club, the pattern contract is in fact a more restrictive means of achieving the objectives than the restrictions imposed on young players in the 2001/2005 regulations. Nevertheless, should Article 20 fail to achieve the goal of incentivising the training of young players, the pattern contract may become appealing. A second alternative is for a system of revenue sharing in which a central solidarity fund is established to which all clubs would contribute. Training clubs would then be compensated from this fund. FIFPro recommended that this fund should comprise a proportion of gate receipts, television revenues and merchandising. This system does not entail a restriction on free movement and it addresses the concerns of the Court in *Bosman* that transfer fees could not be relied on as a stable source of income for clubs. Whilst the solidarity pool raises no free movement objections, the question remains whether it would create sufficient incentives for clubs to invest in youth training.

Other alternatives may be considered. Dabscheck argues that the aims of Articles 20 and 21 could be better achieved by the adoption of a simple rule placing an upper limit on the size of club squads.[721] This would prevent the top clubs from hoarding talent and ensure a more equitable distribution of that talent. Dubey proposed combining elements of both a solidarity fund and a system of training compensation.[722] Without entering into detailed discussion of all possible alternatives, the key legal issue is that if the Court maintains its view that it is legitimate to devise a system which encourages the education and training of young players, restrictions on labour

---

[719] S. Weatherill, 'Sport as Culture in EC Law', in R. Craufurd Smith, *Culture and European Union Law* (Oxford, Oxford University Press 2004) pp. 123-124.

[720] S. Van den Bogaert, *Practical Regulation of the Mobility of Sportsmen in the EU Post Bosman* (The Hague, Kluwer 2005) pp. 247-249, 269-271.

[721] B. Dabscheck, 'The Globe at the Feet: FIFA's New Employment Rules – II', 9(1) *Sport in Society* (January 2006) p. 14.

[722] S. Van den Bogaert, *Practical Regulation of the Mobility of Sportsmen in the EU Post Bosman* (The Hague, Kluwer 2005) pp. 272-273.

mobility that flow from that system can be objectively justified. There demonstrably remain concerns that Article 20 may be susceptible to condemnation, and a possibility exists that more restrictive measures than those currently imposed may be justified in the future. Much depends on the operation of Article 20 and the issue of whether the system has created sufficient incentives for clubs to invest and whether the absence of these incentives has had a deleterious effect on football. Further research is required on these questions.

7.1.5. Maintenance of contractual stability

The need to maintain contractual stability in football is defended by the governing bodies with reference to the need to preserve the regularity, proper functioning and competitive balance of competitions, to allow clubs to build squads, to facilitate supporters' identification with teams and to provide employment stability for players. In order to address the governing body's desire to ensure that contracts are honoured the FIFA Regulations make provision for contracts to be protected for a period of 3 years up until the age of 28 and 2 years thereafter. Article 13 of the FIFA Regulations states that a contract between a professional and a club may only be terminated on expiry of the duration of the contract or by mutual agreement.[723] Financial compensation will be payable if a contract is breached unilaterally by club or player. Should a club unilaterally breach a contract, various sanctions can also be imposed such as a ban on registering new players, deduction of points and exclusion from competitions. For players unilaterally terminating their contract within the protected time, sporting sanctions, such as a limited suspension, can be applied. Unilateral breaches of contract can occur in the case of 'just cause' or 'sporting just cause'.[724] An example of just cause would be a club breaching a contract by, for example, failing to pay monies owed to a player. Sporting just cause can be cited when an established professional has, in the course of the season, appeared in less than 10% of the official matches in which his club has been involved. In such a case, sporting sanctions shall not be imposed, though compensation may be payable. A professional may only terminate his contract on this basis in the 15 days following the last official match of the season of the club for which he is registered.[725]

Whilst the provisions on contract stability and sporting sanctions enhance player mobility in comparison to the pre-*Bosman* system, they still act to potentially deter a Member State national from leaving their home state for the purpose of taking up employment in another Member State. The rules therefore constitute a restriction on free movement and require justification. Furthermore, the rules may be susceptible to action under national law. The rules differentiate players from normal employees who, under national labour law, would be able to resign based on contractual notice periods or unilaterally terminate their contract and provide compensation to the employer.

---

[723] Art. 13, FIFA Regulations for the Status and Transfer of Players, July 2005.
[724] Ibid. Arts. 14-15.
[725] Ibid. Art. 15.

The normalisation of players' contracts was first attempted in 1999 by Arsenal player Nicolas Anelka who was advised by Jean-Louis Dupont, Bosman's lawyer. Anelka wished to leave Arsenal and considered unilaterally breaching his contract and paying compensation to Arsenal for the breach. Having satisfied the requirements of national law, Anelka would have been theoretically free to leave. However, as *Bosman* only condemned out-of-contract payments, the registration system for players under contract would have prevented Anelka from playing elsewhere. Anelka was eventually sold by Arsenal thus avoiding a legal test to the 'Anelka doctrine'.[726]

The post-*Bosman* regulations do not amount to a normalisation of players' contracts and an acceptance of the Anelka doctrine although players do have greater scope for affecting unilateral breaches. For example, former Hearts player Andy Webster made use of Article 17(3) of the FIFA Regulations in order to end his contract with the Scottish club and move to English club Wigan Athletic. Article 17(3) provides that a unilateral breach without just cause after the protected period will not result in sporting sanctions although disciplinary measures may be imposed for failure to give sufficient due notice of termination. This amounts to fifteen days following the last match of the season. The FIFA Dispute Resolution Chamber (DRC) decides on the compensation payable and in doing so takes into account the remuneration and other benefits due to the player under the existing contract and/or the new contract, the time remaining on the existing contract up to a maximum of five years and the fees and expenses paid or incurred by the former club.[727] Assuming the compensation amount does not amount to a mask for a transfer fee, it should not amount to a breach of Article 39. Of course, a player could consent in exchange for financial reward to a contractual assignment clause which imposes a high compensation fee in order to trigger their transfer. In these circumstances, Article 39 is not invoked. Invoking Article 17 may be of assistance to some high-profile players in order to secure a move to another large club. However, the effect may be felt most acutely in the lower leagues in which the calculation of compensation will not be as great and therefore not act as a disincentive to a unilateral breach.

Webster's case can be contrasted with that of Philippe Mexès, a player who moved from French club Auxerre to Italian club Roma. The FIFA DRC found that, unlike Webster, Mexès had unilaterally breached his contract within the protected period. The FIFA regulations provide that in addition to the obligation to pay compensation, sporting sanctions (a ban of up to six months) can also be imposed on any player found to be in breach of contract during the protected period.[728] The DRC permitted Mexès to register for Roma with immediate effect but imposed a six week ban on his eligibility to play for the club. In July 2005, the CAS upheld the ban on Mexès and sanctions imposed on Roma.[729]

---

[726] A. Caiger and J. O'Leary, 'The End of the Affair: The Anelka Doctrine – the Problem of Contract Stability in English Professional Football', in A. Caiger and S. Gardiner, eds., *Professional Sport in the EU, Regulation and Re-regulation* (The Hague, T.M.C. Asser Press 2000).

[727] Art. 17(1), FIFA Regulations for the Status and Transfer of Players, July 2005.

[728] Ibid. Art. 17(3).

[729] CAS 2005/A/902 & 903, *Mexès and AS Roma* v. *AJ Auxerre*.

Resisting freedom to contract continues to be a major concern for the governing bodies. The FIFA Regulations state that the minimum length of a contract shall be from the date of its entry into force to the end of the season, while the maximum length of a contract shall be five years.[730] In the 2001 edition of the regulations, the minimum contract length was one year.[731] The minimum length requirement amounts to a theoretical restriction of free movement although is in principle justifiable in that it pursues the legitimate objective of preserving the regularity of sporting competitions.[732] More contentious is the provision for a protected contract period and the imposition of sporting sanctions. The imposition of sporting sanctions on a player represents another potential impediment on a player's ability to exercise his right of free movement. Having satisfied national law on compensation for breach, the player should not be subject to a sanction. Of course, the specificity of sport argument reveals itself in this context. It naturally falls within the recognised territory of sporting autonomy for governing bodies to impose sanctions on participants for not following agreed rules. The provision is defended by reference to the need to preserve the regularity, proper functioning and competitive balance of competitions, to allow clubs to build squads, to facilitate supporters' identification with teams and to provide employment stability for players. The issue turns on whether these objectives are deemed legitimate and whether the imposition of sporting sanctions for unilateral breach is necessary for the attainment of them and proportionate. Clearly, much depends on the definition of a sporting just cause. The more narrowly this provision is construed, the greater the likelihood that the restriction on the players freedom of movement will not be justified.

The squad-building defence is questionable given the apparent short-termism evident in modern football, as is the supporters' identification justification. Football attendances appear to be experiencing continual growth in an age of labour mobility for players.[733] The question of player security is a legitimate consideration but requires endorsement from FIFPro. On the wider question of the impact of free agency on the regularity, proper functioning and competitive balance of sporting competitions, academics have long cast doubt on such claims.[734] Rottenberg argued that the US reserve system, which is akin to the European retain and transfer system, left the distribution of talent unaffected as the best players still migrated to the best teams. This is an example of the invariance principle which asserts that 'restrictions on the player labour market, such as the retain and transfer system, do not change the distribution of the playing talent among clubs in a league, compared to a competitive 'free agency' player market, if clubs behave like profit maximisers'.[735] It has been argued that follow-

---

[730] Art. 18(2), FIFA Regulations for the Status and Transfer of Players, July 2005.

[731] Art. 4(2), FIFA Regulations for the Status and Transfer of Players, 2001.

[732] *Lehtonen* Para. 53.

[733] Deloitte, *Annual Review of Football Finance* (2007).

[734] S. Rottenberg, 'The Baseball Players' Labor Market', 64 *Journal of Political Economy* (1956).

[735] S. Késenne, 'The Bosman Case and European Football', in W. Andreff and S. Szymanski, *Handbook on the Economics of Sport* (Cheltenham, Edward Elgar 2006) p. 637.

ing free agency in baseball, competition remained relatively balanced despite a clear revenue advantage for the larger teams.[736] Szymanski reviewed the literature on the impact of free agency on competitive balance in US baseball which was introduced in 1976 for players who completed six years of service.[737] Contrary to the claims of club owners, Szymanski finds either no evidence of a negative impact on competitive balance or evidence that it positively affects it, although Szymanski urges caution in how the data is to be interpreted.

The ECJ alluded to the invariance principle in *Bosman* by noting that the transfer system does not preclude the richest clubs from securing the services of the best players.[738] Rather than promoting competitive balance, restrictions on the player market resulting from transfer systems have been viewed as a means through which profit maximising clubs can control wages. Késenne argues that the introduction of free agency in US sports in the 1970's ended the underpayment of players, a scenario being replicated in Europe post-*Bosman*.[739] A less restrictive means of achieving contractual stability would be for clubs to load contractual benefits such as bonuses towards the end of a player's contract, or for players to have assignment clauses in their contract.[740] An assignment clause specifies an amount of money one club would need to pay to acquire a player under contract with another. To be lawful, the assignment (better termed buy-out) figure would need to represent a genuine estimation of the club's losses under the contract and not simply an arbitrary figure. Caiger and O'Leary also question whether contractual stability could be achieved outside the law of contract. They cite the English tort of interference with contractual performance which could be employed to dissuade clubs from poaching players under contract with other clubs.[741]

The principle of non-interference is also contained within the rules of the governing bodies. Article 14(c) of the FIFA Players' Agents Regulations state that a licensed players' agent must never 'approach a player who is under contract with a club with the aim of persuading him to terminate his contract prematurely or to flout the rights and duties stipulated in the contract'. The English Football Association Premier League also prohibits interference with contractual performance, known colloquially as tapping-up. Rule K3 provides that '[a]ny club which by itself, by any of its officials ... makes an approach either directly or indirectly to a contract player ... shall be in breach of these Rules'. Rule K5 provides that '[s]ubject to Rule K6, a contract player,

---

[736] J. Vrooman, 'A General Theory of Professional Sports Leagues', 61(4) *Southern Economic Journal* (1995).

[737] S. Szymanski, 'The Economic Design of Sporting Contests', 41 *Journal of Economic Literature* (2003) pp. 1159-1161.

[738] *Bosman* Para. 107.

[739] S. Késenne, 'The Bosman Case and European Football', in W. Andreff and S. Szymanski, *Handbook on the Economics of Sport* (Cheltenham, Edward Elgar 2006) p. 637.

[740] A. Caiger and J. O'Leary, 'The End of the Affair: The Anelka Doctrine – the Problem of Contract Stability in English Professional Football', in A. Caiger and S. Gardiner, eds., *Professional Sport in the EU, Regulation and Re-regulation* (The Hague, T.M.C. Asser Press 2000) p. 212.

[741] Ibid. p. 213.

either by himself or by any Person on his behalf, shall not either directly or indirectly make any such approach as is referred to in Rule K4 without having obtained the prior written consent of his Club'. In June 2005 Chelsea, its manager Jose Mourinho and then Arsenal player Ashley Cole were found guilty of breaching the above rules by the FA Premier League Independent Disciplinary Commission.

The Disciplinary Panel in the Cole case received evidence that rule K5 was an unlawful restraint of trade and that it could not be enforced against Cole even if he had breached it. Rule K5 denies an employee of a club the opportunity to advance their careers by considering alternative employment opportunities.[742] The application of EC law was not considered even though rule K5 could deter a player from seeking employment with a club in another league. In this connection, K5 would be considered a restriction under Article 39 EC although could be justified on the grounds that it promotes contractual stability and competitive balance. In defence of the rules Gordon Taylor, Chief Executive of the Professional Footballers Association, stated in a written submission to the Cole Commission that '[t]he rules speak for themselves with regard to the specificity of sport ... and to try to achieve fair competition and to avoid the biggest, richest clubs looking to destabilise players of rival clubs'. He also explained that the rule benefits players and was negotiated as part of a collective bargaining agreement which sought to 'achieve a fair balance between the rights of the players, the rights of the clubs as employers and the need to bear in mind special consideration appertaining to sport in order to try to achieve a fair and competitive balance and in order to protect the image of the game in front of the paying public'. The Commission agreed by finding that whilst the rule K5 amounts to a restraint of trade, it was reasonable as it promoted contractual stability and the stability of players. The decision was upheld by the FAPL Appeals Committee, although the sanctions were reduced. In August 2005 Cole appealed to the Court of Arbitration for Sport which decided that the appeal was inadmissible as the CAS had no jurisdiction in the dispute.[743]

7.1.6. Transfer windows

The 2005 FIFA Regulations make provision for one transfer period per season, and a further limited mid-season window, with a limit of one transfer per player per season. Transfer windows restrict the ability of players to seek alternative employment and restrict the ability of clubs to hire them. Consequently, the use of transfer windows can be considered an issue for both free movement and competition law. Their use is not a feature found in other industries. The legal robustness of this measure has been strengthened by the case law of the ECJ. In *Lehtonen*, the Court was asked to provide guidance on a case involving a Finnish Basketball player who was transferred from a Finnish team to a Belgian basketball team.[744] The Belgian bas-

---

[742] Football Association Premier League Disciplinary Commission, in the matter of Ashley Cole, Chelsea Football Club and Jose Mourinho.

[743] CAS 2005/A/952 *Ashley Cole* v. *FAPL*, award 24 January 2006.

[744] Case C-176/96 *Lehtonen* [2000] *ECR* I-2681.

ketball federation refused to register the player on the grounds that the transfer had not taken place within the permitted transfer window and as an un-registered player, Lehtonen was unable to compete in Belgian competitions. Lehtonen had, in fact, already represented his team, Castors Braine and the resulting win was overturned due to the breach of transfer rules. Lehtonen and Castors Braine applied to the Tribunal de Première Instance, Brussels for an interim order on the over-turned match and the sanctions imposed on Lehtonen. The national court requested guidance from the ECJ on the question of whether transfer windows breached Articles 12, 39, 81 and 82 of the Treaty.

The ECJ first examined the nature of the restriction and concluded that transfer windows did amount to such a restriction on a players' mobility even though the restriction related to fielding players and not employing them.[745] On the question of objective justification, the Court agreed with the submissions of the Basketball Federation that late transfers could substantially alter the sporting strength of teams in the course of the championship thus calling into question the proper functioning of sporting competition.[746] However, the differential treatment of players from inside and outside Europe, which the rules promoted, went beyond what was necessary and as such the rules were prohibited by Article 39.[747] Players from a federation outside the European zone were subject to a transfer deadline of March 31, whereas players inside the European zone were subject to a transfer deadline of February 28. The question of competition law was not addressed by the Court. In answer to the questions referred by the Tribunal de Première Instance, Brussels, on 13 April 2000, the ECJ held that such rules were prohibited by Article 31 '... unless objective reasons concerning only sport as such or relating to differences between the position of players from a federation in the European zone and that of players from a federation not in that zone justify such different treatment'.

Consequently, it seems logical that the FIFA transfer windows regulations are compatible with Article 39. Even though amounting to a restriction on free movement, the rule ensures the proper functioning of sporting competition. The stipulation limiting a player to one transfer per season similarly pursues this objective although it might be questioned whether this provision goes beyond what is necessary to achieve that objective. A less restrictive means of achieving the objective would be for a player to be allowed to move more than once in a season but to be prevented from playing for two different teams which are competing with each other in the same competition during the course of one season.[748] The referring court in *Lehtonen* also asked for, but did not receive, guidance on the application of EU competition law to the use of transfer windows. Unlike under Article 39, transfer windows are unlikely to be defined as a restriction at all under competition law. Preventing clubs from acquiring talent towards the end of a season derives from a need inherent in the proper functioning of

---

[745] *Lehtonen* Para. 50.

[746] Ibid. Para. 54.

[747] Ibid. Para. 58.

[748] S. Van den Bogaert, *Practical Regulation of the Mobility of Sportsmen in the EU Post Bosman* (The Hague, Kluwer 2005) p. 303.

a championship. Such rules are therefore likely to be found incapable of being defined as a restriction providing they do not go beyond what is necessary in the achievement of that objective.

7.1.7. Third party influence on player mobility

Not all restrictions on player mobility derive from the rules of the sports governing bodies. In football, it has become common for investment companies to own the economic rights of a player. This means the investment company owns the player's registration and claims entitlement to any transfer fee received. An investor receives a return on their investment once a player is transferred. According to the 2005 European Parliament Report Professional Sport in the Internal Market, Article 39 EC could be invoked if the third party has a decisive influence, by way of a contractual clause or some other influence, in the player's transfer.[749] This legal assessment is distinct from that which has so far been conducted in relation to the influence of investment funds in football. In 2007, English club West Ham United were fined by the Football Association Premier League for breaching league rule U18 on the influence of third parties, which seeks to prevent third parties from materially influencing a club's policies and/or the performance of its teams in League matches and/or the competitions.

7.2. NATIONALITY RESTRICTIONS

The clearest example of rules designed to segment the European sports labour market along national lines are those concerning nationality restrictions, as is discussed in detail in Chapters 3-5. It is a fundamental principle of Community law that any discrimination on the grounds of nationality shall be prohibited. In *Walrave*, two Dutch professional pacemakers in motor-paced cycle races brought an action before a national court following a rule change by the Union Cycliste Internationale (UCI) on the national composition of cycling teams. From 1973, the two elements of the cycling team, the pacemaker and the stayer, were required to be of the same nationality. Although the UCI justified the change of rule on the grounds that World Championships are intended to be competitions between national teams, the two complainants objected on the grounds that it would break up their successful relationship with non-Dutch stayers and amounted to a breach of the principle of non-discrimination on the grounds of nationality. The ECJ held that 'having regard to the objectives of the Community, the practice of sport is subject to Community law only in so far as it constitutes an economic activity within the meaning of Article 2 of the Treaty'.[750] However, the prohibition on discrimination 'does not affect the composition of sport teams, in particular national teams, the formation of which is a question of purely

---

[749] European Parliament, *Professional Sport in the Internal Market*, Commissioned by the Committee on the Internal Market and Consumer Protection of the European Parliament on the initiative of Toine Manders, Project No. IP/A/IMCO/ST/2005-004 (2005), p. 89.

[750] *Walrave* Para. 4.

sporting interest and as such has nothing to do with economic activity'.[751] The ECJ added that 'this restriction on the scope of the provisions in question must however remain limited to its proper objective'.[752]

In *Donà* the ECJ heard a case involving nationality rules in Italian football. Under Article 28(g) of the Italian Football Federation (FIGC) rules, normally only players of Italian nationality, residing in Italy, could be issued with a membership card permitting them to play professional football. In a somewhat contrived case, the objective of which was to open the Italian football league to foreign players, an agent who had attempted to recruit players from abroad challenged the federation's rules.[753] The national court requested a preliminary ruling from the ECJ. In his opinion delivered on 6th July 1976, Advocate General Trabucchi considered that

> 'there is ... nothing to prevent considerations of purely sporting interest from justifying the imposition of some restriction on the signing of foreign players or at least on their participation in official championship matches so as to ensure that the winning team will be representative of the state of which it is the champion team'.[754]

The ECJ took a different view by finding that nationality rules in sport are incompatible with the non-discrimination principle in Community free movement rules 'unless such rules or practice exclude foreign players from participation in certain matches for reasons which are not of an economic nature, which relate to the particular nature and context of such matches and are thus of sporting interest only'.[755]

UEFA persisted with nationality restrictions in club football despite continued objections from the Directorate General for the Internal Market.[756] Further discussions took place between the Commission and UEFA resulting in UEFA adopting the 1991 3+2 rule, an agreement concluded with Martin Bangermann, the Vice-President of the Commission. From July 1992, national associations and UEFA could limit to three the number of foreign players whom a club may field in any first division match in their national championships and in UEFA competitions, plus two assimilated players who have played in the country in question for five years uninterruptedly, including three years in junior teams.

The 3+2 rule was condemned in *Bosman*. The ECJ repeated that Article 39 guarantees freedom of movement for workers and requires the abolition of discrimination based on nationality between workers of the Member States as regards employment, remuneration and conditions of work.[757] Whilst nationality quotas relate to the fielding of players and not to their employment, a restriction still exists as a restriction

---

[751] Ibid. Para. 8.

[752] Ibid. Para. 9.

[753] R. Blanpain and R. Inston, *The Bosman Case. The End of the Transfer System?* (Leuven, Peeters and Sweet and Maxwell 1996).

[754] *Donà*, Opinion of Advocate General Trabucchi, at p. 1344.

[755] *Donà* Para. 14.

[756] E. Grayson, *Sport and the Law*, 2nd edn. (London, Butterworth & Co. 1994) p. 274.

[757] *Bosman* Para. 117.

on participation and also directly affects the prospects of employment.[758] The Court reviewed a series of arguments presented by UEFA, URBSFA and some national governments seeking to justify nationality restrictions on non-economic grounds. On the question of whether nationality restrictions were necessary to maintain a link between club and country, the ECJ argued that a football club's link with the Member State in which it is established cannot be regarded as any more inherent in its sporting activity than its links with its locality, town or region where no rules exist designed to maintain the connection.[759] Second, on the justification relating to nationality restrictions being necessary to ensure a pool of players eligible to play for the national team, the ECJ considered that labour mobility enhances the prospects of players playing in other national associations and that no rules exist limiting a national team's choice of players to one association.[760] Third, the ECJ held that nationality restrictions are inadequate for maintaining a competitive balance between clubs because the richer teams can still recruit the best national players.[761] Finally, in relation to UEFA's argument that nationality restrictions were sanctioned by the European Commission, the ECJ reiterated that the Commission does not possess the power to authorise practices that are contrary to the Treaty.[762] Consequently, in answer to the question referred by the national court, the Court held that 'Article 39 of the EC Treaty precludes the application of rules laid down by sporting associations under which, in matches in competitions which they organize, football clubs may field only a limited number of professional players who are nationals of other Member States'.[763]

From the early sporting exception cases, considered in detail in Chapter 4, an argument for the condemnation of nationality restrictions in the economic activity of club football can be extracted. In the context of activity which is economic, and thus fails the *Walrave* paragraph four criterion, rules can still be exempt from the prohibitions on nationality discrimination if their purpose is the organisation of sport on the basis of nationality, such as is the case where nationality rules serve to structure competition on that basis. The *Walrave* paragraph eight distinction, namely that nationality rules in national team sports constitute 'purely sporting rules with nothing to do with economic activity', is unsatisfactory in light of modern practice. In some sports such as cricket, players are issued central contracts in order to represent the national team. As employees, this clearly satisfies the definition of economic activity. At issue is the legal reasoning for maintaining national eligibility criteria and not the principle, for without such criteria there could be no meaningful national competition.

In *Meca-Medina*, the Court reinterpreted the notion of rules of 'purely sporting interest', accepting that it was difficult to divine such rules which had 'nothing to do with economic activity'.[764] It reiterated that in this respect, the Treaty provisions

---

[758] Ibid. Para. 120.

[759] Ibid. Para. 131.

[760] Ibid. Paras. 133-134.

[761] Ibid. Para. 136.

[762] Ibid. Para. 136.

[763] Ibid. Para. 137.

[764] *Meca-Medina* Paras. 25-26.

concerning freedom of movement 'do not preclude rules or practices justified on non-economic grounds which relate to the particular nature and context of certain sporting events' and are 'limited to [their] proper objectives'.[765] The Court therefore accepted that even where competitions structured on the basis of nationality could constitute economic activity and economic impacts may be inevitable consequences of such rules, if motives were not based on economic grounds and genuinely related to the structuring of competition on the basis of nationality, these could still be exempt from the Treaty prohibition. However, the facts of *Meca-Medina* involved the economic impacts of 'inherent' anti-doping rules, which were neither discriminatory nor primarily economic in purpose. It has as yet to rule on a case involving direct nationality discrimination in that context. It is submitted that the Court is not likely to accept direct nationality discrimination in the context of competition law where it is not related to the sporting exception in free movement, and arguably therefore also 'inherent'.

7.2.1. The rights of third country nationals

The liberalisation of the European players market has under limited circumstances been extended to non-EU nationals playing within the territory of the EU/EEA. The EU has entered into a number of international agreements with third states. Some of these contain rules similar to the EC Treaty prohibitions on discrimination which often lead to similar legal outcomes in this context.[766] EU free movement rules can only be relied on by non-EU nationals if there such an international agreement is in place and the non-discriminatory provision is directly effective thus allowing nationals of the state subject to the agreement to rely on it before a national court. This requirement will be satisfied if the provision contains a clear and precise obligation which does not rely on the adoption of subsequent measures, and a number of cases have established firmly a presumption that prohibitions on nationality discrimination in many of those agreements have direct effect. These provisions do not, however, confer a right of free movement to third country nationals but merely prohibit discriminatory working conditions in the Member State in which they are already legally employed.[767] It also appears that some agreements are more likely to have direct effect than others, since the wording is not identical and some obligations such as for example those in the Association Agreements with Ukraine and Moldova require Member States to merely 'endeavour to ensure' the removal discriminatory restrictions.[768]

The *Bosman* judgment ended the practice of footballers from the Member States of the Union being tied to clubs beyond the term of their contracts without another club paying a transfer fee. However, the question of its effects on non-EU nationals was uncertain. This was raised in the reference made to the court in the *Balog* case.[769] Tibor Balog was a Hungarian footballer legally employed at Belgium first division

---

[765] Ibid. Para. 26 relying on *Donà* Paras. 14-15.
[766] See the Opinions of Advocate General Stix-Hackl in *Kolpak* and *Simutenkov*.
[767] *Kolpak* Para. 42.
[768] *Simutenkov*, Opinion of Advocate General Stix-Hackl, points 23 and 24.
[769] Case C-264/98 *Balog*, reference removed from the register, 2 April 2001.

side, Charleroi. At the end of his contract he refused a one year contract extension and sought to move from Charleroi who refused him a free transfer on the basis that *Bosman* was only applicable to EU nationals. Consequently, Balog's next employer would be required to purchase his registration from Charleroi, a scenario raising the same issues addressed in *Bosman*. Balog brought action in the Belgian courts and the national court referred the matter to the ECJ.[770] At issue was also part of the unanswered referred question in *Bosman* concerning the application of competition law. The Court was asked to interpret Article 81 of the EC Treaty and Article 53 of the EEA Agreement with reference to the conduct of a sports club which, on the basis of the rules of the national, European and world football federations, demands payment of a transfer sum on the occasion of the engagement of one of its former professional players of non-Community nationality who has reached the end of his contract by another club established in the same Member State, another EU/EEA Member State or a non-member country. In late March 2001, the case was settled shortly before Advocate General Stix-Hackl was due to deliver her Opinion. This Opinion was expected to be supportive of Balog's claim and it is clear that just three weeks after the transfer system settlement between FIFA and the Commission, the football authorities could not tolerate a negative Court decision.[771]

The *Malaja* case concerned a Polish basketball player playing professionally in France. The French Basketball Federation only permitted two non-EEA nationals to be fielded in each match. For the 1998/99 season, Racing Club de Strasbourg had already registered two such players thus limiting Ms Malaja's prospects of play. At the time, Poland was not a Member State of the EU but had concluded an Association Agreement with the EU. Article 37(1) of that agreement provided a non-discrimination clause stating that Polish workers should not be discriminated against on the grounds of nationality. The Administrative Court of Appeal in Nancy held that the provision satisfied the requirements enabling Ms Malaja to rely upon Article 37(1).[772]

A similar set of circumstances arose in *Kolpak*. Maros Kolpak, a Slovak national, was a handball goalkeeper playing in the second division handball club TSV Ostringen in Germany. He concluded a contract with the club in 1997 which was subsequently renewed until June 2003. Kolpak was legally employed in Germany. The national governing of handball, the German Handball Federation (DHB), issued Kolpak with players' licence marked with the letter A, a letter indicating non-EU/EEA players. At the time the Slovak Republic was not a Member State of the EU. According to Article 15 of the DHB regulations, clubs in the Bundesliga or Regionalligen were only permitted to field two players with A-licences per competition match. Kolpak successfully challenged the decision before the Landgericht arguing that he should not be issued with an A license due to the non-discriminatory provisions contained in the EU/Slovak Agreement. The DHB appealed against the decision and the *Oberlandesgericht* (Higher Regional Court) made a reference to the ECJ.

---

[770] Ibid.

[771] S. Van den Bogaert, *Practical Regulation of the Mobility of Sportsmen in the EU Post Bosman* (The Hague, Kluwer 2005) p. 107.

[772] Case No. 99NC00282, judgment of 3 February 2000.

Article 38(1) of the EU / Slovak Association Agreement provided that 'subject to the conditions and modalities applicable in each Member State treatment accorded to workers of Slovak Republic nationality legally employed in the territory of a Member State shall be free from any discrimination based on nationality, as regards working conditions, remuneration or dismissal, as compared to its own nationals'. The ECJ found that Article 38(1) did hold direct effect and confirmed that the prohibition of discrimination applies to rules laid down by sporting bodies which determine the conditions under which professional sportsmen can engage in gainful employment. Consequently, the Court held that Article 38(1) precludes

'the application to a professional sportsman of Slovak nationality, who is lawfully employed by a club established in a Member State, of a rule drawn up by a sports federation in that State under which clubs are authorised to field, during league or cup matches, only a limited number of players from non-member countries that are not parties to the Agreement on the European Economic Area'.[773]

The Court found that the discrimination could not 'be regarded as justified on exclusively sporting grounds' and that no other arguments were advanced 'capable of providing objective justification for the difference in treatment' between nationals and non-nationals.[774] This, together with equally awkward forms of words of the Grand Chamber of the ECJ in *Simutenkov* and the treatment of nationality discrimination in the context of objective justification in *Bosman* suggest that even the Court itself has doubts as to the analytical framework of free movement and objective justification, the legal implications which are considered in greater detail in Chapters 3 and 4. Nevertheless, the outcome of the case was that Article 38 entitled Slovak nationals to treatment equal to that of the nationals of the Member States in whose territory they are legally employed. This equal treatment extends to working conditions, remuneration and dismissal. Article 38 and similar non-discriminatory provisions contained in Association Agreements do not establish a principle of free movement for non-EU workers within the Community as Article 39 EC does for EU nationals. Although there is no case law as to whether those provisions also subject non-discriminatory obstacles to free movement to scrutiny, it should be noted that in practice the liberalisation of the EU player market may have this effect in intra-state transfers since the differential treatment of players from Member States would in effect make those rules discriminatory in relation to domestic players. This does not fall within the notion of a 'purely internal' situation because the Association State national has exercised his rights of free movement. However, where that national seeks to transfer to another State, the act would constitute access to that State's labour market and as such would not fall within the scope of the Accession Agreement's prohibition on discrimination in working conditions.

At issue in *Simutenkov* was a dispute between a Russian footballer legally employed in Spain and the Ministry of Education and Culture and the Royal Spanish

---

[773] *Kolpak* Para. 58.
[774] Ibid. Paras. 56 and 57.

Football Federation. Igor Simutenkov played for Spanish league side Club Deportivo Tenerife as a non-EU player. In 2001 the player submitted through that club an application to the Royal Spanish Football Federation requesting the replacement of that status with a license granting him the same status as Community nationals. The request was rejected on the grounds that the rules of the Spanish Football Federation precluded the issuance of such licences to non-EU/EEA nationals. Simutenkov was therefore classed as a non-EU player and subject to nationality restrictions in force in Spain. Three non-EU players could participate in division one matches in the 2000/01 season. Simutenkov brought an action before the Central Court for Contentious Administrative Proceedings challenging the Federation's refusal to alter his status. The Court dismissed the application in October 2002 and Simutenkov appealed to the High Court, which made a reference to the ECJ. At issue was Article 23(1) of the EU/Russia partnership which provided for the same protection for Russian nationals as Article 38 did for Slovak nationals. A difference between the two lay in the purpose of each Agreement. Unlike with the Slovak Agreement, the Russian Agreement was never intended to act as the basis for the gradual integration of that state into the EU but rather as a platform for co-operation. Nevertheless, the statement on non-discrimination was clear regardless of the purpose of the Agreement. As in *Kolpak*, the ECJ found that the non-discrimination provision in Article 23(1) had direct effect and confirmed that the issuance of a license did amount to a working condition and was more than a mere administrative permit as was argued by the Spanish Government and the Football Federation.[775] The Court came to the same conclusion as in *Kolpak*, substituting the words 'of Slovak nationality' with 'of Russian nationality'. By analogy, Article 23 of the EU/Russia Agreement offered Russian sportspersons protection from discrimination in terms of working conditions, remuneration or dismissal when legally employed in the territory of the EU.[776]

7.2.2. Home-grown players

It is clear that the EU has limited UEFA's scope to continue to structure the European sports labour market along national lines. UEFA argues that the rulings in *Bosman* and *Kolpak* have generated three serious externalities for football. First, the rulings have promoted financial instability in European football and competitive balance has been undermined. Labour mobility has promoted a trade in players and encouraged clubs to spend heavily on attracting new talent. This has promoted wage inflation, financial instability and a diminution of competitive balance as financial disparities between clubs widen. The free market approach has not led to a more even distribution of talent because clubs simply hoard players, a position strongly discouraged under the pre-*Bosman* 3+2 agreement. This commercialisation of the game has also contributed to larger clubs resisting attempts to redistribute money and this has serious consequences in terms of a concentration of wealth and a diminution of the

---

[775] *Simutenkov* Para. 18.
[776] *Simutenkov*.

solidarity principle which connects football at all levels. Second, the judgments have encouraged clubs to rely on the market to attract players thus creating disincentives for clubs to invest in the education and training of local talent. This has consequences for the future development of talent and may undermine national team sports. It also further heightens financial stability, competitive imbalance and short-termism. Third, UEFA claim that the proliferation in international player transfers has severed the link between clubs and their localities, a link strongly favoured by supporters.

In response to these concerns, UEFA adopted new regulations at their Ordinary Congress in April 2005 in Estonia and these were subsequently incorporated into the 2006/07 UEFA regulations.[777] The new rule provides that squad lists for UEFA club competitions will continue to be limited to 25 players for the main 'A' list. From season 2006-2007, the final four places are reserved exclusively for 'locally trained players'. A locally trained player is either a 'club trained player' or an 'association trained player'. In the following two seasons, one additional place for a club trained player and one additional place for an association trained player is reserved on the A list with the final numbers of four club trained and four association trained players in place for the 2009 season. A club trained player is defined as a player who, irrespective of his nationality and age, has been registered with his current club for a period, continuous or non-continuous, of three entire seasons or of 36 months whilst between the ages of 15 and 21. An association trained player fulfils the same criteria but with another club in the same association. In the event that a club fails to meet the new conditions for registration, the maximum number of players on the 'A' list will be reduced accordingly. Should a club list an ineligible player in the places reserved for home-grown players, those players will not be eligible to participate for the club in the UEFA club competition in question and the club will be unable to replace that player on list 'A'. UEFA made the recommendation for national associations to apply the same rule for domestic competitions.

The home-grown player rule is crafted in such a way as to avoid direct reference to nationality. It is legally distinguishable from the 3+2 rule in the sense that the Bangermann compromise amounted to a directly discriminatory restriction on labour mobility whilst the effect, and one might conclude objective, of the home-grown rule is to impose a residency requirement on players. UEFA's approach to the issue of home-grown players is sharply contrasted to that of FIFA. In November 2006 FIFA and FIFPro published a joint Memorandum of Understanding which, *inter alia*, contained joint support for the 'protection of national teams by FIFA introducing, over several seasons, the 6+5 system regarding eligibility for national teams'.[778] This initiative was approved by the FIFA Congress in May 2007 and if implemented will require clubs to field at least six players qualified to represent the national team in the association in which they play.

In law this initiative is conceptually different to UEFA's rule in that it amounts to direct nationality discrimination and potentially seriously limits the justificatory field,

---

[777] UEFA, *Regulations of the UEFA Champions League 2006/07 competition, Conditions for Registration* (2005) p. 22.

[778] FIFA/FIFPro, Memorandum of Understanding (November 2006) p. 5.

as is detailed in Chapters 3 and 4. The Court has consistently held that directly discriminatory rules in the context of the fundamental economic freedoms are justifiable
only with reference to the Treaty derogations, or the public service exceptions. Whilst
it has recognised the possibility of rules that are 'inherent' in the organisation of sport
and thus do not constitute restrictions of either free movement or of competition, this
category appears limited to non-discriminatory, indistinctly applicable rules that bear
no relationship, even if indirect, to nationality discrimination.[779] It is true that the
Court has in Paragraph 8 of *Walrave* accepted that the prohibition on discrimination
itself did not apply to nationality rules in national team sports. However, it has consistently denied the extension of this category of sporting exception to other nationality
rules, particularly in the context of economic sporting activities such as professional
football. It could be argued that the Court has implied in principle the objective justifiability of such rules in the context of sport due to its placement of this analysis in
the context of nationality rules in *Bosman, Kolpak* and *Simutenkov*. Nevertheless,
the case remains that nationality rules in professional sports have never been found
justified on the facts of any decided case, and that it seems increasingly unlikely that
given its harsh view of the rule in *Bosman*, a similar rule could survive such as the
6+5 rule proposed by FIFA. However, UEFA's home-grown player rule only amounts
to indirect discrimination on the grounds of nationality and is therefore in any case
capable of objective justification beyond the Treaty grounds. The question then arises
what legitimate grounds could possibly be such that a home-grown player rule would
constitute the least restrictive measure capable of satisfying that objective.

Maintaining a competitive balance between clubs and promoting the education
and training of young players are objectives which UEFA can legitimately pursue.[780]
UEFA will need to establish a connection between the home-gown rule and these
objectives. Késenne argues that competitive balance across Europe could be negatively affected if labour market liberalisation is not matched by a de-regulation in the
product market, namely the structure of European football in which the market is segmented along national lines.[781] The better players will simply migrate from the small
to the large markets thus impairing competitive balance between national leagues.
This has particularly pronounced effects on the top clubs in small markets such as the
Netherlands. Here, Ajax Amsterdam previously competed to a high level in European
competitions but now struggle to compete internationally.

UEFA's arguments require careful construction. Assuming UEFA does not want
to de-regulate the product market and establish a number of European leagues, they
need to re-regulate the labour market and reintroduce greater national segmenta-

---

[779] S. Miettinen and R. Parrish, 'Nationality Discrimination in Community Law: An Assessment
of UEFA Regulations Governing Player Eligibility for European Club Competitions (The Home-grown
Player Rule)', 5(2) *Entertainment and Sports Law Journal* (2007).

[780] *Bosman* Para. 106.

[781] S. Késenne, 'The Bosman Case and European Football', in W. Andreff and S. Szymanski, *Handbook on the Economics of Sport* (Cheltenham, Edward Elgar 2006) p. 638; S. Késenne, 'The Peculiar International Economics of Professional Football in Europe', 54(3) *Scottish Journal of Political Economy*
(2007).

tion without reference to nationality eligibility. From a political perspective, UEFA's home-grown rule is therefore well crafted. Yet, their desire to intervene in the labour market by way of the rule reveals a deeper regulatory anxiety. If Késenne is correct, one can envisage growing discontent within small to medium sized leagues whose clubs find themselves unable to compete with clubs from larger markets. This may lead some clubs to consider cross-border territorial relocation into larger markets or forming supranational leagues capable of competing with the big five leagues of England, Italy, Germany, Spain and France. Such a model, whilst conceivable under UEFA control, could seriously undermine UEFA's regulatory control of the game. If the home-grown rule is challenged, UEFA would therefore need to convince a court that the rule does seek to promote competitive balance and is not a mask for continued regulatory strength.

Whilst the rule places some requirement on clubs to train their own young players, it struggles to make a convincing case on its indispensability in incentivising youth training schemes and maintaining competitive balance. It does not impede the richer clubs in their efforts to recruitment and remunerate the best players. Furthermore, these clubs will still be in a stronger position to invest in academies and recruit association trained players, thus maintaining their position of competitive superiority. As the ECJ found in *Bosman*, nationality clauses 'are not sufficient to achieve the aim of maintaining a competitive balance, since there are no rules limiting the possibility for such clubs to recruit the best national players, thus undermining that balance to just the same extent'.[782] Whilst UEFA claim the rule is neutral in terms of nationality, the restriction amounts to indirect discrimination and consequently the *Bosman* reasoning still applies. Nor does it follow that the rule will deter the hoarding of players. Squad size limits are already in operation in UEFA competitions and players who do not play regularly can invoke the FIFA regulations on 'sporting just cause' to seek contract termination without the imposition of sanctions.[783]

A concern which could potentially limit the justificatory strength of the home-grown rule is the prospect of clubs searching internationally to recruit young foreign players to their academies in order to qualify them as home-grown players. This contradicts the EU's desire to protect young players from commercial exploitation as expressed in Paragraph 13 of the Nice Declaration on Sport. The protection of young sportsmen and sportswomen was recognised in the Constitutional Treaty and continues as an express policy objective in the draft Reform Treaty. It was also a concern raised in the European Parliament's Belet Report on The Future of Professional Football in Europe. Whilst the Report expressed strong support for UEFA's home-grown rule, it remained 'convinced that additional arrangements are necessary to ensure that the home-grown players initiative does not lead to child trafficking, with some clubs giving contracts to very young children'.[784]

---

[782] *Bosman* Para. 135.

[783] Art. 15, 2005 FIFA Regulations on Status and Transfer of Players.

[784] European Parliament, rapporteur: Ivo Belet, *Much Work Remains to be Done,* European Parliament Committee on Culture and Education, 2006/2130(INI), Para. 18.

UEFA contends that the proliferation in international player transfers has severed the link between the club and its locality and that supporters favour a strong link. A UEFA survey on the home-grown player rule attracted 5,600 responses.[785] 83% agreed that '[i]t is important that clubs maintain their local/regional identity'. 69% agreed that '[t]he link between clubs and their local community (or region) depends partly on fans being able to identify with the players in the team'. 66% agreed that '[t]here is an increasing loss of local/regional identity in clubs – as fewer locally trained players are used by clubs'. UEFA's survey, whilst as yet not confirmed by independent sources, is a contribution not to be immediately dismissed. With Community law placing a significant emphasis on evidence based justifications for *prima facie* restrictive rules, the governing bodies of sport need to engage more actively with research. Despite the findings of the survey, it does not seem that the appearance of migrant workers within leagues has affected attendance at games or the value of broadcasting and other commercial rights. For instance, the 2007 Deloitte Review of Football Finance revealed that the big five leagues in Europe generated revenues of EUR 6.7 billion in 2005/06 which represented 7 per cent growth on the preceding year. In England, Premier League attendances and capacity utilisation experienced continued growth.[786] As Késenne argues, '[i]f European supporters would hate the mobility of players, they would have turned away from football, which would have stopped the international transfers because clubs do not shoot themselves in the foot'.[787] Whilst Késenne may be underestimating just how deep-seated and non-substitutable a club brand may be, on balance consumers have not responded to these transfers by abandoning their clubs. Whether clubs are utility maximising or profit maximising, they recruit players according to their needs. For Ranc, there is no evidence that the *Bosman* ruling put an end to supporters' identification with their club because players are not the only means through which fans can attach to their club.[788] Ranc argues that whilst clubs may symbolise a local, and not a national identity, that does not necessarily support the thesis that fans favour local players. Indeed, when local groups are from different nationalities, the presence of foreigners can actually be a means to attract support from such communities.

It is unlikely that the ECJ would accept as legitimate UEFA's connection between the home-grown rule and the promotion of local links. As described above, the rule will not necessarily lead to a higher proportion of genuinely local players representing their local club as the rule is neutral in terms of nationality and it places no restriction on the number of home-grown players that must be fielded in a starting eleven. In *Bosman*, the ECJ decided that a football club's link with the Member State in which it is established cannot be regarded as any more inherent in its sporting activity than its links with its locality, town or region where no rules exist designed to maintain the

[785] *UEFA proposals win fan backing*, see at <www.uefa.com> (11 July 07).

[786] Deloitte, *Annual Review of Football Finance* (2007).

[787] S. Késenne, 'The Peculiar International Economics of Professional Football in Europe', 54(3) *Scottish Journal of Political Economy* (2007) p. 397.

[788] D. Ranc, *Vectors of Identification and Markets of Identity in Contemporary European Football*, XIth International CESH Congress (Vienna 2006).

connection.[789] It added that 'in international competitions, moreover, participation is limited to clubs which have achieved certain results in competition in their respective countries, without any particular significance being attached to the nationalities of their players'.[790] This fact remains unchanged as UEFA has only recommended that national associations implement the rule for domestic competition whilst it is compulsory for teams competing in European competitions.

UEFA also contend that international labour mobility in football is affecting the quality of national teams by discouraging investment in youth, narrowing the pool of talent available for national associations from which to select and causing problems over how national associations monitor the progress of players who play in other national associations. As described above, the protection of national team sports has been acknowledged by the Court as a legitimate objective.[791] In *Deliège*, Advocate General Cosmas remarked, that 'the pursuit of a national team's interests constitutes an overriding need in the public interest which, by its very nature, is capable of justifying restrictions on the freedom to provide services'.[792] Nevertheless, in *Bosman* the Court rejected the notion that directly discriminatory nationality restrictions are necessary to ensure a pool of players eligible to play for the national team. It noted that labour mobility enhances the prospects of players playing in other national associations and that national associations remain free to select players playing in other associations.[793] Furthermore, the unexpected victory of Greece in the 2004 European Championships revealed the strength of competitive balance in European football. Nevertheless, the Court's faith in the opportunities a single market offers to players may be somewhat exaggerated given the presence of strong cultural, linguistic and economic barriers to the migration of players from larger markets to smaller markets.

The justifications presented by UEFA also need to satisfy the proportionality test and in this connection a number of alternatives should be considered, the details of which are examined in the next chapter and elsewhere in this book. These include internal revenue sharing mechanisms, the use of salary caps to promote competitive balance, the use of a strengthened club licensing scheme, an agreement concluded by way of social dialogue or even changes in governing body governance structures such as the abolition of the Champions League and the de-regulation of the product market in which a number of European leagues would operate. In 2006 the UEFA-commissioned Independent European Sport Review provided strong support for UEFA's rule. The Review argued that the link between the financial budget of a club and its playing strength will become less direct as a result of the rule and concluded that 'such a system, which promotes education and training and competitive balance should be

---

[789] *Bosman* Para. 131.
[790] Ibid. Para. 132.
[791] *Walrave* Para. 8.
[792] *Deliège*, Opinion of Advocate General Cosmas, point 84.
[793] *Bosman* Paras. 133-134.

seen as compatible with Community law'.[794] Similarly, the Belet Report expressed
support for the rule 'on the condition that these measures remain proportionate and
are not linked to players' nationality'.[795] Clearly, the Belet Report was signalling its
support for UEFA's approach rather than that of FIFA. Nevertheless, in the Commission Staff Working Paper accompanying the White Paper on Sport, the Commission
reported that it was still analysing the home-grown rule and was waiting the results
of a Commissioned study on the training of young sportsmen and sportswomen in
Europe.[796]

7.2.3. The rights of amateur players

Even nationality restrictions in amateur sport are under investigation. Here, these
persist despite the Court's finding that that access to leisure activities is a corollary to
freedom of movement[797] and Article 12 of the EC Treaty which prohibits nationality
discrimination in relation to those areas of the Treaty that are not linked to fundamental economic freedoms. A worker's right to be joined by its family in the host country,
and the integration of that family into their new surroundings, may not be undermined
by directly discriminatory nationality rules employed by sports governing bodies.
The Commission has investigated nationality discrimination in the context of amateur
sports, and has concluded that citizenship entitles to non-discriminatory access to
amateur sport within the new state of residence.[798]

   However, the issue of amateur sportspersons' rights raises an interesting question
from the point of view of the original sporting exception in Paragraph 4 of *Walrave.*
Although the ECJ has subsequently altered and refined the legal formulae which are
employed to permit sporting rules to continue to operate even in the shadow of the application of the Treaty, it has continued to make reference to the Paragraph 4 distinction between sporting activity which is non-economic, and that which is economic in
its recent case law up to and including *Meca-Medina.*[799] Its reiteration of the exact
form of words in that paragraph suggests that the Court is still prepared to consider
non-economic sporting activity outside the scope of the Treaty and thus exempt from
other Treaty provisions. Thus it may be that the combined effects of Article 12 and
Article 18(1), which together prohibit discrimination against citizens exercising their
non-economic free movement rights, do not apply in relation to non-economic sporting activity. This in practice requires free movement rights in the sporting context
to be derived from either a primary economic freedom, or from a secondary right
based on a relationship between the individual and a person exercising such rights.

---

[794] J. Arnaut, *Independent European Sport Review* (2006), see at <www.independentfootballreview.
com>, p. 50.

[795] European Parliament, rapporteur: Ivo Belet, *Much Work Remains to be Done,* European Parliament Committee on Culture and Education, 2006/2130(INI), Para. 17.

[796] Commission of the European Communities, *White Paper on Sport*, COM(2007) 391 Final, p. 13.

[797] Case C-334/94 *Commission* v. *France* [1996] *ECR* I-1307 Para. 21.

[798] Commission Press Release IP/04/1222 Brussels, 13 October 2004.

[799] *Meca-Medina* Para. 22.

Another consequence of this is that in the context of non-economic sporting activity, discrimination on the basis of grounds other than nationality may not be contrary to Community law. In principle, the Court could find that activity pursued without the prospect of direct remuneration constitutes a service, following indications to this effect given in *Deliège*. However, this raises the thorny question of what its stance will be towards activity without even a spurious economic dimension. Also, the appreciation of facts and the determination of whether such a dimension exists is within the powers of national courts, rather than the ECJ, so they, too, have a considerable role in the development or otherwise of the rights of amateur sportspersons in EC law. As yet no comprehensive study exists on how these rules are applied by national courts.

7.3. CONCLUSIONS

In theory there are two sustainable models of labour market organisation within sport. First is the perfectly liberalised model in which players' contractual position with their clubs is normalised with that of traditional workers. This entails freedom to contract and the absence of discrimination on the grounds of nationality. The second model is the protectionist model in which players are considered a unique category of worker subject to restrictions akin to the pre-*Bosman* regime. In reality, neither of these models is likely to prevail in the medium term. Interventions in the player market will continue to be tolerated by the EU as long as it can be demonstrated that such interventions are an effective and proportionate means of achieving legitimate objectives. In this connection, more research is required on the factual evidence of connections between restraining player mobility and the objectives of ensuring competitive balance, providing training incentives, protecting national teams, and connecting with local communities. In the absence of evidence-based justificatory support, the players market will continue to be liberalised and this will cause some significant governance issues for the governing bodies. Two issues are of particular interest. The first is whether a liberalised player market will continue to promote contractual freedom and migratory flows to such an extent that the competitive balance between national league systems and incentives to train young players are lost altogether. The second is whether that market will force a change in the product market itself, for instance as large clubs from smaller markets challenge rules on territorial relocation in order to compete with teams from larger markets. Some of these issues are crystallised within the home-grown player debate. UEFA assert that the post-*Bosman* liberalised player market disturbs competitive balance, creates financial instability in the game as clubs rely on the market to bring in new players which has a consequential impact on training programmes and the strength of the national team. Some economists cast doubt on these fears although where they are recognised to be legitimate, de-regulation in the product market is recommended as the solution rather than the reintroduction of restrictions on players' mobility. This is as unappealing to UEFA as de-regulation in the player market as it further erodes its regulatory control. Consequently, UEFA have sought to re-regulate the player market through the adoption of the home-grown player rule. Strategically, this rule enables UEFA to gradually re-partition the players market along national lines without the need to make structural changes in the product market. As the rule amounts to indirect nationality discrimination, their ability to succeed rests on them connecting the rule to the proportionate pursuit of the legitimate objectives discussed above and does not raise questions as to the currently unsettled question of how directly discriminatory restrictions in the context of sport can be objectively justified. In this connection, more research must be conducted on the value of the rule and it remains likely that in the absence of further evidence based justificatory support, the Court would condemn the rule regardless of the Commission's conciliatory stance.

Chapter 8
Legal Issues in the Governance of Sport

Governance issues in sport raise questions of EC competition law. The Commission has acquired considerable experience of applying competition rules to sporting contexts but its method in this sector had not been specifically reviewed by the European Court of Justice. In *Meca-Medina* the Court established a definitive methodology for applying competition law to sport. The judgment is notable for its constriction of the use of the sporting exception in which rules alleged to have only sporting relevance were excluded from the application of the Treaty's competition provisions. Instead, the Court held that 'it is apparent that the mere fact that a rule is purely sporting in nature does not have the effect of removing from the scope of the Treaty the person engaging in the activity governed by that rule or the body which has laid it down'.[800] Relying on the judgment in *Wouters*, the Court stated the importance of taking into account the overall context in which the dispute rules were taken or produce their effects, assessing the objectives of the rules, examining whether the restrictive effects are inherent in the pursuit of those objectives, and whether the rules were proportionate in that they did not go beyond what was necessary to achieve the objectives.

This analysis was employed by the Court to remove the disputed anti-doping rules from challenge under Article 81(1). The context in which the doping rules were made related to the legitimate pursuit of clean sport. The restrictions imposed on the swimmers were considered inherent in the pursuit of these objectives and they did not go beyond what was necessary to achieve them. This analysis would also remove such rules from the scope of Article 82. Where the Court is unable to make the determination that a rule is inherent in the organisation or proper conduct of sport, it will be defined as a restriction under Article 81(1) and condemned unless the exemption criteria contained in Article 81(3) can be applied.

In relation to governance standards in European sport, governing bodies will pursue a number of related legitimate objectives including the laying down of the rules of the game, ensuring the effective organisation of sport, ensuring the proper conduct of sport, ensuring competitive balance and uncertainty of result, maintaining the integrity of sport, protecting the well-being of young athletes, encouraging the education and training of young players, ensuring the viability of competition, maintaining the financial stability of sport and maintaining a safe environment for spectators and participants. Whilst some of these features relate to the operation of the European model of sport, restrictions purporting simply to be in conformity with the European model cannot be regarded as pursuing a legitimate objective. In order to escape the reach of competition law, contested rules pursuing the above legitimate objectives must be deemed inherent. Thus far only rules limiting multiple club ownership and those re-

---

[800] *Meca-Medina* Para. 27.

lating to anti-doping measures have been considered such. The rule must still remain proportionate in relation to the attainment of those legitimate objectives. In particular, the Court will examine whether the rule has been applied in a transparent, objective and non-discriminatory manner. It may also be material whether it allows relevant stakeholders a reasonable input into the decision making process.

This chapter examines three contentious issues relating to the governance of sport in Europe. First, it debates the lawfulness of rules designed to structure the product market. In this connection a number of features are examined including the promotion and relegation system, rules regulating territorial location of clubs, rules preventing break-away leagues, rules preventing multiple club ownership and club licensing rules. Second, the chapter questions whether proposals to regulate players' pay by way of a salary cap are lawful. It also explores the pending *Charleroi/Oulmers* litigation rising out of mandatory player release clauses.[801] Finally, the chapter interrogates current patterns of player agent regulation with reference to the EC Treaty's provisions on competition law and free movement.

8.1. STRUCTURING THE PRODUCT MARKET

Chapter 7 described how commercial and legal forces have liberalised the European player market. Players are able to migrate across frontier with limited restrictions imposed upon them by way of the transfer system and nationality restrictions. Player market liberalisation is a policy actively pursued by the Court and the Commission but thus far they have been reluctant to pursue a concurrent policy of de-regulation in European product market. As a result, whilst national segmentation in the player market has been dismantled, the organisational basis of sporting competition remains national. Although contrary to the principles of a single market, the Commission has its indicated political support for the maintenance of national segmentation in the product market.

In 1998 the Commission referred to the commitment to a national identity in terms of organising sport in Europe as 'one key feature of the European model' and added that 'the monopolistic role of federations is not called into question, as their institutional structure is recognised to be the most efficient way of organising sport'.[802] Furthermore, in the White Paper on Sport the Commission stated that the organisation of football on a national territorial basis was not called into question by Community law and that it supported 'the organisation of sport on a national basis, and the principle of a single federation per sport'.[803] Also in the White Paper the Commission considered that the 'organisation of sport and of competitions on a national basis is part of the historical and cultural background of the European approach to sport, and

---

[801] Case C-243/06 *Charleroi/Oulmers, OJ* C 212, 2 September 2006, p. 11.

[802] Commission of the European Communities, *Developments and Prospects for Community Activity in the Field of Sport*, Commission Staff Working Paper (1998), Directorate General X, p. 8.

[803] Commission of the European Communities, *White Paper on Sport*, COM(2007) 391 Final, p. 13.

corresponds to the wishes of European citizens'.[804] The Arnaut Report supports this line of reasoning, arguing that Community law should not extend a right to clubs to 'cherry pick' the events it plays in within the overall pyramid structure.[805] The Report claims this would undermine the proper functioning of national and international competitions and compromise the financial solidarity system on which the pyramid model of European sport is based. On these grounds, the Report argues that rules related to the participation or non-participation in sporting competitions in the European sports pyramid do not conflict with European Community law. National segmentation is therefore a central feature of the European model of sport. Nevertheless, rules designed to maintain this structure do impact on the commercial freedoms of undertakings operating within the sector.

8.1.1. Promotion and relegation

A key feature distinguishing the European and US models of sport is the existence of a system of promotion and relegation. In the US leagues are closed, but the European system is based on open vertical channels of mobility for clubs. This system rewards excellence through promotion and punishes under-performance through relegation. Some argue that this European system is inferior to the US model in terms of team profitability, its discouragement of revenue sharing and its resultant propensity to promote competitive imbalance.[806] Faced with the strong incentive to avoid relegation, or to achieve promotion, teams forfeit profit for on-the-pitch success and this can lead to financial instability. However, it enhances the competitive nature of sport and may thus be responding to consumer preferences. Ultimately, this can result in one or more of the larger clubs actually being relegated thus further reducing the overall profitability of the league and reducing consumer welfare. The promotion and relegation system can also lead to an underinvestment in infrastructure, such as stadium facilities, as clubs value playing talent over facilities. As all clubs stand a theoretical chance of progressing up the organisational pyramid, promotion and relegation also removes the need for a franchise system in which clubs relocate from small to large markets. Not only is this discouraged under the European system, it is prohibited by the governing bodies. Prohibitions on club relocation, either intra-state or inter-state, and prohibitions on breakaway structures impose restrictions on clubs as undertakings and may be susceptible to legal challenge.

Promotion and relegation requires rules regulating the conditions under which a team is promoted or relegated. Whilst this is determined on the basis of a points tally, other technical criteria may be imposed which could be subject to legal challenge. For example, Stevenage Borough challenged stadium criteria imposed on teams entering the Football League following their winning of the championship in the top

---

[804] Ibid. p. 14.

[805] J. Arnaut, *Independent European Sport Review* (2006), see at <www.independentfootballreview. com> p. 37.

[806] S. Szymanski, 'The Economic Design of Sporting Contests', 41 *Journal of Economic Literature* (2003) p. 1175.

non-league division.[807] As promotion allows for the theoretical prospect that a lower league club could enter European competitions, a cross border dimension would be evident and Community law potentially engaged. Should such a question arise in EC competition law, a rule which imposes minimum stadium requirements on promoted clubs might be considered inherent in the operation of safe sport and removed from the scope of Articles 81 and 82 as long as the rule was proportionate. However, a rule requiring levels of investment or bureaucratic compliance far beyond the means of all non-league clubs wishing to enter the league system could be considered a means of protecting the status of league clubs. Other entry conditions linked to club licensing schemes are discussed below.

Nevertheless, the principle of promotion and relegation can be defended on the grounds that it imposes a fiercely competitive sporting mentality on clubs which has a positive impact on competitive balance as smaller clubs have strong incentives to compete throughout the whole season. This requires them to attract talent which in turn creates a more equal distribution of talent throughout the league. Their tenacity is particularly evident towards the end of the season when issues of relegation are brought into sharper focus. Under a closed league system, games towards the end of a season can often be meaningless for those whose prospect of winning a championship or entering post-season competition is non-existent. In addition, Szymanski notes that sports leagues with promotion and relegation tend to be governed by bodies which have an interest in the development of sport at all levels.[808] A closed league system does not have this grassroots solidarity mentality. Consequently, promotion and relegation can be defended on the grounds that it promotes competitive balance, solidarity and that consumers benefit from a better contest, although these issues only really arise in the context of a debate over the formation of a closed breakaway league. Hornsby argues that rules in closed leagues effectively shutting out competition can be challenged only if there is room for only one such system, and that the league structure can therefore be considered an 'essential facility' to which potential competitors must be afforded access.[809]

8.1.2. Home and away rule

In the *Mouscron* case, Belgian football club Excelsior Mouscron made a request to UEFA to stage the home leg of a 1997/98 UEFA Cup tie against French side F.C. Metz in a nearby Stadium in Lille, France. Mouscron's ground capacity was restricted by UEFA to more than half its usual capacity and Mouscron wanted to play the game in a larger stadium thus satisfying consumer demand and maximising revenues. UEFA blocked the move referring to the home and away structure of its competitions which

---

[807] *Stevenage Borough FC Ltd* v. *Football League Ltd.* (1997) 9 Admin LR 109, Times August 1st, 1996.

[808] S. Szymanski, 'Revenue Sharing', in W. Andreff and S. Szymanski, *Handbook on the Economics of Sport* (Cheltenham, Edward Elgar 2006) p. 687.

[809] S. Hornsby, '"Closed Leagues": A Prime Candidate for the "Sporting Exception" in European Competition Law', 2 *International Sports Law Review* (June 2001).

required clubs to play their home matches on the ground of the home club or on another ground in the same or another city within the territory of its national association. The French Communauté Urbaine de Lille lodged a complaint challenging UEFA's home and away rule on the grounds that it breached Article 82 EC. The Commission rejected the complaint.[810] In the press release accompanying the unpublished decision, the Commission found that the rule constituted a sporting rule that did not fall within the scope of Articles 81 and 82 EC.[811] Commenting on the case in the White Paper on Sport, the Commission stated that the 'the organisation of football on a national territorial basis was not called into question by Community law' as the rule was indispensable for the organisation of national and international competitions in view of ensuring equality of chances between clubs and that it did not go beyond what was necessary.[812] *Meca-Medina* introduces the possibility of articulating this as a rule 'inherent' in the organisation and proper functioning of sport. Whilst the Commission favours such a solution, the Court has as yet to accept that the organisation of sport along national lines is an objective that ought legitimately to trump all other, foundational policy aims of Community law.

8.1.3. Club relocation

The open model of league organisation discourages club relocation as clubs in small markets are still able, with investment or skill, to progress through the leagues in order to satisfy their ambitions. The *Mouscron* decision concerned the temporary relocation of a club into another Member State. In other instances, clubs have sought to relocate permanently to another Member State but continue to play in the league of the home state. This was considered by English league side Wimbledon and Scottish league side Clydebank who explored the possibility of relocating to Dublin but wished to continue playing in their respective leagues.[813] It may be possible in principle to consider this rule 'inherent'. However, even if that is the case, it may be doubted that the prohibition amounts to a rule inherent in the maintenance of nationally rooted sporting competition given that the club would continue to play in the same league. Much depends on the circumstances of the case. For example, Berwick Rangers, a club based in an English town, play in the Scottish league yet this does not impede the effective organisation of either Scottish or English football nor inconvenience football supporters as Berwick is a border town. By contrast, when London side Wimbledon FC proposed a move to Dublin, the impact on the League of Ireland may have been considerable as would the effect on supporters of the London club who would have

---

[810] Case 36851, *C.U. de Lille/UEFA (Mouscron)* Unpublished Commission Decision of 9 December 1999.

[811] Commission Press Release IP/99/965, 9 December 99, 'Limits to Application of Treaty Competition Rules to Sport: Commission Gives Clear Signal'.

[812] Commission of the European Communities, *Commission staff working document. The EU and Sport: Background and Context*, SEC (2007) 935, p. 71.

[813] A. Duff, 'Scottish Update: A Brief Synopsis of Newsworthy Matters Concerning Football, Rugby & Others from August 1998 to Date', 6(3) *Sport and the Law Journal* (1998) p. 54.

faced an expensive round trip to attend their 'home' match. In Wimbledon's defence, the club made the calculation that they needed to move to a larger market in order to compete more effectively within the English league and that their presence in Ireland would have heightened interest in football generally.

Whilst the Wimbledon model was predicated on the club remaining in the English league, some large clubs in smaller markets may want to permanently relocate into a league in another national association whilst remaining based in the home state. For example, Rangers and Celtic are reportedly interested in playing in the English Premier League whilst continuing to be located in Glasgow and some Dutch clubs may be interested in playing in the German Bundesliga. Liberalisation of the player market has resulted in the leading teams from the smaller markets haemorrhaging talent to the larger markets thus seriously undermining their ability to compete in UEFA competitions. Permitting cross border relocation of this kind would undermine the national segmentation of the product market on which the European model is based. In the White Paper on Sport, the Commission argued that the in the Mouscron case 'the organisation of football on a national territorial basis was not called into question by Community law'. Nevertheless, if maintaining the national segmentation of the product market is to be considered a legitimate objective, then transparent and proportionate rules maintaining this segmentation could be considered 'inherent' in the pursuit of that objective. Adopting the counterfactual argument, there could be no truly national league system if clubs were able to establish themselves in another Member State. This could seriously destabilise national competition. The counter-argument is that player market liberalisation in the absence of product market liberalisation seriously undermines competitive balance in Europe and clubs require the commercial freedom to attract new sources of revenue in larger markets.

In conclusion a number of legal mechanisms may be employed to prevent a finding that the rule infringes Community law. First, given circumstances similar to those in Mouscron, the rule may be considered as having such a limited effect on cross border trade that it would be considered *de minimis* and there would be no Community interest in intervening. Second, if the rule is found to pursue legitimate objectives such as ensuring competitive balance and facilitating the efficient operation of the competition, the restriction imposed on the club could be considered inherent in the organisation of club competitions so long as it remained proportionate. Third, in the absence of a finding of inherency, the Commission could exempt the rule under Article 81(3) as it contributes to the production of the sporting contest whilst allowing consumers to benefit in the sense that the club is tied to the locality were most of its supporters are based.

However, the fact that the Commission possesses the analytical means to accept this rule within the context of its competition investigations and that it has in the past utilised those means is not in itself proof that the rule is compatible with Community law in either the field of competition or of free movement. No case has been brought before the Court of Justice in respect of the compatibility of this rule with free movement, or indeed with competition law, perhaps for good reasons on the part of the governing bodies. As potential service providers, clubs could also rely on Articles 43 or 49 EC, depending on the permanence of the relocation. As discussed in detail in Chapter 3, a rule 'inherent' in the organisation of sport does not constitute a 'restriction' to free movement. However, the home and away rule bears the hallmarks of market segmentation. It is therefore not beyond dispute that this objective can constitute an 'inherent' one. For similar reasons, it may encounter difficulties in the context of objective justification. It is for the governing bodies to articulate within this legal framework why abolishing the home and away rule would seriously destabilise the game, evidence of which has as yet not been forthcoming.

8.1.4. A breakaway European 'super-league'

Article 49(1) of the UEFA Statutes provides that 'UEFA shall have the sole jurisdiction to organise or abolish international competitions in Europe in which Member Associations and/or their clubs participate'. Article 49(3) states that '[i]nternational competitions and international tournaments which are not organised by UEFA shall require the approval of the latter'.[814] Alternative models of organising football in Europe must therefore receive the approval of UEFA and clubs participating in unsanctioned competitions would normally be expected to resign from their national association. Késenne argues that competition across Europe will become unbalanced if labour market liberalisation is not matched by a de-regulation in the product market.[815] Késenne argues for the establishment of one or more European leagues in which the best national teams leave their respective leagues and compete with one another in the new European league.[816] Furthermore, he argues that the Champions League should be abolished 'because of its devastating impact on the competitive balance between and within countries'.[817] This system would allow large clubs from small markets to compete more effectively on the international stage and would re-balance competitive forces within national leagues as the large clubs who previously dominated championships now played in the new European leagues, assuming that is they left the national league. Competitive balance could also be promoted by the creation of re-distributional policies such as the rookie draft system or a salary cap which are difficult to implement in an open league system.

Two super-league models could be pursued. In the first, smaller regional leagues could be established, such as the proposed Atlantic league. In 2001 it was reported that this league would be founded by Ajax Amsterdam, PSV Eindhoven and Feyenoord from the Netherlands, Rangers and Celtic from Scotland, Benfica and Sport-

---

[814] *UEFA statutes, rules of procedure of Congress, regulations governing the implementation of the statutes*, edition June 2007.

[815] S. Késenne, 'The Bosman Case and European Football', in W. Andreff and S. Szymanski, *Handbook on the Economics of Sport* (Cheltenham, Edward Elgar 2006) p. 638; S. Késenne, 'The Peculiar International Economics of Professional Football in Europe', 54(3) *Scottish Journal of Political Economy* (2007).

[816] See also T. Hoehn and S. Szymanski, 'The Americanisation of European Football', 28 *Economic Policy* (1999).

[817] S. Késenne, 'The Peculiar International Economics of Professional Football in Europe', 54(3) *Scottish Journal of Political Economy* (2007) p. 399.

ing from Portugal, Anderlecht and Bruges from Belgium, IK Gothenburg and AIK Stockholm from Sweden and Brondby and FC Copenhagen from Denmark.[818] Clubs would leave their unbalanced domestic leagues and compete with relative equals. The increased revenues that would be generated from this competition would enhance the ability of clubs of this stature to compete with the leading clubs from larger markets. Competitive balance would therefore be enhanced both within the new league and in terms of pan European competition. The second model is for the creation of a top-flight super-league in which the leading clubs from the largest markets left their respective national associations to form such a league, or they continued playing in their domestic leagues but established a rival to the Champions League independent of UEFA control. The UEFA Champions League was established to head off such a threat. In 1998 Italian marketing firm Media Partners International Limited lodged a complaint to the European Commission concerning UEFA's approval policy for alternative competitions. This, it was alleged, amounted to an abuse of a dominant market position. Media Partners then notified the Commission of their intention to establish a new European Football Super-league, independent of UEFA.[819] The Media Partners Super-league proposal was for 18 founder clubs to be given three years exclusive participation with membership being based on market strength as opposed to merit based criteria. To encourage clubs to participate, Media Partners offered a total of GBP 1.2 billion to the participants.[820]

The Media Partners proposal was not implemented as the top European clubs accepted UEFA's proposal to establish the Champions League in 1991/92. Under the old European Cup model, only winners of national championships would qualify for the European Cup, leaving other clubs to enter the less prestigious UEFA Cup. As the two Cups were based on a knock-out basis, a club could be faced with elimination after playing just one two-leg tie. This system, whilst popular with supporters, did not satisfy the larger clubs' desire to maximise revenues through repeat encounters with other large clubs. Repeat encounters facilitate their longer term financial planning. By widening the entry criteria to the Champions League and adopting a league system, more large clubs would compete with each other more often. For the clubs, this partly satisfied their financial objectives and removed questions of sanctions being imposed on them by UEFA and national associations for participation in an un-sanctioned league. In particular, whilst the larger clubs wish to engage in repeat supranational encounters, they also want to maintain lucrative domestic rivalries.

Serious consequences have flowed from the creation of the Champions League which amounts to a UEFA Super-league. Teams entering this competition are able to invest significantly more in squads than those not qualifying. This has implications for competitive balance in national competitions as the richer Champions League teams continue to compete with the poorer teams who do not qualify. This leads to

---

[818] 'UEFA Warns Clubs over Atlantic League', see at <www.sportbusiness.com> (27 September 2001).

[819] Case No. IV/37.400 – Project Gandalf, *OJ* C 70, 13. March 1999.

[820] J.P. Van den Brink, 'EC Competition Law and the Regulation of Football: Part 1', 21(8) *European Competition Law Review* (2000) p. 365.

a concentration of teams regularly qualifying for the Champions League and a progressive diminution of domestic competitive balance. It has also prompted a talent arms race in football as clubs attempt to break into the Champions League qualification places. This has had serious consequences on the financial stability of European football. Some argue for a European breakaway super-league in which the breakaway members leave their respective national leagues.[821] Only under this model would a competitive equilibrium have been found within both the super-league and the domestic leagues.

From a Community competition law perspective, it is not objectionable in itself for clubs to resign from national associations and establish a super-league. The question would rest on the nature of the newly established structure. The adoption of a Media Partners style closed league system would have been a significant departure from the traditional promotion and relegation system in Europe. Even though the Commission did not form a judgment on the Media Partners proposal, the closed league model may be objected to on the grounds that as a cartel of undertakings, the clubs should be expected to adopt fair and non-discriminatory access rules, either in terms of a promotion and relegation system, or by way of a franchise system most commonly employed in the USA. Articles 81 and 82 could preclude a closed league system without such access conditions as this could foreclose the market to aspiring entrants and amount to an abuse of a dominant market position. Furthermore, collective selling of broadcasting rights in a closed league system would arguably not be sanctioned by way of an exemption decision by the Commission as there would be no commitment, or indeed means, of redistributing revenues to leagues still under the regulatory control of UEFA and the national associations. Where the closed league itself operates clubs or owns the rights, Article 81 may be excluded because the league cannot as a matter of law conspire against itself. Of course, super-league clubs may well profit from individual selling and consequently, the league may not seek to collectively market the rights.

In order to remain with the current regulatory structure, breakaway clubs would need to satisfy UEFA's Article 49 approval policy. This has not yet been the subject of a formal decision by the Commission and opinion differs on its legality. The 2005 European Parliament on Professional Sport in the Internal Market cited the work of Hellenthal on the question of breakaway structures.[822] According to Hellenthal, UEFA's approval policy and the rules of national associations prohibiting clubs participating in unsanctioned competitions is a measure which affects trade between Member States and is one which has as its object restricting competition on the market for the organisation of European club competitions within Europe. Consequently, Hellenthal

---

[821] T. Hoehn and S. Szymanski, 'The Americanisation of European Football', 28 *Economic Policy* (1999); S. Késenne, 'The Peculiar International Economics of Professional Football in Europe', 54(3) *Scottish Journal of Political Economy* (2007).

[822] C. Hellenthal, *Zulässigkeit einer supranationalen Fussball Europaliga nach den Bestimmungen des europäischen Wettbewerbsrechts*, Frankfurt am Main 2000, cited in *Professional Sport in the Internal Market*, project No. IP/A/IMCO/ST/2005-004, Commissioned by the Committee on the Internal Market and Consumer Protection of the European Parliament (September 2005).

argues that the measure is in breach of Article 81 and incapable of being exempt pursuant to 81(3) EC. In addition, as UEFA holds a dominant position in the market for the organisation of European club competitions, it is also abusing its position of dominance in breach of Article 82 EC. A breakaway league based on open, transparent and non-discriminatory access conditions, such as a merit-based open system, would not be objectionable although practical considerations may preclude the adoption of this model. Either pan-European breakaway feeder leagues would need to be established in order to service the promotion and relegation system, or national leagues would need to form part of the structure despite national association rules prohibiting participation in such leagues. Alternatively, a franchise system based on fair and non-discriminatory access conditions would need to be established.

Restrictions imposed of members of bodies analogous to leagues have been considered by the European Court of Justice. In the Danish Co-operatives case, an agricultural co-operative was permitted to prohibit their members from participating in alternative agricultural co-operatives did not go '... beyond what [as] necessary to ensure that the cooperative functions properly'.[823] Following *Meca-Medina* in which the Court emphasised that rules necessary to ensure the integrity of sporting competitions were 'inherent' in the organisation of sport and therefore not 'restrictions' of competition, UEFA's approval policy might be removed from the scope of the EC Treaty's competition and that without such a rule, national competitions could be seriously undermined. If this analysis is unsustainable, the restriction might be exempted from the application of Article 81 as it facilitates the efficient production of the contest and allows consumers to benefit. Nevertheless, Hoehn and Szymanski question in 'The Americanisation of European football' why the European Commission would support the maintenance of national segmentation when the transnational league system appears the most plausible solution to the growing problem of competitive imbalance throughout Europe. Whilst the Danish Co-operatives analysis has application to the sports sector generally, the Commission must examine the nature of the restriction in its proper context.

Prohibitions on breakaway structures cannot simply be removed from the scope of competition law on the grounds that they promote the efficient organisation of the market. In the Formula One case, the Commission objected to the rules of FIA which had a number of consequences on the market for the organisation of motor racing competitions.[824] In particular, the FIA was accused of abusing a dominant position in breach of Article 82 EC by using its regulatory monopoly to maintain its commercial strength. First, the Commission believed that the FIA used its position to block series which compete with its own events by placing undue restrictions on promoters, circuit owners, vehicle manufacturers and drivers. Second, the FIA was accused of using its regulatory strength to force a competing series, the GTR Organisation, out of the market. Third, the Commission maintained that the FIA abused its market strength to acquire all the television rights to international motor sports events thus further

---

[823] *Gøttrup-Klim Grovvareforeninger and Others* Case C-250/92 [1994] *ECR* I-5641 Para. 40.

[824] Commission Press Release IP/99/434, 30 June 1999, 'Commission Opens Formal Proceedings into Formula One and Other International Motor Racing Series'.

contributing to regulatory and commercial concentration. Fourth, the Commission argued the FIA protected the Formula One Championship from competition by hoarding the prerequisites that are needed to stage a rival championship. The promoter's contracts prevented circuits used for Formula One races from being used for races that could compete with Formula One. In addition, the 'Concorde Agreement' prevented Formula One teams from competing in any other series and the agreements with broadcasters placed huge financial penalties on them if they televised anything deemed to be a competitive threat to Formula One.[825]

In 2001, the Commission adopted a Notice under Article 19(3) of Regulation 17/62, signalling its satisfaction with undertakings made by the FIA to the effect of making internal structural changes which were designed to separate the FIA's regulatory function from its commercial exploitation of Formula One, thus reducing restrictions on competitors.[826] Given that no further objections were raised by third parties following publication of the notice, the Commission closed the case in October 2001.[827] The agreement was a political compromise which allowed both the Commission and the FIA to express satisfaction with the outcome but 'it remains difficult to divine any clear legal principle from the settlement of the case'.[828] Nevertheless, it can be deduced that restrictions imposed on participants taking part in alternative competitions must be objectively related to the legitimate requirements of the sport such as ensuring the safe, efficient, fair or orderly conduct of the sport whilst remaining proportionate. The restrictions must not be a mask for the maintenance of commercial dominance.

These commercial questions lie at the heart of the debate on breakaway structures. The European football breakaway league idea is prompted by the desire of Europe's larger clubs to maximise revenues from playing one another on a more regular basis. In this respect, the threat of a breakaway league is more political than legal. UEFA's re-configuration of the European Cup demonstrates the strength of such pressure. In the longer term, it is not inconceivable that a de-regulated product market based on supranational, as opposed to national leagues, could fall under UEFA's regulatory purview. So too could a mixed model in which a super-league operates in conjunction with national leagues, although some argue that this would lead to untenable conflicts of interest.[829] In the meantime, the larger clubs want assurances on access conditions to the lucrative Champions League market.

---

[825] Commission Press Release IP/99/434, 30 June 1999, 'Commission Opens Formal Proceedings into Formula One and Other International Motor Racing Series'.

[826] Notice published pursuant to Art. 19(3) of Council Regulation No. 17 concerning cases COMP/35.163 – Notification of FIA Regulations, COMP/36.638 – Notification by FIA/FOA of Agreements relating to the FIA Formula One World Championship, COMP/36.776 – GTR/FIA & others (2001/C169/03), 13. June 2001.

[827] Commission Press Release, 30 October 2001, IP/01/1523, 'Commission Closes Its Investigation into Formula One and Other Four-wheel Motor Sports'.

[828] A. Bell, A. Lewis and J. Taylor, 'EC and UK Competition Rules and Sport', in A. Lewis and J. Taylor, *Sport: Law and Practice* (London, Butterworths Lexis Nexis 2003) p. 371.

[829] T. Hoehn and S. Szymanski, 'The Americanisation of European Football', 28 *Economic Policy* (1999).

8.1.5.   Access to competitions

UEFA regulates access to European competitions by way of a coefficients table. On the basis of final league standing, each national association enters a number of teams for participation in the Champions League and UEFA Cup. The number of teams each national association enters into these competitions is determined by past results of the clubs in those leagues. Under this formula, Spain, Italy and England are awarded four Champions Leagues places thus meaning that that top four placed clubs in those associations play in the Champions League in the following season. Other national associations enter fewer clubs. This system ensures that the best performing national associations, judged by the performance of their clubs, are rewarded through the most number of places in Champions League and UEFA Cup. However, as a consequence, clubs are dependent on but unable to influence the performance of other clubs in the same country. Entry into the Champions League is a major source of revenue for clubs and the coefficients formula may be caught by Article 81 in that it imposes unfair trading conditions on undertakings. Article 82 may be engaged as the entry conditions are imposed upon clubs and national associations by UEFA. This issue has received added attention since the election in 2007 of Michel Platini as President of UEFA. Platini has stated his preference for the removal of one Champions League place from the larger countries so that a more representative range of teams can enter the competition.[830] If challenged on competition law grounds, the coefficients formula can be defended on the basis that some selectivity is required and UEFA's formula is based on open, transparent and non-discriminatory criteria. Furthermore, decisions on how many places should be awarded to each national association needs to take into account the question of competitive balance in European football. Késenne argues for the abolition of the Champions league because of its effects on competitive balance.[831] Part of the imbalance stems from the number of clubs from leading associations entered into the competition. Platini's plan could result in some rebalancing by allowing larger teams from smaller markets to compete more regularly. On these grounds, the Commission may have grounds to remove the coefficients table from the scope of the Treaty's competition provisions as a rule 'inherent' in the organisation of the competition based on appropriate entry criteria which do not go beyond what is necessary for the attainment of these objectives.

8.1.6.   League organisation and clubs as service providers

The notion of 'inherency' in the organisation of sport has been accepted by the Court of Justice also in the context of free movement in *Deliège*. It is difficult to envisage organisational rules governing access to competitions or breakaway leagues that the Court would accept in the context of only competition law or free movement, but not both. Nevertheless, if the Court were to find that these rules were not 'inherent' in the

---

[830] Euro cash fear for English clubs, see at <www.bbc.co.uk> (11 January 2007).

[831] S. Késenne, 'The Peculiar International Economics of Professional Football in Europe', 54(3) *Scottish Journal of Political Economy* (2007) pp. 388-399.

context of free movement, this raises the question of whether the governing body is in principle within the personal scope of application of those free movement rules in relation to services or establishment. In any event it is clear that the governing bodies, when acting without the authorisation of the state, would not fall within the scope of application of either the services or professional qualifications directives. Should the thresholds for the application of Articles 43 or 49 be fulfilled, it would still be open to governing bodies to provide arguments to the effect that those rules are capable of objective justification.

8.1.7. Club ownership

Article 2 of UEFA's 2007/08 Regulations for both the Champions League and the UEFA Cup provides for measures designed to maintain the integrity of the UEFA competitions. No club participating in a UEFA club competition may hold or deal in the securities or shares of any other club participating in a UEFA club competition, nor be a member of any other club participating in a UEFA club competition. Licensed clubs may not be involved in any capacity in the management or operation of competing clubs. Furthermore, no one person may simultaneously be involved in any capacity in the management, or operation of more than one club participating in a UEFA club competition. Finally, no individual or legal entity may have control or influence over more than one club participating in a UEFA club competition. This control is defined as holding a majority of the shareholders' voting rights, having the right to appoint or remove a majority of the members of any controlling body of the club, being a shareholder and alone controlling a majority of the shareholders' voting rights pursuant to an agreement entered into with other shareholders of the club, or being able to exercise by any means a decisive influence in the decision-making of the club. If two or more clubs fail to meet these criteria, only one of them is entitled to be entered into a UEFA club competition.

Article 2 places a restriction on clubs attracting new investment and a restriction on the ability of undertakings to supply that investment. One such undertaking, the English National Investment Company (ENIC), lodged a complaint to the Commission on the grounds that it had been materially affected by UEFA's rule. Two football clubs owned by ENIC, AEK Athens and Slavia Prague, had qualified for the UEFA Cup Winners Cup along with Vicenza, an Italian club also owned by ENIC. According to UEFA's rule, only one team could participate in the competition. As entry into the competition was financially lucrative, ENIC and the affected club suffered a significant detriment. In 1999, two of the clubs lodged an appeal to the CAS which found for UEFA.[832] ENIC subsequently lodged a compliant with the Commission in February 2000 arguing that the rule restricted competition. The Commission's examination of UEFA's club ownership rule was concluded in July 2002 with the formal rejection of ENIC's complaint.[833] The Commission found that UEFA's rule is a decision taken

---

[832] CAS 98/200 *AEK Athens and Slavia Prague* v. *UEFA,* August 20, 1999, Lausanne, Switzerland.

[833] Case COMP/37 806: *ENIC/UEFA.* Commission Press Release IP/02/942, 27 June 2002, 'Commission Closes Investigation into UEFA Rule on Multiple Ownership of Football Clubs'.

by an association of undertakings and as such is theoretically caught within the scope of Article 81 EC. In a decision notable for its reliance on *Wouters*, the Commission considered that the object of the contested rule was not to distort competition and that the possible effect on clubs and potential investors was inherent to the very existence of credible pan European football competitions. Furthermore, the measure did not go beyond what was necessary to ensure the legitimate aim of protecting the uncertainty of the results and maintaining the integrity of the competition. As such, the rule was incapable of being defined as a restriction and consequently it fell outside the scope of Articles 81 and 82 EC.

8.1.8. Club licensing

It is common practice in sport for access to competitions to be conditional on participants satisfying minimum licensing requirements. UEFA's club licensing manual specifies five categories of minimum criteria to be satisfied by the clubs.[834] These are sporting criteria, infrastructure criteria, personnel and administrative criteria, legal criteria and financial criteria. Failure to meet compulsory criteria results in disqualification from UEFA competitions. In theory such licensing requirements amount to a barrier to entry to the market and are prone to capture within Article 81 and 82 EC. The club licensing system pursues a number of important sporting objectives including improving governance standards, maintaining minimum standards in terms of training and caring for young players, assuring clubs have adequate levels of management and organisation, ensuring that clubs' provide spectators and the media with well-appointed, well-equipped and safe stadiums, improving financial standards, safeguarding the continuity of international competitions, monitoring the financial fair play in the competitions, and allowing the development of benchmarking for clubs in financial, sporting, legal, personnel, administrative and infrastructure related criteria throughout Europe.[835]

These objectives are all argued to derive from a need inherent in the organisation of sporting competitions. Providing that these rules do not go beyond what is necessary for the attainment of these objectives, they could be deemed outside the scope of the Treaty competition provisions. Alternatively, in instances where the determination of inherency cannot be made, the rule may benefit from an exemption under Article 81(3). Clearly, the Commission would need to assess each contested restriction on its merits rather than accepting from the outset that all rules forming the basis of a licensing scheme are compatible with Community law. The club licensing scheme has the potential to act as a less restrictive means of UEFA achieving its legitimate objectives in other contexts. For example, the adoption of the home-grown player rule was designed, *inter alia*, to promote the education and training of young players, although the means of achieving this objective was based on a *de facto* residence requirement which amounted to indirect discrimination of the grounds of nationality. Part of the

---

[834] *UEFA Club Licensing System*, edition 2005.
[835] Id.

UEFA club licensing scheme requires each applicant club to run an approved youth development programme with effective management of this programme contributing to the fulfilment of UEFA's youth training objectives.

The scheme has scope for expansion and greater enforcement. For instance, the objective of encouraging clubs to invest in education and training programmes could potentially be achieved by extending the scheme to require clubs to spend a fixed sum on their youth academies. A minimum spending requirement could be implemented on a hard or soft basis in similar vein to a salary cap with a supplementary fee operating for those not spending the requisite amount. Whilst clubs may object to the imposition of such trading conditions, this licensing requirement could be defended on the grounds described above. In the White Paper on Sport, the Commission acknowledged the 'usefulness of robust licensing systems for professional clubs at European and national levels as a tool for promoting good governance in sport'.[836] It did not, however, acknowledge that good governance necessarily included any notion of economic redistribution. This aspect of the licensing rules appears less likely to satisfy the criteria for 'inherency'. The European Parliament's Belet Report stressed the importance of European club licensing in terms of establishing a level playing field in Europe given that clubs now compete on a supranational level through participation in the Champions League.[837] The Arnaut Report also favoured its use although stressed the importance of diligent enforcement.[838]

8.2. REGULATING PLAYERS' PAY AND RELEASE CCONDITIONS

8.2.1. Salary caps

The *Bosman* judgment liberalised the European player market and by doing so contributed to wage inflation in football. Monies that previously circulated between clubs by way of transfer fees were redirected to the players through higher salaries. For example, in Germany, average player salaries more than doubled between 1996/97 and 2006/07, standing now at over EUR 1 million.[839] The clubs were also seduced by the prospect of lucrative earnings stemming from involvement in the Champions League, and consequently they were encouraged to overspend to attract this new breed of nomadic talent. This overspending was often mistakenly guaranteed against revenues generated from participation in supranational competition and from a very buoyant broadcasting rights market. Clubs' traditional ethos as utility-maximising rather than profit maximising undertakings also encouraged the pursuit of sporting success when

---

[836] Commission of the European Communities, *White Paper on Sport*, COM(2007) 391 Final, p. 17.

[837] European Parliament, rapporteur: Ivo Belet, *Much Work Remains to be Done,* European Parliament Committee on Culture and Education, 2006/2130(INI), point 13.

[838] J. Arnaut, *Independent European Sport Review* (2006), see at <www.independentfootballreview. com>, p. 82.

[839] B. Frick, 'The football Players' Labor Market: Empirical Evidence from the Major European Leagues', 54(3) *Scottish Journal of Political Economy* (2007) p. 426.

financial prudence would urge caution. The system of promotion and relegation contributes to this utility maximising mentality. In sum, these influences appear to have
caused some significant perturbations within the game. Governing bodies claim that
player market liberalisation has caused financial instability in football, has seriously
impaired competitive balance, and has had a negative impact on supporters who pay
higher prices in order to subsidise higher player wages.

One possible solution to these problems is the introduction of a salary cap which
limits the amount a club can spend on player wages. Although salary capping is a
common feature in US sports, it is a relatively new phenomenon in Europe although
caps have been employed in a number of sports throughout Europe including rugby,
basketball and ice hockey. However, it is in the context of European football that the
debate on capping has received most attention.

A hard cap imposes a flat ceiling on the spending of all clubs whilst a soft cap links
spending to a percentage of revenue. As a salary cap restricts the ability of a club to
freely recruit players and on the level of competition for players' services could be
considered a restriction under Article 81 EC. A cap is inherently collusive and may
simply be employed in order to allow clubs to maximise revenues and control player
wages and influence. In this connection, a salary cap may be viewed as a crude means
of reconstructing player restraint mechanisms lost through general labour market liberalisation and on those grounds could not be sanctioned by competition law. Nevertheless, in a state of serious financial dislocation in sport, a strong case might be made
for a salary cap to be considered inherent in ensuring the economic viability of teams
competing in the league, preserving competitive balance between clubs and encouraging the development of young talent. Consequently, following *Meca-Medina*, a
cap might be removed from the scope of Articles 81 and 82 EC. This judgment needs
much closer scrutiny as the implementation of a hard and a soft cap will result in different impacts on the market. A hard cap imposes a much greater restriction on club's
commercial freedom than a soft cap. Nevertheless, some commentators have argued
that the softer the cap the harder the law should intervene.[840] A soft cap may be insufficient to correct competitive imbalance as it disproportionately affects the ability
of small clubs to improve their position. This is because larger clubs would continue
to be able to spend more on salaries thus aggravating income disparities between
clubs. This contrasts with a hard cap which imposes a flat ceiling on the spending
of all clubs thus creates a more level playing field assuming that all teams spend the
maximum permissible amount. Non-financial variables such as the quality of training
regimes are therefore afforded greater prominence. Consequently, whilst a hard cap
is arguably pro-competitive, a soft cap, although less restrictive on undertakings, may
create structural imbalance within a league. On these grounds, and depending on the
economic context in which the cap is imposed, a hard cap is more likely to be considered inherent in ensuring the economic viability of teams competing in the league,
preserving competitive balance between clubs and encouraging the development of
young talent. Thus a hard cap may escape definition as a restriction under Article

---

[840] S. Hornsby, 'The Harder the Cap, the Softer the Law?', 10(2) *Sport and the Law Journal* (2002).

81(1). Clearly removing a cap from the scope of Article 81 renders a discussion on the application of the exemption criteria meaningless. Nevertheless, whilst a soft cap may not be considered an inherent restriction, it may still qualify for an exemption under Article 81(3). For the reasons explained above, it is unlikely that a soft cap would satisfy the exemption criteria.

A potentially less restrictive measure than a cap is the luxury tax in which a soft cap is imposed and any spending over and above the ceiling is subject to a luxury tax, the proceeds of which are redistributed within the game.[841] This has the effect of discouraging clubs acquiring expensive playing talent. A luxury tax is no automatic panacea. The luxury tax which operated in baseball between 1997 and 1999 raised just over USD 30 million for redistribution, a fraction of total Major League spending.[842] Even less restrictive, but potentially as effective, are squad size limits which impose a ceiling on the number of squad players but which leave remuneration questions to the club. This also has the effect of restricting the hoarding of players thus ensuring a more equitable redistribution of playing talent.

The idea of a salary cap was mooted in *Bosman*. In the context of discussing alternatives to the disputed international transfer system for players, Advocate General Lenz remarked, 'it would be possible to determine by a collective wage agreement specified limits for the salaries to be paid to the players by the clubs'.[843] In football, the involvement of the social partners in the construction of a cap would be essential in order to restrict the application of competition law, since a salary cap constitutes a clear example of a restriction with the 'object' of restricting competition, not ordinarily justifiable in the framework of EC competition law and its 'inherency' must be demonstrated by the governing bodies in order for the rule to escape definition as a restriction. A less uncertain legal basis for the salary cap could be found in a collective agreement. In *Brentjens* the Court found that collective labour agreements can escape the reach of competition law if the social partners demonstrate that the agreement improves the employment and labour conditions of those covered by the agreement.[844] However, if the cap restricted a player's right of free movement, it would still be susceptible to challenge under Article 39. As a non-discriminatory restriction it could be justified with reference to the need to ensure the financial viability of the clubs, the need to maintain competitive balance and the need to train young players. However, as Snell points out, '[t]he Court has always insisted that restrictive measures cannot be justified by economic aims'.[845] In the gambling cases where restrictions were sought to be justified by reference to the redistribution of proceeds to benefit some

---

[841] S. Rosen and A. Sanderson, 'Labour Markets in Professional Sports', 111 *Economic Journal* (February 2001); and E. Gustafson, 'The Luxury Tax in Professional Sports', in W. Andreff and S. Szymanski, *Handbook on the Economics of Sport* (Cheltenham, Edward Elgar 2006).

[842] S. Szymanski, 'The Economic Design of Sporting Contests', 41 *Journal of Economic Literature* (2003) p. 1172.

[843] *Bosman,* Opinion of Advocate General Lenz, point 226.

[844] Joined Cases C-115/97 to 117/97 *Brentjens ECR* [1999] I-6025 Para. 56 .

[845] J. Snell, 'Economic Aims as Justification for Restrictions on Free Movement', in A. Schrauwen, ed., *The Rule of Reason: Rethinking Another Classic of European Legal Doctrine* (Groningen, Europa Law Publishing 2005) p. 38.

public interest, the Court was quick to strike down any notion that this constitutes objective justification. The possibility of justifying salary caps in the context of free movement on the basis of their redistributive effects must therefore be seen as questionable. Slightly more plausible is the proposition that the effects of salary caps are too indirect and uncertain to constitute 'obstacles' or 'hindrances', and that therefore when they are applied to clubs in the context of an overall spending limit in the league structure, they do not require justification under free movement rules.

The lack of a supranational collective bargaining culture in Europe is one reason why salary caps have yet to become established in Europe. Clearly the unilateral imposition of a cap in one national market would result in players migrating elsewhere, thus ensuring the league imposing the cap suffered in competitive terms. There would also be difficulties in agreeing to a level appropriate for all leagues, particularly as taxation regimes and inflation vary and not all states use the same currency. Despite these legal and practical concerns, the Arnaut report recommended that a decision on whether to impose a salary cap should fall within the regulatory purview of the sports governing bodies.[846]

The use of salary caps has an established history in the USA. Their use fits into a wider pattern of player restraints designed to address concerns relating to the economic viability of clubs and the maintenance of competitive balance. Nevertheless, Rottenberg's 1956 account of player restrictions revealed that such restrictions in the player labour market do not change the distribution of the playing talent among clubs in a league, compared to a player market characterised by free agency.[847] Fort and Quirk (1995) agree with Rottenberg's analysis but argue that an enforceable salary cap is the only cross-subsidisation scheme currently in use that can be expected to accomplish financial viability while improving the competitive balance in a league.[848] Employing a model similar, Késenne also finds that a salary cap could improve competitive balance, although practical issues of enforcement were acknowledged.[849] In this regard, the experience of US salary caps suggests that capping suffers from a serious enforcement problem and can lead to unstable labour relations.[850] Furthermore, as Vrooman argues, salary caps can in fact lead to competitive imbalance and player exploitation.[851] Summing up the evidence on salary caps, Szymanski argues, 'it is clear in theory that a salary cap should improve competitive balance, and equally clear that making a salary cap effective has proved elusive'.[852]

---

[846] J. Arnaut, *Independent European Sport Review* (2006), see at <www.independentfootballreview. com>, p. 53.

[847] S. Rottenberg, 'The Baseball Players' Labor Market', 64 *Journal of Political Economy* (1956).

[848] R. Fort and J. Quirk, 'Cross-subsidization, Incentives and Outcomes in Professional Teams Sports Leagues', XXXIII *Journal of Economic Literature* (1995).

[849] S. Késenne, 'The Impact of Salary Caps in Professional Team Sports', 47(4) *Scottish Journal of Political Economy* (2000).

[850] D. Marburger, 'Chasing the Elusive Salary Cap', in W. Andreff and S. Szymanski, *Handbook on the Economics of Sport* (Cheltenham, Edward Elgar 2006).

[851] J. Vrooman, 'A General Theory of Professional Sports Leagues', 62(3) *Southern Economic Journal* (1995).

[852] S. Szymanski, 'The Economic Design of Sporting Contests', 41 *Journal of Economic Literature* (2003) p. 1171.

8.2.2. Player release

National team sports are enormously popular with spectators and in some sports such as cricket, international representative competition subsidises the domestic game. The viability of domestic cricket in the Test Match playing countries would be seriously undermined by a diminution of the international game. In the absence of player release rules, or in the case of English cricket the central contracting of leading players, international cricket would be unappealing and become unviable. Whilst international football does not subsidise domestic football to the same extent as in cricket, it is nonetheless an important source of revenue for the governing bodies and national associations. Furthermore, as Allen argues, 'the England national team's performances are important in affecting attendance at Premier League games'.[853] International team sport is also peculiar in that teams from countries with small populations are still able to provide effective competition against countries with larger populations. Szymanski provides the example of the New Zealand All Blacks and the Australian and West Indian cricket teams as examples of countries with high international win ratios despite pronounced population disadvantages.[854] It is appealing to spectators to see a contest take place in which the outcome is less dependent on financial considerations as is often witnessed in club sport. In other sports such as football, larger countries traditionally maintain high win ratios and competitive balance is not as even. The importance of protecting national team sports is acknowledged by the European Court of Justice and the legal form of this recognition has been discussed in detail in Chapter 4.

FIFA rules provide for the mandatory release of players for national association representative matches. For matches on dates listed in the coordinated international match calendar and for all matches for which a duty to release players exists on the basis of a special decision of the FIFA Executive Committee, clubs are obliged to release their registered players for representative teams of the country for which the player is eligible to play on the basis of his nationality.[855] The FIFA regulations do not provide for clubs who are required to release a player to receive financial compensation. The Association calling up a player is expected to bear the costs of travel actually incurred by the player as a result of the call-up. The club for which the player concerned is registered is responsible for his insurance cover against illness and accident during the entire period of his release. This cover must also extend to any injuries sustained by the player during the international match for which he was released.[856] Clubs refusing to comply with the mandatory release clause can be subject to a points or game forfeiture.[857]

---

[853] S. Allen, Satellite Television and Football Attendance: The Not so Super Effect, 11(2) *Applied Economics Letters* (2004) p. 123.

[854] S. Szymanski, 'The Economic Design of Sporting Contests', 41 *Journal of Economic Literature* (2003) p. 1177.

[855] Annex 1, Art. 1, FIFA Regulations for the Status and Transfer of Players, July 2005.

[856] Ibid. Annex 1, Art. 2.

[857] Ibid. Annex 1, Art. 6.

In the pending *Charleroi/Oulmers* case, the ECJ will hear a challenge to FIFA's mandatory player release rule and the structure of the international match calendar brought by Belgian football club Charleroi and the G14 grouping of leading clubs.[858] In this case Charleroi player Abdelmajid Oulmers returned injured from international duty in 2004. According to the FIFA regulations, Charleroi was not entitled to compensation. Justifying their decision to join the litigation, G14 lamented the focus of the current regulations on the interests of federations to the detriment of some of their members.

'[P]rofessional clubs have no direct representation on the bodies that make the rules and, not surprisingly, these regulations favour federations over clubs. The *Charleroi/Oulmers* case is an example of how a lack of representation can lead to rules which favour one party over another. G14 believes that these rules, which are imposed on all clubs without their consent, are unfair, undemocratic and must change.'[859]

This statement from G-14 reveals the real source of the litigation. The major clubs feel disenfranchised by existing governance standards in football. This system vests monopoly power in the governing bodies and prevents horizontal channels of communication between stakeholders and the governing body. In short, existing governance structures in football are undemocratic and this impedes the larger clubs in their desire to control the considerable wealth generated within the sector. This decision-making system resulted in two rules concerning player release and the fixing of the international match calendar which itself causes disruption and financial loss to clubs. The manner in which these rules are imposed on clubs, it is argued, contradicts paragraph seven of the EU's Nice Declaration on Sport which grants sports governing bodies conditional autonomy based on 'a democratic and transparent method of operation'. It also contradicts Arnaut's desire to see sporting autonomy traded for a commitment to ensure participatory democracy in sport.[860] These rules have significant economic effects on the clubs and strengthen the commercial value of international football tournaments even though it is the clubs who are providing the talent without recompense. In other words, a regulatory function of the governing body, namely the efficient organisation of international football, may mask commercial objectives.

The referring court in *Charleroi/Oulmers* has asked the ECJ to consider whether

'the obligations on clubs and football players having employment contracts with those clubs imposed by the provisions of FIFA's statutes and regulations providing for the obligatory release of players to national federations without compensation and the unilateral and binding determination of the coordinated international match calendar constitute unlawful restrictions of competition or abuses of a dominant position or obstacles to the exercise of the fundamental freedoms conferred by the EC Treaty and are they therefore

---

[858] Case C-243/06 *Charleroi/Oulmers, OJ* C 212, 2 September 2006, p. 11.

[859] See <www.g14.com>.

[860] J. Arnaut, *Independent European Sport Review* (2006), see at <www.independentfootballreview. com>.

contrary to Articles 81 and 82 of the Treaty or to any other provision of Community law, particularly Articles 39 and 49 of the Treaty?'.[861]

The case is expected to be heard in spring 2008 and represents the first major sports case before the ECJ since *Meca-Medina*.

On the basis of *Meca-Medina*, and assuming that the real legal question lies in the interpretation of Articles 81 and 82 EC, FIFA would argue that the player release system and the fixing of the international match calendar are inherent in the operation of international football. In international football tournaments, national teams from large countries traditionally have a high win ratio. The football World Cup is usually won by a large country with a robust tradition in the sport such as Italy, Brazil, Germany and Argentina. There is hope that national teams from emerging markets such as Australia, Africa and Central and Eastern Europe may be able to challenge this concentration, although from a financial perspective FIFA arguably benefits from teams from larger markets progressing to the latter stages of the World Cup. France won the World Cup for the first time in 1998 and Greece won the European Championships in 2004. If player release clauses were not mandatory, smaller national associations would not be able to select their best players as they would be unable to compensate the clubs or afford the insurance premiums for players who play at some of Europe's top clubs. This would have a negative impact on competitive balance and further strengthen the concentration of success in the larger countries and has the potential to undermine interest in international competition. Spectators in the dominant regional market, Europe, can see the best world players in club football as a consequence of the liberalisation in the player market. The very viability of the international game would be called into question. In this connection, the clubs would suffer a detriment as they benefit from the exposure their employees receive whilst on international duty. Generally, a player with a place on a national team has a higher market value than one without. Furthermore, international football tournaments raise very significant amounts of revenue for the governing bodies and much of this revenue is re-invested into football at all levels. The international match calendar forms a crucial aspect of the international system. Fixing this calendar can only be done centrally as issues relating to climate need taking into consideration.

Weatherill suggests that it is not the principle of player release which is at issue but the nature of the regime and the manner in which the rule is imposed on clubs by FIFA. He considers that '[i]t is doubtless necessary that a system of players release to which clubs are bound be put in place, or else international representative football could not survive'.[862] However, the rules as they are currently constituted are not necessary in the pursuit of the legitimate objective of protecting national team sport. Weatherill sees value in a less restrictive player release system in which clubs receive some compensation for the use of their employees, even if this does not amount to full market value. For those national associations too poor to compensate clubs, a revenue

---

[861] Case C-243/06 *Charleroi/Oulmers, OJ* C 212, 2 September 2006, p. 11.

[862] S. Weatherill, 'Is the Pyramid Compatible with EC Law?', 3-4 *International Sports Law Journal* (2005) p. 6.

sharing scheme could be devised comprising a proportion of the revenues generated from international football. On the procedural question concerning stakeholder representation within international football governance, Weatherill makes the case for the establishment of a committee in which relevant stakeholders have a genuine ability to influence decisions having a direct impact on their activities.[863] The substantive and procedural changes suggested by Weatherill would almost certainly result in the new player release system being considered compatible with competition law. Most likely, the Commission or Court would remove the rule from the scope of Articles 81 and 82 EC on the grounds that the inherent nature of the rule precludes its definition as a restriction. Alternatively, the Commission could issue a favourable exemption decision. On the question of the setting of the international match calendar, Weatherill argues that whilst issues of climate are important, the governing bodies use the match calendar to avoid its tournaments competing with domestic competitions, thus raising the value of broadcasting rights. Potentially, this is anti-competitive as a regulatory function acts as a mask for commercial protectionism.

Weatherill's prescience on the question of stakeholder representation was demonstrated by two developments in the summer of 2007. In July, the Commission published a White Paper on sport in which it called for the development of a common set of principles for good governance in sport such as transparency, democracy, accountability and representation of stakeholders.[864] In June, UEFA approved the establishment of the Professional Football Strategy Council which includes amongst its membership representatives of the EPFL, representatives of the European Club Forum whose members represent the interests of the clubs participating in the UEFA competitions, and representatives of FIFPro (Division Europe) who represent professional players in Europe. At the time of writing, the terms of the new committee are unknown although its composition would indicate that the question of player release and the international match calendar could be discussed.

The establishment of the Professional Football Strategy Council is a significant move and is motivated by two factors. First, UEFA hope that by addressing G14's criticisms over stakeholder representation in the governance of football, they can placate some of the more moderate G14 members. By causing a split in G14, UEFA hope that the organisation disbands and withdraws its challenge in *Charleroi/Oulmers*. The move also responds to the themes contained in the Nice Declaration and the Arnaut Report, both of which recommended that UEFA afford stakeholders sufficient representation with their structures. In a rather unfortunate turn of phrase, UEFA President Michel Platini invited representatives of major clubs to join: 'Presidents and heads of the major clubs – let [UEFA] profit from your great experience and your ideas. Tell us about your convictions.'[865] UEFA's second motivation involves pre-empting the possible threat of social dialogue taking place between the EPFL and FIFPro within the context of the EC Treaty and outside the formal regulatory structure of UEFA.

---

[863] Ibid. p. 7.

[864] Commission of the European Communities, *White Paper on Sport*, COM(2007) 391 Final, p. 12.

[865] 'Platini Asks Clubs to Disband G14', see at <www.bbc.co.uk> (28 May 2007).

UEFA's new committee can be interpreted as a means of internalizing social dialogue under UEFA's oversight.

8.3.   REGULATING PLAYERS' AGENTS

A consequence of liberalising the European player market is the increasing influence players' agents have in sport, particularly football. A players' agent is a person authorised by a player to act for him or her with respect to their dealings with third parties. At one level a player's agent is no more than an intermediary ensuring the supply and demand for labour within sport is met. For a fee commonly referred to as a commission, an agent assists a player in finding a club. They also perform so-called related management services for players. This can include providing advice on housing, taxation, social security, work permits, general financial planning, legal advice, career development, health advice, media relations and representation in cases of a dispute with a third party. Agents are also instructed by a club for the purpose of finding a particular type of player on particular terms. Despite being of potential benefit to both players and clubs, their role within football has been criticised. Since the liberalisation of the labour market following *Bosman*, agents have been accused of encouraging the nomadic instincts of players thus contributing to contractual instability in football. They have also been criticised for negotiating large fees for their services thus taking large sums of money out of the game which could have been better spent elsewhere. Furthermore, agents have been cited in many instances of conduct which is in breach of the rules of the governing bodies, and/or national law.[866]

Agents face four tiers of regulation. First, their activities fall under the International Labour Organisation Convention C181 (1997) on Private Employment Agencies. Ten Member States of the EU are signatories to this convention. Second, agents are regulated by national law. Some traditionally sporting interventionist states such as France, Greece and Portugal require agents to be licensed whilst other states do not require agents to hold state licenses in order to carry out their activities although general statutory frameworks regulate agency work. For example, in the Netherlands the Labour Market Intermediaries Act (*Wet Allocatie Arbeidskrachten door Intermediairs* – WAADI) regulates employment agencies generally although specific rules are absent in the field of sports agents and agents are no longer required to hold a state licence.

The third tier of regulation is provided by FIFA's Players' Agent Regulations. This is a unique tier of regulation in that as private sporting body, FIFA would not normally be able to regulate a profession normally only controllable by body which has received a public mandate. According to Article 1 of the current regulations, amended following a complaint lodged with the Commission, clubs and players can only call upon the services of agents who are licensed by national associations although this prohibition does not apply if the agent acting on behalf of a player is a parent, a sibling

---

[866] R. Siekmann, R. Parrish, R. Branco-Martins and J. Soek, eds., *Players' Agents Worldwide: Legal Aspects* (The Hague, TMC Asser Press 2007).

or the spouse of the player in question or if the agent acting on behalf of the player or club is legally authorised to practise as a lawyer in compliance with the rules in force in his country of domicile. The procedure under Article 2 for being granted a licence involves a formal application to the national association and a requirement to have an impeccable reputation. Article 4(2) imposes a requirement to sit a competence examination covering relevant national laws and the rules of football. If a candidate passes the examination, Article 6 requires the agent to conclude professional liability insurance with an insurance company in his country. If the players' agent cannot conclude a professional liability insurance policy in country in which he passed the examination, he is required under Article 7 to deposit a bank guarantee to the amount of CHF 100,000. Article 8 requires every agent who passes the examination to sign a Code of Professional Conduct. If these requirements are met the competent national association issues a licence. A register of licensed agents is created under Article 10.

Having regulated access to the profession the FIFA Regulations then specify certain requirements of conduct for licensed agents. These include the need, detailed in Article 12, to follow set procedures and terms when an agent enters into contractual relations with clubs or players, Article 14 prohibitions on tapping up and dual representation coupled with a requirement to give, at request, the relevant body at each national association and/or FIFA all of the requisite information and to send in the necessary papers. The sanctions for breaches under Article 15 of the regulations can include a warning, fine, suspension or withdrawal of license. Article 22 provides that disputes involving agents, which are wholly internal to a national association, are dealt with by that association with all other disputes being heard by the FIFA Players' Status Committee. FIFA's Regulations require national associations to make their own Regulations for Players' Agents based on the guidelines provided by FIFA and such guidelines must be approved by the FIFA Players' Status Committee.

Arguably, the EU represents a fourth tier of agent regulation. In particular, FIFA's authority to regulate the profession has been challenged by private parties. In 1996 the Commission received a complaint from Multiplayers International Denmark concerning the incompatibility of the FIFA Regulations with EC competition law. In 1998 French agent Laurent Piau complained also and lodged a complaint adding that the Regulations were also contrary to Article 49 EC on the freedom to provide services. A statement of objections was sent to FIFA based on a potential breach of Article 81. The Commission objected to the license requirements, the requirement that an agent deposited a bank guarantee and the sanctions regime imposed on clubs, players and agents for breaching the rules. FIFA amended the Regulations to those described above, although new regulations are being prepared.

Piau maintained his objection to the requirement to sit an examination in order to receive a licence and the requirement to take out professional liability insurance. He added that the new regulations introduced new restrictions by way of the rules on professional conduct, the use of a standard contract and the rules on the determination of remuneration. These, he argued, were in breach of Article 81 and possibly Article 82 although Piau appeared to have ceased his complaint relating to Article 49. Piau's complaint was rejected by the Commission in April 2002. Piau lodged an appeal to the Court of First Instance. The CFI found that the license system did not result in competition being eliminated as the system resulted in a qualitative selection process rather than a quantitative restriction on access to that occupation. This was necessary in order to raise professional standards for the occupation of players' agent, particularly as players' careers were short and they needed protection. The current conditions governing the exercise of the occupation of players' agent were characterised as a nearly total absence of national rules or collective organisation for players' agents.[867] The CFI disagreed with the Commission's assessment that FIFA did not hold a dominant position in the market of services of players' agents. However, the CFI found no abuse of dominance. On appeal, the European Court of Justice rejected Piau's request that the Commission Decision and the decision of the CFI be annulled. The ECJ did not explore the substance of Piau's claim relating to Article 49 but dismissed this as a new argument which it could not address as the Commission acted on the basis of Regulation 17/62 and was therefore only obliged to consider competition law.

Notwithstanding current challenges to national player agent regulations before national courts, there are a number of remaining questions concerning the application of Community law. In *Piau*, the CFI stated that the legitimacy of a private body such as FIFA to regulate a profession such as agents is 'open to question' given that FIFA have not received a mandate from a public authority.[868] The CFI held that '[t]he very principle of regulation of an economic activity concerning neither the specific nature of sport nor the freedom of internal organisation of sports associations by a private-law body, like FIFA, which has not been delegated any such power by a public authority, cannot from the outset be regarded as compatible with Community law, in particular with regard to respect for civil and economic liberties'.[869] Branco Martins questions the Court's reasoning to allow such regulation to continue.[870] The Court noted that only questions of competition law could be heard and that the rule-making power exercised by FIFA was legitimate as there was an almost complete absence of national rules on player agent regulation. Players' agents were not organised collectively and consequently did not constitute a profession with its own internal organisation. Branco Martins observes that within the EU 16 out of the 25 Member States have in fact established some type of legislation or legally structured framework for regulating the profession of players' agent and that a collective organization of players' agents does exist, namely the International Association of FIFA Agents. Since the *Piau* case, a new collective organisation has emerged, the European Football Agents Association (EFAA). Consequently, players' agents are increasingly organised collectively and those collective organisations should be consulted by FIFA.

On these grounds, FIFA's players' agent regulations may be susceptible to challenge on both inherency and proportionality grounds. The rules cannot be considered

---

[867] *Piau*, CFI.

[868] Ibid. Para. 76.

[869] Ibid. Para. 77.

[870] R. Branco Martins, 'The Laurent Piau Case and the Basis for Regulations of the Profession of Players' Agents in the European Union', in R. Siekmann, R. Parrish, R. Branco-Martins and J. Soek, eds., *Players' Agents Worldwide: Legal Aspects* (The Hague, TMC Asser Press 2007).

inherent in terms of raising professional standards as agents are already regulated by national law. This undermines FIFA's claims to possess a mandate to regulate. Second, even if FIFA is considered to have such a mandate, the measures may go beyond what is necessary in the pursuit of the legitimate objective as the collective body representing player's agents has not been consulted. This cannot be considered to be a rule devised in a transparent, objective and non-discriminatory manner, in which the relevant stakeholders are afforded a reasonable input.

Furthermore, Piau's initial question on the application of Article 49 remains alive. The Commission's White Paper package contained an undertaking to police more carefully the line between legitimate state regulation and private professional regulation. As a matter of principle the CFI has deemed private professional regulation questionable. The practical effects of this undertaking remain to be seen. FIFA regulations are not state-sanctioned in any Member State. As a consequence they must be considered carefully from the point of view of services provision. The professional qualifications regime requires Member States to grant recognition even to professionals who have practiced for a period of time in a Member State without formal requirements, and whilst it can only affect state bodies, the Directive itself largely echoes case law which is derived from Articles 43 and 49. Where those articles can be relied upon by private parties, as would appear to be the case in relation to collective private regulators, rules restricting free movement must be justified. In effect, both the conditional grants of authorisation and requirements for particular qualifications must be justified. As Davies has pointed out, the Services Directive contains no objective justifications for temporary services despite retaining these in relation to Article 43 establishment.[871] This calls into question many of the sporting-related grounds on which such rules could be justified. In sum, the compatibility of professional rules in relation to the freedom of establishment and the free movement of services requires some judicial clarification which has as yet not been forthcoming. The weight of the arguments against private regulation and the principled stands of both the Commission and the CFI suggest that unless specificity arguments are reinvigorated in the form of a sporting exception rather than an objective justification, the market for players' agents stands to undergo considerable liberalisation in the medium term. It is difficult to see how an argument for the 'inherency' of such rules could be sustained, considering the diversity of current national regimes which itself suggests that less restrictive methods of indirect regulation satisfy the concerns highlighted by sports governing bodies.

Despite persisting doubts as to the legality of the current pattern of agent regulation, the Arnaut Report concluded that 'that rules concerning players' agents are inherent to the proper regulation of football and therefore compatible with Community law'.[872] Nevertheless, Arnaut recommended that the current pattern of agent regulation should be formalised through the adoption of a specific Directive on sports agents, perhaps in

---

[871] G. Davies, 'The Services Directive: Extending the country of origin principle and reforming public administration', 32(2) *European Law Review* (2007).

[872] J. Arnaut, *Independent European Sport Review* (2006), see at <www.independentfootballreview. com> p. 40.

part to overcome the current difficulties in establishing the legitimacy of purely private regulation. In the White Paper on Sport, the Commission responded to the Arnaut recommendation by proposing to carry out an impact assessment to provide a clear overview of the activities of players' agents in the EU. It will evaluate whether action at EU level is necessary beyond that provided by the Professional Qualifications Directive, which itself establishes rules requiring mutual recognition of qualifications rather than reinforces the legitimacy of regulation as such.[873]

8.4. CONCLUSIONS

Following *Meca-Medina*, the governing bodies lamented the ECJ's condemnation of the *Walrave* sporting exception in the context of competition law. The governing bodies maintained that questions of governance go to the heart of sporting autonomy. In the absence of a regulator able to take sporting decisions in the best interest of sport generally, rather than the narrow commercial considerations of a small number of stakeholders, there could be no sport. However, this is exactly the counterfactual argument promoted by *Meca-Medina*. Modern sports governance involves governing bodies making choices at the margins between sport and the economy. In other words, choices defended on regulatory grounds often involve significant effects in commercial markets. Rather than making artificial distinctions at these margins, *Meca-Medina* refocuses the analytical attention on the context in which the rule is formed, the inherency of the rule in pursuing legitimate objectives and the proportionality of the measure.

Ostensibly sporting rules which nonetheless contain significant economic effects can therefore be removed from the scope of competition law whilst leaving the exemption criteria to dispose of rules which, whilst not inherent, still possess pro-competitive features. The protection of these rules will serve to maintain present conditions, including the segmentation of markets where such segmentation already exists. There may be competitive dangers for sport inherent in the deregulation of the labour market where this occurs without deregulating the product market. The Commission has lent strong political support to the European model. This seems to lead to the expectation of a justificatory regime based on the current structure of the market. In other words, a pre-existing condition is in itself proposed to be the justification for its continued existence. Instability in the sport sector can lead to calls for either further deregulation, or the prospect of an attempt at re-regulating player markets.

---

[873] Commission of the European Communities, *White Paper on Sport*, COM(2007) 391 Final, p. 16.

Chapter 9
Conclusions

9.1.   THE BIRTH OF THE SPORTING EXCEPTION

In *Walrave* the European Court of Justice recognised that certain sporting activities were not subject to Community law. In Paragraph 4, the Court made a distinction between economic and uneconomic sporting activity. The latter was declared to fall altogether outside the scope of Community law. Despite the development of Community competences since the 1974 judgment to include areas with less pronounced economic dimensions, the Paragraph 4 formula remains a staple of the Court's recent case law. In *Meca-Medina*, the ECJ continues to maintain that uneconomic sporting activity remains beyond the scope of Community law. The *Walrave* judgment also introduced in Paragraph 8 the notion of 'purely sporting' reasons which 'have nothing to do with economic activity'. Although in that context those 'purely sporting' reasons were used only to limit the prohibition on nationality discrimination, this line of reasoning has in the argumentation of sports governing bodies been developed into a more general attempt to remove sport from legal scrutiny. This part of the ruling heralded the beginning of problematic distinctions between the economy and sport, and 'purely sporting motives' and their economic consequences.

9.2.   THE CURRENT FRAMEWORK

9.2.1.   Scope of the sporting exception

As Chapters 3 and 4 demonstrate, Community free movement law has metamorphosed in the lifetime of the 'sporting exception'. Originally only a narrow principle of equality on the basis of nationality applied, and only to the Member States. 'Restrictions' and 'obstacles' to free movement must now be justified, often even where the state bears no direct responsibility for their imposition. In relation to sport, four categories of sporting rules can be identified. The ECJ still recognises in its modern case law that sport which does not constitute 'an economic activity within the meaning of Article 2 EC' remains outside the scope of Community law. This potentially limits the rights of citizens and the scope of Community regulatory competence where it might otherwise arise. The ECJ also still recognises the Paragraph 8 distinction in the context of nationality discrimination in national team sports, where the rule was originally conceived. Although this has now been restricted to those circumstances where sport is structured on an exclusively national basis, both limbs of the 'sporting exception' strictly so-called remain valid. The Court has, of course, denied its extension to categories not recognised in *Walrave*. Third, rules 'inherent' to the organisation of sport may not constitute 'restrictions'. Finally, 'restrictions' may be capable of objective justification.

9.2.2. Restrictions, objective justification, and 'inherent' rules

Contemporary free movement rules apply to at least some non-discriminatory restrictions, and to at least some rules not emanating from the state. To compensate for this expansion in the scope of what can fall within Community law, the Court has developed categories of objective justifications to compensate for the breadth of the free movement rules. In *Bosman*, it recognised a number of categories relevant to sport. The Court also hinted in this and some later cases that despite its orthodox position in other sectors, it might be willing to consider directly discriminatory sporting rules capable of objective justification. In *Deliège*, the Court developed a category of 'inherent' rules related to the organisation and proper functioning of sport which were not *de jure* considered 'restrictions' of free movement despite *de facto* restricting the opportunities of athletes. This can be considered the final blow against any argument that sporting rules were somehow disconnected from economic impacts, or indeed that they must be 'purely sporting' to be either exempt from or justifiable under Community law. In *Meca-Medina*, the Court retained this framework and indeed transposed the 'inherency' criterion to EC competition law despite formally rejecting any convergence between the analytical framework of free movement and competition. Modern legislative initiatives such as the Services Directive have cast shadows over some of the sporting-related objective justifications, and therefore also the rules which sports governing bodies impose within professional sporting activities. Nevertheless, many of these cannot be applied to sports governing bodies due to the constitutional constraints of Community secondary legislation. It remains to be seen whether the Court is willing to derive similar rules from the Treaty articles themselves.

9.2.3. 'Purely sporting' rules and proportionality

When sporting activity is not 'an economic activity within the meaning of Article 2 EC' or 'rules or practices excluding a foreign player from participating in certain matches for reasons which are not of an economic nature', the 'sporting exception' is an exception properly so called from the scope of the Treaty. Community law simply does not apply to non-economic sport, and the prohibition on nationality discrimination is not applicable to that limited set of circumstances, thus far accepted by the Court only in the context of nationality rules in national team sports. This has sometimes been argued to lead to a lack of Community competence to interfere in these areas, and to greater margins of appreciation in relation to those rules. Whilst it would be inappropriate to use the language of 'justification', it must be pointed out that 'purely sporting' rules in these senses must nevertheless be limited to their proper objectives. As a consequence, whilst the margin of appreciation may be greater, such rules cannot therefore be entirely disproportionate, and must be demonstrated in any event to fulfil the criteria for exemption.

9.2.4. Competition law

Sport raises some specific questions in relation to competition law which do not present in other sectors. Sports competitions and leagues in particular demonstrate a certain degree of interdependence between competitors and requires central organisation, both of which are unusual features from economic points of view. Market exit is not a natural consequence of a successful sporting league, and driving one's sporting competitors permanently out of competition is not necessarily a reward for the successful, more economically efficient firm but instead destabilises the possibility of retaining any kind of sporting competition at all. Also, sports markets often feature arrangements which would in other sectors raise suspicions of illegitimate activity. Collective selling, fixing criteria for competitors and the exploitation of governance powers to further economic goals of redistribution all run counter to the liberal philosophy of efficiency maximisation.

Once the applicability of competition law to sport was established, sports governing bodies consistently argued that efficiency maximisation should not be the purpose of Community competition policy in the sector. Instead, various arguments have been put forward to the effect that sport pursues other public policy interests, and that in any event the maximisation of welfare could not in that sector be best achieved by the maximisation of short-term economic efficiencies. Competition law has demonstrated itself to be a sufficiently flexible tool in the hands of the Commission to facilitate recognition of these concerns. At the same time the Commission avoids in its formal language entering into debates on the relationship between sport and competition law on a more principled basis. The Commission has historically made much of the sensitive application of competition law to sport, but in practice it has managed to keep its legal analysis within the limits of the pre-existing Treaty framework. This can be effected for example through broad market definition and a consequential application of appreciability thresholds such as in relation to UEFA's blocking rules. In some cases the Commission has simply stated that rules are 'not called into question by Community law' or too insignificant to warrant an investigation, as in *Mouscron*. Since competition law only applies to 'undertakings' carrying out economic activity, the pursuit and regulation of non-economic sport is outside its scope even without reference to a specific sporting exception such as that in Paragraph 4 of *Walrave*.

When the Court finally expressly considered the relationship of competition law and sporting rules for the first time in its 2006 *Meca-Medina* judgment, it confirmed the orthodoxy that free movement and competition required separate analytical frameworks but that on those particular facts, the same outcome was achieved. In doing so, it applied the notion of 'inherency'. This had been established in the sporting context in the *Deliège* free movement case. In competition law this had been introduced outside the sporting context in case law exploring the context and purpose of rules which resulted in restrictive effects on competition. In line with that case law, the Court recognised that restrictions which were 'inherent' in the pursuit of legitimate non-competition objectives were not in fact 'restrictions' of competition. Even where rules are not 'inherent' and constitute *prima facie* restrictions, those rules may be justified on Article 81(3) grounds. It is submitted that similar analytical principles apply to the notion of what constitutes 'abuse' of a sports governing body's dominant position.

9.2.5. The state, competition and sport

Competition law does not apply to public law. There is as a consequence some move within governing bodies to have sports rules enshrined in national legislation. Some have gone so far as to explore the possibility that sport might constitute a 'service of general economic interest'. These are not arguments to be made, or indeed to be accepted without serious consideration. For one, to constitute services of general economic interest sports must be given express public obligations enshrined in law. This initiative would run counter to the thus far prevalent arguments that sport is a private matter and therefore should encounter minimal direct state regulation. Even if successful, the Commission has articulated a vigorous approach to public service regulation and indicates that it prefers competition in these areas, even if occasionally mitigated by other concerns. Definition as a public service provider may also have the consequence of subjecting an otherwise private organisation to the Court's definition of 'Member State' for the purposes of the horizontal direct effect of directives. As a consequence of this, the detailed provisions of some secondary legislation could apply to sports bodies even though some, such as the Services Directive, expressly exclude SGEIs from their scope.

Other concerns arising out of the allegedly public nature of sport revolve around the dichotomous treatment of sports broadcasting under Community law. A premise of the Television Without Frontiers and proposed Audiovisual and Media Services Directives is that there is a 'public good' dimension to sporting events, and that as a consequence the broader public is entitled to some sporting coverage irrespective of their direct contributions to its provision. Specificity arguments are nevertheless often accommodated in the application of broadcasting rules to economic arrangements with sporting dimensions. Whilst the Commission avoids reference to these in its formal decisional practice, a sensitive recognition of the concerns of sports governing bodies and others involved in the regulation of sporting activity can be recognised.

Overall, many sporting concerns fit well within the general framework without recourse to sporting-specific rules. The uncertainty decried by sports governing bodies is partly due to their and the Commission's historical preference for informal settlements. Their often legally ambiguous formulations attempt to balance political needs with the manifest lack of sporting competence in the present constitutional framework. The national application of EC competition law following Regulation 1/2003 is likely to cause considerable difficulties also in the sport sector, because there is little by way of formal guidance to national competition authorities on the application of the exemption criteria relevant to sporting concerns. The Commission and the Court have both demonstrated a willingness in this field to afford wide margins of appreciation to sports governing bodies in areas with direct impacts on the regulation of sporting issues. Nevertheless, in an era of increasing commercialisation, it is also clear that when governing bodies engage in economic activity, they may not abuse their dominant positions or regulatory authority to extract economic advantage. In this respect, the period of uncertainty is over, and the Commission has intimated that pleas of past uncertainty will no longer be causes for future leniency in its decisional practice on penalties.

9.2.6. Convergence theories and sport

The application of EC law to sport has seen the emergence of a number of strands of convergence between free movement and competition. This echoes more generalised arguments that have been presented to justify such reasoning in broader contexts. The *Meca-Medina* judgment demonstrates that although the material outcomes of cases may be similar under both frameworks of analysis, the Court will insist on a formal separation of free movement and competition. This is also sometimes an inevitable result of the process of appeal from Commission decisions originally made under competition enforcement powers. The time has yet to come for convergence of analytical frameworks despite the common convergence of outcomes.

9.3.   LEGAL QUESTIONS ARISING FROM THE SPORTING EXCEPTION

The sporting-specific rules of EC law raise questions of principle that have yet to be answered with satisfactory clarity. The persistent repetition of Paragraph 4 of *Walrave* in the Court's modern case law suggests that the Court may indeed be willing to restrict rights of non-discrimination that Union citizens might otherwise enjoy. The Court has also been less than clear as to the legal effects of direct nationality discrimination outside the context of team composition in national team sports. This analysis and its location in the *Bosman*, *Kolpak* and *Simutenkov* frameworks suggests that whilst direct nationality discrimination cannot be objectively justified in other sectors, sport may be exceptional in this respect. Another question of scope is that of the rule on 'inherency'. In free movement, such rules have so far been recognised in relation to the organisation and proper functioning of sporting competition. This could potentially constitute an expansive category, and its boundaries have yet to be judicially explored in either competition or free movement. It is submitted that some distinction between economic motives and incidental economic effects may be helpful but is likely to prove as elusive as the bounds of the 'purely sporting' rule. In this respect, 'inherency' is the new 'purely sporting' rule. One remaining question is whether national market segmentation is 'inherent' simply because it reflects the pre-existing regulatory frameworks for professional sport. It is submitted that here, too, the Court is likely to develop some qualification on the scope of 'inherency' and at the very least will scrutinise the proportionality of such rules with some intensity.

Sports governing bodies often raise the protest that sport is a private matter, rather than one which should be regulated by public rules. Questions of horizontality raised in Chapter 3 remain live in the broader context of free movement and also highlight some particular difficulties in the application of EC law to sport. It is clear that directives and therefore much of the detailed regime of modern free movement law do not apply to bodies that are not performing state functions. Nevertheless, the Commission and the Court have both identified private regulation as objectionable in principle. In those areas of professional regulation there may be a close relationship between Treaty-derived rules and those codified in directives. This may assist in determining the substance of Treaty-derived rules. However, the contours of the personal scope of even Treaty provisions on free movement remain uncertain. If it is accepted that *Angonese* represents an extension of Article 39 to all private bodies even where their rules do not constitute collective regulation of employment, it must nevertheless be questioned whether this reasoning can be transposed to the other fundamental economic freedoms. Thus far there is no indication that similar horizontal applications can be found in the application of the Treaty citizenship rights.

9.4.   REMAINING POLICY ISSUES

The present state of affairs raises a number of policy issues that remain unresolved. The first is the extent to which sports governing bodies should be permitted to regulate sporting-related activity in the interests of justice or efficiency, namely on the grounds that they are best placed to consider the merits of legal issues raised within sport. It is beyond dispute that the Community rules have gradually deregulated and liberalised player markets. Sports governing bodies have argued that this has caused serious destabilisation in the European model of sport. This claim presents sports governing bodies and regulatory institutions with two key policy choices. They may continue with deregulation and witness a consequential crisis in a product market that continues to be rigidly structured. Alternatively, they may attempt to re-regulate the player market in an effort to support the ailing structures of competitive sports in Europe. It is unlikely that the asymmetries between deregulation and regulation can coexist in the long term without considerable detriment to sport. Early indications are that the Commission is prepared to accept some re-regulation. After the *Bosman* judgment it entered into the 2001 agreement that introduced measures partly compensating for the Court's rejection of the international transfer system. It remains to be seen whether such progressive re-regulation of the player market is lawful. So far the Court has not accepted nationality discrimination beyond the tightly restricted realm of national eligibility rules in national team sports despite paying lip service to such claims by expressly considering nationality rules in professional sports under the framework for objective justification. It has always found other reasons to reject their legality, and it is submitted that if pressed on the point, the Court will continue to do so whilst consistently refusing to declare nationality discrimination in professional sport unjustifiable in principle. The home-grown player's framework, however, raises slightly different legal issues. This is because the rules are not directly discriminatory, but are instead modelled on other criteria which closely correlate with nationality. Under the present analytical framework of free movement, they can be argued to constitute rules which can be justified with reference to objective criteria unrelated to nationality, such as needs to encourage the training of young players.

9.5.   ANALYSIS OF SPORTING RULES

As has been identified, a number of sporting-related objectives have been recognised by the Court as warranting special treatment under Community law. These include the need to maintain some competitive balance and that of ensuring the regularity and proper functioning of those competitions. These justifications enable sports bodies to govern sport. Encouraging the training and education of young players, the protection of national teams, and ensuring the integrity and uncertainty of sporting competition are likewise recognised in the Court's case law. However, the Court has demonstrated that despite this list, it is not prepared to accept every reason put forward. In particular, it has expressed doubts where the facts of a claim are not supportive of the reasons put forward. For example, in *Bosman*, it struck down the proposition that nationality restrictions were maintaining a link between players and the representative nature of the team, observing that those links were no more inherent than club's links with the localities or regions in which they played.

Within the current framework, and according to existing Court jurisprudence, only national eligibility criteria remain within a territory of rule removed from the scope of the Treaty on 'purely sporting' grounds under *Walrave* Paragraph 8. Rules labelled inherent are incapable of definition as a restriction. These have included selection criteria and anti-doping rules, both recognised by the ECJ, and club ownership rules, recognised by the Commission. All other sporting rules have required justification under either competition law or free movement. In competition law, the collective sale of broadcasting rights satisfies the exemption criteria under Article 81(3). In free movement law, only transfer windows have been successfully justified. Thus far, nationality restrictions in club sport, the use of end of contract transfer payments, breaches of non-discrimination provisions in Association Agreements, excessive periods of exclusivity and regulatory rules designed to protect commercial positions have all been struck down in Community law.

9.6.   PROSPECTS FOR SPORT WITHIN THE LEGAL FRAMEWORK

9.6.1.   **White Paper on Sport**

The Commission's White Paper Package identifies a number of concurrent approaches that it will take in relation to the governance of sport. This despite the failure of the 2005 Constitutional Treaty to come into force and the uncertain future of the substantially similar Reform Treaty. In the White Paper itself, the Commission identified a lack of conclusive evidence in relation to the many claims thus far made by sports governing bodies. To remedy this, it identified funding streams to support research in the field and particular projects which it considered to be prioritised. Its action plan has identified a number of discrete projects for investigation as well as areas where the Commission will prepare for the prospect of enforcement actions. Due to the present lack of an express Treaty legal base in sport, many of these will be funded through other means or involve mere co-ordination of national or private action.

In relation to public health, the Commission's proposals include support for an EU network and research within the frameworks for existing projects. In doping, the Commission will support networking and co-ordination efforts. Education and training involves a Community competence, and in relation to home-grown players, the Commission has undertaken to complete the analysis which it has commenced as to their legality. The Commission also pledges support for volunteering in sport, and has undertaken to launch a study on volunteering in sport. Social inclusion initiatives are centered on mainstreaming sport in social inclusion, and using sport as a vehicle for furthering social inclusion targets. In relation to the campaign against racism, the Commission undertaken to analyse possibilities of new legal instruments to prevent public disorder at sport events, and to strengthen cooperation between law enforcement services and stakeholders in sport. Sport is also being raised a potential vehicle for external relations and the promotion of sustainable development.

The economic dimensions of sport have since *Walrave* been problematic as markers between the contours of Community competence and 'purely sporting' questions. Nevertheless, these form a key component of the White Paper's action plan. The Commission's lack of conclusive information will be corrected with a number of specific sport-related surveys, the development of European methods to measure the economic impacts of sports, and studies to assess sport as a vehicle for the broader goals of the Lisbon agenda. The Commission has undertaken to study grassroots financing and to defend the pre-existing possibilities for reduced VAT within the Community's tax rules. In relation to free movement, the Commission claims that it will combat discrimination based on nationality in all sports through political dialogue but also through infringement procedures. In this connection, it is worth noting that the Commission has undertaken to commence infringement proceedings against Member States not only where they infringe EC law, but also where they permit private parties to continue doing so by ineffectively enforcing Community rules relevant to economic sporting activity. This relates in particular to players' agents, where the Commission has made a commitment to carry out an impact assessment to evaluate whether specific EU action is necessary. Similar scrutiny of general legislation and its application to the sporting field is promised in relation to the protection of minors and combating financial crime.

Licensing systems, despite their obvious risk of anti-competitive objects or effects, will merely be considered through a dialogue with sport organisations and conferences between stakeholders in sports starting with football. In media, too, the Commission offers only a continuation of its existing practice, namely recommending that sport organisations maintain solidarity mechanisms but not expressly suggesting that the legality of arrangements with restrictive effects should be further studied. Its follow-up to the White Paper will emphasise the pursuit of structured dialogue with stakeholders, cooperation with Member States, and the encouragement of social dialogue.

9.6.2. Reform Treaty

Like the 2005 Treaty Establishing a Constitution for Europe, the draft Reform Treaty proposes to include a specific competence for the Union to pursue a sports policy. This is technically restricted to a contribution on the promotion of European sporting issues, and due to its nature as a category of supporting, coordinating or complementary action, excludes direct harmonisation of the laws of Member States. Within the letter of the proposed Article 176b, the Union is obliged to take account of the specific nature of sport only in relation to the promotion of European sporting issues. This express Treaty base is likely to resolve many of the technical constitutional grounds which have prevented the Community thus far from creating a coherent European sports policy. Its action related to European sporting issues could indirectly impact upon national laws. A soft and limited competence could in time harden into a statutory competence and possibly a 'sporting exception' based on this field. Indeed, the Court of Justice was presented with similar arguments in *Bosman,* based on the cultural aspects of sport which on those facts the Court was not prepared to recognise. Given an express competence in sport, its conclusions may very well differ.

9.6.3. Services of General Economic Interest

The prospect of sport constituting a service of general economic interest raises a number of legal challenges. Such services must enjoy express state mandates. These would defeat many of the objectives of the 'Service of General Economic Interest' (SGEI) designation that sports governing bodies might harbour. Definition as a SGEI may also have the inadvertent consequences of subjecting sporting organisations to detailed obligations that bind Member States such as those enshrined in directives on free movement. As yet the arguments to the effect that sports are SGEIs or that a particular body is a provider of such SGEIs have not been well articulated by those bodies. This label may well impose obligations more onerous than those from which it exempts service providers. Furthermore, the increasing application of market competition values even to SGEIs will subdue any desire on the part of sporting bodies to be subject to regulation as SGEIs rather than as ordinary economic activities.

9.6.4. Social dialogue

Social dialogue remains a vehicle through which specificity of sport arguments can be channelled as long as the content of a collective agreement pertains to the employment relationship and satisfies the conditions imposed on social partners by Article 137. The content of discussions taking place in a social dialogue committee could include contractual terms, transfer windows, the transfer system, image rights, pension funds and doping rules. In *Brentjens* the Court established that the social policy objectives of collective agreements would be undermined if agreements seeking to improve conditions of work and employment were subject to competition law. This immunity from the application of Treaty principles is not extended to free movement rights in relation to which the court would examine the clause which restricts free movement and proceed to examine whether the restriction is 'inherent' or objectively justified.

Social dialogue, too, is fraught with difficulties despite in principle offering a method for both greater legal certainty and the express exemption of particular rules from the scope of other areas of Community law. First, the social partners must be genuinely representative. There are questions as to the representative nature of some potential social partners. The conclusions of that dialogue must satisfy clear legal requirements. This legislative process does not in itself enable the circumvention of other Community policy areas. In particular, the Commission has the function of acting as a conduit for legislation based on social dialogue. As a consequence of this it has the power to preclude the formalisation of agreements that are contrary to Community policy aims.

9.6.5. **Block exemption**

The White Paper makes clear that the Commission is currently not prepared to consider the prospect of block exemptions relevant to sport. This is in itself sufficient to abandon this line of reasoning, since only the Commission is able to make such a categorisation and to take that initiative. It may be that given a hardening and development of its decisional practice, the time for a sports-related block exemption will in due course arrive. That time has not yet come.

9.7.   AREAS OF REMAINING UNCERTAINTY

A number of specific issues are clearly still subject to debate as to their position within the present framework. Club licensing conditions, UEFA's coefficients formula, the use of a hard salary cap, player release clauses, rules on geographical tying, a closed breakaway league and rules protecting sports governing bodies from competition are likely to be discussed in the context of the *Meca-Medina* inherency test. Clearly, the context in which the rules are formed, the connection with the pursuit of legitimate objectives and the existence of less restrictive means of achieving such objectives will determine whether such rules are labelled inherent and thus removed from the scope of the Treaty. In the absence of a finding of 'inherency', these rules will need to be justified pursuant to the Article 81(3) criteria. In free movement law the key remaining issues concern the home-grown players rule and the free movement elements of the FIFA regulations on players' agents. Both of these elements require objective justification. In addition, the Commission approved international transfer system has yet to be judicially tested. Rules unlikely to satisfy either the inherency or justificatory tests are closed system breakaway leagues based on unfair and discriminatory access criteria and soft salary caps. The Commission's uneasy position on the axis between sporting considerations and conventional EC law has contributed to the uncertainties still facing sport. Refusals to investigate issues, informal closures of investigations, and the occasional disparities between its official press releases and its formal reasoning likewise contribute to legal uncertainty. The Commission has not always acted in accordance with Community law, and its decisional practice should therefore be considered carefully against the recognised legal framework. The Court of Justice has in the past revisited such arrangements. The White Paper recognises that one of the key difficulties facing the Commission is a current lack of evidence as to the substance of the arguments put forward by interested parties. To this end, the Commission has clarified that it will not only expect such evidence to be produced, but that it will itself fund a number of studies.

BIBLIOGRAPHY

Allan, S., 'Satellite Television and Football Attendance: The Not so Super Effect', 11(2) *Applied Economics Letters* (2004) pp. 123-125.

Andenas M. and W-H. Roth (eds.), *Services and Free Movement in EU Law* (Oxford, Oxford University Press 2002).

Arnaut, J., *Independent European Sport Review*, see at <www.independentfootballreview.com> (2006).

Arnull, A., 'Competition, the Commission and Some Constitutional Questions of More Than Minor Importance', 23(1) *European Law Review* (1998) pp. 1-2.

Arnull, A., *The European Union and Its Court of Justice*, 2nd edn. (Oxford: Oxford University Press 2006).

Baimbridge, M., S. Cameron and P. Dawson, 'Satellite Television and the Demand for Football: A Whole New Ball Game?', 43(3) *Scottish Journal of Political Economy* (1996) pp. 317-33.

Barnard, C., *The Substantive Law of the EU: The Four Freedoms* (Oxford: Oxford University Press 2004).

Barnard, C., *EC Employment Law*, 3rd edn. (Oxford: Oxford University Press 2006).

Barnard, C., *The Substantive Law of the EU: The Four Freedoms*, 2nd edn. (Oxford: Oxford University Press 2007).

Barnard, C. and J. Scott (eds.), *The Law of the Single Market: Unpacking the Premises* (Oxford: Hart 2002).

Bell, A., A. Lewis and J. Taylor, 'EC and UK Competition Rules and Sport', in A. Lewis and J. Taylor, *Sport: Law and Practice* (London: Butterworths Lexis Nexis 2003).

Beloff, M., T. Kerr and M. Demetriou, *Sports Law* (Oxford: Hart 1999).

Beloff, M., 'Is There a Lex Sportiva', 3 *International Sports Law Review* (2005) pp. 49-60.

Bennett, M., 'They Think It's All Over ... It Is Now! How Extra Time Was Required to Finally Settle Football's Transfer Saga', 9(3) *Sport and the Law Journal* (2001) pp. 180-185.

Blanpain, R. and R. Inston, *The Bosman Case. The End of the Transfer System?* (Leuven: Peeters and Sweet & Maxwell 1996).

Bolotny, F. and J-F Bourg, 'The Demand for Media Coverage', in W. Andreff and S. Szymanski, *Handbook on the Economics of Sport* (Cheltenham: Edward Elgar 2006).

Bourgeois, J. and J. Bocken, 'Guidelines on the Application of Article 81(3) of the EC Treaty, or How to Restrict a Restriction', 32 *Legal Issues of Economic Integration* (2005) pp. 111-122.

Branco Martins, R., 'The *Laurent Piau* Case of the ECJ on the Status of Players' Agents', in R.C.R. Siekmann et al. (eds.), *Players' Agents Worldwide: Legal Aspects* (The Hague: T.M.C. Asser Press 2007).

Breillat, J-C. and F. Lagarde, 'The Specificity of Sport and European Community Law: The Example of Nationality', in W. Andreff and S. Szymanski, *Handbook on the Economics of Sport* (Cheltenham: Edward Elgar 2006).

Burainmo, B., 'The Demand for Sports Broadcasting', in W. Andreff and S. Szymanski, *Handbook on the Economics of Sport* (Cheltenham: Edward Elgar 2006).

Caiger, A. and J. O'Leary, 'The End of the Affair: The Anelka Doctrine – the Problem of Contract Stability in English Professional Football', in A. Caiger and S. Gardiner, (eds)., *Professional Sport in the EU, Regulation and Re-regulation* (The Hague: T.M.C. Asser Press 2000).

Carmichael, F., 'The Player Transfer System in Soccer', in W. Andreff and S. Szymanski, *Handbook on the Economics of Sport* (Cheltenham: Edward Elgar 2006).

Cave, M. and R. Crandall, 'Sports Rights and the Broadcast Industry', 111 *Economic Journal* (February 2001) pp. F4-26.

Chaker, A.N., *Study of National Sports Legislation in Europe* (Strasbourg: Council of Europe 1999).

Chalmers, D. et al., *EU Law* (Cambridge: Cambridge University Press 2006).

Collins, R., *Broadcasting and Audio-Visual Policy in the European Single Market* (London: John Libby 1994).

Commission of the European Communities, 'A People's Europe, Reports from the ad hoc Committee' (1984), COM (84) 446 Final.

Commission of the European Communities, 'The European Community and sport' (1991), SEC (91) 1438 of 31 July 1991.

Commission of the European Communities, 'Information on the Bosman case' (1996), Sport Info Europe, DG X, Brussels.

Commission of the European Communities, 'Developments and prospects for Community activity in the field of sport' (1998), Commission Staff Working Paper, Directorate General X.

Commission of the European Communities, *The European Model of Sport* (1998), Consultation Document of DG X.

Commission of the European Communities, 'Promoting and adapting the social dialogue' (1998), COM(98) 322 final.

Commission of the European Communities, 'Report from the Commission to the European Council with a view to safeguarding sports structures and maintaining the social significance of sport within the Community framework: The Helsinki Report on Sport' (1999), COM (1999) 644.

Commission of the European Communities, 'Commission Communication on Services of General Economic Interest' (2001), OJ 2001 C 17/4.

Commission of the European Communities, 'Green Paper on Services of General Economic Interest' (2003), COM(2003) 270.

Commission of the European Communities, 'Education of young sportspersons, Final Report' (August 2004), A report by PMP in partnership with the Institute of Sport and Leisure Policy, Loughborough University.

Commission of the European Communities, 'Report on competition in professional services' (2004), Commission Communication COM(2004) 83 final.

Commission of the European Communities, 'White Paper on Services of General Economic Interest' (2004), COM(2004) 374 final.

Commission of the European Communities, 'The citizens of the European Union and sport' (2004), special Eurobarometer survey.

Commission of the European Communities, 'Issues paper for the audiovisual conference in Liverpool. Right to information and right to short reporting', (July 2005).

Commission of the European Communities, 'Professional services-scope for more reform Commission Communication', COM(2005) 405 final.

Commission of the European Communities, 'State aid action plan', COM(2005)107 final.

Commission of the European Communities, 'Université Catholique de Louvain study on the representativeness of the social partner organisations in the professional football players sector', project No. VC/2004/0547 (February 2006), research project conducted on behalf of the Employment and Social Affairs DG of the European Commission.

Commission of the European Communities, 'White Paper on Sport', COM(2007) 391 Final.

Commission of the European Communities, 'Commission staff working document. The EU and sport: Background and context', SEC (2007) 935.

Commission of the European Communities, 'Commission staff working document. Impact assessment accompanying the White Paper on Sport', SEC 932, 11/07/2007.

Commission of the European Communities, 'Action Plan 'Pierre de Coubertin', SEC(2007) 934.

Coopers and Lybrand, 'The impact of European Union activities on sport' (1995), Study for DG X of the European Commission.

Craig, P. and G. deBurca (eds.), *Evolution of EU Law* (Oxford: Oxford University Press 1999).

Crauford Smith, B. and B. Böttcher, 'Football and Fundamental Rights: Regulating Access to Major Sporting Events on Television', 8(1) *European Public Law* (2002) pp. 107-133.

Dabscheck, B., 'The Globe at the Feet: FIFA's New Employment Rules – II', 9(1) *Sport in Society* (January 2006) pp. 1-18.

Davies, G., *Nationality Discrimination in the European Internal Market* (The Hague: Kluwer Law International 2003).

Davies, G., 'Can Selling Arrangements Be Harmonized?', 30(3) *European Law Review* (2005) pp. 371-385.

Davies, G., 'The Services Directive: Extending the Country of Origin Principle and Reforming Public Administration', 32(2) *European Law Review* (2007) pp. 232-245.

Deloitte, Annual Review of Football Finance (2007).

Dobson, S. and J. Goddard, 'Performance, Revenue and Cross-Subsidisation in the Football League, 1927-1994', LI (4) *Economic History Review* (1998) pp. 763-785.

Drolet, J-C., 'Extra Time: Are the New FIFA Transfer Rules Doomed?', 1-2 *International Sports Law Journal* (2006) pp. 66-73.

Duff, A., 'Scottish Update: A Brief Synopsis of Newsworthy Matters Concerning Football, Rugby & Others from August 1998 to Date', 6(3) *Sport and the Law Journal* (1998) pp. 93-191.

Duthie, M., 'European Community Sports Policy', in A. Lewis and J. Taylor, J. (eds.), *Sport: Law and Practice* (London: Butterworths Lexis Nexis 2002).

European Broadcasting Union (EBU), 'Public consultation by the European Commission on the Review of the Television Without Frontiers Directive (July 2003).

European Parliament, rapporteur: J. Van Raay, Report for the Committee on Legal Affairs and Citizen's Rights, on the freedom of movement of professional footballers in the Community (1989).

European Parliament, rapporteur: J. Larive, Report on the European Community and sport (1994).

European Parliament, rapporteur: D. Pack, Report on the role of the European Union in the field of sport (1997).

European Parliament, Report on the Commission Report to the European Council with a view to safeguarding current sports structures and maintaining the social function of sport within the Community framework- The Helsinki Report on Sport (2000).

European Parliament, Professional sport in the internal market (2005), commissioned by the Committee on the Internal Market and Consumer Protection of the European Parliament on the initiative of Toine Manders. Project No: IP/A/IMCO/ST/2005-004.

European Parliament, rapporteur: Ivo Belet, The future of professional football in Europe (2006), European Parliament Committee on Culture and Education, 2006/2130(INI).

European Publishers News Association (ENPA), ENPA response to the Issue Paper for the audiovisual conference in Liverpool. Right to information and right to short reporting (August 2005).

Feess, E. and G. Mühlheußer, 'Economic Consequences of Transfer Fee Regulations in European Football', 13 *European Journal of Law and Economics* (2002) pp. 221-237.

Feess, E. and G. Mühlheußer, 'The Impact of Transfer Fees on Professional Sports: An Analysis of the New Transfer System for European Football', 105(1) *Scandinavian Journal of Economics* (2003) pp. 139-154.

Feess, E. and G. Mühlheußer, 'Transfer Fee Regulations in European Football', 47 *European Economic Review* (2003) pp. 645-668.

FIFPro, 'Time for a new approach. The international player transfer system', FIFPRO Report to the European Commission (February 9th 2001).

Fleming, H., 'Television Without Frontiers: The Broadcasting of Sporting Events in Europe', 8(8) *Entertainment Law Review* (1997) pp. 281-285.

Flynn, L., 'Coming of Age: The Free Movement of Capital Case Law 1993-2002', 39(4) *Common Market Law Review* (2002) pp. 773-805.

Flynn, M. and R. Gilbert, 'The Analysis of Professional Sports Leagues as Joint Ventures', 111 *Economic Journal* (February 2001) pp. F27-46.

Forrest, D. and R. Simmons, 'New Issues in Attendance Demand. The Case of the English Football League', 7(3) *Journal of Sports Economics* (2006) pp. 247-266.

Fort, R. and J. Quirk, 'Cross-Subsidization, Incentives and Outcomes in Professional Teams Sports Leagues', XXXIII *Journal of Economic Literature* (1995) pp. 1265-1299.

Foster, K. (1993), 'Developments in Sporting Law', in L. Allison, (ed.), *The Changing Politics of Sport* (Manchester: Manchester University Press 1993).

Foster, K. (2000), 'How Can Sport Be Regulated?', in S. Greenfield and G. Osborn (eds.), *Law and Sport in Contemporary Society* (London: Frank Cass 2000).

Foster, K., 'What is International Sports Law?', 5(6) *Sports Law Bulletin* (2002) pp. 14-16.

Foster, K., 'Is There a Global Sports Law?', 2(1) *Entertainment Law* (2003) pp. 1-18.

Foster, K., 'Lex Sportiva and Lex Ludica: The Court of Arbitration for Sport's jurisprudence', 3(2) *Entertainment and Sports Law Journal* (2006), and also in I.S. Blackshaw, R.C.R. Siekmann and J.W. Soek, eds., *The Court of Arbitration for Sport 1984-2004* (The Hague: T.M.C. Asser Press 2006) pp. 420-440.

Frick, B., 'The Football Players' Labor Market: Empirical Evidence From the Major European Leagues', 54(3) *Scottish Journal of Political Economy* (2007) pp. 422-446.

Goyder, D. G., *EC Competition Law*, 4th edn. (2003), Oxford: Oxford University Press.

Gray, J., 'Regulation of Sports Leagues, Team, Athletes and Agents in the United States', in Caiger, A. & Gardiner, S. (eds.), *Professional Sport in the EU, Regulation and Re-regulation* (2000), The Hague: T.M.C. Asser Press.

Grayson, E., *Sport and the Law,* 2nd edn. (London: Butterworth & Co 1994).

Gustafson, E., 'The Luxury Tax in Professional Sports', in W. Andreff and S. Szymanski, *Handbook on the Economics of Sport* (Cheltenham: Edward Elgar 2006).

Halgreen, L., *European Sports Law, a Comparative Analysis of the European and American Models of Sport* (Copenhagen: Forlaget Thomson 2004).

Harbord, D. and S. Szymanski, 'Restricted View. The Rights and Wrongs of FA Premier League Broadcasting', Report for the Consumers' Association, London (2003).

Hatton, C., C. Wagner and H. Armengod, 'Fair play: How Competition Authorities Have Regulated the Sale of Football Media Rights in Europe', 28(6) *European Competition Law Review* (2007) pp. 346-354.

Helberger, N., 'The "Right to Information" and Digital Broadcasting – About Monsters, Invisible Men, and the Future of European Broadcasting Regulation', 17(2) *Entertainment Law Review* (2006) pp. 70-80.

Hellenthal, C., Zulässigkeit einer supranationalen Fussball Europaliga nach den Bestimmungen des europäischen Wettbewerbsrechts (2000), Frankfurt am Main. Cited in: Professional Sport in the Internal Market, Project No. IP/A/IMCO/ST/2005-004, Commissioned by the Committee on the Internal Market and Consumer Protection of the European Parliament (September 2005).

Hoehn, T. and D. Lancefield, 'Broadcasting and Sport', 19(4) *Oxford Review of Economic Policy* (2003) pp. 552-568.

Hoehn, T. and S. Szymanski, 'The Americanisation of European Football', 28 *Economic Policy* (1999) pp. 205-240.

Hornsby, S., '"Closed Leagues": A Prime Candidate for the "Sporting Exception" in European Competition Law', 2 *International Sports Law Review* (June 2001) pp. 161-167.

Hornsby, S., 'The Harder the Cap, the Softer the Law?', 10(2) *Sport and the Law Journal* (2002) pp. 142-149.

Hoskins, M. and M. Gray, 'EC Free Movement Rules and Sport', in A. Lewis and J. Taylor, (eds.), *Sport: Law and Practice* (London: Butterworths Lexis Nexis 2002).

Humphreys, P., Mass Media and Media Policy in Western Europe (Manchester: Manchester University Press 1996).

Infantino, G., 'Meca-Medina: A Step Backwards for the European Sports Model and the Specificity of Sport?', INF (2 October 2006).

Johnson, E. and D. O'Keeffe, 'From Discrimination to Free Movement: Recent Developments Concerning the Free Movement of Workers 1989-1994', 31(6) *Common Market Law Review* (1994) pp. 1313-1346.

Jones, A. and B. Sufrin, *EC Competition Law: Text, Cases and Materials,* 2nd edn. (Oxford: Oxford University Press 2004).

Kerr, T., 'Is Sport Special?', 9(1) *Sport and the Law Journal* (2001) pp. 78-80.

Késenne, S., 'The Impact of Salary Caps in Professional Team Sports', 47(4) *Scottish Journal of Political Economy* (2000) pp. 422-430.

Késenne, S., 'The Bosman Case and European Football', in W. Andreff and S. Szymanski, *Handbook on the Economics of Sport* (Cheltenham: Edward Elgar 2006).

Késenne, S., The Peculiar International Economics of Professional Football in Europe, 54(3) *Scottish Journal of Political Economy* (2007) pp. 388-399.

Komninos, A., 'Non-competition concerns: Resolution of conflicts in the integrated Article 81', Oxford Centre for Competition Law and Policy Working Paper (L) 08/05 part IV (2005).

Kuypers, T., 'The Beautiful Game? An Econometric Study of Why People Watch Football', University College London Discussion Paper in Economics (1996) pp. 96-101.

Levermore, R. and P. Millward, 'Using Sport as a Vehicle to Help Build a Pan-European Identity' (July 2004), paper presented to Europe in the World Centre International Workshop, University of Liverpool.

Lindström-Rossi, L., S. de Waele, and D. Vaigauskaite, 'Application of EC antitrust rules in the sport sector: an update', 3 *EC Competition Policy Newsletter* (Autumn 2005) pp. 72-77.

Loozen, E., 'Professional Ethics and Restraints of Competition', 31(1) *European Law Review* (2006) pp. 28-47.

Marburger, D., 'Chasing the Elusive Salary Cap', in W. Andreff and S. Szymanski, *Handbook on the Economics of Sport* (Cheltenham: Edward Elgar 2006).

Mash, J., 'Is There an EU "Sporting Exception"', 13(2) *Sport and the Law Journal* (2005) pp. 25-32.

Massey, P., 'Are Sports Cartels Different? An Analysis of EU Commission Decisions Concerning the Collective Selling Arrangements for Football Broadcasting Rights', 30(1) *World Competition* (2007) pp. 81-106.

Mattera, A., 'The Principle of Mutual Recognition and Respect for National, Regional and Local Identities and Traditions', in F. Padoia (ed.), *The Principle of Mutual Recognition in the European Integration Process* (Basingstoke: Palgrave MacMillan 2005) pp. 1-24.

Meier, H.E., 'The Rise of the Regulatory State in Sport', paper presented at the 3rd ECPR Conference (8-10 September 2005) Budapest.

Miettinen, S., 'The Internal Market Legislative Programme and Sport', in S. Gardiner, R. Parrish, and R. Siekmann (eds), *Professional Sport in the European Union, Regulation, Reregulation and Representation* (The Hague: TMC Asser Press forthcoming 2008).

Miettinen, S. and R. Parrish, 'Nationality Discrimination in Community Law: An Assessment of UEFA Regulations Governing Player Eligibility for European Club Competitions (The Home-Grown Player Rule)', 5(2) *Entertainment and Sports Law Journal* (2007).

Monti, G., 'Article 81 EC and Public Policy', 39(5) *Common Market Law Review* (2002) pp. 1057-1099.

Mortelmans, K., 'Towards Convergence in the Application of the Rules on Free Movement and on Competition?', 38 *Common Market Law Review* (2001) pp. 613-649.

Nafziger, J., 'International Sports Law as a Process for Resolving Disputes', 45 *International and Comparative Law Quarterly* (1996) pp.130-149.

Nafziger, J., *International Sports Law* (Ardsley, New York State: Transnational 2004).

Nazzini, R, 'Article 81 EC Between Time Present and Time Past: A Normative Critique of Restriction of Competition in EU Law', 43 *Common Market Law Review* (2006) pp. 497-536.

Nicolaides, P., 'The Balancing Myth: The Economics of Article 81(1) and 81(3)', 32 *Legal Issues of Economic Integration* (2005) pp. 123-146.

Noll, R., 'Broadcasting and Team Sports', 54(3) *Scottish Journal of Political Economy* (2007) pp. 400-421.

Nys, J-F., 'Central Government and Sport', in W. Andreff and S. Szymanski, *Handbook on the Economics of Sport* (Cheltenham: Edward Elgar 2006).

O'Loughlin, R., 'EC Competition Rules and Free Movement Rules: An Examination of the Parallels and Their Furtherance by the ECJ Wouters Decision', 24(2) *European Competition Law Review* (2003) pp. 62-69.

Odudu, O., 'A New Economic Approach to Article 81(1)?', 27(1) *European Law Review* (2002) pp. 100-105.

Odudu, O., 'Article 81(3), Discretion and Direct Effect', 23(1) *European Competition Law Review* (2002) pp. 17-25.

Odudu, O., *The Boundaries of EC Competition Law: The Scope of Article 81* (Oxford: Oxford University Press 2006).

Parlasca, S., 'Collective Selling of Broadcast Rights in Team Sports', in W. Andreff and S. Szymanski, *Handbook on the Economics of Sport* (Cheltenham: Edward Elgar 2006).

Parrish, R., *Sports Law and Policy in the European Union* (Manchester: Manchester University Press 2003).

Parrish, R., 'The EU's Draft Constitutional Treaty and the Future of EU Sports Policy', 3 *International Sports Law Journal* (2003) pp. 2-4.

Pinder, J., 'Positive and Negative Integration. Some Problems of Economic Union in the EEC', 24 *World Today* (1968) pp. 88-110.

Pollack, M., 'Creeping Competence: The Expanding Agenda of the European Community', 14(2) *Journal of Public Policy* (1994) pp. 95-145.

Prechal, S., *Directives in EC Law*, 2nd edn. (Oxford: Oxford University Press 2005).

Prosser, T., *The Limits of Competition Law: Markets and Public Services* (Oxford: Oxford University Press 2005).

Ranc, D., 'Vectors of Identification and Markets of Identity in Contemporary European Football', XIth International CESH Congress (2006), Vienna.

Ratliff, J., 'EC competition Law and Sport', 6(3) *Sport and the Law Journal* (1998) pp. 4-17.

Reeb, M., 'The Role and Functions of the Court of Arbitration for Sport (CAS)', 2 *International Sports Law Journal* (2002) pp. 21-24.

Report for the Commission of the European Communities, 'Promoting the social dialogue in European professional football' (EFFC/T.M.C. Asser Institute, September 2004).

Report for the Commission of the European Communities, 'Promoting the social dialogue in European professional football (candidate EU Member States)', (The Hague: T.M.C. Asser Institute November 2004).

Ritter, C., 'European Union Purely Internal Situations, Reverse Discrimination, Guimont, Dzodzi and Article 234', 31(5) *European Law Review* (2006) pp. 690-710.

Roche, M., 'The EU and TV sport: perspectives on cultural Europeanisation with particular reference to football' (August 2003), paper presented at the European sport roundtable, University Association for Contemporary European Studies Annual Conference, Newcastle United Football Club.

Rosen, S. and A. Sanderson, 'Labour Markets in Professional Sports', 111 *Economic Journal* (February 2001) pp. F47-F68.

Ross, M., 'Article 16 EC and Services of General Interest: From Derogation to Obligation', 25(1) *European Law Review* (2000) pp. 22-38.

Ross, S., 'Competition Law as a Constraint on Monopolistic Exploitation by Sports Leagues and Clubs', 19(4) *Oxford Review of Economic Policy* (2003) pp. 569-584.

Rottenberg, S., 'The Baseball Players' Labor Market', 64 *Journal of Political Economy* (1956) pp. 242-58.

Schrauwen, A. (ed.), *The Rule of Reason: Rethinking Another Classic of European legal Doctrine* (Groningen: Europa Law Publishing 2005).

Sher, B., 'The Last of the Steam Powered Trains: Modernising Article 82', 25(5) *European Competition Law Review* (2004) pp. 243-246.

Shuibhne, N., 'Free Movement of Persons and the Wholly Internal Rule: Time to Move on?', 39(4) *Common Market Law Review* (2002) pp. 731-771.

Siekmann, R., 'Labour Law, the Provision of Services, Transfer Rights and Social Dialogue in Professional Football in Europe', 1-2 *The International Sports Law Journal* (2006) p. 117.

Siekmann, R.C.R., R. Parrish, R. Branco-Martins and J.W. Soek, (eds.), *Players'Agents World-wide: Legal Aspects* (The Hague: TMC Asser Press 2007).

Sloane, P., 'The European Model of Sport', in W. Andreff and S. Szymanski, *Handbook on the Economics of Sport* (Cheltenham: Edward Elgar 2006).

Smismans, S., 'The European Social Dialogue Between Constitutional and Labour Law', 32(3) *European Law Review* (2007) pp. 341-364.

Snell, J., *Goods and Services in EC Law* (Oxford: Oxford University Press 2001).

Snell, J., 'Who's Got the Power? Free Movement and Allocation of Competences in EC Law', 22 *Yearbook of European Law* (2003) pp. 323-351.

Snell, J., 'Economic Aims as Justification for Restrictions on Free Movement', in a. Schrauwen (ed.), *The Rule of Reason: Rethinking Another Classic of European Legal Doctrine* (Groningen: Europa Law Publishing 2005).

Spaventa, E., 'From Gebhard to Carpenter: Towards a (Non-)Economic European Constitution', 41(3) *Common Market Law Review* (2004) pp. 743-773.

Stix-Hackl, C. and A. Egger, 'Sports and Competition Law: A Never-ending Story?', 23(2) *European Competition Law Review* (2002) pp. 81-91.

Szamuley, H., 'The Golf Ball as a Symbol of Integration,' see at <www.brugesgroup.com>.

Szymanski, S., 'The Economic Design of Sporting Contests', 41 *Journal of Economic Literature* (2003) pp. 1137-1187.

Szymanski, S., 'Baseball Economics', in W. Andreff and S. Szymanski, *Handbook on the Economics of Sport* (Cheltenham: Edward Elgar 2006).

Szymanski, S., 'Revenue Sharing', in W. Andreff and S. Szymanski, *Handbook on the Economics of Sport* (Cheltenham: Edward Elgar 2006).

Szymanski, S. and S. Késenne, 'Competitive Balance and Gate Revenue Sharing in Team Sports', 52 *The Journal of Industrial Economics* (2004) pp. 165-177.

Szyszczak, E., 'Competition and Sport', 32(1) *European Law Review* (2007) pp. 95-110.

Thomas, D., 'The Retain and Transfer System', in W. Andreff and S. Szymanski, *Handbook on the Economics of Sport* (Cheltenham: Edward Elgar 2006).

Tokarski, W. et al. (eds.), *Two Players One Goal? Sport in the European Union* (Oxford: Meyer and Meyer 2004).

Toner, H., 'Non-Discriminatory Obstacles to the Exercise of the Treaty Rights – Articles 39, 43, 49 and 18 EC', 23 *Yearbook of European Law* (Oxford: Oxford University Press 2004).

Tridimas, T., *General Principles of EU Law* (Oxford: Oxford University Press 2006).

Van den Bogaert, S., *Practical Regulation of the Mobility of Sportsmen in the EU Post Bosman* (The Hague: Kluwer 2005).

Van den Brink, J.P., 'EC Competition Law and the Regulation of Football: Part I', 21(8) *European Competition Law Review* (2000) pp. 359-368.

Van den Brink, J.P., 'EC Competition Law and the Regulation of Football: Part II', 21(9) *European Competition Law Review* (2000) pp. 420-427.

Vrooman, J., 'A General Theory of Professional Sports Leagues', 61(4) *Southern Economic Journal* (1995) pp. 339-360.

Weatherill, S., 'Discrimination on Grounds of Nationality in Sport', 9 *Yearbook of European Law* (Oxford: Oxford University Press 1989).

Weatherill, S., 'Resisting the Pressures of "Americanisation": The Influence of European Community Law on the "European Model of Sport"', in S. Greenfield and G. Osborn (eds.), *Law and Sport in Contemporary Society* (London: Frank Cass 2000).

Weatherill, S., 'Fair Play Please! Recent Developments in the Application of EC Law to Sport', 40 *Common Market Law Review* (2003) pp. 51-93.

Weatherill, S., 'Sport as Culture in EC Law', in R. Craufurd Smith, *Culture and European Union Law* (Oxford: Oxford University Press 2004).

Weatherill, S., 'Anti-Doping Rules and EC Law', 26(7) *European Competition Law Review* (2005) pp. 416-421.

Weatherill, S., 'Is the Pyramid Compatible with EC law?', 3-4 *International Sports Law Journal* (2005) pp. 3-7.

Weatherill, S., 'Anti-Doping Revisited: The Demise of the Rule of Purely Sporting Interest', 27(12) *European Competition Law Review* (2006).

Weatherill, S., 'The Sale of Rights to Broadcast Sporting Events under EC Law', 3-4 *International Sports Law Journal* (2006) pp. 3-27.

Weatherill, S., *European Sports Law: Collected Papers* (The Hague: T.M.C. Asser Press 2007).

Weatherill, S. 'The Challenge of Better Regulation', in S. Weatherill (ed.), *Better Regulation* (Oxford: Hart 2007).

Weiler, J. H. H., 'Functional Equivalence and Harmonization', in F. Padoia (ed.), *The Principle of Mutual Recognition in the European Integration Process* (Basingstoke: Palgrave MacMillan 2005) pp. 25-84.

Whish, R., *Competition Law*, 5th edn. (London: Butterworths Lexis Nexis 2003).

White, R., *Workers, Services and Establishment* (Oxford: Oxford University Press 2004).

Wise, A. and B. Meyer, *International Sports Law and Business* (The Hague: Kluwer Law International 1997).

Annex
COMMISSION OF THE EUROPEAN COMMUNITIES
WHITE PAPER ON SPORT

Brussels, 11.7.2007
(presented by the Commission)

1. INTRODUCTION

"Sport is part of every man and woman's heritage and its absence can never be compensated for."

Sport[874] is a growing social and economic phenomenon which makes an important contribution to the European Union's strategic objectives of solidarity and prosperity. The Olympic ideal of developing sport to promote peace and understanding among nations and cultures as well as the education of young people was born in Europe and has been fostered by the International Olympic Committee and the European Olympic Committees.

Sport attracts European citizens, with a majority of people taking part in sporting activities on a regular basis. It generates important values such as team spirit, solidarity, tolerance and fair play, contributing to personal development and fulfilment. It promotes the active contribution of EU citizens to society and thereby helps to foster active citizenship. The Commission acknowledges the essential role of sport in European society, in particular when it needs to bring itself closer to citizens and to tackle issues that matter directly to them.

However, sport is also confronted with new threats and challenges which have emerged in European society, such as commercial pressure, exploitation of young players, doping, racism, violence, corruption and money laundering.

This initiative marks the first time that the Commission is addressing sport-related issues in a comprehensive manner. Its overall objective is to give strategic orientation on the role of sport in Europe, to encourage debate on specific problems, to enhance the visibility of sport in EU policy-making and to raise public awareness of the needs and specificities of the sector. The initiative aims to illustrate important issues such as the application of EU law to sport. It also seeks to set out further sports-related action at EU level.

This White Paper is not starting from scratch. Sport is subject to the application of the *acquis communautaire* and European policies in a number of areas already have a considerable and growing impact on sport.

The important role of sport in European society and its specific nature were recognised in December 2000 in the European Council's Declaration on the specific characteristics of sport and its social function in Europe, of which account should be taken in implementing common policies (the "Nice Declaration"). It points out that sporting organisations and Member States have a primary responsibility in the conduct of sporting affairs, with a central role for sports

---

[874] For the sake of clarity and simplicity, this White Paper will use the definition of "sport" established by the Council of Europe: "all forms of physical activity which, through casual or organised participation, aim at expressing or improving physical fitness and mental well-being, forming social relationships or obtaining results in competition at all levels."

federations. It clarifies that sporting organisations have to exercise their task to organise and promote their particular sports "with due regard to national and Community legislation". At the same time, it recognises that, "even though not having any direct powers in this area, the Community must, in its action under the various Treaty provisions, take account of the social, educational and cultural functions inherent in sport and making it special, in order that the code of ethics and the solidarity essential to the preservation of its social role may be respected and nurtured." The European institutions have recognised the specificity of the role sport plays in European society, based on volunteer-driven structures, in terms of health, education, social integration, and culture.

The European Parliament has followed the various challenges facing European sport with keen interest and has regularly dealt with sporting issues in recent years.

In preparing this White Paper, the Commission has held numerous consultations with sport stakeholders on issues of common interest as well as an on-line consultation. They have demonstrated that considerable expectations exist concerning the role of sport in Europe and EU action in this area.

This White Paper focuses on the societal role of sport, its economic dimension and its organisation in Europe, and on the follow-up that will be given to this initiative. Concrete proposals for further EU action are brought together in an Action Plan named after Pierre de Coubertin which contains activities to be implemented or supported by the Commission. A Staff Working Document contains the background and context of the proposals, including annexes on Sport and EU Competition Rules, Sport and Internal Market Freedoms, and on consultations with stakeholders.

2.   THE SOCIETAL ROLE OF SPORT

Sport is an area of human activity that greatly interests citizens of the European Union and has enormous potential for bringing them together, reaching out to all, regardless of age or social origin. According to a November 2004 Eurobarometer survey,[875] approximately 60% of European citizens participate in sporting activities on a regular basis within or outside some 700,000 clubs, which are themselves members of a plethora of associations and federations.

The vast majority of sporting activity takes place in amateur structures. Professional sport is of growing importance and contributes equally to the societal role of sport. In addition to improving the health of European citizens, sport has an educational dimension and plays a social, cultural and recreational role. The societal role of sport also has the potential to strengthen the Union's external relations.

2.1   Enhancing public health through physical activity

Lack of physical activity reinforces the occurrence of overweight, obesity and a number of chronic conditions such as cardio-vascular diseases and diabetes, which reduce the quality of life, put individuals' lives at risk and are a burden on health budgets and the economy.

The Commission's White Paper "A Strategy for Europe on Nutrition, Overweight and Obesity related health issues"[876] underlines the importance of taking pro-active steps to reverse the decline in physical activity, and actions suggested in the area of physical activity in the two White Papers will complement each other.

---

[875]   Special Eurobarometer (2004): The Citizens of the European Union and Sport.
[876]   COM(2007)279 final of 30.5.2007.

As a tool for health-enhancing physical activity, the sport movement has a greater influence than any other social movement. Sport is attractive to people and has a positive image.

However, the recognised potential of the sport movement to foster health-enhancing physical activity often remains under-utilised and needs to be developed.

The World Health Organisation (WHO) recommends a minimum of 30 minutes of moderate physical activity (including but not limited to sport) per day for adults and 60 minutes for children. Public authorities and private organisations in Member States should all contribute to reaching this objective. Recent studies tend to show that sufficient progress is not being made.

(1) The Commission proposes to develop new physical activity guidelines with the Member States before the end of 2008.

The Commission recommends strengthening the cooperation between the health, education and sport sectors to be promoted at ministerial level in the Member States in order to define and implement coherent strategies to reduce overweight, obesity and other health risks. In this context, the Commission encourages Member States to examine how to promote the concept of active living through the national education and training systems, including the training of teachers.

Sport organisations are encouraged to take into account their potential for health-enhancing physical activity and to undertake activities for this purpose. The Commission will facilitate the exchange of information and good practice, in particular in relation to young people, with a focus on the grassroots level.

(2) The Commission will support an EU Health-Enhancing Physical Activity (HEPA) network and, if appropriate, smaller and more focussed networks dealing with specific aspects of the topic.

(3) The Commission will make health-enhancing physical activity a cornerstone of its sportrelated activities and will seek to take this priority better into account in relevant financial instruments, including:

- The 7th Framework Programme for Research and Technological Development (lifestyle aspects of health);
- The Public Health Programme 2007-2013;
- The Youth and Citizenship programmes (cooperation between sport organisations, schools, civil society, parents and other partners at local level);
- The Lifelong Learning Programme (teacher training and cooperation between schools).

2.2 Joining forces in the fight against doping

Doping poses a threat to sport worldwide, including European sports. It undermines the principle of open and fair competition. It is a demotivating factor for sport in general and puts the professional under unreasonable pressure. It seriously affects the image of sport and poses a serious threat to individual health. At European level, the fight against doping must take into account both a law-enforcement and a health and prevention dimension.

(4) Partnerships could be developed between Member State law enforcement agencies (border guards, national and local police, customs, etc.), laboratories accredited by the World Anti-Doping Agency (WADA) and INTERPOL to exchange information about new doping substances and practices in a timely manner and in a secure environment. The EU could support such efforts through training courses and networking between training centres for law enforcement officers.

The Commission recommends that trade in illicit doping substances be treated in the same manner as trade in illicit drugs throughout the EU.

The Commission calls on all actors with a responsibility for public health to take the healthhazard aspects of doping into account. It calls on sport organisations to develop rules of good practice to ensure that young sportsmen and sportswomen are better informed and educated of doping substances, prescription medicines which may contain them, and their health implications.

The EU would benefit from a more coordinated approach in the fight against doping, in particular by defining common positions in relation to the Council of Europe, WADA and UNESCO, and through the exchange of information and good practice between Governments, national anti-doping organisations and laboratories. Proper implementation of the UNESCO Convention against Doping in Sport by the Member States is particularly important in this context.

(5) The Commission will play a facilitating role, for example by supporting a network of national anti-doping organisations of Member States.

2.3 Enhancing the role of sport in education and training

Through its role in formal and non-formal education, sport reinforces Europe's human capital. The values conveyed through sport help develop knowledge, motivation, skills and readiness for personal effort. Time spent in sport activities at school and at university produces health and education benefits which need to be enhanced.

Based on experience gained during the 2004 European Year of Education through Sport, the Commission encourages support for sport and physical activity through various policy initiatives in the field of education and training, including the development of social and civic competences in accordance with the 2006 Recommendation on key competences for lifelong learning.[877]

(6) Sport and physical activity can be supported through the Lifelong Learning programme. Promoting participation in educational opportunities through sport is thus a priority topic for school partnerships supported by the Comenius programme, for structured actions in the field of vocational education and training through the Leonardo da Vinci programme, for thematic networks and mobility in the field of higher education supported by the Erasmus programme, as well as multilateral projects in the field of adult training supported by the Grundtvig programme.

(7) The sport sector can also apply for support through the individual calls for proposals on the implementation of the European Qualifications Framework (EQF) and the European 5 Recommendation of the European Parliament and of the Council, of 18 December 2006, on key competences for lifelong learning (Official Journal L 394 of 30.12.2006).

Credit System for Vocational Education and Training (ECVET). The sport sector has been involved in the development of the EQF and has been selected for financial support in 2007/2008. In view of the high professional mobility of sportspeople, and without prejudice to Directive 2005/36/EC on the mutual recognition of professional qualifications, it may also be identified as a pilot sector for the implementation of

---

[877] Recommendation of the European Parliament and of the Council, of 18 December 2006, on key competences for lifelong learning (Official Journal L 394 of 30.12.2006).

ECVET to increase the transparency of national competence and qualification systems.

(8) The Commission will introduce the award of a European label to schools actively involved in supporting and promoting physical activities in a school environment.

In order to ensure the reintegration of professional sportspersons into the labour market at the end of their sporting careers, the Commission emphasises the importance of taking into account at an early stage the need to provide "dual career" training for young sportsmen and sportswomen and to provide high quality local training centres to safeguard their moral, educational and professional interests.

The Commission has launched a study on the training of young sportsmen and sportswomen in Europe, the results of which could feed into the abovementioned policies and programmes. Investment in and promotion of training of young talented sportsmen and sportswomen in proper conditions is crucial for a sustainable development of sport at all levels. The Commission stresses that training systems for talented young sportsmen and sportswomen should be open to all and must not lead to discrimination between EU citizens based on nationality.

(9) Rules requiring that teams include a certain quota of locally trained players could be accepted as being compatible with the Treaty provisions on free movement of persons if they do not lead to any direct discrimination based on nationality and if possible indirect discrimination effects resulting from them can be justified as being proportionate to a legitimate objective pursued, such as to enhance and protect the training and development of talented young players. The ongoing study on the training of young sportsmen and sportswomen in Europe will provide valuable input for this analysis.

2.4   Promoting volunteering and active citizenship through sport

Participation in a team, principles such as fair-play, compliance with the rules of the game, respect for others, solidarity and discipline as well as the organisation of amateur sport based on non-profit clubs and volunteering reinforce active citizenship. Volunteering in sport organisations provides many occasions for non-formal education which need to be recognised and enhanced. Sport also provides attractive possibilities for young people's engagement and involvement in society and may have a beneficial effect in helping people steer away from delinquency.

There are, however, new trends in the way people, particularly the young, practice sport. There is a growing tendency to practise sport individually, rather than collectively and in an organised structure, which is resulting in a declining volunteer base for amateur sport clubs.

(10) Together with the Member States, the Commission will identify key challenges for non-profit sport organisations and the main characteristics of services provided by these organisations.

(11) The Commission will support grassroots sport through the Europe for Citizens programme.

(12) The Commission will furthermore propose to encourage young people's volunteering in sport through the Youth in Action programme in fields such as youth exchanges and voluntary service for sporting events.

(13) The Commission will further develop exchange of information and best practice on volunteering in sport involving Member States, sport organisations and local authorities. (14) In order to understand better the specific demands and needs of the voluntary sport sector in national and European policy making, the Commission will launch a European study on volunteering in sport.

2.5   Using the potential of sport for social inclusion, integration and equal opportunities

Sport makes an important contribution to economic and social cohesion and more integrated societies. All residents should have access to sport. The specific needs and situation of under-represented groups therefore need to be addressed, and the special role that sport can play for young people, people with disabilities and people from less privileged backgrounds must be taken into account. Sport can also facilitate the integration into society of migrants and persons of foreign origin as well as support inter-cultural dialogue.

Sport promotes a shared sense of belonging and participation and may therefore also be an important tool for the integration of immigrants. It is in this context that making available spaces for sport and supporting sport-related activities is important for allowing immigrants and the host society to interact together in a positive way.

The Commission believes that better use can be made of the potential of sport as an instrument for social inclusion in the policies, actions and programmes of the European Union and of Member States. This includes the contribution of sport to job creation and to economic growth and revitalisation, particularly in disadvantaged areas. Non-profit sport activities contributing to social cohesion and social inclusion of vulnerable groups can be considered as social services of general interest.

The Open Method of Coordination on social protection and social inclusion will continue to include sport as a tool and indicator. Studies, seminars, conferences, policy proposals and action plans will include access to sport and/or belonging to social sport structures as a key element for analysis of social exclusion.

(15)   The Commission will suggest to Member States that the PROGRESS programme and the Lifelong Learning, Youth in Action and Europe for Citizens programmes support actions promoting social inclusion through sport and combating discrimination in sport. In the context of cohesion policy, Member States should consider the role of sports in the field of social inclusion, integration and equal opportunities as part of their programming of the European Social Fund and the European Regional Development Fund, and they are encouraged to promote action under the European Integration Fund.

The Commission furthermore encourages Member States and sport organisations to adapt sport infrastructure to take into account the needs of people with disabilities. Member States and local authorities should ensure that sport venues and accommodations are accessible for people with disabilities. Specific criteria should be adopted for ensuring equal access to sport for all pupils, and specifically for children with disabilities. Training of monitors, volunteers and host staff of clubs and organisations for the purpose of welcoming people with disabilities will be promoted. In its consultations with sport stakeholders, the Commission takes special care to maintain a dialogue with representatives of sportspeople with disabilities.

(16)   The Commission, in its Action Plan on the European Union Disability Strategy, will take into account the importance of sport for disabled people and will support Member State actions in this field.

(17)   In the framework of its Roadmap for Equality between Women and Men 2006-2010, the Commission will encourage the mainstreaming of gender issues into all its sports-related activities, with a specific focus on access to sport for immigrant women and women from ethnic minorities, women's access to decision-making positions in sport and media coverage of women in sport.

2.6 Strengthening the prevention of and fight against racism and violence

Violence at sport events, especially at football grounds, remains a disturbing problem and can take different forms. It has been shifting from inside stadiums to outside, including urban areas. The Commission is committed to contributing to the prevention of incidents by promoting and facilitating dialogue with Member States, international organisations (e.g., Council of Europe), sport organisations, law enforcement services and other stakeholders (e.g., supporters' organisations and local authorities). Law enforcement authorities cannot deal with the underlying causes of sport violence in isolation.

The Commission also encourages the exchange of best practice and of operational information on risk-supporters among police services and/or sport authorities. Particular importance will be given to police training on crowd management and hooliganism. Sport involves all citizens regardless of gender, race, age, disability, religion and belief, sexual orientation and social or economic background. The Commission has repeatedly condemned all manifestations of racism and xenophobia, which are incompatible with the values of the EU.

(18) As regards racist and xenophobic attitudes, the Commission will continue to promote dialogue and exchange of best practices in existing cooperation frameworks such as the Football against Racism in Europe network (FARE).

The Commission recommends sport federations to have procedures for dealing with racist abuse during matches, based on existing initiatives. It also recommends strengthening provisions regarding discrimination in licensing systems for clubs (see section 4.7).

The Commission will:

(19) Promote, in accordance with the domestic and EU rules applicable, the exchange of operational information and practical know-how and experience on the prevention of violent and racist incidents between law enforcement services and with sport organisations;

(20) Analyse possibilities for new legal instruments and other EU-wide standards to prevent public disorder at sport events;

(21) Promote a multidisciplinary approach to preventing anti-social behaviour, with a special focus given to socio-educational actions such as fan-coaching (long-term work with supporters to develop a positive and non-violent attitude);

(22) Strengthen regular and structured cooperation among law enforcement services, sport organisations and other stakeholders;

(23) Encourage the use of the following programmes to contribute to the prevention of and fight against violence and racism in sport: Youth in Action, Europe for Citizens, DAPHNE III, Fundamental Rights and Citizenship and Prevention and Fight against Crime;

(24) Organise a high level conference to discuss measures to prevent and fight violence and racism at sport events with stakeholders.

2.7 Sharing our values with other parts of the world

Sport can play a role regarding different aspects of the EU's external relations: as an element of external assistance programmes, as an element of dialogue with partner countries and as part of the EU's public diplomacy.

Through concrete actions, sport has a considerable potential as a tool to promote education, health, inter-cultural dialogue, development and peace.

(25) The Commission will promote the use of sport as a tool in its development policy. In particular, it will:
 • Promote sport and physical education as essential elements of quality education and as a means to make schools more attractive and improve attendance;
 • Target action at improving access for girls and women to physical education and sport, with the objective to help them build confidence, improve social integration, overcome prejudices and promote healthy lifestyles as well as women's access to education;
 • Support health promotion and awareness-raising campaigns through sport.
 When addressing sport in its development policies, the EU will make its best effort to create synergies with existing programmes of the United Nations, Member States, local authorities and private bodies. It will implement actions that are complementary or innovative with respect to existing programmes and actions. The memorandum of understanding signed between the Commission and FIFA in 2006 to make football a force for development in African, Caribbean and Pacific countries is an example in this respect.

(26) The EU will include, wherever appropriate, sport-related issues such as international players' transfers, exploitation of underage players, doping, money-laundering through sport, and security during major international sport events in its policy dialogue and cooperation with partner countries.
 Rapid visa and immigration procedures for, in particular, elite sportspersons from non-EU countries are an important element to enhance the EU's international attractiveness. In addition to the on-going process of concluding visa facilitation agreements with third countries and the consolidation of the visa regime applicable to members of the Olympic family during Olympic Games, the EU needs to develop further (temporary) admission mechanisms for sportspersons from third countries.
 The Commission will pay particular attention to the sport sector:

(27) When implementing the recently presented Communication on circular migration and mobility partnerships with third countries;

(28) When elaborating harmonised schemes for the admission of various categories of third country nationals for economic purposes on the basis of the 2005 Policy Plan on Legal Migration.

2.8 Supporting sustainable development

The practice of sport, sport facilities and sport events all have a significant impact on the environment. It is important to promote environmentally sound management, fit to address, *inter alia*, green procurement, greenhouse gas emissions, energy efficiency, waste disposal and the treatment of soil and water. European sport organisations and sport event organisers should adopt environmental objectives in order to make their activities environmentally sustainable. By improving their credibility on environmental matters, responsible organisations could expect specific benefits while bidding to host sport events as well as economic benefits related to a more rationalised use of natural resources.
 The Commission will:

(29) Use its structured dialogue with leading international and European sport organisations and other sport stakeholders to encourage them and their members to participate in the Eco Management Audit Scheme (EMAS) and Community Eco-Label Award schemes, and promote these voluntary schemes during major sport events;

(30) Promote green procurement in its political dialogue with Member States and other concerned parties;
(31) Raise awareness, through guidance developed in cooperation with relevant stakeholders (policy makers, SMEs, local communities), about the need to work together in partnership at the regional level to organise sport events in a sustainable way;
(32) Take sport into account as part of the "Information and Communication" component of the new LIFE+ programme.

3. THE ECONOMIC DIMENSION OF SPORT

Sport is a dynamic and fast-growing sector with an underestimated macro-economic impact, and can contribute to the Lisbon objectives of growth and job creation. It can serve as a tool for local and regional development, urban regeneration or rural development. Sport has synergies with tourism and can stimulate the upgrading of infrastructure and the emergence of new partnerships for financing sport and leisure facilities.

Although sound and comparable data on the economic weight of sport are generally lacking, its importance is confirmed by studies and analyses of national accounts, the economics of large-scale sporting events, and physical inactivity costs, including for the ageing population.

A study presented during the Austrian Presidency in 2006 suggested that sport in a broader sense generated value-added of 407 billion euros in 2004, accounting for 3.7% of EU GDP, and employment for 15 million people or 5.4% of the labour force.[878] This contribution of sport should be made more visible and promoted in EU policies.

A growing part of the economic value of sports is linked to intellectual property rights. These rights relate to copyright, commercial communications, trademarks, and image and media rights. In an increasingly globalised and dynamic sector, the effective enforcement of intellectual property rights around the world is becoming an essential part of the health of the sport economy. It is also important that recipients are guaranteed the possibility to have distance access to sport events at cross-border level within the EU.

On the other hand, notwithstanding the overall economic importance of sport, the vast majority of sporting activities takes place in non-profit structures, many of which depend on public support to provide access to sporting activities to all citizens.

3.1 Moving towards evidence-based sport policies

The launch of policy actions and enhanced cooperation on sport at EU level needs to be underpinned by a sound knowledge base. The quality and comparability of data need to be improved to allow for better strategic planning and policy-making in the area of sport. Governmental and non-governmental stakeholders have repeatedly called upon the Commission to develop a European statistical definition of sport and to coordinate efforts to produce sport and sport-related statistics on that basis.

(33) The Commission, in close cooperation with the Member States, will seek to develop a European statistical method for measuring the economic impact of sport as a basis for national statistical accounts for sport, which could lead in time to a European satellite account for sport.

---

[878] D. Dimitrov / C. Helmenstein / A. Kleissner / B. Moser / J. Schindler: *Die makroökonomischen Effekte des Sports in Europa*, Studie im Auftrag des Bundeskanzleramts, Sektion Sport, Wien, 2006.

(34) In addition, specific sport-related information surveys should continue to take place once every few years (e.g., Eurobarometer polls), in particular to provide non-economic information which cannot be provided on the basis of national statistical accounts for sport (e.g., participation rates, data on volunteering, etc.).

(35) The Commission will launch a study to assess the sport sector's direct contribution (in terms of GDP, growth and employment) and indirect contribution (through education, regional development and higher attractiveness of the EU) to the Lisbon Agenda.

(36) The Commission will organise the exchange of best practices among Member States and sports federations concerning the organisation of large sport events, with a view to promoting sustainable economic growth, competitiveness and employment.

3.2 Putting public support for sport on a more secure footing

Sport organisations have many sources of income, including club fees and ticket sales, advertising and sponsorship, media rights, re-distribution of income within the sport federations, merchandising, public support, etc. However, some sport organisations have considerably better access to resources from business operators than others, even if in some cases a well-functioning system of redistribution is in place. In grassroots sport, equal opportunities and open access to sporting activities can only be guaranteed through strong public involvement. The Commission understands the importance of public support for grassroots sport and sport for all, and is in favour of such support provided it is granted in accordance with Community law.

In many Member States sport is partly financed through a tax or levy on state-run or state-licensed gambling or lottery services. The Commission invites Member States to reflect upon how best to maintain and develop a sustainable financing model for giving long-term support to sports organisations.

(37) As a contribution to the reflection on the financing of sport, the Commission will carry out an independent study on the financing of grassroots sport and sport for all in the Member States from both public and private sources, and on the impact of on-going changes in this area.

In the field of indirect taxation, the EU's VAT legislation is laid down in Council Directive 2006/112/EC, which aims at ensuring that the application of Member State legislation on VAT does not distort competition or hinder the free movement of goods and services. The Directive provides for both the possibility for Member States to exempt certain sport-related services and, where exemption does not apply, the possibility to apply reduced rates in some cases.

(38) Given the important societal role of sport and its strong local anchoring, the Commission will defend maintaining the existing possibilities of reduced VAT rates for sport.

4. THE ORGANISATION OF SPORT

The political debate on sport in Europe often attributes considerable importance to the so-called "European Sport Model". The Commission considers that certain values and traditions of European sport should be promoted. In view of the diversity and complexities of European sport structures it considers, however, that it is unrealistic to try to define a unified model of organisation of sport in Europe. Moreover, economic and social developments that are common to the majority of the Member States (increasing commercialisation, challenges to public spending, increasing numbers of participants and stagnation in the number of voluntary work-ers) have resulted in new challenges for the organisation of sport in Europe. The emergence of new stakeholders (participants outside the organised disciplines, professional sports clubs, etc.) is posing new questions as regards governance, democracy and representation of interests within the sport movement.

The Commission can play a role in encouraging the sharing of best practice in sport gov-ernance. It can also help to develop a common set of principles for good governance in sport, such as transparency, democracy, accountability and representation of stakeholders (associa-tions, federations, players, clubs, leagues, supporters, etc.). While doing so the Commission will draw on previous work.[879] Attention should also be paid to the representation of women in management and leadership positions.

The Commission acknowledges the autonomy of sporting organisations and representative structures (such as leagues). Furthermore, it recognises that governance is mainly the respon-sibility of sports governing bodies and, to some extent, the Member States and social partners. Nonetheless, dialogue with sports organisations has brought a number of areas to the Commis-sion's attention, which are addressed below. The Commission considers that most challenges can be addressed through self-regulation respectful of good governance principles, provided that EU law is respected, and is ready to play a facilitating role or take action if necessary.

4.1 The specificity of sport

Sport activity is subject to the application of EU law. This is described in detail in the Staff Working Document and its annexes. Competition law and Internal Market provisions apply to sport in so far as it constitutes an economic activity. Sport is also subject to other important as-pects of EU law, such as the prohibition of discrimination on grounds of nationality, provisions regarding citizenship of the Union and equality between men and women in employment.

At the same time, sport has certain specific characteristics, which are often referred to as the "specificity of sport". The specificity of European sport can be approached through two prisms:

- The specificity of sporting activities and of sporting rules, such as separate competitions for men and women, limitations on the number of participants in competitions, or the need to ensure uncertainty concerning outcomes and to preserve a competitive balance between clubs taking part in the same competitions;
- The specificity of the sport structure, including notably the autonomy and diversity of sport organisations, a pyramid structure of competitions from grassroots to elite level and organ-ised solidarity mechanisms between the different levels and operators, the organisation of sport on a national basis, and the principle of a single federation per sport; The case law of the European courts and decisions of the European Commission show that the specificity of sport has been recognised and taken into account. They also provide guidance on how EU law applies to sport. In line with established case law, the specificity of sport will continue to be recognised, but it cannot be construed so as to justify a general exemption from the application of EU law.

As is explained in detail in the Staff Working Document and its annexes, there areorganisa-tional sporting rules that – based on their legitimate objectives – are likely not to breach the

---

[879] E.g. the "Rules of the Game" conference organised in 2001 by FIA and the EOC and the Inde-pendent European Sport Review carried out in 2006.

anti-trust provisions of the EC Treaty, provided that their anti-competitive effects, if any, are inherent and proportionate to the objectives pursued. Examples of such rules would be "rules of the game" (e.g., rules fixing the length of matches or the number of players on the field), rules concerning selection criteria for sport competitions, "at home and away from home" rules, rules preventing multiple ownership in club competitions, rules concerning the composition of national teams, anti-doping rules and rules concerning transfer periods. However, in respect of the regulatory aspects of sport, the assessment whether a certain sporting rule is compatible with EU competition law can only be made on a case-by-case basis, as recently confirmed by the European Court of Justice in its Meca-Medina ruling.[880] The Court provided a clarification regarding the impact of EU law on sporting rules. It dismissed the notion of "purely sporting rules" as irrelevant for the question of the applicability of EU competition rules to the sport sector.

The Court recognised that the specificity of sport has to be taken into consideration in the sense that restrictive effects on competition that are inherent in the organisation and proper conduct of competitive sport are not in breach of EU competition rules, provided that these effects are proportionate to the legitimate genuine sporting interest pursued. The necessity of a proportionality test implies the need to take into account the individual features of each case. It does not allow for the formulation of general guidelines on the application of competition law to the sport sector.

4.2 Free movement and nationality

The organisation of sport and of competitions on a national basis is part of the historical and cultural background of the European approach to sport, and corresponds to the wishes of European citizens. In particular, national teams play an essential role not only in terms of identity but also to secure solidarity with grassroots sport, and therefore deserve to be supported.

Discrimination on grounds of nationality is prohibited in the Treaties, which establish the right for any citizen of the Union to move and reside freely in the territory of the Member States. The Treaties also aim to abolish any discrimination based on nationality between workers of the Member States as regards employment, remuneration and other conditions of work and employment. The same prohibitions apply to discrimination based on nationality in the provision of services. Moreover, membership of sports clubs and participation in competitions are relevant factors to promote the integration of residents into the society of the host country.

Equal treatment also concerns citizens of States which have signed agreements with the EU that contain non-discrimination clauses, and who are legally employed in the territory of the Member States.

(39) The Commission calls on Member States and sport organisations to address discrimination based on nationality in all sports. It will combat discrimination in sport through political dialogue with the Member States, recommendations, structured dialogue with sport stakeholders, and infringement procedures when appropriate.

The Commission reaffirms its acceptance of limited and proportionate restrictions (in line with EU Treaty provisions on free movement and European Court of Justice rulings) to the principle of free movement in particular as regards:
- The right to select national athletes for national team competitions;

---

[880] Case C-519/04P, *Meca Medina* v. *Commission*, *ECR* 2006, I-6991. For more details, see the Staff Working Document.

- The need to limit the number of participants in a competition;
- The setting of deadlines for transfers of players in team sports.

(40) As regards access to individual competitions for non-nationals, the Commission intends to launch a study to analyse all aspects of this complex issue.

4.3 Transfers

In the absence of transfer rules, the integrity of sport competitions could be challenged by clubs recruiting players during a given season to prevail upon their competitors. At the same time, any rule on the transfer of players must respect EU law (competition provisions and rules on the free movement of workers).

In 2001, in the context of the pursuit of a case concerning alleged infringements of EC competition law and after discussions with the Commission, football authorities undertook to revise FIFA Regulations on international football transfers, based on compensation for training costs incurred by sports clubs, the creation of transfer periods, the protection of school education of underage players, and guaranteed access to national courts.

The Commission considers such a system to constitute an example of good practice that ensures a competitive equilibrium between sport clubs while taking into account the requirements of EU law.

The transfer of players also gives rise to concerns about the legality of the financial flows involved. To increase transparency in money flows related to transfers, an information and verification system for transfers could be an effective solution. The Commission considers that such a system should only have a control function; financial transactions should be conducted directly between the parties involved. Depending on the sport, the system could be run by the relevant European sport organisation, or by national information and verification systems in the Member States.

4.4 Players' agents

The development of a truly European market for players and the rise in the level of players' salaries in some sports has resulted in an increase in the activities of players' agents. In an increasingly complex legal environment, many players (but also sport clubs) ask for the services of agents to negotiate and sign contracts.

There are reports of bad practices in the activities of some agents which have resulted in instances of corruption, money laundering and exploitation of underage players. These practices are damaging for sport in general and raise serious governance questions. The health and security of players, particularly minors, has to be protected and criminal activities fought against.

Moreover, agents are subject to differing regulations in different Member States. Some Member States have introduced specific legislation on players' agents while in others the applicable law is the general law regarding employment agencies, but with references to players' agents. Moreover, some international federations (FIFA, FIBA) have introduced their own regulations.

For these reasons, repeated calls have been made on the EU to regulate the activity of players' agents through an EU legislative initiative.

(41) The Commission will carry out an impact assessment to provide a clear overview of the activities of players' agents in the EU and an evaluation of whether action at EU level is necessary, which will also analyse the different possible options.

4.5   Protection of minors

The exploitation of young players is continuing. The most serious problem concerns children who are not selected for competitions and abandoned in a foreign country, often falling in this way in an irregular position which fosters their further exploitation. Although in most cases this phenomenon does not fall into the legal definition of trafficking in human beings, it is unacceptable given the fundamental values recognised by the EU and its Member States. It is also contrary to the values of sport. Protective measures for unaccompanied minors in Member State immigration laws need to be applied rigorously. Sexual abuse and harassment of minors in sport must also be fought against.

(42)   The Commission will continue to monitor the implementation of EU legislation, in particular the Directive on the Protection of Young People at Work. The Commission has recently launched a study on child labour as a complement to its monitoring of the implementation of the Directive. The issue of young players falling within the scope of the Directive will be taken into account in the study.

(43)   The Commission will propose to Member States and sport organisations to cooperate on the protection of the moral and physical integrity of young people through the dissemination of information on existing legislation, establishment of minimum standards and exchange of best practices.

4.6   Corruption, money laundering and other forms of financial crime

Corruption, money laundering and other forms of financial crime are affecting sport at local, national and international levels. Given the sector's high degree of internationalisation, corruption in the sport sector often has cross-border aspects. Corruption problems with a European dimension need to be tackled at European level. EU anti-money laundering mechanisms should apply effectively also in the sport sector.

(44)   The Commission will support public-private partnerships representative of sports interests and anti-corruption authorities, which would identify vulnerabilities to corruption in the sport sector and assist in the development of effective preventive and repressive strategies to counter such corruption.

(45)   The Commission will continue to monitor the implementation of EU anti-money laundering legislation in the Member States with regard to the sport sector.

4.7   Licensing systems for clubs

The Commission acknowledges the usefulness of robust licensing systems for professional clubs at European and national levels as a tool for promoting good governance in sport. Licensing systems generally aim to ensure that all clubs respect the same basic rules on financial management and transparency, but could also include provisions regarding discrimination, violence, protection of minors and training. Such systems must be compatible with competition and Internal Market provisions and may not go beyond what is necessary for the pursuit of a legitimate objective relating to the proper organisation and conduct of sport.

Efforts need to concentrate on the implementation and gradual reinforcement of licensing systems. In the case of football, where a licensing system will soon be compulsory for clubs entering European competitions, action needs to concentrate on promoting and encouraging the use of licensing systems at national level.

(46) The Commission will promote dialogue with sport organisations in order to address the implementation and strengthening of self-regulatory licensing systems.

(47) Starting with football, the Commission intends to organise a conference with UEFA, EPFL, Fifpro, national associations and national leagues on licensing systems and best practices in this field.

4.8 Media

Issues concerning the relationship between the sport sector and sport media (television in particular) have become crucial as television rights are the primary source of income for professional sport in Europe. Conversely, sport media rights are a decisive source of content for many media operators.

Sport has been a driving force behind the emergence of new media and interactive television services. The Commission will continue to support the right to information and wide access for citizens to broadcasts of sport events, which are seen as being of high interest or major importance for society.

The application of the competition provisions of the EC Treaty to the selling of media rights of sport events takes into account a number of specific characteristics in this area. Sport media rights are sometimes sold collectively by a sport association on behalf of individual clubs (as opposed to clubs marketing the rights individually). While joint selling of media rights raises competition concerns, the Commission has accepted it under certain conditions. Collective selling can be important for the redistribution of income and can thus be a tool for achieving greater solidarity within sports.

The Commission recognises the importance of an equitable redistribution of income between clubs, including the smallest ones, and between professional and amateur sport.

(48) The Commission recommends to sport organisations to pay due attention to the creation and maintenance of solidarity mechanisms. In the area of sports media rights, such mechanisms can take the form of a system of collective selling of media rights or, alternatively, of a system of individual selling by clubs, in both cases linked to a robust solidarity mechanism.

5. FOLLOW-UP

The Commission will follow up on the initiatives presented in this White Paper through the implementation of a structured dialogue with sport stakeholders, cooperation with the Member States, and the promotion of social dialogue in the sport sector.

5.1 Structured dialogue

European sport is characterised by a multitude of complex and diverse structures which enjoy different types of legal status and levels of autonomy in Member States. Unlike other sectors and due to the very nature of organised sport, European sport structures are, as a rule, less well developed than sport structures at national and international levels. Moreover, European sport is generally organised according to continental structures, and not at EU level.

Stakeholders agree that the Commission has an important role to play in contributing to the European debate on sport by providing a platform for dialogue with sport stakeholders.

Wide consultation with "interested parties" is one of the Commission's duties according to the Treaties.

In view of the complex and diverse sports culture in Europe, the Commission intends to involve notably the following actors in its structured dialogue:

- European Sport Federations;
- European umbrella organisations for sport, notably the European Olympic Committees (EOC), the European Paralympic Committee (EPC) and European non-governmental sport organisations;
- National umbrella organisations for sport and national Olympic and Paralympic Committees;
- Other actors in the field of sport represented at European level, including social partners;
- Other European and international organisations, in particular the Council of Europe's structures for sport and UN bodies such as UNESCO and the WHO.

(49) The Commission intends to organise the structured dialogue in the following manner:
  - EU Sport Forum: an annual gathering of all sport stakeholders;
  - Thematic discussions with limited numbers of participants.
(50) The Commission will also seek to promote greater European visibility at sporting events. The Commission supports the further development of the European Capitals of Sport initiative.

5.2 Cooperation with Member States

Cooperation among Member States on sport at EU level takes place in informal ministerial meetings, as well as at the administrative level by Sport Directors. A Rolling Agenda for sport was adopted by EU Sport Ministers in 2004 to define priority themes for discussions on sport among the Member States.

(51) In order to address the issues listed in this White Paper, the Commission proposes to strengthen existing cooperation among the Member States and the Commission.
  Based on a proposal from the Commission, Member States may wish to reinforce the mechanism of the Rolling Agenda, for example:
  - To jointly define priorities for sport policy cooperation;
  - To report regularly to EU Sport Ministers on progress.
  Closer cooperation will require the regular organisation of Sport Ministers and Sport Directors meetings under each Presidency, which should be taken into account by future 18-month Presidency teams.
(52) The Commission will report on the implementation of the "Pierre de Coubertin" Action Plan through the mechanism of the Rolling Agenda.

5.3 Social dialogue

In the light of a growing number of challenges to sport governance, social dialogue at European level can contribute to addressing common concerns of employers and athletes, including agreements on employment relations and working conditions in the sector in accordance with EC Treaty provisions.

The Commission has been supporting projects for the consolidation of social dialogue in the sport sector in general as well as in the football sector. These projects have created a basis for social dialogue at European level and the consolidation of European-level organisations. A Sectoral Social Dialogue Committee can be established by the Commission on the basis of a joint request by social partners. The Commission considers that a European social dialogue in the sport sector or in its sub-sectors (e.g., football) is an instrument which would allow social partners to contribute to the shaping of employment relations and working conditions in an active and participative way. In this area, such a social dialogue could also lead to the establishment of commonly agreed codes of conduct or charters, which could address issues related to training, working conditions or the protection of young people.

(53)   The Commission encourages and welcomes all efforts leading to the establishment of European Social Dialogue Committees in the sport sector. It will continue to give support to both employers and employees and it will pursue its open dialogue with all sport organisations on this issue.
The support that the Member States should make available for capacity building and joint actions of social partners through the European Social Fund in the convergence regions should also be used for capacity building of the social partners in the sport sector.

6.   CONCLUSION

The White Paper contains a number of actions to be implemented or supported by the Commission. Together, these actions form the "Pierre de Coubertin" Action Plan which will guide the Commission in its sport-related activities during the coming years.

The White Paper has taken full advantage of the possibilities offered by the current Treaties.

A mandate has been given by the European Council of June 2007 for the Intergovernmental Conference, which foresees a Treaty provision on sport. If necessary, the Commission may return to this issue and indicate further steps in the context of a new Treaty provision.

The Commission will organise a conference to present the White Paper to sport stakeholders in the autumn of 2007. Its findings will be presented to EU Sport Ministers by the end of 2007. The White Paper will also be presented to the European Parliament, the Committee of the Regions and the Economic and Social Committee.

NATIONAL AND INTERNATIONAL LEGISLATION

NATIONAL LEGISLATION

REGULATIONS OF SPORTS FEDERATIONS

TABLE OF CASES

COMMISSION DECISIONS

COURT OF ARBITRATION FOR SPORT

BELGIUM

FRANCE

UNITED KINGDOM

UNITED STATES

SUBJECT INDEX

Asser International Sports Law Series

Editors
Robert C.R. Siekmann and Janwillem Soek

ISSN 1874–6926

Basic Documents of International Sports Organisations, R.C.R. Siekmann and J.W. Soek, eds. (The Hague/Boston/London, Kluwer Law International 1998)

Doping Rules of International Sports Organisations, R.C.R. Siekmann, J.W. Soek and A. Bellani, eds. (The Hague, T.M.C.ASSER PRESS 1999)

Arbitral and Disciplinary Rules of International Sports Organisations, R.C.R. Siekmann and J.W. Soek, eds. (The Hague, T.M.C.ASSER PRESS 2001)

Professional Sport in the European Union: Regulation and Re-regulation, A. Caiger and S. Gardiner, eds. (The Hague, T.M.C.ASSER PRESS 2001)

Mediating Sports Disputes: National and International Perspectives, I.S. Blackshaw (The Hague, T.M.C.ASSER PRESS 2002)

The European Union and Sport: Legal and Policy Documents, R.C.R. Siekmann and J.W. Soek, eds. (The Hague, T.M.C.ASSER PRESS 2005)

Sports Image Rights in Europe, I.S. Blackshaw and R.C.R. Siekmann, eds. (The Hague, T.M.C.ASSER PRESS 2005)

The Court of Arbitration for Sport 1984–2004, I.S. Blackshaw, R.C.R. Siekmann and J.W. Soek, eds. (The Hague, T.M.C.ASSER PRESS 2006)

The Strict Liability Principle and the Human Rights of Athletes in Doping Cases, J.W. Soek (The Hague, T.M.C.ASSER PRESS 2006)

The Council of Europe and Sport: Basic Documents, R.C.R. Siekmann and J.W. Soek, eds. (The Hague, T.M.C.ASSER PRESS 2007)

Players' Agents Worldwide: Legal Aspects, R.C.R. Siekmann, R. Parrish, R. Branco Martins and J.W. Soek, eds. (The Hague, T.M.C.ASSER PRESS 2008)